TABLE OF CONTENTS

FOREWORD..5

PREFACE – Our Earliest Inhabitants.........7

INTRODUCTION..9

SECTION ONE – Escaping Shadows of Oppression
SECTION TWO – Seeds of a New Identity
SECTION THREE – The Dream Takes Root

CHAPTER ONE – Flames of Faith..............................30

SECTION ONE – Perils of the Old World
SECTION TWO – Voyage to Hope
SECTION THREE – Blending Beliefs

CHAPTER TWO – Generations of Growth......................47

SECTION ONE – Early Ties To Europe
SECTION TWO – Mid-Generational Shifts
SECTION THREE – Diminishing Allegiance

CHAPTER THREE – Heroes of the Revolution................70

SECTION ONE – Early Agitators
SECTION TWO – Financiers and Diplomats
SECTION THREE – Warriors and Unsung Heroes

CHAPTER FOUR – Grievances and Resolve...................85

SECTION ONE – Echoes of Past Tyrannies
SECTION TWO – Moral Imperative For Change
SECTION THREE – Path to Independence

CHAPTER FIVE – Ancient Echoes..............................100
Lessons from Fallen Empires

SECTION ONE – Greek and Roman Declines
SECTION TWO – Eastern Empires' Falls
SECTION THREE – Founder's Applications

CHAPTER SIX – Convention's Crucible.......................122

SECTION ONE – Diverse Colonies Converge
SECTION TWO – Slavery's Shadow
SECTION THREE – Knowledge and Compromise

I0833063

CHAPTER SEVEN – Partisan Perils....................................140
SECTION ONE – Federalist Visions
SECTION TWO – Republican Responses
SECTION THREE – Electoral Resolutions

CHAPTER EIGHT – Shadows of Compromise....................166
SECTION ONE – Convention's Bargains
SECTION TWO – Escalating Tensions
SECTION THREE – War's Inevitable Dawn

CHAPTER NINE – Expansion and Innovation....................196
SECTION ONE – Westward Expansion and Native Struggles
SECTION TWO – Innovations and Cultural Shifts

CHAPTER TEN – Nets of Dependency...............................203
SECTION ONE – Early Expansions
SECTION TWO – The Era of Wilson Begins America's Era of Entitlement
SECTION THREE – Franklin Roosevelt's New Deal

CHAPTER ELEVEN – The Second Half of the 20th Century..242
SECTION ONE – Mid-Century Burdens
SECTION TWO – The Turbulent 1960s Lead to War's End
SECTION THREE – Debt's Shadow

CHAPTER TWELVE – Strength's Renewal........................265
SECTION ONE – Reagan's Deterrence
SECTION TWO – The 1990s and Moral Decay in the Presidency
SECTION THREE – The New Millenium Opens with Tragedy

CHAPTER THIRTEEN – Hope and Change Turns to Hope For Change..279
SECTION ONE – False Promises and Polarization
SECTION TWO – Trump's America First Agenda
SECTION THREE – Forward Paths

CONCLUSION – Eternal Flame.......................................310
America's Promise to Humanity
EPILOGUE – Keeping the Faith......................................312
REFERENCES...316
DISCLAIMER..327
ABOUT THE AUTHOR..328

**This book is dedicated to the memory of my father,
Maynard Lee Sisler, M.D., F.A.C.P.,
Captain, United States Navy,
a decorated World War II veteran,
and to every man and woman in American history
who gave their final measure of devotion,
sacrificing their lives so that we can live free.
Let us carry them in our hearts and honor them all by
preserving our liberties for future generations.**

Flames of Freedom

America's Resilient Dream and Why it is Humanity's Last Hope

Igniting Patriotic Renewal Through Stories of Faith, Courage, and Sacrifice on our 250th Anniversary

America 250

FAITH AND FREEDOM MASTERY SERIES

VOLUME ONE

By Tad Sisler

FOREWORD

My father, Maynard Lee Sisler, MD, FACP, was an avid historian and a Renaissance man. He reveled in teaching me History, particularly American History, and I soaked it up because his teaching wasn't about dates and times. It was about alliterative stories of courage and sacrifice, transporting me through time into the moment, and I was always transfixed! And he had lived it, serving valiantly in battle in the Second World War.

Maynard Lee Sisler, MD

When I was growing up, my dad was a doctor in the United States Navy. When I was 8, we were transferred to the largest Army-Navy Hospital in the world at the time, in Corpus Christi, Texas, where he served as Chief of Medicine. We lived in a lovely, large house on the Army/Navy base with a spacious yard. Down the street from my home was an obstacle course where young recruits trained. My friends and I would run the course when no one else was around, pretending we were soldiers. Across from the course was a "graveyard" of downed airplanes and helicopters, brought home from the Vietnam conflict halfway around the world and dumped into a field for scrap metal and parts. This pile of metal, reeking still of burnt flesh, was our playground.

We sat in cockpits, pretending we were valiant pilots flying in a war zone, oblivious to the fact that war is a terrible, ugly thing, and men had probably died in the aircraft where we were blithely playing.

What I gained most from my experience as a Navy brat was an extreme sense of patriotism. My father often took me on his rounds at the Army-Navy Hospital in Corpus Christi, and again when he was transferred to Balboa Naval Hospital in San Diego. I met brave soldiers without limbs, not much older than me, really, reduced to half of their original stature, with unbelievable courage masking the pain in their eyes. My dad had fought beside many of these soldiers, and he now medically treated the Admirals he had served under with deep respect.

He introduced me to many of these towering men, now with bodies failing from years of over-exertion and stress (and many from heavy drinking). I understood first-hand what sacrifice for love of country is.

My father also signed "Conscientious Objector" applications for many of my older sister's friends, helping them to serve in other ways than the meat grinder of Vietnam. He understood, as they did, that one can serve in many ways.

Mostly, he taught me to abhor even the idea of war and what it does to humanity. He told a thousand stories about how our nation came to be and why it is the last, best hope for the world.

Later, when I was in High School, my father and his older brother, my Uncle Bill, would take one side of any argument and have me argue the other side (for instance, the Monroe Doctrine and whether Manifest Destiny was good for our country... or did the Civil War start because of slavery or was it States' Rights?). As valiantly as I argued any point, they would always win and then switch to the other side of the argument, and beat me that way, too. It was an excellent lesson in open-mindedness, to say the least. I gleaned much of his book from dad's stories and our many debates, along with other stories I loved, as I delved deeply into what America is truly about. I hope you read this and derive a deeper sense of patriotism from the experience. We cannot, as a nation, afford to be a house divided against itself anymore. Although this book is written for the 250th anniversary of America, it encompasses American history over a 500-year period to date.

Share your sentiment with your colleagues, family, and friends. Don't be afraid to be proud of America. However imperfect our system is, it remains the model for everyone who craves freedom worldwide. Our fierce independence from oppression is in our DNA. I hope you enjoy the experience of reading this as much as I did, writing it!

PREFACE
OUR EARLIEST INHABITANTS

In the vast expanse of time, long before the sails of European ships dotted the horizon, the story of America's first people began with a great journey across a frozen land bridge. Around 20,000 to 25,000 years ago, during the height of the last Ice Age, sea levels plummeted, exposing a wide corridor between what is now Siberia and Alaska—known as Beringia. Nomadic hunters, following herds of mammoth and bison, crossed this icy path, likely in small family groups, seeking new hunting grounds. These early migrants, often called Paleo-Indians, didn't know they were stepping onto a new continent; they were simply surviving and adapting to the harsh, changing world. Over generations, they spread southward, following rivers and coastlines, reaching as far as South America by around 15,000 years ago. Archaeological sites like Monte Verde in Chile and Meadowcroft Rockshelter in Pennsylvania whisper of their presence, with tools and fire pits dating back millennia.

These ancient inhabitants lived in harmony with the land, as nomadic hunter-gatherers who moved with the seasons. They crafted stone tools for hunting woolly mammoths and giant sloths, gathered wild plants, berries, and nuts, and built temporary shelters from animal hides and wood. Family and clan bonds were strong, with oral traditions passing down knowledge of the stars, weather, and survival. As the ice receded around 12,000 years ago, diverse cultures blossomed—the Clovis people with their distinctive spear points, followed by settled communities that farmed maize, built earthen mounds, and created intricate pottery. For over 15,000 years, they thrived across the continent, from the Arctic tundra to the Amazon rainforests, developing rich spiritual beliefs tied to nature, without the metal tools or written languages of later civilizations.

This era of untouched abundance lasted until 1492, when Christopher Columbus's arrival marked the beginning of European contact. For millennia, these first Americans had shaped the landscape through controlled burns that created prairies or trade networks spanning continents—building societies that numbered in the tens of millions by the time outsiders came. Their legacy endures in the land itself, a testament to human resilience long before the stars and stripes flew.

When I was 12, my sister Judy was traveling through New Mexico. The van she was in carried nine people, and in the dead of night, a logging truck swerved to avoid an animal in the road. The chains broke, and the logs fell on the van carrying my sister. Six died, my sister's boyfriend lapsed into a coma, and when he finally awoke, he found he had become a paraplegic. Another passenger broke a leg. My sister's back was badly broken, and she was airlifted to a hospital in Santa Fe, where she was nursed back to health over several months by an Arapahoe family. After a time, she married one of the sons and had a son of her own, which technically made me part of their extended family.

Because of this, I was allowed to attend the Sundance in Wyoming when I was 14. Only Native Americans are allowed into this sacred festival. We lived in teepees for the week I was there. There was no evidence of modern culture in sight. Dressed in traditional clothing, men hunted deer, skinned them, hung the hides, and prepared the meat for food. Native dances and peyote meetings were plentiful. For a short time, I was thrust back 2,000 years to a different world, one that exists now only in customs passed down through generations. I was fortunate to get a glimpse of how America must have been before the earliest European settlers. Although I was raised Christian, the experience gave me an appreciation for the depth of Native American culture, and I am better because of it. In this book, I will outline the lessons we learned from them and the ones they learned from us, including the tragic ones.

This land belongs to all of us now; it belongs to a patchwork of natives and immigrants from every corner of the world. But we owe the original Americans a deep debt of gratitude for the lessons they taught us and for the timeless ideas they contributed, which became woven into our own laws and culture.

"The most common trait of all primitive peoples is a reverence for the life-giving earth, and the Native American shared this elemental ethic: The land was alive to his loving touch, and he, its son, was brother to all creatures." – Stewart Udall

INTRODUCTION

"By looking into more details of American history, we can make more sense of what's happening today." – Christoph Waltz

It's late autumn 1607. Three small, battered ships limp into a marshy river mouth in Jamestown, Virginia. The men who stumble ashore are little more than skeletons wrapped in rags. Scurvy has blackened their gums, fever has burned half of them hollow, and the ones still on their feet know the odds: most won't see another Christmas. Yet the instant their boots hit that cold, sucking mud, something irreversible begins. Not drums or trumpets—just a quiet, stubborn spark that will one day set the world on fire.

Those early settlers in Jamestown had gone through real nightmares back in England, where kings like James I made sure everyone followed their church rules or paid the price with the whip.

These weren't explorers chasing gold. They were families fleeing for their lives. Back in England, King James had made worship a crime. Pray the wrong way—or pray without a bishop's permission—and the king's men could break down your door. One farmer, John, never forgot the night soldiers dragged his neighbor away for reading the Bible aloud with friends. Weeks later, the man's body was tossed in a ditch, ribs showing through the skin, face unrecognizable. As John's ship lurched through storm after storm, he held his wife in the stinking dark and whispered, "I'll take my chances with the sea and whatever waits on the other side before I let them do that to us." They weren't after adventure. They just wanted space to breathe without a boot on their throat.

Thirteen years later, in the dead of winter 1620, the Mayflower finally dropped anchor off a windswept cape the passengers named Plymouth. Below deck, a father named William wrapped his shivering children in whatever rags were left. They'd already spent years hiding in Holland because the king called their simple faith treason.

Night after night on that brutal crossing, William repeated an old line to keep them going—"the obstacle is the way"—while waves smashed the ship like God's own hammer and sickness took hold in the hold. When they finally staggered onto land, half the company was dead before spring. The survivors dropped to their knees on the frozen ground and wept in gratitude, because they were still alive and still free to pray.

That first winter was a slow-motion nightmare—skin splitting from cold, bellies so empty strong men cried like babies. Then one spring morning, a native man named Squanto walked out of the trees, speaking English he'd learned through his own kidnapping and slavery. He was not afraid of the new settlers because he had lived among their people in a distant land. Squanto had compassion for these people fleeing the same tyranny he had personally experienced, so he taught them to bury a fish with every corn seed. His quiet kindness, mixed with desperate prayer, pulled them through. The harvest feast we still remember started there: two peoples who had every reason to fear each other sitting down together, sharing deer meat and corn, grateful simply to be breathing.

From that raw beginning, something took root. The Bible's fierce insistence that every person is made in God's image met native understanding that the earth is a gift to be honored, not owned. Together, they planted the first fragile seed of an idea almost no one else on the planet believed yet: ordinary men and women can govern themselves.

Jump forward four generations from the first pilgrims who set foot on American soil. In this same "New World," a young mother named Anne stood in her doorway watching a tax collector ride off with her family's only plow horses—payment for a faraway war she had nothing to do with.

Old memories flood back: stories of Roman emperors throwing Christians to lions while crowds roared approval, of empires that looked invincible until cruelty rotted them from the inside. Anne pulled her children close and said, voice steady, "We're finished being pieces on somebody else's board. From now on, we make the rules that keep us alive." That same iron refusal to bow is the blood in America's veins.

By 1776, that seed had become a wildfire. Men and women who had never laid eyes on England stood up straight and said their rights came from their Creator, not from any crown. And they meant it enough to fight for it.

This book is their story—and ours.

We'll walk it together: the desperate beginnings on frozen shores, the slow, stubborn growth of a people who learned to feed themselves, govern themselves, worship as their conscience demanded. We'll meet the everyday men and women who gave everything—homes burned, fortunes lost, lives laid down—so their children would never again have to kneel to a tyrant.

We'll see how that fire almost flickered out many times and how it always roared back hotter, because it was forged in faith and refusal to quit.

And we'll talk straight about what it takes to keep it burning today: guarding our borders, using the gifts God put in this ground, standing watch over truth so no new tyranny can smother the light.

Because in a world sliding back into darkness, this stubborn, God-given American freedom isn't just our story.

It's the world's last real hope.

Come with me. Let's keep the flame alive.

INTRODUCTION - SECTION ONE:
ESCAPING SHADOWS OF OPPRESSION

THE CALL ACROSS THE OCEAN

It's hard for us today to wrap our heads around it, but there was a time—not that long ago—when a King could throw you in a hole for life just for praying the "wrong" way or saying the "wrong" thing about the government. We get upset now when a social media post gets taken down or an account gets suspended, and rightly so, but that's nothing compared to what our ancestors lived with every single day.

Take a simple tailor named Richard, a quiet man in England with a family to feed. One rainy night in 1606, the door to his little house crashed open. Soldiers stormed in, accused him of meeting with friends to read the Bible without a priest looking over their shoulders. They dragged him out into the mud, whipped him until the skin hung off his back in strips, then chained him, and threw him into a cell so dark and wet he couldn't tell day from night. Weeks or months later—nobody kept good count—he was carried out barely breathing. The only crime on the books: wanting to worship God the way his conscience told him to.

Richard survived, but the scars never let him forget the message loud and clear: keep your head down or lose it.

He couldn't do it. He'd seen too many neighbors disappear. So, when word came of ships leaving for a raw, wild place called Virginia, Richard looked at his wife and children and said, "I'll take my chances with fever and Indians over living like this." They sold what little they had, climbed aboard, and sailed away from a country where faith could get you killed.

That kind of fear was normal back then. Speak against the King's church, print the wrong pamphlet, even whisper the wrong prayer—doors got kicked in, families got torn apart, and people vanished into prisons most never walked out of.

We're starting to feel echoes of that again. In England today, people are actually being arrested and jailed for social-media posts the government labels "hate speech." Peaceful grandmothers, comedians, even just folks venting frustration—handcuffs, court dates, prison cells. It's not the rack and the whip yet, but the chill is the same: shut up or we'll make you shut up. This kind of tyranny (and worse) happens all over the world today, but too many people like Richard sacrificed everything so it wouldn't happen here in America. But this was a time when America was just a faraway place on a map.

George Santayana nailed it: "Those who cannot remember the past are condemned to repeat it." Our ancestors remembered the past all too well—that's why they risked everything to get away from it. They crossed an ocean in leaky wooden boats so their kids wouldn't have to grow up afraid of their own thoughts.

We owe it to them—and to our own children—not to let that darkness creep back in. The fight for freedom didn't end in 1776. It's still on. And it starts with refusing to be silent when silence is precisely what the new tyrants want.

The crossing itself was its own kind of hell.

The ships were small, overcrowded, and the Atlantic didn't care. Waves taller than houses slammed the hulls day after day. Below deck, it was pitch black, wet, and stank of vomit and fear. Sickness spread like wildfire—people coughing their lungs up, fevers burning hot enough to make strong men cry for their mothers. Families squeezed together on narrow benches, sharing the last scraps of hard bread and whatever hope they had left.

A young mother named Mary held her baby so close she could feel its little heartbeat racing against her own. The fever had already taken hold below deck, and she didn't know if either of them would live to see morning. Between the groans of the ship and the crying of the sick, she whispered a promise into her child's ear: "If we make it through this, we'll build a place where nobody ever has to hide what they believe again."

The Susan Constant—the biggest of the three ships headed for Jamestown—creaked and leaked like it might split apart any minute. But the people on board kept going. They told each other stories of the whips and prisons they'd left behind, reminded one another why the risk was worth it, and somehow that shared stubbornness pushed them forward.

When they finally staggered onto the muddy banks of Virginia, the nightmare didn't end—it changed. Mosquitoes swarmed thick as smoke. Strange fevers came next. Food ran out fast. One by one, friends and family were buried in shallow graves along the river. But every morning the survivors got up, said their prayers, and went back to work—because giving up meant the tyrants had won after all.

"There is something inexpressibly sad in the thought of the children who crossed the ocean with the Pilgrims and the fathers of Jamestown, New Amsterdam, and Boston, and the infancy of those born in the first years of colonial life in this strange new world." – Alice Morse Earle

FAITH AS ANCHOR

Thirteen years later, the same story played out again on the Mayflower.

Down in the dark hold, families huddled around a single lantern that swung wildly with every roll of the ship. They passed around worn Bibles from hand to hand—books that could have gotten them hanged back home. A young woman named Elizabeth never forgot the night soldiers kicked in her family's door, dragged her brother away for praying without the King's permission, and dumped his broken body in the street days later.

As the storm howled and the main beam cracked overhead, water pouring in like judgment day, she clung to her husband and said through chattering teeth, "We'll find a place where God's word isn't a crime."

The storm was so fierce that grown men thought the ship would rip in two. They bailed water with buckets, hats, anything they could grab, praying out loud while the kids cried. When the Mayflower finally scraped bottom off Cape Cod, half the passengers were already dead or dying. The rest crawled onto the frozen beach, fell to their knees in the snow, and thanked God they were still breathing.

That winter finished off most of the rest. Cold, hunger, sickness—no mercy. But the ones who lived through it came out different—tougher, quieter, grateful for every sunrise.

Both groups—Jamestown and Plymouth—learned the same hard lesson: this new land didn't give anything away. It demanded everything. And in giving everything, they discovered something the old world never offered: the chance to build a life where faith was a strength, not a crime, and where a person's word and work mattered more than which King sat on a faraway throne.

They weren't heroes in shining armor. They were scared, seasick, grieving people who refused to let fear own them. And because they refused, the rest of us get to live free.

That's the fire that started on those freezing, lonely shores. It's been burning ever since.

Those same Bibles they'd smuggled aboard became more than comfort—they became the colony's first law book. They were all simple rules, straight from the Ten Commandments and the Golden Rule: don't steal, don't kill, don't lie, treat your neighbor the way you want to be treated. In a place where one bad decision could doom everybody, those verses were the only thing standing between them and total chaos.

That first winter at Plymouth was brutal beyond cruel. By March, half the company—50 out of 100—lay in graves dug in frozen ground. William Bradford was chosen as governor because he remained steady when everyone else broke.

From his journal, we know he felt that he had seen God's hand guiding them, even through the dying. "The Lord watched over the sparrow," he wrote, "and He has not abandoned us." Faith, for Bradford, wasn't a feeling. It was the lifeline they all held onto when despair tried to drag them under. It turned grief into grit and kept them planting, building, believing that something lasting could still come out of all that loss.

I know exactly how that feels.

When I lost my young wife far too early, those same words were the only thing that kept me from going under. Life isn't fair—never has been—but I've come to believe our loved ones don't really leave us. They stand watch in ways we can't always see, the way Bradford felt God standing watch over a handful of freezing pilgrims.

That kind of trust didn't just help the pilgrims survive. It shaped everything they built. The laws they wrote into the Mayflower Compact and later into town charters weren't fancy—they were biblical and practical: protect the weak, punish the wrongdoer quickly and fairly, make sure every man has a voice. The Ten Commandments and "do unto others" weren't slogans; they were the foundation under their feet when there was nothing else.

And that foundation—the one laid in frozen ground by people who had nothing left but faith and each other—is the Ten Commandments—and it ended up holding up what was to become the freest nation the world has ever known.

It still does, if we remember where it came from.

FIRST ENCOUNTERS WITH NATIVE AMERICANS

This story is about America's beginnings, but I can't tell it completely without honoring the people who were already here—the ones who had walked this continent for thousands of years before a single European sail appeared on the horizon. Some of their nations built great cities and traded across half the continent; others lived light on the land, moving with the seasons. They were the first Americans, many of our laws are based upon theirs, and what they knew about surviving here saved the newcomers more than once. We owe them a debt most of us have forgotten, and later chapters will face the hard truth of what happened when thankfulness turned to taking. For now, though, let's go back to the moment two very different worlds met—and chose, for a little while, to help each other alive.

Imagine you've just survived the worst voyage of your life. For sixty-six brutal days, the Mayflower has pitched and rolled, seasick children crying below deck, food rotting, drinking water turning slimy. When the ship finally stops, your legs feel like a stranger's. You step onto a narrow strip of sand with pine trees marching clear to the sky and no sign of another human soul. The air smells clean for the first time in months, but the silence is frightening. You know half your friends won't live to see spring.

That's exactly how it was for the little band of English families we call the Pilgrims when they landed at Plymouth in December 1620.

They threw up rough shelters, but winter hit like a hammer. Snow piled to the eaves, food ran out, and a sickness swept through that left bodies stacked like cordwood because the ground was too frozen to bury them properly. By March, only half were left alive.

Then, on a raw morning when hope was almost gone, an Indian named Samoset walked straight into their settlement and said in clear English, "Welcome." A week later, he came back with a man the Pilgrims called Squanto.

Squanto's own story could break your heart. Seven years earlier, an English captain had lured him and twenty-six other Patuxet men aboard a ship with promises of trade, then clapped them in irons and sailed for the slave markets in Spain. Then came the worst day of his life.

The slave market in Málaga was a chaos of shouting men, chains clanking, and the stink of fear. Squanto—barely twenty-five, strong, confused, and a long way from home—was shoved onto the block like a horse or a bolt of cloth. Bidders poked him, opened his mouth to check his teeth, and argued over his price in a language he didn't know. His freedom was gone, sold for a handful of coins.

But God hadn't forgotten him.

Some Franciscan friars were in the crowd that day—quiet men in rough brown robes who made their living helping the poor and the lost. Something about the young Indian's eyes moved them. They scraped together what little money they had, bought him out of that market, and took him back to their monastery.

There, for the first time since the chains went on, someone treated him like a human being. They fed him, taught him Spanish, and told him about a God who loved the broken and set captives free. Squanto listened. The Jesus they described sounded a lot like the caring spirit his own people had always known. He asked to be baptized. When the priest poured water over his head and gave him a Christian name, Squanto clung to the words of the 23rd Psalm like a lifeline: "The Lord is my shepherd; I shall not want."

Those verses carried him through the years that followed—years of hard work, of learning new languages, of waiting for a ship that would take him home. He crossed to England, lived in London, learned the ways and words of the very people who had stolen him. All the while, he kept one thought burning: get back to his village, back to his family.

In 1619, he finally stepped onto a ship headed west again. He stood at the rail every day, eyes fixed on the horizon, dreaming of the moment he'd run up the beach and feel his mother's arms around him.

He never got that moment.

When the ship dropped anchor off the coast he'd known as a boy, he saw smoke rising from no cookfires, heard no children laughing, no dogs barking. His entire village—every man, woman, and child of the Patuxet people—was gone, wiped out by a sickness brought by earlier ships. The homes he remembered were collapsing into the sand. The trails were overgrown. He was alive... and completely alone.

Most men would have broken. Squanto didn't.

A year later, when half-starved English families stumbled ashore at Plymouth, cold, scared, and dying by the day, Squanto walked out of the woods and chose to help them—the same kind of people who had kidnapped him, enslaved him, and unknowingly destroyed everything he loved.

He didn't do it for revenge. He did it because something bigger than hate had taken root in his heart on the other side of the world: a belief that a merciful God could turn even the worst pain into a way to help others. And he saw that same quiet faith and resolve in their hearts that he had witnessed with the friars in Spain who had saved him from a life of slavery.

That's the man who saved the Pilgrims. Not some distant figure in a history book—a real flesh-and-blood human who had every reason to walk away... and chose mercy instead.

He could have vanished into the woods and let the English starve. Plenty would have. Instead, he stayed.

Picture him in the spring mud, kneeling beside William Bradford and the others, showing them how to plant corn the way his mother taught him: drop a fish in the hole with the seed so the soil stays rich, then plant beans and squash around it so the three sisters grow together—one climbs, one shades, one feeds the dirt.

He showed them where the eels ran thick in the creeks, how to trap beaver for warm robes, and which berries wouldn't poison you. When the Wampanoag chief Massasoit came to talk peace, Squanto stood between the two peoples and made the words work.

Because of him, that little settlement didn't die. One Pilgrim wrote later that Squanto was "a special instrument sent of God for their good beyond their expectation."

Squanto himself caught a fever and died only two years later, still helping the English on a trading trip. His last words asked William Bradford to pray for him, that he might go to the Englishmen's God in Heaven.

Those first quiet acts of friendship—sharing food, teaching how to live on the land—became the bridge between two worlds. The Pilgrims brought their Bible and their hunger for freedom. The native people brought knowledge of this continent that had kept their nations alive for centuries. Together, for a little while, they made something stronger than either could alone.

That spirit—faith in a higher plan, respect for the earth that feeds us, and the simple courage to help a stranger when you've got every reason not to—is woven deep into what America was meant to be.

Later, we forgot too much of it. That's part of the story too, and we'll face it honestly. But it started with open hands instead of clenched fists, with a man who had lost everything choosing mercy anyway.

And that choice lit a flame that still burns.

SECTION TWO:
SEEDS OF A NEW IDENTITY

LOYALTY'S SLOW FADE

At first, the colonists still felt British to the bone. They said the King's name in church every Sunday and loaded ships with tobacco, timber, and furs headed straight for London. A portrait of the King hung in more than one tavern, and folks raised a mug to his health without thinking twice.

But three thousand miles of ocean has a way of changing things.

News from England took months to arrive—if it arrived at all. When a hurricane ripped the roof off your house or a drought baked your corn to dust, no royal governor was riding to the rescue. When wolves came down from the hills or a bear smashed through the fence, a proclamation from London wasn't going to help. You fixed what was broken with your own hands, or you called the neighbors, and everybody showed up with hammers and hope.

Little by little, people started handling their own problems. They met in the meetinghouse after Sunday service to argue over property lines or whose turn it was to repair the bridge. Rough-handed farmers and shopkeepers who smelled of pipe smoke and leather sat shoulder to shoulder and talked it out until something fair got decided. No need to write a letter to England and wait a year for an answer. They took care of it themselves, right there.

That habit changed how they saw the world. If God made every man equal in His sight—and the preacher said so every week—then why should one man three thousand miles away get the final say over their lives?

The hurt came when London finally noticed them again—and only to send the bill. Years of the first settlers' backbreaking work were starting to pay off, and many towns were becoming prosperous, so the King's men came with their hands out.

Taxes were levied for wars that the colonists never voted on—duties on tea, paper, glass—everyday things a family couldn't do without. Redcoats marched in to ensure the money was collected. Families who'd fought Indians on the frontier to protect the King's land now watched those same soldiers kick open doors looking for smuggled goods.

Seven generations is a long time. Grandparents still remembered swearing loyalty to the crown. Their children had learned to get by without it. The grandchildren started asking questions. And the great-grandchildren? Most of them had never laid eyes on England. It was a story, not a home.

Take Ebenezer Mackintosh, a shoemaker in Boston. His grandfather had come over from Scotland, his father had scratched out a living on these streets, and now Ebenezer sat at his bench hammering soles from dawn to dark. He was a quiet man who loved his wife, his kids, and the little church where he heard sermons about resisting evil.

When the Stamp Act hit in 1765—taxes on every piece of paper, every contract, every newspaper—it squeezed him hard. Customers who used to bring boots to fix now had to choose between food and the tax stamp.

Ebenezer didn't start out looking for trouble. But one August night, he found himself walking with a crowd of regular workingmen—carpenters, ropemakers, sailors—carrying an effigy of Andrew Oliver, the King's new stamp master. They hanged the dummy from a tree, then tore down Oliver's fancy new office, papers flying everywhere like angry snow. Ebenezer's hands shook the whole time—not from fear of the soldiers, but from knowing what he'd just done. He'd crossed a line for his children's future.

London answered with more troops and harsher laws. Families lost homes because they couldn't pay the new taxes. Men rotted in jail while their kids went hungry. Ebenezer stepped back into the shadows after that night, but the fire he helped light kept spreading.

Ordinary people were waking up to a simple truth: they'd already learned to run their own lives. They protected their towns, fed their families, worshiped as their hearts told them—all without a King's permission. So why keep sending their money and their freedom across the ocean to a man who treated them like strangers?

The old loyalty didn't snap all at once. It wore away, slow and steady, like a rope fraying strand by strand.

And when enough strands were gone, the people left weren't subjects anymore.

They were Americans.

Ready to stand on their own.

CULTURAL BLENDING BEGINS

People call America a melting pot now—a place where folks from everywhere come together and, over time, turn into one people. But that didn't start with the big waves of immigrants in the 1800s. It started way back, in the quiet spaces between settlers' campfires and native villages, when nobody from the king was watching.

Out on the frontier, far from any governor or priest, something simple and real began to happen. A settler might bow his head over a rough table and thank the God of the Bible for the deer on his plate. A native hunter a mile away might stand at dawn and offer tobacco to the Great Spirit for the same deer. Different words, different ways—but both men looking up at the same sky, grateful to be alive in a rugged land.

Those moments led to talk. And talk led to meals.

The Pilgrims and the Wampanoag in 1621 were starving after a winter that killed half of them. When the corn finally came in—thanks to native friends teaching them how to plant it—they threw a feast—Venison, wildfowl, corn bread, maybe some clams.

Englishmen in wool coats sat on the ground next to Wampanoag warriors in deerskin. Somebody said grace from the Bible. Somebody else gave thanks to the spirits who made the harvest grow. Guns fired in celebration, kids ran wild, and for three days, nobody worried about tomorrow.

Edward Winslow, one of the settlers, wrote home about it: they ate together, played games, and gave thanks to God "that He might make us all one in the end." It wasn't perfect harmony—there were old hurts and new fears on both sides—but for a little while, two entirely different cultures who had every reason to fight chose to share a table instead.

Ideas started crossing that table, too.

The settlers told stories of a God who said, "Love your neighbor and forgive those who wrong you." The natives talked about living in balance—hurt the land or your brother, and it comes back on you. Neither side changed everything overnight, but the best parts started rubbing off on each other: be fair, be kind when you can, stand firm when you have to.

It wasn't all smooth. Not every tribe was friendly, just like not every settler was honest. As the colonies grew, terrible fights and terrible wrongs occurred on both sides. We'll face that honestly later. But in those first quiet years, something powerful took root: the idea that people from different worlds could take the best from each other and build something stronger together.

POCOHONTAS

Pocahontas's story really captures how delicate the connections between different cultures can be. She was born around 1596 as Matoaka, the daughter of Chief Powhatan, in Virginia's Tidewater area—a place full of rivers and forests where her Algonquian community lived off hunting, farming, and shared traditions. By the time she was 11 or 12, she got pulled into the world of the Jamestown settlers. According to John Smith's later account, she stepped in to stop her father from executing him, an act that—whether fully accurate or not—stood for a brief moment of understanding amid rising conflicts.

She handled the cultural divide with real poise, picking up English customs while staying true to her own background. Eventually, she converted to Christianity, took the name Rebecca, and in 1614 married tobacco farmer John Rolfe. That union helped ease tensions between the Powhatan and the English for a while, and they had a son, Thomas, whose lineage would blend the two worlds and ripple through American history.

She didn't live long, dying at just 21 in 1617 while in England, on a ship about to head back home. As she held her husband's hand, she asked him to make sure their son grew up knowing both sides—the untamed freedom of her Virginia homeland and the ordered life of English society. Pocahontas had gone to London as something of an ambassador, dressed in elegant European clothes and introduced at court, where people saw her as a "civilized" Native princess and were fascinated by her.

But she fell ill, likely from smallpox or pneumonia, and never made it back. In those last days, she represented the heartbreaking side of cultural encounters: someone who traveled across the world to create links, only to be taken by the very diseases that came with those exchanges.

She never got to see the full impact of her life, but it was huge. By putting herself on the line to help a stranger and then bridging vast differences, she wove her courage into the fabric of America. Through descendants like Thomas Rolfe, her influence spread into colonial families and beyond, touching everyone from Virginia's leaders to people today. Even if myths and stories have softened the edges, Pocahontas stands as a real example of strength and coming together. It's a reminder that big shifts in history often start with one person's choices, cutting through divides to point toward something shared.

That early mixing wasn't perfect. It was messy, sometimes painful. But it planted the idea that people who look different, pray differently, and eat differently can still sit down together, share what's good, and come out stronger.

That's where the melting pot really began—not in some government plan, but around campfires and harvest tables where folks decided to help each other instead of hating each other.

KNOWLEDGE AS POWER

A few brave souls decided the best way to fight back wasn't with muskets—at least not yet—but with words on paper.

Printers who usually turned out Bibles, almanacs, and the occasional wedding invitation started working late into the night.

They churned out cheap pamphlets—thin little things you could fold and slip in your pocket—that laid everything bare in plain English. No fancy talk, just the facts: the King's laws were unfair, his officials were crooked, and the colonies were getting robbed blind. Those pages flew from hand to hand faster than gossip. A farmer would read one after supper, shake his head, and pass it to the blacksmith. By Sunday, the preacher was quoting lines he'd never seen in print.

The King's men called it troublemaking and tried to stamp it out. Didn't matter. Another press fired up in the next town. All that printing did something huge: it let ordinary people see the whole picture for themselves. No more swallowing whatever story came down from the governor's mansion. Folks gathered in taverns and on village greens, reading the latest sheet aloud, arguing, thinking—regular farmers and shopkeepers who'd never questioned authority before started asking hard questions.

And once people start thinking for themselves, it's mighty hard to herd them back.

The men who would later write our Constitution knew exactly how powerful that was. They made sure a free press got written into the very first amendment—because they'd seen what happens when truth gets muzzled.

We're fighting the same fight today. Posts get taken down, accounts frozen, whole ideas labeled "dangerous" before anyone can read them. It's not chains and dungeons yet, but the chill feels familiar. A free press isn't some nice extra. It's the alarm bell that warns us when something's wrong. And words like "disinformation" and "misinformation" may mask censorship.

John Peter Zenger learned that the hard way.

He was a German immigrant who landed in New York as a boy in 1710, learned the printing trade, married, and set up his own shop. In 1733, he started the New York Weekly Journal—basically the only paper willing to call out Governor William Cosby for the crook he was. Cosby fixed trials, stole land, and crushed anyone who complained. Zenger's paper printed the truth: rigged elections, grabbed wages, the works.

Cosby lost his mind. He had copies burned in the street and threw Zenger in jail on "seditious libel"—a charge that said it didn't matter if the words were true; saying them was the crime.

Zenger sat in a damp cell for eight months while his wife Anna kept the paper running. The trial was a joke—his first lawyers got thrown off the case for daring to defend him. Then an old Philadelphia lawyer named Andrew Hamilton stepped up. He looked the jury—twelve ordinary New Yorkers—in the eye and said, "This isn't about one poor printer. It's about whether truth gets to walk free or stays locked up forever." He told them, "The question before you is not the cause of a poor printer... it is the cause of liberty."

The courtroom was dead quiet. Then the jury came back in minutes: not guilty.

People cheered in the streets. Printers across the colonies took it as a green light. Tell the truth, and no governor can touch you. Zenger went home, kept printing, and died a quiet man in 1746. But what he started echoed all the way to the First Amendment.

Those pamphlets and that one brave printer didn't win the war, but they woke people up. They turned grumbles into questions, questions into convictions, and convictions into courage.

Once regular people could read the truth for themselves, the King's lies didn't stand a chance.

And a people who know the truth are a people ready to fight for it.

SECTION THREE:
THE DREAM TAKES ROOT

OPPORTUNITY'S PROMISE

Step off the ship back then, and the land just stretched out forever—wild, rough, and wide open. No lords fencing it off, no King saying you couldn't touch it. All it asked was sweat and stubbornness. Clear the trees, break the soil, plant your seed, and what grew was yours. That was the deal, plain and simple, and it changed everything.

There's an old story that nails it. A traveler comes across a beautiful farm—neat fields, fat cattle, orchards heavy with fruit. He says to the farmer, "God has blessed you with an amazing place." The farmer looks around, spits, and answers, "Yeah, He has now, but you should've seen it when God had it all to Himself."

That was America. Raw dirt and endless work, but if you stuck with it, the ground gave back more than you ever put in.

You didn't need a title or a rich daddy. A poor kid with nothing but a strong back and a sharp mind could end up owning hundreds of acres. Immigrants who arrived with one shirt on their back built houses, barns, and businesses that fed whole towns. By the time their grandchildren came along, they weren't servants or tenants anymore. They were free men and women who answered to nobody but God and their own conscience.

From sunrise to sunset, it was hard, bone-tiring work. Men swung axes until their hands bled, women hoed rows under a sun that felt close enough to touch, and kids hauled water and gathered firewood. But at the end of the day, when the family gathered around a table they'd built themselves, eating food they'd grown themselves, in a house they'd raised with their own neighbors—there was a quiet pride no king could give or take away.

Faith kept it honest. The Bible they read by firelight didn't promise easy.

It pledged that work done right, with clean hands and a clean heart, mattered to God. "Whatever your hand finds to do, do it with all your might." That wasn't a suggestion. It was a way of life.

Robert Morris lived it better than most.

He was born dirt-poor in Liverpool in 1734. At thirteen, a stray cannonball during some harbor celebration killed his father and left him an orphan. He crossed the ocean as an indentured boy—no money, no family, just a sharp mind and a willingness to work. In Philadelphia, he started at the bottom: sweeping floors, copying ledgers, hauling crates until his hands were raw.

But Robert believed what the Bible said about using what God gave you. He kept his eyes open, learned fast, and by thirty had his name on the company sign. Ships, warehouses, land—he built one of the biggest fortunes in the colonies. Most men would have stopped there, sat back, and enjoyed it.

When the war came, Robert didn't.

He signed the Declaration of Independence, knowing King George had already put a price on his head. Then he opened his ledgers and poured his money into the fight—over a million dollars of his own cash to feed barefoot soldiers, buy guns, keep the army from falling apart. When Congress was broke, he melted his family's silver into bullets. By the end, he was ruined financially, but he never complained. "A man who won't serve his country when its credit is low," he said, "doesn't deserve to be called a citizen."

He died almost forgotten by the country he helped create, but the freedom we enjoy today? A big chunk of it was paid for with Robert Morris's fortune—and his faith that giving everything was the only way to keep it.

That's what the land did. It took poor immigrants, orphans, and dreamers with nothing but callused hands and turned them into a people who believed they could do anything if they worked hard and kept their word.

It wasn't perfect. There was heartache, failure, and loss along the way. But every cleared field, every new barn, every child who went to bed with a full belly proved the same thing:

Out here, what you built with your own hands stayed yours. And nobody—no king, no lord—could take it away without a fight.

That promise pulled people across oceans. It turned settlers into citizens. And it lit a fire inside them that said, "If we can do this for ourselves, maybe we don't need a King at all."

The flame was growing. And it was starting to warm the hearts of those ready to stand on their own.

MORAL COMPASS SET

As the colonies grew, people needed something solid to guide them day to day—something stronger than a far-off King's whim. They found it in the Bible and in the quiet wisdom of the native people around them.

The settlers leaned hard on Scripture. The Ten Commandments and the Golden Rule weren't just words for Sunday—they were the rules that kept neighbors from tearing each other apart over a stray cow or a crooked fence line. Be honest. Don't steal. Treat the other person the way you'd want to be treated if the tables were turned. Simple stuff, but in a place where one selfish act could bring the whole settlement down, those verses were life or death.

The native tribes brought their own profound truths. Everything was connected—the land, the animals, the people. Hurt one, you hurt them all. Take care of the earth that feeds you. Settle fights with talk before weapons. Look out for the whole village, not just yourself. Those ideas weren't preached from pulpits; they were lived, passed down around campfires for generations.

When those two ways of seeing the world started rubbing up against each other, something new was born. The Bible's call to love your neighbor lined up with the native belief that we're all tied together. Personal responsibility met community care. Mercy met justice.

It gave people a code strong enough to stand against any tyrant who thought he could rule by fear.

My uncle Ted Witt used to tell a story that always stuck with me. As a teenager, he was a handful—always in trouble, constantly testing limits. After one too many scrapes, he told me he finally figured something out: doing the wrong thing hurt him worse than any punishment ever could. From then on, he chose the harder road because it was easier in the long run. Ted grew up to be the kind of dentist everybody trusted and the kind of neighbor you'd call at two in the morning if your kid had a terrible toothache.

William Penn's story reminds me a lot of Uncle Ted's wake-up call.

Penn was born rich in 1644, the son of a big-shot English admiral. He had money, manners, everything going for him. But young William couldn't stomach the fancy religion everyone pretended to follow while treating poor folks like dirt. He got kicked out of Oxford for refusing to wear the right clothes to chapel and started listening to Quaker preachers who talked about an inner light from God that made every person equal.

His father was furious—cut him off cold. Penn ended up in prison more than once, crammed into filthy cells where men coughed their lives away on the straw. But he kept writing, kept preaching peace and fairness, kept quoting Micah: "Do justly, love mercy, walk humbly with your God." King Charles II laughed at his plain coat and hat, but Penn never backed down.

In 1681, the King owed Penn's family a huge debt and paid it off with a chunk of wilderness across the ocean. Penn saw it as God's open door. He sailed over in 1682 and did something almost nobody else bothered to do: he treated the Lenape natives like equals. Under a big elm tree at Shackamaxon, he sat down with their leaders—no soldiers, no threats—just talked. He paid fair prices for the land, promised honest dealings, and swore his people would live in peace. The Lenape, who'd been burned before, looked him in the eye and believed him. That treaty lasted for over seventy years, longer than most "civilized" agreements.

Penn named the place Pennsylvania—"Penn's woods"—and wrote laws that banned slavery, guaranteed fair trials, and welcomed anyone who wanted to worship God in their own way. It wasn't perfect—troubles came later—but for a shining moment, it showed what happens when you treat people the way the Bible and basic human decency say you should.

That blend of biblical justice and native respect for the common good became the quiet backbone of everything America would stand for. It gave people the strength to look a distant king in the eye and say, "No more."

Because when your moral compass points true—toward fairness, mercy, and looking out for each other—no tyrant can spin you off course.

The flame was burning steadily now, ready for the storms ahead.

IDENTITY EMERGES

By the 1700s, most children growing up in the colonies had never seen England. It was a place their great-great-grandparents talked about in fading stories—foggy streets, stone churches, a King who lived in a palace. To them, it felt like a fairy tale from another life. What felt real was the farm they woke up on before dawn, the neighbors who'd drop everything to help raise a barn, the scars on their fathers' hands from years of chopping trees and plowing rocky ground.

Seven generations of sweat had changed everything.

Those old ties to the crown were fraying. Grandparents might still pray for the King out of habit. Still, their grandchildren heard different heroes around the supper table: the grandfather who'd buried half his children that first winter yet kept planting, the uncle who'd stood off a war party with nothing but an old musket and a prayer, the mother who'd crossed an ocean rather than let soldiers kick in her door again.

Take Josiah Quincy, born in 1744 outside Boston. His family went all the way back to the Puritans who'd stepped off the Arbella in 1630. Growing up, Josiah worked the stony fields beside his father from the time he could swing a hoe. He heard the stories at night—how his ancestors clung to their faith through storms that almost sank the ship, through forests full of wolves and worse. Hard work and quiet talks with God were just how you stayed alive.

But as Josiah grew older, something began to burn inside him. He watched tax collectors ride off with money his neighbors had scratched from the dirt. He saw British redcoat soldiers marching down Boston streets like they owned the place. And he sat in candlelit rooms where men—farmers, merchants, preachers—whispered about things that could get them hanged.

One night, a traveling preacher came through during the Great Awakening. The man thundered about tyranny being the devil's tool and standing against it a Christian duty. Josiah felt those words land like a spark on dry grass.

He thought of the Mayflower Compact his ancestors had signed—promising to govern themselves under God's laws, not some far-off King's. Right then, it clicked: their loyalty wasn't to a throne across the ocean. It was to the principles those first freezing settlers had planted, watered with blood and prayer.

The change didn't happen overnight. It crept in, family by family, town by town. From Philadelphia wharves to Virginia tobacco fields, people started feeling a new bond—stronger than blood, deeper than old oaths.
They weren't Englishmen living in America anymore. They were Americans, tied together by the land they'd tamed and the God they answered to.

Town meetings turned into something fierce. Regular people—hands cracked from work—stood up and picked their own leaders. They made rules that fit their lives, not some lord's whim. Revival preachers packed barns and fields, shouting that true authority came from heaven, not a palace. When the Stamp Act hit and crowds tore down tax offices, it wasn't just anger. It was people finally saying out loud who they'd become.

The flame that started as a desperate flicker on frozen shores had taken root deep in American soil. It had a new name now, spoken with pride around kitchen tables and campfires:

American.

And once a people know exactly who they are, no King can tell them who they must be.

CHAPTER ONE
FLAMES OF FAITH

ESCAPING PERSECUTION'S GRIP

In the cold, damp prisons of old England, ordinary men and women huddled in the dark, whispering prayers through cracked lips. Their only crime? Wanting to worship God in their own simple way, without a King or bishop telling them how. Many never walked out alive. But the ones who did escape—climbing aboard leaky ships with nothing but faith and a Bible—carried a fire inside them that would one day light up a whole new nation.

This chapter is about those brave souls. We'll follow their desperate voyages across stormy seas, watch them land on wild shores where everything wanted to kill them, and see how meeting the native people here—sometimes with kindness, sometimes with tragedy—helped shape who we became. Through their stories of raw courage, quiet faith, and refusal to bow, we'll discover the moral backbone that still holds America together. It's the same backbone the world needs now more than ever—because real freedom isn't just about land or laws. It starts with hearts bold enough to trust God and stand tall, no matter what comes.

SECTION ONE:
PERILS OF THE OLD WORLD

RELIGIOUS CHAINS BROKEN

Let's step back to England in the early 1600s, when the King and his bishops controlled every part of how people lived their faith. You had to go along with the Anglican Church's rules exactly, or you'd face serious trouble. Think about it: all you wanted was to follow your beliefs in a straightforward way, maybe just sitting down with the Bible and taking in the words as they were, without even sitting in a church, hearing a preacher, or any of the extra ceremonies. But that could get you pulled away from everything you knew, locked in a freezing, lonely prison, away from your loved ones, with no idea if you'd ever walk free again.

This had nothing to do with helping people grow in their spirit; it was all about holding onto control, where even a small question made you seem like a threat to the throne.

Laws like these broke families apart, making it illegal to meet quietly if it didn't fit the King's version of events. A father might be grabbed right in the middle of a family prayer, leaving his wife and kids to struggle through on their own, their hearts full of worry that he might be gone for good. These rules turned everyone suspicious—people reporting on their own neighbors just to stay safe—and homes that used to feel warm and secure turned into places filled with fear, where a simple knock could change everything. No one thought they could really trust anyone anymore.

Gathering in secret to study the holy writings? That meant risking real horror, like having your thumbs twisted in metal clamps until they broke, or getting burned with hot irons that left scars you'd carry forever. Tormented people would crowd into dark, hidden spots, trying to keep their breathing steady, aware that if they got caught, the pain would spread to everyone they cared about. Even so, they didn't give up, held together by this strong feeling that such profound truths couldn't be repressed, no matter how much it hurt.

For those going through all that, deciding to pack up and sail across the vast ocean became more than just running away. It was like hearing a call from something greater—a way to protect what they believed in, in a new place where no ruler could interfere. They moved ahead on pure trust, leaving that tight grip behind to build a life that felt real and pure. The fear of what lay ahead was not as terrible a thought as the circumstances they were already enduring.

Stories like the one about William Prynne really hit home to me. He was a dedicated Puritan back in the 1630s, someone who couldn't force himself to follow the Anglican ways. He was a brilliant lawyer deeply tied to his values. William would stay up late reading scripture, convinced that true worship came from the heart, not from fancy shows put on because you had to. What kept him going was this rock-solid honesty—he saw changing sacred words to please the King as the worst kind of wrong. So, he wrote pieces that called out the bishops for their over-the-top displays, saying it was like watching actors in a show that made a joke out of genuine faith.

The leaders didn't stand for it. They brought him before the Star Chamber, a court that only answered to the King, and came down hard: a fine so big he couldn't possibly pay it, time behind bars, and then shame in front of everyone in the stocks. With crowds yelling insults, they cut into his ears with rough knives, blood flowing down, while he held back his shouts, all for turning away from those required practices. They kept going, burning his face with hot tools to mark "S.L." for causing trouble, the sharp smoke hurting his eyes as he repeated to himself, "Blessed are they which are persecuted for righteousness' sake." Then they beat him with whips through the streets, each hit tearing his skin, the sound ringing out while some in the crowd laughed and others looked away, unable to watch.

He could've said what they wanted and stopped it all, but he didn't budge—he knew that would mean turning his back on so many others dealing with the same breaks from rules against free belief, families much like his carrying the load.

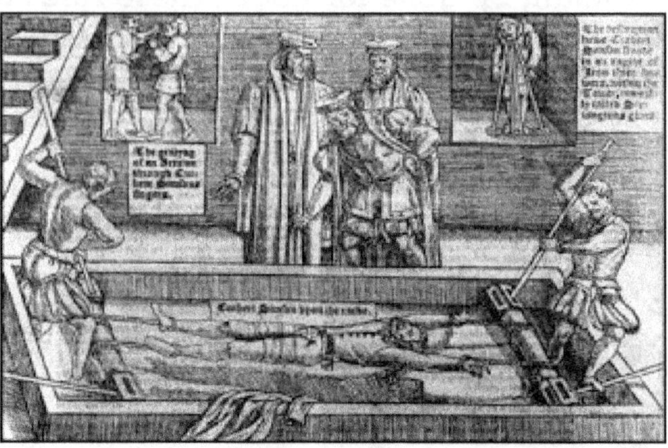

With Kings like Charles I acting as harsh rulers who wanted complete obedience, this kind of cruelty showed what happens when power has no limits: men twisted on machines for private Bible talks, women wasting away in dirty pits for not saying words that went against their souls. It shows why a system rooted in freedom, where beliefs aren't forced, is the better road—giving people room to live out what they hold true without always fearing the whip or something even worse.

That spark of resistance didn't die out; it crossed the sea and came alive again when oppression followed. Take Penelope Barker in the colonies around 1774—her stand was like an echo of those early breaks for freedom. Raised in North Carolina, she married young, endured the loss of her first husband while raising the kids alone, and then found solid ground in another marriage full of quiet strength. She saw that the British laws were more than just taking money; they crushed the spirit, mixing government force with leftovers from that old religious control, where standing up to the King felt like going against God's order.

What moved her was a genuine concern for the people nearby, the families hurt by rules that limited what they could do, and the memories of England's blocks on personal worship—hearing about relatives from the past thrown in jail for their faith pulled at her, pushing her to do something. In Edenton, she brought 51 women together—other wives, mothers, friends—to her house, all of them focused and determined as they talked about the King's latest demands. Drawing from the same unbreakable drive as those who escaped pain to seek plain truth, she led them to promise they'd stop buying British tea and goods, a bold choice that could mean getting locked up or called a traitor, especially back when women didn't often speak out.

"We cannot be indifferent," she wrote in their statement, nodding to the spiritual drive that led those runs from suffering. It was coming together out of real caring, helping tired families by standing as one against the chains trying to hold them down again. Her courage broke through the doubt, turning worries into a strong bond, showing that cutting those ties of faith and rule wasn't something that happened once—it was a lasting fight, passed along to keep safe what really mattered.

Men and women came together, acting as equals in the New World, and working towards a new life based on simple principles of faith, family, love, and community.

By breaking away from those old bindings, they made way for a new start, where beliefs could grow strong and free, building up the strength to face whatever hard times were coming—and setting the stage for the next part of our journey into the magic and blessing we call America today.

ECONOMIC STRANGLEHOLDS

So much of the freedom we hold close to our hearts today was born from the oppression and misery people experienced during those hard times in 17th-century England, when a King's orders could wreck a family's whole life without a second thought. This is a real story from back then, about a farmer named Robert Garth, and how the pain of losing everything pushed him toward something better—if you had the strength and belief to go after it.

Think of a place shrouded in mist and strict laws, where people like Robert got up before dawn, plowing fields that fought back every step. He was in his forties, built solid from years of battling the tough soil in Lincolnshire, his hands rough and marked from the work. He'd inherited his father's small farm—just enough land to support his wife Mary and their four kids, with a little extra to sell at the local market. A desire for more didn't drive Robert. His faith kept him going, drawn from his Bible, which he read every evening. As he fixed fences or planted seeds in the early light, he'd remind himself, "Whatever you do, work at it with all your heart." Those weren't empty words—they guided him, showing that real effort meant something greater than any ruler's demands.

But life turned against people like him. Distant Kings, who never knew the feel of mud under their boots or the pull of a heavy load, were taxed on taxes that hit these hard-working, decent people like a punch to the gut. It wasn't just paperwork; it meant rough collectors dragging away your last bit of grain on horseback, or taking your cow to fill royal barns, while your kids cried themselves to sleep hungry. One dry summer, when no rain came, the tax men showed up regardless, leaving Robert's home filled with the sound of empty stomachs and quiet tears. And it didn't stop there—the lords, dressed fancy and always wanting more, began enclosing the common lands. These were the shared fields where everyone let their animals graze or picked up wood for the fire, no permission needed. Now, under Charles I's rule, barriers went up like walls, turning open ground into private spots for rich men profiting off wool. Robert saw it unfold one sharp fall morning: enforcers riding in hard, flashing official papers, while workers hammered posts into the earth that had fed his family line for ages. His sheep went hungry on what was left, no milk for the winter, and the cold settled in deep, making their house feel like a place of endless struggle.

"This isn't fair," Robert said to Mary that evening by the fading fire, his voice steady but angry, thinking back to stories of ancient Roman rulers who grabbed lands and left people starving in the streets, watching their worlds fall apart from the inside. He remembered the Bible's lessons on greed, how it spread like poison through everything. Greed, envy, anger, and jealousy are all acids that eat their own container. Robert saw that their greed was fueling his own anger, and he felt himself being eaten alive from within.

But even more pain came. The "ship money" tax, supposed to build ships but extended unfairly to folks like him far from the coast, called for money he couldn't scrape together. One rainy dawn, men burst into his barn, seizing his strongest ox and most of his stored food, leaving him kneeling in the dirt. Robert begged these men for even the slightest kindness, but they scoffed at him and ignored his pleas. The worst followed: his youngest son, that lively boy with hair like ripe grain, grew weak from the lack of food and the biting cold. Robert stayed by his side through the long nights, holding onto words from the Psalms—"The Lord will provide"—but the child passed quietly, marked only by a small grave that couldn't hold all the sorrow. It was the king's far-off battles that caused this, decisions from a place that never cared about ordinary lives. Gradually, his grief and depression turned to even more anger and rage.

But that loss didn't break Robert completely—it hardened him into action. In the dim taverns and during church gatherings, quiet talk spread about a New World over the ocean, vast and wild, with land plentiful and free from taxes or enclosures. Ground ready for anyone willing to work it, under open skies that promised release from old burdens. Robert felt it deep inside, like a clear signal. "We can't stay and let our family line end like this," he told Mary, his resolve matching that of figures like John Winthrop, who talked of creating a "city upon a hill"—a light standing against the oppression.

They scraped together what they could: tools traded for ship fare, packs bundled with shaky hands. Robert joined other families carrying the same wounds, facing the sea's fury—storms pounding like enemies, disease creeping through the crowded ship. But his faith steered him, changing his fear into determination, those old scriptures protecting him from despair. When they finally reached the rough coasts of Massachusetts Bay, he set foot on fertile dirt, free from a ruler's grasp. There, his bravery took root—through planting, building, and giving up comforts for a future without chains. Robert's experience wasn't unique; it inspired many more to follow, proving that harsh treatment could shape a tough spirit, ready to blend with the challenges and connections ahead, sparking a freedom that warms us even now.

That spark grew stronger as settlers crossed paths with the people who'd cared for that land long before, their ways mixing in tests that made the light endure. And with each new shipload of settlers, the struggle became slightly easier, with additional help to build warm homes and tend the land to feed all the settlers. But more on that soon—what matters is holding onto that fire in our own lives. If we, as Americans, can remember each day the actual struggle and sacrifice our ancestors made to flee oppression and tyranny, we can better appreciate the fragile gift of the freedoms and comparative comfort we enjoy today.

POLITICAL TYRANNY'S TOLL

It's difficult to explain to someone who experiences our freedoms today about the raw edge of power back in 17th-century England, where Kings like James I and Charles I held sway with a grip that left no room for questions or second thoughts. Normal people lived under a system where one wrong word could land you in irons, your life turned upside down on a whim from the throne. Arbitrary arrests were the norm. A loving family, already struggling, but finally huddling around a wooden table, eating a warm dinner the mother had scratched together, suddenly heard a knock on the door. Soldiers came and snatched away their weary father. His crime was that he spoke out against the Crown's heavy hand, about how his children were starving, and they were taking away his means of surviving. But his pleas fell on ears bent on silencing voices before they could spread. No one had a say in the laws that chained their daily lives. Heartless decrees were handed down from on high, binding everyone without a whisper of input from those who had to live by them. Corruption ran deep, tilting everything toward the elite, the connected few who pocketed favors while ordinary people suffered. Under that iron rule, the spark of liberty flickered low, nearly snuffed out by fear and force, pushing many to dream of a place where a man's conscience could stand tall.

It's hard to grasp now, but picture the toll it took on real lives, like Henry Barrow's, a man whose quiet determination made him a target around 1590. Henry worked hard to become a sharp-minded lawyer in London, well-educated and full of promise. He delved into the law while studying at Cambridge, but in his research, he came across holy writings and ideas about God that seemed to run counter to the narrative pushed by the Crown.

He dove deep into Scripture, seeing a call for pure worship free from the state's meddling. In reading, he realized that the King had twisted these teachings into tools to manipulate people. The aim was not to praise the Lord but to control the masses. What drove him wasn't rebellion for its own sake, but a burning belief that true devotion answered to God alone, not to Kings or bishops who played favorites. "The church is Christ's kingdom," he'd argue in his writings, pulling from ancient truths that echoed the Stoic idea that we all must stand firm in our principles, no matter the storm.

But speaking that truth came at a price. Arrested without warning for gathering with like-minded souls who questioned the Queen's authority over faith—Elizabeth I at the time, though the same shadows loomed under her successors—Henry found himself thrown into the Fleet Prison. In this dank hole, damp walls and chains wore down stronger men. From behind bars, he didn't back down; he scribbled fierce defenses of separation from the corrupt church, smuggling them out to inspire others. The Crown saw it as sedition, a direct slap at their power. Henry was tried in a hurry, with no real chance to defend his heart's convictions. Unbelievably, simply because he believed in a just God, Henry faced the gallows on a chill April morning in 1593. As the noose tightened, Henry held his ground, his last words a prayer for those left behind, sacrificing everything for the hope that one day faith could flourish unchecked. His execution, alongside his friend John Greenwood, sent ripples of fear, but also resolve—reminding folks of tyrants like those in ancient Rome, who beheaded dissenters in public squares, their blood staining the stones as crowds watched in forced silence, empires rotting from unchecked cruelty.

Stories like Henry's fueled the desperation to flee, dimming liberty's light back home but kindling it anew across the sea. Each time the state tore a family apart or killed a man of character for his beliefs, it gave other people of faith the courage to break away. That same unyielding spirit, forged in this darkness, would blend with the harmonies of this new land's first British settlers, laying a foundation for freedom's flame to burn bright and steady.

SECTION TWO: VOYAGE TO HOPE

SEAS OF UNCERTAINTY

I can only imagine what that ocean crossing really meant for those early souls chasing freedom—the ships packed tight with families full of hope, yet facing a sea that seemed bent on breaking them. Wooden vessels like the Mayflower groaned under the weight of over a hundred frightened people, crammed below decks in spaces meant for far fewer, where the air grew thick with the smell of unwashed bodies and salt spray. These courageous souls were dreamers, risking everything for a chance to worship without chains. Their eyes were fixed on a new dream, a distant, unknown world that promised pain and hardship, but that meant nothing when compared to the fact that they were finally free of the King's unyielding grasp.

But first they had to get there. The unforgiving sea had its own tests, whipping up storms that slammed waves like giants' fists against the hull, testing every ounce of their resolve. Sickness crept through the holds like a thief, claiming lives one by one—fevers that burned hot, coughs that rattled bones, leaving families to bury loved ones in the cold depths.

Children died in their mother's arms, an insanely heavy price for anyone to pay just for a taste of freedom. But this might help us understand how horrible it was in the land they left behind. And, when I think of a parent in a dark, scary ship holding their sick child in their arms, I cannot fathom how someone who lives today is not taught properly about the sacrifice our ancestors made so that we can take our freedoms for granted.

When they finally sighted land, ragged and weary, their first act was often dropping to their knees in tearful prayers of thanks, that flame of hope flickering brighter against the unknown ahead.

Take the Brewster family as an example—their experiences show how faith can help people get through tough times. By 1620, William Brewster was in his fifties and had already faced many challenges. He'd left England for Holland years earlier with his wife Mary and their children to escape spies and arrests, all because his views on a purer church didn't align with what the crown required. What sustained him was a strong belief in God's plan. He saw enduring persecution as part of building a better life, much as the Stoics did, who believed absolute freedom comes from within. He often turned to Scripture, like "Endure hardness as a good soldier of Jesus Christ," which helped him lead underground meetings back in England, even knowing a mistake could lead to execution. Mary stood by him through it all—she'd raised six children during the chaos—and together they sailed on the Mayflower with their younger sons, Love and Wrestling, plus two wards, while leaving their older daughters in Holland for their safety. The ship departed in September, but leaks and storms forced two returns, wearing everyone down before the full Atlantic crossing began.

In the dark hold, as storms raged for days, the Brewsters and others held on tightly while the ship rocked violently. Water leaked in, drenching everything, and the motion caused widespread seasickness—those who could worked to plug the leaks. Illness spread quickly—scurvy affected mouths and gums, fevers rose in the cramped space—and William saw people around him weaken, die, and be buried at sea. But he and Mary recited Psalms to comfort the scared children, verses like "He commandeth and raiseth the stormy wind, which lifteth up the waves thereof... Then they cry unto the Lord in their trouble, and he bringeth them out of their distresses." These weren't just words; they offered real support, recalling how God had helped others in the past. William organized Bible readings and songs, keeping his composure when others panicked, motivated by care for his family and the hope of a place where his children could live without constant threats from rulers who publicly punished dissenters to maintain control.

After 66 difficult days, the Mayflower reached Cape Cod, and the survivors, including the Brewsters, offered prayers of thanks.

The struggles weren't over—a brutal winter killed half of them—but the journey had strengthened their resolve. As they landed on that rocky coast, that endurance led to alliances with the area's native people, contributing to the early foundations of freedom in the new land.

FIRST STEPS ON NEW SOIL

Let me paint a picture of those first shaky moments on American soil. The settlers came upon a land stretched out, barren and unforgiving, testing every primal survival instinct these newcomers had. The land they entered was nothing like the land they left. Thick forests and swampy grounds greeted them. They immediately started clearing the woods and building shelter, forcing the weak travelers to hack through underbrush with aching arms and to learn fast how to hunt, fish, or forage to stay alive. Those initial hardships—biting cold, scarce food, strange fevers—pulled them all together like nothing else. After all they had already been through, they forged bonds that turned strangers into family, sharing what little they had in a fight against the wild.

Prayers for guidance filled the air each day, simple pleas rising at dawn and dusk, seeking strength from above to face the unknowns. And when the first small victories came—a successful hunt or a sturdy shelter—they saw it as clear signs of God's favor, that hand of providence guiding them toward a freer life. Edward Winslow lost his wife, Elizabeth, during that brutal first winter in Plymouth, and Susanna White lost her husband, William White. After a period of grieving, they married each other on May 12, 1621, becoming the first couple to wed in the Plymouth Colony. They went on to have five children together, though only two—Josiah (born around 1629) and Elizabeth (born around 1630)—survived to adulthood. It was just that way. They were in a strange land, and they made the best of their circumstances, somehow, knowing how blessed they were to survive.

Women were the ones who really held things together back then, working quietly in the background with an inner strength that kept entire communities from falling apart. Martha Washington is a great example—she was born Martha Dandridge in 1731 down in Virginia's tidewater area, and her story shows what real staying power looks like during those tough early days in the colonies. Growing up on a plantation taught her young how to run a home and handle land, skills that proved enormously handy as the fight for independence ramped up. When she married George in 1759, she stepped right into managing Mount Vernon, keeping everything running smoothly while he took on all sorts of public roles. It wasn't about chasing glory or control for her; what kept her steady was this solid faith from her Anglican roots. Anglicans viewed tough times as part of a larger plan from above, like the old Stoics did, who saw hardships shaping who you are.

"I am still determined to be cheerful and happy, in whatever situation I may be," she once said, and those words nail how she always managed to spot a bit of hope even in the roughest spots.

NATIVE AMERICANS WELCOMES AND WARNINGS

"American History is not history without Native history." – Lily Gladstone

It would be remiss to write the story of America without including the contributions and struggles of the Natives who inhabited this continent for generations before Europeans stepped foot onto the shores.

Let me draw you into those early days when the wide-open lands of North America were already alive with Native American communities full of life, families raising kids, tending fields, and sharing stories around fires—long before any English sails appeared on the waves. Their unique culture and their relationship with nature were unparalleled. That's when the Spanish Conquistadors barreled in around the early 1500s, fueled by this raw craving for riches and power that tore through everything in their path, leaving heartbreak in their wake.

Men like Juan Ponce de León stepped onto Florida's beaches in 1513, staking a claim for Spain with weapons ready, sparking a chain of brutal clashes with tribes that cut deep into Native lives like a knife through skin. Pánfilo de Narváez tried to seize the Gulf Coast in 1528, but his group crashed along shores from Florida to Texas, scrambling against local tribes in frantic fights for scraps and spoils. Down south, Hernán Cortés brought down the Aztec world in Mexico from 1519 to 1521—it was pure chaos, with thousands lost in brutal sieges and clashes, bodies filling the streets of Tenochtitlán as people starved and suffered. Then Hernando de Soto charged northward from 1539 to 1543, storming through the Southeast all the way to the Mississippi, his crew raping women, raiding villages for supplies, and forcing folks into chains, walking away from broken homes and smoldering ruins where families once thrived.

"While the Pilgrims landed on 'Plymouth Rock' in 1620, the Spanish had already settled in to the Southwest beginning in the late 1500s, and with the coming of Europeans, some tribes suffered massive declines in populations due to disease and violence. Some Tribes were wiped out by 90 percent, while others were completely decimated." – Deb Haaland

The cost in human lives was heartbreaking—thousands cut down outright in those ruthless conquests. Meanwhile, Spanish rules, including the "encomienda system," locked Native people into a nightmare of forced work. Basically, it was a setup where Spanish settlers were "issued" groups of Natives by the crown, supposedly to "protect" and teach them Christianity in return for their labor and goods. Still, in reality, it turned into outright exploitation that crushed lives. Folks ended up trapped in exhausting tasks, their backs giving out under brutal whippings as they mined silver deep in the earth or slaved away in fields under the hot sun for their Spanish overseers. And brutal rape was used as a heartless method of domination. Women were ripped from their families and violated to shatter any spirit of resistance, leaving emotional scars that rippled through generations and tore apart the fabric of their communities. Many modern Mexicans are descendants of Spaniards and Indians.

Over in the Caribbean, the Taíno folks were nearly wiped out in just a few short decades, their communities dropping from hundreds of thousands to almost none, torn apart by chains and brutality that left villages in ashes, and the few who hung on worked until they dropped. The looting hit just as hard—priceless gold and silver hauled off to Spain in amounts that'd be worth billions now, holy items from generations past just tossed into fires and melted like they meant nothing. Estimates put Native deaths under Spanish hands at millions in that first century, though disease played its part; the cruelty mirrored despots like those in ancient tyrannies, who impaled rebels on stakes for public terror, empires crumbling under their own vicious weight. These terrible men brought with them the very same oppression that their English counterparts were fleeing, and subjected scores of Native Americans to brutality. Yet amid the horror, some exchanges trickled through—the Columbian Exchange brought metal tools, horses that transformed hunting for tribes like the Plains Indians, and crops like wheat that mixed into surviving diets. Missionaries offered coerced education, believing that Native American customs that had lasted for millennia were "savage" and needed to be replaced with Christianity. A handful of actually decent people, like Bartolomé de las Casas, witnessed these crimes and pushed for reforms banning the worst abuses in 1542. Intermarriages birthed blended societies, and trade alliances, like French fur partnerships, sparked mutual gains, though often at the cost of Native ways fading under pressure.

When the English and other Europeans arrived later, they weren't always the kinder alternative—their hands carried the same stains of violence and land hunger, varying by place and time but often leading to displacement and clashes. The Spanish charged in with military might, enslaving and converting by force, earning a dark reputation spread by English rivals. English settlers in Virginia or New England began with uneasy pacts, such as those with the Powhatan or Wampanoag.

Still, wars erupted—most clashes stemmed from fear and misunderstanding—because when you don't grasp another culture, you are prone to reject it. One incident can spark a war. The Pequot War in 1636-1638 saw villages massacred. Survivors were sold into slavery. King Philip's War in 1675-1676 claimed thousands of lives. Lands were seized as Natives were pushed aside like obstacles. The French mainly focused on trading up in Canada, forging partnerships with local tribes instead of launching full-on takeovers, even if they still got into fights and dealt in enslaved people. The Dutch around New York stuck to bargaining when they could, but they turned vicious in a clash if someone pushed back. None of these newcomers came in total peace; a thread of taking advantage wove through every group, though the Spanish struck with the most extraordinary brutality right from the start.

Diseases ravaged everything—Europeans from Spain onward unwittingly unleashed smallpox, measles, and more on populations with no defenses, wiping out up to 90 percent in some areas. Diseases brought by the Spanish starting in the 1520s hit Mexico and the Caribbean like a storm, wiping out whole communities in ways that still ache to think about; de Soto's journey carried those invisible killers through the Southeast, leaving entire groups of people and their ways of life just gone. The English and other arrivals only made it worse later, with outbreaks like the one from 1616 to 1619 that devastated the coastal tribes in New England, hollowing out villages that had thrived for ages. Altogether, this wave of sickness cut Native populations by half or more across the Americas by 1650—a quiet devastation that cleared paths for the takers who followed. This is a common tragedy in the history of the world. Conquests have wiped out entire civilizations since the beginning of recorded time.

But even in those early, uneasy moments when the English arrived, some fragile connections started to take shape—simple swaps of beads for warm furs or handy tools for tips on the land sparked a bit of trust, little acts that bridged the gaps where no common words existed. They would sometimes communicate with hand signals and sketches in the soil, pointing out dangers like brutal winters or spots teeming with fish, slowly turning strangers into something more. Shared meals around fires hinted at possible alliances, bowls of corn stew passed with nods that eased fears. But misunderstandings flared into conflicts—differing views on land sparked skirmishes, trust fracturing like dry earth underfoot. Everyone was always on edge.

One moment that cut through the tension was Pocahontas's bold stand in 1608. As I briefly mentioned in this book's introduction, she was a young Powhatan woman whose quick thinking saved Captain John Smith from her father's warriors. Born Matoaka around 1596, she grew up amid her tribe's rhythms, curious and spirited, drawn to the strange newcomers at Jamestown.

When Smith stared down death, with those clubs hovering ready to strike, she flung herself over him, her desperate words shifting rage into a moment of grace—maybe out of pure kindness or a deep urge for harmony, but either way, it bridged that chasm between worlds in an instant. That bold move gave everyone a chance to breathe and talk things through, leading her to embrace their faith later and marry John Rolfe, tying together English ways with her Native roots, all while dealing with pushback from folks on both sides who didn't get it. Her bravery came from this quiet drive to bring people together, much like those old wise ones who believed real strength shows up when you stare down fear for something bigger. As the Stoics put it, true guts means stepping up despite the terror. Even though she died too soon in 1617, what she left behind cracked open doors to shaky agreements, mixing steadfast spirit with the deep knowledge of the land's first people to keep that budding spark of freedom alive, paving the way for stronger ties down the road.

During the Revolutionary War, with George Washington out leading the Continental Army, his wife, Martha, really stepped in. She made a difference in ways that brought the whole fight down to a personal level—trekking hundreds of miles every winter to be with him at places like Valley Forge, where the men were freezing in tatters and hunger never let up. She'd rally other women to stitch up shirts and patch socks, tend to the ill herself, and share kind words that boosted morale when things looked bleak. Her bravery stood out in those icy stretches, sharing the dangers of sickness and raids, all fueled by her deep care for her husband and the push for freedom, and by her willingness to give up her own ease to back the men standing against oppression. Compared to the brutal kings back in England, who had rebels torn apart and hanged in gruesome shows to scare everyone silent, Martha's steady resistance felt even more powerful—women like her mixing sheer determination with lessons from the Bible to hold the line at home. What she did went beyond just getting by; it embedded strong values at the heart of this emerging country, proving that one person's belief could lift everyone around them.

Those hard-fought wins, earned through that kind of toughness, started opening people up to the folks who'd been on the land first, mixing their know-how with the newcomers' drive to keep that spark of enduring freedom burning strong. We must never forget the pain endured by Native Americans and cherish the contributions to our current way of life of their customs, laws, and culture.

SECTION THREE:
BLENDING BELIEFS

JUDEO-CHRISTIAN CORE

Think about what really powered those early days in America—the solid grounding from Judeo-Christian ideas that gave people a real sense of value and fairness, right from Genesis, where it says everyone's created in God's image, putting the thought out there that nobody's inherently better than anyone else. These people had experienced religious persecution first-hand. They'd watched close friends get killed just for holding onto their beliefs, so religious freedom wasn't some abstract idea—it was everything to them, a lifeline worth dying for. That deep conviction shaped how the settlers viewed equality, seeing it as a basic right—handed down from God Himself, putting kings and everyday people on equal footing.

Micah, the Old Testament prophet who called people to live out God's will through simple, powerful guidance, urged them to do justice, love mercy, and walk humbly—and those words seeped right into the laws they built, creating rules designed to protect the weak and hold the powerful accountable. Proverbs offered practical advice for everyday living—like putting in honest effort, speaking kindly, and avoiding foolish choices—that helped guide them through the tough job of carving out homes in an untamed place. And the one common denominator in their lives was faith, the reliable spark that kept them pushing forward when things got rough, turning tough breaks into chances to move ahead, all with the belief that a greater force was steering the way. We can help this country to last forever if we just remember where we came from and do everything we can to hold on to these same beliefs for our children's sake.

A time when this all came to life was the Great Awakening in the 1740s. Dynamic men like George Whitefield preached to huge groups in spots like Philadelphia, their words booming across open fields filled with all sorts of people—farmers brushing off dirt from a long day, shop owners stepping away from their counters, even doubters who showed up anyway. George was someone completely dedicated to his mission, born in 1714 in England to a family running a small inn, but losing his dad young meant scraping by and searching for meaning early on. What got him going was a powerful shift in his twenties, a deep faith experience that fired him up and sent him sailing across the ocean seven times, ignoring his weak health, rough seas, and pushback from folks who thought he was rocking the boat too much. "I am willing to go to prison and to death for Jesus Christ," he'd declare, tapping into that old stoic toughness of tackling hard times for a cause worth more than personal safety.

During one of those massive outdoor meetings, with storm clouds gathering and wind gusts picking up, George spoke of coming together under God. He opened his Bible and spoke his truth in passages that bridged gaps—between wealthy and struggling, between fresh arrivals and long-timers—showing how their shared beliefs could create a bond no oppressor could break. People who normally kept to their own circles ended up side by side, some with tears running down their faces as it sank in, building a surge of determination that pulled the colonies closer and turned individual faith into a group defense against control.

Compared to kings across the water who'd order dissenters torched alive at the stake, screams filling the air to force total obedience, that kind of spiritual fire was untouchable. George's messages did more than soothe; they got people living out fairness and compassion in real ways, folding those principles right into the spirit that was becoming America.

With that base in place, it was easy for our early settlers to incorporate a similar wisdom from the land's original inhabitants, adding depth to that growing flame of resilient liberty and making it even tougher to put out.

NATIVE HARMONIES

Think about how Native ways of life added depth to the settlers' world, like how their communal circles—gathering in rings to talk things out as equals—shaped how early Americans came together in town meetings. Everyone had a voice without one person towering over the rest. That respect for nature and community, seeing the land as a gift to care for rather than use up, fostered a sense of stewardship that helped them all make decisions about farming and sharing their resources. People learned to live in balance so future generations could thrive. Peace pipes, passed in solemn rituals to seal agreements, became symbols of covenants built on trust. They were like oaths sworn on sacred ground. And those wisdom circles, where Native American elders shared stories and lessons around fires, were very similar to the assemblies settlers formed. This was their way of passing down knowledge that strengthened their fragile communities against hard times.

One story that brings this blending to life is the meeting under the great elm tree in 1682, when William Penn sat down with Tamanend, a wise Lenape leader whose calm presence commanded respect from his people, earned through years of guiding them through harsh winters and rival threats.

Penn was a man who'd faced his own storms—he had been jailed back in England for his Quaker beliefs that put faith above kings' decrees—Penn arrived in Pennsylvania driven by a vision of peace, seeing the land as a divine chance to build fairly. What moved him was a deep conviction that true strength comes from humility and fairness. Penn had developed these convictions by reading the works of ancient stoics who taught that we must endure trials with quiet resolve for the sake of harmony. As they gathered, the Lenape shared their pipe, smoke rising as a sign of honest intentions, while Penn offered words from his Scriptures about loving neighbors and walking justly.

Tamanend had been humanized by his own losses in conflicts with earlier settlers who were not as accommodating. But he trusted Penn's earnestness, so he chose courage over suspicion, sealing a treaty that promised mutual respect—no stealing land, fair trades, and handling disputes like kin. "We meet on the broad pathway of good faith and goodwill," Penn is said to have declared. He kept his voice steady as he bridged two worlds together. He had seen the devastation caused by Kings across the ocean, who'd ordered villages destroyed and families scattered in bloody conquests to crush any defiance. William Penn deeply desired a pact with the Natives, born from shared rituals.

Reaching out a hand to each other in an untamed world held communities steady. These early actions sparked a resilient liberty that grew stronger, lighting the way toward a nation where individual grit and collective care turned adversity into enduring hope.

THE LIGHT OF KNOWLEDGE

After centuries of repression, where anyone could be dragged away and tortured or murdered simply for speaking what they believed, it must have been amazing to see how knowledge became a beacon in those early days. Many people experienced, for the first time, unbiased news flying through the colonies—simple printed sheets tacked up in taverns or passed hand to hand, cutting through rumors to deliver straight facts that everyone could grasp. That free press shone a light on hidden truths, uncovering corruption and lies from the Old Country an ocean away, empowering ordinary folks to question and stand firm. Citizens were finally informed, becoming guardians of liberty. Now it seemed like everybody was staying vigilant against any shadow that threatened their hard-won rights. And propaganda? They saw it for what it was—a tyrant's sneaky weapon, twisting words to control minds. They remembered too well these terrible overlords who'd force false confessions through torture, bones cracking under racks until victims echoed the lies or faced the flames. In sixth grade, I had a very aware teacher who taught us the various types of propaganda, like 'testimonials' where someone will attest to a product or idea with a personal endorsement; 'bandwagon' appealing to the idea that "everyone is doing it", like peer pressure to join the majority to avoid feeling left out; 'name-calling' labeling opponents or ideas with negative terms like "radical" or "unpatriotic"; or 'glittering generalities' using vague, emotionally appealing words like "freedom," "honor," or "progress" to associate their cause with positive values, without specific details or proof. Even a sixth-grader with eyes wide open could see when he or she was being manipulated. So many people are gullible to propaganda. It's human nature.

One person who learned to use propaganda gently and effectively for the American cause is Ben Franklin, during his time behind the printing press in Philadelphia around the 1730s. Ben was a man whose clever mind and steady hands turned ink into a force for clarity. He started young, born in 1706 to a large Boston family where money was tight, apprenticing as a printer under his brother but hating the harsh treatment—enough to run away at 17, landing in Philadelphia with little more than his youthful drive, ambition, and a love of books. He was driven by a quiet faith shaped by his Puritan roots. Franklin voiced a practical wisdom that saw truth as a divine tool for better living, again like the ancient stoics who urged seeking knowledge to navigate life's storms. "Lost time is never found again," he'd later write in his almanack, a reminder born from his own hustles to remind folks to use every moment wisely. Running his shop, Ben didn't just print jobs; he exposed scandals, like when he published pieces challenging the governor's shady deals, risking arrest but holding firm because he believed an informed public was the best defense against overreach. His courage showed in quiet ways—dodging censors by using satire, humanizing the fight for free speech as an everyday battle anyone could join. Kings across the sea would silence printers by seizing presses and hanging them as traitors in public squares. But Ben helped spread the light of free speech, born from the blood that soaked the ground of England from people less fortunate who tried to speak out. Now, nothing could dim that light Ben helped spread.

With newly spread knowledge fanning the flames of awareness, our resilient idea of liberty grew brighter, carrying the colonies from faithful beginnings into a new era where old ties faded and a bold American identity rose to confront far-off rulers.

CHAPTER TWO
GENERATIONS OF GROWTH

FROM SUBJECTS TO SOVEREIGNS

Seven generations passed like seasons, each one quietly wearing away the old chains of loyalty—until, by 1776, a new kind of people stood on this soil, heads high, no longer waiting for a distant king to tell them who they were or what they could become.

SECTION ONE:
EARLY TIES TO EUROPE

Picture it: you finally stagger off the ship after weeks of being tossed around like cargo. Your legs are shaky, your stomach is empty, and the smell of the ocean is still stuck in your nose.

The shore in front of you is nothing but mud, mosquitoes, and endless trees. And the very first thing the men do—before they even unload the sick or bury the dead—is climb the rickety palisade they've thrown together and run up the flag. Not some new banner. The same flag with a red cross, they grew up saluting back home. That sight must have meant everything to them: a piece of England planted right there in the wilderness, proof they hadn't really left the mother country—they'd just stretched her farther than anyone thought possible.

In those early years, from Jamestown's swampy riverbanks all the way up to the cold harbors of New England, people still felt English to the bone. They'd fled persecution, yes—some had seen friends whipped or thrown in jail for praying the "wrong" way—but that didn't mean they hated England, far from it. They loved her the way you love a difficult parent: fiercely, painfully, even when she hurt you. They'd been taught since childhood that the King ruled by God's own appointment, that to honor him was to honor the Lord Himself. So they named their muddy little settlements after English towns, drank to His Majesty's health with whatever passed for wine, and sent long letters home describing how they were carrying the light of true faith and English law into the darkness.

BRITISH ROOTS CLING

Those first survivors never thought of themselves as starting a new nation. They were Englishmen doing what Englishmen had always done—pushing the borders of the realm outward. When a supply ship finally showed up after months of silence, you'd see grown men running down to the water like boys on Christmas morning, shouting and waving their hats as crates of real bread, iron pots, and news from London came ashore. That connection felt like breathing after holding your breath for half a year.

Their laws were English laws. Their courts ran the way courts ran in Dorset or Yorkshire—twelve honest men deciding guilt or innocence, no nobleman able to seize your farm on a whim. In Virginia, the House of Burgesses argued about tobacco prices and land grants the same way county gentlemen argued back home, convinced they were extending England's glory across the sea. Trade tied them even tighter: great hogsheads of tobacco rolled down to the rivers on English-built ships, and in return came plows from Birmingham, cloth from Manchester, and the latest word on the King's wars with Spain or France. A planter out in the tidewater country could hitch his ox to a plowshare made in Sheffield and feel, for a moment, that the old world wasn't so far away after all.

Holidays followed the old calendar too. On the King's birthday, they'd fire off muskets in salute, roast whatever meat they'd managed to cure, and dance the same way their ancestors had danced under English oaks. Those nights around the fire, with fiddles playing familiar music and voices raised in songs everybody knew by heart, kept the homesickness from swallowing them whole.

SAMUEL THORNE

Let me tell you about a young man named Samuel Thorne—he feels real to me because so many like him left bits of their stories behind in faded courthouse records and yellowed letters. Samuel grew up in a narrow London street where his father made barrels for the brewers. In 1635, at nineteen, he signed away seven years of his life for the price of a passage to Virginia. He wasn't escaping the hangman or running from debt; he just wanted land of his own, and he believed the King's colonies were the place an honest Englishman could get it.

When their ship, battered and leaking, finally nosed into the James River, half the passengers were too weak to stand. Samuel was one of the few still on his feet. While others retched over the rail, he and a couple of sailors climbed the mainmast in a swaying wind and nailed up the red ensign. He wrote later that the instant the flag caught the breeze, he felt the ground steady under him, like the ship had finally remembered which kingdom it belonged to. That night, sitting in a dirt-floor hut with smoke stinging his eyes, he scratched out a letter by firelight: "We have raised His Majesty's colors over a proper English fort, and though the wilderness presses close, we are not afraid.

God and King Charles have brought us safe thus far, and with their help we shall make this place a new shire of England."

Samuel's faith wasn't some gentle thing—it was iron-hard. He'd sat in London churches listening to preachers thunder that England was God's chosen nation, set apart to carry true religion to the heathen. Samuel felt every blister on his hands from hoeing tobacco. Every night he spent protecting his humble shack, gripping his musket while wolves howled beyond the palisade, he told himself it was part of the same sacred work his ancestors had done. Samuel was an Englishman above all, and he felt he was doing his part like his forefathers, just like when they drove back the Armada or stood firm against Catholic plots. When fever came through the settlement the following summer and the graveyard filled faster than they could dig it, Samuel helped carry the dead and still found words to steady the living: "We are English. We do not break."

The years went by more quickly than anyone expected. Samuel finished his seven years of service, took the fifty acres he'd earned with his sweat, and started building a real life. He married a quiet girl named Elizabeth who'd crossed on the ship after his. She understood the ache of leaving everything behind, but they both still believed they were planting England in new ground. Together, they built their own frame house with a proper brick chimney that actually drew the smoke instead of choking the room, a small thing that felt like triumph after years of dirt-floor huts.

On the ridgepole above the door, Samuel hung a little Union Jack flag he'd pieced together from scraps of red and blue cloth traded from a passing ship. Every morning when the wind caught it, he'd pause on his way to the fields and feel that same steadiness he'd known the day he nailed the big ensign to the mast.

Whenever the settlement came together—whether to raise a neighbor's barn before the rains came or to baptize a new baby in the little log meetinghouse—the hard work always ended the same way. Tools went quiet, a fire got built, and supper was passed around on wooden platters. By the time the stars came out, everybody was worn out, arms aching, hands blistered and black from handling rough timber all day.

But no one headed home yet.

They'd fill whatever cups or horns they had with cider or small beer, stand up together, and lift them high. Tired, hoarse from laughing and shouting instructions over the wind, they'd shout the same words they'd known since childhood: "God save the King!"

And they meant every syllable. To them, that far-away man on the throne was still the protector of all they held dear—their laws, their faith, their right to start over. He felt like the distant head of the family they were all part of, and they were proud to be building his empire on new ground. That toast wasn't just a habit. It was love.

But here's the thing nobody saw coming, not even men like Samuel: every year the supply ships took a little longer, every letter from home felt a little more like reading about someone else's life. When Native Americans raided or crops failed or fever came again, no royal troops were riding over the hill—just the men standing next to you in the cornfield, the preacher in the log meetinghouse, the neighbors who showed up with axes and rifles because that's what you did when trouble knocked. Slowly, without speeches or declarations, people started solving their own problems. And with every problem they solved themselves, the old habit of looking across the ocean for answers faded just a little more.

The roots were still deep. The love hadn't died. But something new was pushing up through the soil—something stubborn, quiet, and unstoppable. The same hands that once raised the King's flag were starting to wonder why they couldn't raise their own families, make their own rules, and protect their own futures without waiting for permission from a throne three thousand miles away.

That wondering took seven generations to grow into words, and then into action. But it started right there, under that proud red cross snapping in the salt wind, while men like Samuel Thorne believed with all their hearts they were being good Englishmen. Little did they know the flame they were tending wasn't England's anymore. It was becoming something the world had never seen before.

EUROPEAN INFLUENCES LINGER

Not every ship that came over the Atlantic to the New World was English. By the time the 1620s and 30s rolled around, you could already find little clusters of people scattered along the coast who didn't sound anything like the folks in Virginia or Massachusetts.

Swedes were putting up solid log houses along the Delaware River before the English even bothered to claim it. Germans began arriving in large numbers in Pennsylvania, farming the land as they had always done and singing their old hymns in the fields. And the Dutch—practical, tough traders—had taken a swampy island at the mouth of the Hudson, drained it, built canals, thrown up windmills, and turned the whole place into a busy little port called New Amsterdam. It looked more like home than anything the English had managed.

If you walked the dirt paths in those settlements, the air was full of different languages. English got mixed in with the thick, guttural Dutch you'd hear in the markets, German out in the barns, and French from the Huguenots down south. Go to church on Sunday, and it wasn't the same prayer book everywhere.

In New Amsterdam, the minister preached from a massive Dutch Bible under a roof that could have been lifted straight out of Utrecht, and the congregation answered back in the accents they'd brought from Friesland or Zeeland. Kids learned to read from primers printed in Amsterdam or Geneva, not London. Weddings were still done the old way—long tables, rye bread, spiced meat, the bride in a lace cap, everybody toasting with genever, the original Dutch and Flemish gin, instead of ale. Even the farms looked different: long narrow strips running back from the water, houses with those stepped gables you'd see all over Holland. And as the colonies grew, so did their diversity. It was almost as if many small worlds were coexisting, but entirely different and not interacting all that much with each other.

These people weren't trying to invent something brand new. They were trying to keep what they already had—safe from meddling Kings and church courts that wanted everyone to pray and live the same way.

JAN VAN DER HEYDEN

Take Jan van der Heyden, a bricklayer from Amsterdam. Jan was the everyday kind of man who could lay a straight wall and feed a family doing it. In 1645, he packed his wife, Anna, and their three young children into the stinking hold of a West India Company ship and sailed west. He wasn't fleeing troops or a dungeon the way some of the English separatists were. Jan just wanted ground he could call his own, a place where the elders couldn't drag him into court for missing a service he didn't believe in, and where his kids could grow up speaking Dutch without getting sideways looks.

The crossing was rough. Fever ran through the ship, storms ripped the sails, and for weeks they ate hard biscuit crawling with bugs and drank water that turned their stomachs. Anna went into labor somewhere out in the open Atlantic and delivered a little girl they named Neeltje while the ship rolled and groaned. Jan held that tiny baby in his hands, raw from salt and rope, whispering the exact words his father had taught him: "If I dwell in the uttermost parts of the sea, even there shall thy hand lead me." When the ship finally limped into the harbor and the cannon on the fort fired its welcome, Jan stepped onto the wharf and went down on his knees, crying like a man who'd just been pulled out of deep water.

They found a narrow lot of land just outside the town wall. Jan built a small brick house with his own hands—the first real home they'd ever owned outright. On Sundays, the family walked to the church inside the fort, picking their way past pigs in the lane, and sang the old psalms in Dutch while the organ wheezed. Every Pinkster (that old Dutch Pentecost feast), they'd close the shutters tight, roast a fat goose until the whole house smelled like heaven, and clear the kitchen floor for dancing. Jan would scrape away on a beat-up fiddle while the children spun and stomped until they collapsed in a heap, breathless and giggling.

When Neeltje turned six, Jan spent evenings after work whittling her a pair of little wooden skates, just like the ones he'd had as a boy back on the Dutch canals.

The first hard freeze that winter, he bundled everybody up and marched them down to the Collect Pond. They spent the whole day out there—falling, sliding, grabbing each other to stay upright, laughing so hard their ribs ached and their cheeks burned from the cold. For one afternoon, the wilderness felt a million miles away, and they were just a family on a frozen canal in Holland again.

Everybody knew the English were coming. Word drifted in that the King had handed the whole area to his brother and that warships were on the way. Some Dutch families sold what they could and sailed home. Others just waited, angry and scared. Jan looked at the house he'd built, the garden Anna had wrestled out of strange soil, the children already picking up a few English words from the docks, and decided. One night, he told Anna, quietly so the kids wouldn't hear, "The Lord brought us across the water. If the flag changes, we'll learn the new language and pay whatever they ask. But faith and family and honest work—those stay ours."

In 1664, English ships arrived. The governor surrendered without firing a shot, and the next morning, New Amsterdam was New York. The church bells rang the same as always, only now the preacher slipped in a little English. Jan's oldest boy went to work for an English trader to pick up the language faster. But on Sunday nights, the family still sat around the hearth while Jan read from the big Dutch Bible they'd carried over like it was made of gold.

Jan died in 1698 and was buried in the Dutch churchyard. By then, his grandchildren spoke English without thinking about it, voted in an assembly nobody in London took seriously yet, and—when the time came—stood right alongside the Adamses and the Washingtons. The Dutch words faded, the skates became outgrown, the little brick house was torn down for something taller. But what Jan carried across the ocean stayed: the rock-hard belief that a man ought to be able to work, worship, and raise his family without some far-off ruler deciding how it's done.

You saw it everywhere—in German farmhouses, Swedish trading posts, French vineyards down south. People held on to the old ways long enough for the best parts to sink deep into this new ground. And out of that stubborn grip on what was good from the past came something Europe never saw coming: a people who decided the only King worth answering to ruled from a lot higher throne than any palace in London, Amsterdam, or anywhere else.

That slow mixing, that quiet refusal to let go of faith and freedom—it was how the fire started. Small embers at first, but steady. And steady fires are the hardest ones to put out.

INITIAL LOYALTIES TESTED

T.S. Eliot, in "The Hollow Men," opines that the world will not end with a bang, but a whimper.... The early settlers did not have a sudden revelation that they were living in oppressive conditions. It was a slow roll-out, the pain of a thousand small wounds.

The break didn't start with muskets or declarations. It began with a ship pulling into harbor carrying a packet of papers from London—another tax, another regulation, another bill for somebody else's war. At first, people just shook their heads over supper, poured another cup of cider, and paid it. They were still Englishmen (or Dutchmen or Germans who had learned to live under the English crown), and paying the king's duties felt like the natural order of things.

But the complaints got louder. A new governor would step ashore, powdered and buckled, expecting the same instant bowing and scraping he'd have gotten in some sleepy shire back home. Out here, a man had to patch his own roof after a hurricane, round up his own militia when raiders hit the next farm, and wait half a year for an answer to a letter. Being told to sit quietly and open his purse started to feel less like respect and more like a yoke.

The taxes themselves weren't crushing—not yet. A little extra on molasses here, a stamp on every deed and newspaper there, a duty on window glass and paint. What stung was that the money vanished across the ocean, and nothing came back but more orders. Governors like Berkeley, down in Virginia, or Bernard, up in Boston, didn't help. When the assemblies pushed back, the governors shut them down, sent the members home, and quartered redcoats in towns that had never asked for soldiers. On the frontier, people were still burying neighbors scalped by Native Americans or ravaged by disease, yet the governor's answer too often felt like a hand on their throat instead of a shield at their back.

Robert Beverley—most folks just called him Major Beverley, though he never made a fuss about rank—was the kind of man who believed order came from the top down, straight from the throne and from God Himself. Born sometime in the 1630s, raised on a tidewater plantation, he'd worked the tobacco fields as a boy, married into good land, and built a solid brick house near Jamestown. He sat on the Governor's Council, took his oaths to the king seriously, and every Sunday rode to Bruton Parish Church to hear the parson read from Romans about the powers that be being ordained of God.

Then came 1676.

The frontier was on fire.

Tribes hit settlement after settlement, and people were dying faster than the militia could ride out. Governor Berkeley wanted caution—treaties with the friendly tribes, forts along the falls, no wild offensives that would bring every nation down on their heads. But Nathaniel Bacon and a lot of angry young planters wanted blood and land, and they wanted it now.

When Bacon raised his army anyway, Berkeley branded him a traitor.

Beverley sided with the governor. He called out the militia from Middlesex County, saddled up with his old sword and a brace of pistols, and rode into the swamps. He fought men he'd known for years—neighbors he'd shared meals with, stood beside at baptisms. They looted his plantation, drove off his cattle, and left his wife and children hiding in the woods while torches lit the night. One morning, he came home to find his barns still smoldering and a scrap of paper nailed to his door: "Berkeley's dog."

He could have changed sides. Plenty of men did—one quiet ride to Bacon's camp and the raids on his place would stop. His family would be safe. But at night, with the house dark and the Bible open on the table, Beverley read the same verses he'd grown up on and felt that old loyalty like a weight on his chest. "The Lord sets up kings," he told his wife, voice low and tired. "If we pull that down, what's left but chaos?" So he kept riding, kept fighting, kept believing the crown would make it right in the end.

It didn't. Bacon torched Jamestown itself. He died of fever soon after, but the rebellion dragged on until royal troops finally arrived and hanged the ringleaders. Berkeley was called home in disgrace, and men like Beverley were left staring at blackened fields and empty barns, wondering what any of it had been worth.

He rebuilt, retook his seat in the assembly, and lived out his days as a respected planter. But the hurt never left him—the knowledge that decent men he'd called friends had looked him in the eye and chosen the other side. And somewhere, deep down, he must have wondered if they'd had cause.

That was the real crack—quiet, personal, painful. Not some grand battle, just a thousand families like Beverley's, torn between the king they'd been taught to revere and the neighbors they'd bled beside. Those early taxes, those high-handed governors, those unanswered raids—they didn't start the revolution. They just forced ordinary men to look hard at where their hearts truly lay.

For some, loyalty held right to the end, no matter the cost. For others, the cost finally became too high.

Either way, something shifted in those years. A small flame started burning in kitchens and churchyards and lonely rides home through the dark. It didn't roar yet. It just glowed, steady and warm, waiting for the wind that would one day make it blaze. The whimper was slowly becoming a bang.

SECTION TWO:
MID-GENERATIONAL SHIFTS

LOCAL GOVERNANCE RISES

By the middle of the 1700s, England was little more than a name to most people in the colonies. A few old folks could still remember stepping off the ship, but their grandchildren had never seen so much as a picture of London. To them, the King was a face on a coin, a name in a prayer, someone who lived on the other side of a vast ocean. What felt real was the dirt road out front, the neighbor who'd ride over when your ox went lame, and the plain wooden meetinghouse where everybody gathered when something needed deciding.

Those town meetings were the pulse of everything. A bell would clang from the steeple, or a boy on horseback would come tearing past the farms, yelling that there was business at the hall. Men would set down their plows mid-furrow, wipe their hands on their breeches, and head in. Sometimes a wife or two stood in the back doorway listening, arms crossed, ready to weigh in if things got stupid. They argued about whose cow had wrecked whose corn, who was going to fix the bridge before spring floods washed it away, and how much the minister ought to be paid this year. Votes were taken by a show of hands or by dropping a white bean for yes and a black one for no. It was loud, it was slow, and half the time, nobody was completely happy, but when the meeting ended, the matter was settled—no waiting for some clerk in England to stamp a paper.

Doing it that way, over and over, changed people. A farmer who'd stood up in front of two hundred neighbors and told the wealthiest man in town his idea was hogwash began to feel his own weight in the world. When the next packet ship brought another thick bundle of royal orders—raise this tax, quarter these troops, close that port—people didn't just bow their heads anymore. They measured the order against everything they already knew how to handle on their own.

SAMUEL ALLYNE OTIS

Then came a raw day in March 1772 that turned everything on its head.

Governor Hutchinson had dissolved the Massachusetts assembly again—simply shut the doors because the representatives had the nerve to complain about taxes. The members came stomping out into the cold, coats flapping, faces red with anger. Most men would have gone home to nurse their pride over a mug of flip.

Instead, they marched straight down to Faneuil Hall, the big brick hall Boston had built with its own money, no help from the crown.

Samuel Allyne Otis—merchant, church deacon, brother-in-law to the fiery James Otis—was the one who climbed the stairs that day. He wasn't the shouting kind. He was a practical man who liked his account books balanced and his supper on time. But when he saw Hutchinson's soldiers blocking anyone from passing through the State House door, something settled hard in his gut. He thought about his kids asleep at home, about the customs men who searched cellars without warrant, about the frontier families still digging graves after raids the King's troops never showed up to stop. He banged a gavel on an old crate and called the crowd to order. No governor had told them to meet. No charter said they could. Three hundred men packed in so tight their breath hung like smoke, and in that cold hall they voted to create the Committee of Correspondence—a way for every town to talk to every other town without asking London's permission first.

It wasn't dramatic. Nobody fired a shot. They just refused to go home.

Word flew from steeple to steeple. Within weeks, committees were meeting in little villages you've never heard of and big ports alike. Farmers, shopkeepers, preachers in dusty black coats—ordinary men—sat up late writing letters, copying them by hand, sending riders out in the dark. A governor could padlock a state house, but he couldn't padlock a whole countryside talking to itself.

Samuel spent the following years doing the quiet work—keeping the minutes, sealing the letters, riding half-frozen roads with dispatches tucked inside his coat. He never made the history books the way Sam Adams or Hancock did. When independence finally came, he served as secretary of the Continental Congress, standing in the shadows while louder men made the speeches. But on that cold day in Faneuil Hall, he and hundreds like him took the first real step: they decided the people's business couldn't wait on a King's mood.

All over the colonies, the same thing was happening, one meetinghouse at a time. Men who once prayed for the King on Sunday were voting on Wednesday to stock powder and shot, just in case. The habit of running their own lives had become muscle memory.

The wide ocean that once carried commands now mostly carried excuses and delays. And in the space those delays created, something new took root—authority that didn't come down from a throne but rose up from the ground itself, stubborn and practical and impossible to scare back into silence.

That flame of resilient liberty had been only a glow for a long time. Now it was catching—steady, warm, and growing. Once people learn they can govern themselves, no one can convince them again that they need a master.

ECONOMIC SELF-RELIANCE

While the town meetings were teaching people how to run their own affairs, the ground under their feet was teaching them something even more dangerous: they didn't need a King to get rich.

A single farm that once barely survived by growing just enough tobacco to fill a handful of barrels now produced so much extra wheat and corn that wagon after wagon rumbled down to the docks, loaded to the top. Shipyards in Boston and Philadelphia were turning out fast, beautiful ships—brigs and snows—that could sail circles around anything the British navy had, and they sold them for half what it cost to build the same thing in England.

Give a hardworking man forty acres of good river-bottom soil, and here's what he could do: Year one, cut down the trees and sell the timber: year two, plant apple trees in the cleared ground. By year three, he'd be distilling apple brandy and shipping barrels straight to Dutch sugar planters in Curaçao, who paid in heavy Spanish silver.

The Navigation Acts, back in London, said every barrel had to go to England first, be taxed coming and going, and only then could it be sold anywhere else. Three thousand miles of ocean made that rule easy to ignore.

The sharp traders figured out the system fast. They'd load the legal cargo up top where the customs officers could see it, then pack the good stuff down low where no one looked. If a British revenue cutter came sniffing too close, a couple of "accidental" crates would tumble over the side in the dark. Pennsylvania iron went straight to the French islands because the French paid cash, no questions asked. Rhode Island distilleries turned cheap molasses from Africa or the French Caribbean into rum without ever sending a penny—or a drop—to England.

The profits never left America. Farmers built bigger barns. Others bought the businesses from the people who'd had enough of the rules. Fed up, many people sold out cheap and sailed home, and sons who once would have been shipped off as apprentices in London now stayed put and learned Latin at little colleges that didn't answer to any King.

In short, people were making real money on their own terms—and once you've done that, bowing to someone three thousand miles away starts to feel optional.

JOHN HANCOCK

John Hancock felt the change in his bones before most others.

He was only twenty-seven when his uncle Thomas—the man everyone in Boston called the merchant prince—slumped over his desk one afternoon and died. Just like that, young John inherited everything: the tall counting houses on the waterfront, the long wharves crowded with masts, a whole fleet of ships with pretty names like Boston Packet and Lydia. Most fellows handed a fortune that size would have hired managers, bought fancy clothes, and spent their days playing cards at the tavern.

Not John.

He was out on the docks every morning before the sun came up, coat flapping in the salt wind, asking grizzled captains, "Where's the real money this season?" In ten short years, he took a large inheritance. He turned it into something almost embarrassing—warehouses bursting, ships coming and going in a constant parade, silver piling up faster than he could count it.

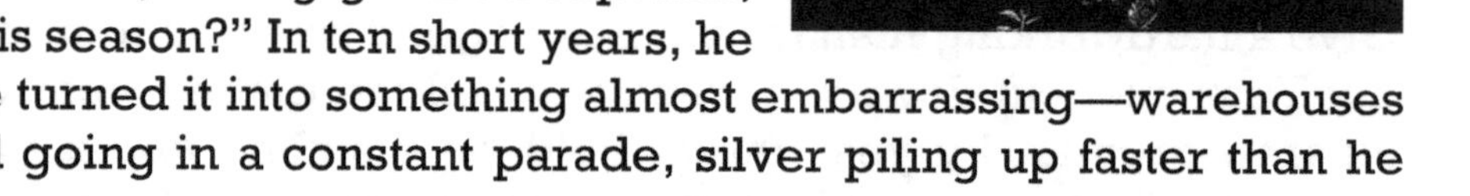

He didn't get there by being perfect. He knew precisely which customs officer liked a quiet cask of good Madeira left on his doorstep at Christmas, which clerk would "lose" a shipping manifest if you bought him a new suit. But every Sunday evening, he still sat at the long table in his uncle's house (now his house), listening to the older man's voice echo in his head: close the ledgers, open the big family Bible, and read about the talents God gives a man and what He expects you to do with them.

When London started slapping new taxes on everything—stamps on newspapers and legal papers, duties on paint, glass, even tea—John saw it for what it was: robbery with a fancy law behind it. In 1768, the revenue men seized his favorite sloop, Liberty, on some trumped-up charge. Most merchants would have grumbled, paid the fine, and gone back to business. John hired the best lawyer in Boston—John Adams—who fought the case in open court and made the King's officers look like fools in front of the whole town. The crowd hoisted him onto their shoulders and carried him home like a hero.

But that night, he sat alone in the counting house long after everyone else had gone to bed. The candles burned low while he stared at columns of numbers that could vanish tomorrow if the crown decided to play rough. He could keep his mouth shut, slip the right people the right gifts, and stay the richest man from Maine to Virginia.

Or he could draw a line in the sand.

He pulled the big Bible toward him, hands shaking just a little, and turned to Proverbs, and read the words he'd known since childhood: "The fear of man lays a snare, but whoever trusts in the Lord is safe." He closed the book, snuffed the candle, and went upstairs.

The next morning, the crates rolling into his warehouses weren't tea or wine anymore. They were long pine boxes packed with muskets, kegs of gunpowder, and cannonballs wrapped in straw.

Seven years later, in April 1775, British General Gage sent eight hundred redcoats marching out of Boston with orders to arrest John Hancock and Sam Adams. John kissed his fiancée goodbye, swung into the saddle with a price on his head, and rode off into the night. He left behind a mansion full of silk wallpaper, silver candlesticks, and wine older than he was. British officers later chopped his furniture for firewood and used his wine cellar for target practice.

Almost everything his uncle had spent a lifetime building was gone by the end of the war—burned, sunk at sea, or loaned to a new country too broke to pay him back.

But somewhere on that wild ride through the darkness, a messenger caught up with him. The farmers at Concord Bridge had stood their ground. They'd fired on the regulars and held.

Hancock pulled his horse to a stop, threw his head back, and laughed—one big, free, joyous laugh that rang through the trees.

"It's begun!" he shouted into the night. "The king can't stop it now!"

He lived another eighteen years—served as governor, helped write Massachusetts' constitution, stayed comfortable, though never again the wealthiest man in America. When he died in 1793, people remembered him as the Patriot Merchant.

He had traded warehouses full of goods for a warehouse full of liberty, and he never once regretted the deal. That enormous, looping signature at the bottom of the Declaration of Independence—the one so big King George supposedly needed spectacles to read it—was John Hancock's final message to the crown:

Bill settled. Paid in full. By one man willing to risk everything for everyone else's freedom.

"Taxation without representation is tyranny." – James Otis

Thousands of ordinary people were living the same shift in consciousness, just without the big houses or famous names.

A farmer up in Connecticut once figured he was doing well if he shipped enough barrels of salt pork to cover London's taxes. Now he smiled at harvest time when most of the crop stayed right there on his own shelves—and his family ate better than ever. Down in Charleston, a rice planter quietly loaded his crop onto a Portuguese ship bound straight for Lisbon because the price was double what the British factors offered. A captain out of Salem kept a locker full of different flags; he'd run up whatever colors got him into the best port fastest and brought home the fattest profit.

The money no longer vanished across the ocean. It paid local carpenters to raise sturdier barns. It built one-room schoolhouses and simple white-steepled churches that belonged to the people who nailed every board in place. It bought books, plows, wedding dresses—things earned and spent by the same hands.

Every dollar that stayed home was a quiet vote: "We can take care of ourselves."

When a man can put supper on the table, shoes on his kids' feet, and still hear silver clink in his pocket at the end of the week—all without waiting for some lord in Westminster to say yes or no—the old question flips upside down. It stops being "How do we obey the King?" and turns into "Why exactly are we still obeying him?"

That question didn't thunder from pulpits or pamphlets at first. It rose from kitchen tables where wives tallied the household accounts, from taverns where captains swapped stories about the latest run, barns where neighbors helped raise rafters and wondered out loud why they needed permission to live the way they already lived.

"Taxation without representation" was the battle cry, but in reality, people were just wanting to live their lives without being stolen from by a distant King who didn't have a clue who they were or what they were all about. Sure, there were still English subjects throughout the colonies and they didn't want to rock the boat, but as the flame of freedom spread, their numbers became smaller and smaller.

It was the same flame that had started in those crowded town meetings, only now it smelled of pine tar from new shipyards and sweet rum from island stills.

It was fed by plain, everyday sweat—the sweat of people who had discovered they could prosper without a king's blessing.

And once a fire learns it doesn't need someone else's breath to keep burning, it starts looking around for new ground to light.

CULTURAL EVOLUTION

The longer families put down roots on this side of the Atlantic, the more England began to feel like a story someone else used to tell.

Kids born here didn't grow up walking tidy English lanes between ancient hedgerows. They ran barefoot through cornfields their grandfathers had carved out of solid forest, chasing fireflies at dusk while owls called from trees that had never heard a church bell until the settlers brought one. They learned to read from a hornbook or the big family Bible balanced on a stump, not from some wigged schoolmaster droning Latin in a stone schoolhouse older than their whole bloodline. When they sang on Sunday, it was simple psalms rising from rough pine benches that still smelled of the axe, not fancy hymns bouncing off cathedral vaults built when knights were still riding around in armor.

The tales at the hearth changed, too. Sure, an old grandmother might still whisper about Robin Hood or King Arthur. Still, the stories that really held the room now were about the grandfather who buried half his children that first terrible winter yet kept planting, or the neighbor who stood off a Shawnee war party with an old fowling piece and a heart full of prayer, or the circuit rider who showed up half-frozen and preached for three days in a barn until hardened men were weeping at the altar.

And holidays—those changed more than anything.

In the old country, Election Day was a quiet affair for a handful of landowners who rode in, voted, and rode home. Out here, it became the biggest party of the year.

Imagine the Hartford Common Square on a bright May morning in the 1750s. Wagons roll in from every direction, piled high with wives, kids, and barrels of cider. Men wear their Sunday-best homespun and gather under the giant elm to shout their votes aloud—no secret ballots, every name called out clearly so the clerk can mark it down. Once the counting's done, the real fun starts.

Long tables appear like magic, loaded with roast beef, cornbread, and pumpkin pie still warm from the ashes. Fiddlers scrape out "Yankee Doodle" until toes can't stay still. Young bucks wrestle in a roped-off ring while old men argue politics loud enough to scatter the crows. A preacher climbs on a stump and gives thanks for the harvest, for the right to choose their own leaders, and for the strength to keep both. At twilight, the militia companies line up and fire three thundering volleys into the sky, powder smoke drifting like sweet incense while everybody cheers for the new governor—whoever he turns out to be—because come tomorrow, he'll have to face the same crowd again.

One of those Election Days still gets talked about years later.

Israel Putnam—everyone called him Old Put even though he wasn't thirty yet—came riding in from Pomfret with his wife, Hannah, and a wagon full of children. Put was already a legend for killing the last wolf in Connecticut. In the dead of winter, he'd tracked the beast to its den, tied a rope around his waist so his neighbors could pull him out if things went bad, crawled in on his belly with nothing but a torch and a musket, and shot the wolf right between the eyes when it charged. Folks loved that story almost as much as they loved watching him wrestle.

That day, he took on every comer in the ring—huge teamsters, cocky sailors fresh off the West Indies run—and tossed them all into the dirt like sacks of grain. When the last man hit the ground, the cheering was so loud they say it carried clean across the Connecticut River. Old Put just laughed, wiped his face with his sleeve, and hollered for a mug of flip. Later, when the preacher asked who'd lead the evening prayer, Put stepped right up—still dusty from the ring—and thanked God out loud for the harvest, for the privilege of choosing their own rulers, and for the muscle to defend both.

A lot of the men who followed him to war a few years later said they never forgot that prayer. When the news of Lexington reached Pomfret, Put left his plow in the middle of the field and rode straight to Cambridge, still wearing his farm clothes. The same fellows who'd watched him wrestle and pray on Election Day grabbed their muskets and rode after him. They knew they had a chance as long as he was on their side.

Election Day wasn't just about picking leaders. It was the colonies growing into their own skin—loud, rough-edged, full of faith and muscle and plain joy. The old English holidays were still observed, but they felt thin and far away next to a day when the whole countryside came together to vote, feast, wrestle, and thank God they got to do it their own way.

The same thing happened everywhere, quietly and steadily. German hymns rang out in Pennsylvania barns right alongside English psalms. Dutch Pinkster celebrations up the Hudson started serving cornbread and maple sugar with the goose. Frontier weddings mixed Scottish reels with rhythms brought from Africa, and nobody thought twice about it. The faith never wavered—it was still the same Bible—but now preachers rode hundreds of miles on horseback instead of waiting in stone churches, and their sermons promised heaven and liberty in the same breath. This was truly a New World.

Bit by bit, people stopped talking, dressing, singing, or celebrating quite like Europeans. They were turning into something the old world didn't have a name for yet.

That new way of living didn't get handed down by some King's order or dreamed up in fancy London parlors. It just grew—wild and rugged—like one of those giant oaks you see out in a pasture that started from a single acorn nobody even remembers planting.

Every laugh shared over a jug of cider, every wrestling match that ended with two muddy friends grinning at each other, every militia volley cracking the May sky—it all poured fuel on the same fire that had first sparked in those crowded town meetings and busy local get-togethers.

It was becoming their fire now. And it wasn't going out.

Now it had its own voice, its own song, its own kind of courage—one that belonged entirely to this ground.

And a flame that speaks with its own voice is a flame ready to shout its own name.

SECTION THREE: DIMINISHING ALLEGIANCE

GRIEVANCES MOUNT

By the 1760s, the letters sailing back to England weren't polite suggestions anymore. They were flat-out warnings.

Parliament kept cranking out laws that sounded reasonable in some London office but felt like a punch in the gut over here. Shut down Boston's harbor until every penny for that spoiled tea was paid. Force families to cook, wash, and give up their own beds for soldiers who might shove them aside like they owned the place. Drag a man three thousand miles across the ocean to stand trial for treason, with no friend or neighbor allowed to speak for him. Slap a tax stamp on every newspaper, every contract, even a deck of cards. And the whole time, not one single person from the colonies got a seat—or a voice—in the place making those rules.

"No taxation without representation" didn't start as a catchy phrase on a sign.

It was a question men shouted in taverns after a long day's work, voices raw: "Why are we handing over our money to a government that treats us like dirt?"

"A wise and frugal government, which shall restrain men from injuring one another, shall leave them otherwise free to regulate their own pursuits of industry and improvement, and shall not take from the mouth of labor the bread it has earned." – Thomas Jefferson

Words only held the anger for so long.

Then came a freezing night in March 1770. A couple of boys started heaving snowballs and oyster shells at a British sentry posted outside the customs house in Boston. Taunts turned to shoves. More redcoats came running. Somebody yelled "Fire!"—nobody ever proved who—and the muskets roared. When the smoke cleared, five men were down on the icy cobblestones, blood soaking the snow around them: Crispus Attucks, Samuel Gray, James Caldwell, Samuel Maverick, and Patrick Carr. Church bells rang through the night. The next day, thousands walked behind the coffins in dead silence except for the slow beat of muffled drums.

That night changed everything.

Abigail Adams stood at her window watching the funeral procession wind through the streets, holding her children a little tighter. John was away again—always away—riding circuits, writing letters, trying to keep the peace before it exploded. Abigail kept the farm running, the children fed and safe, and poured everything she was feeling into the letters she sent him.

She didn't hold back. In one she wrote, "I long to hear that you have declared an independency—and by the way, in the new Code of Laws which I suppose it will be necessary for you to make, I desire you would Remember the Ladies... Do not put such unlimited power into the hands of the Husbands. Remember, all Men would be tyrants if they could."

She wasn't begging. She was reminding him—and every man who'd soon be writing new laws—that if a king could treat grown Englishmen like enslaved people, a husband could do the same to his wife. Liberty had to start at home. While John argued in halls, Abigail nursed wounded men after the shooting, hid patriots when patrols came knocking, and melted the family's pewter spoons into bullets when powder got scarce—all while raising five kids and keeping the farm feeding half of Braintree. She might have spoken for scores of other women, but she certainly wasn't alone in her feelings.

Years later, when John Adams came home worn out from helping draft the Massachusetts constitution, Abigail poured him tea, sat him by the fire, and said quietly, "If particular care and attention is not paid to the ladies, we are determined to foment a rebellion of our own." John laughed—he always laughed when her eyes flashed like that—but he listened. The laws they wrote gave married women more rights than almost anywhere else on earth. It was a start.

The fight wasn't about tea or stamps anymore. It was about dignity. About a man keeping what he earned with his own hands. About a family sleeping safely under their own roof. About a woman being more than someone else's property while her husband risked his life for everybody else's freedom.

That anger rolled south to north like a wave. Farmers who'd never cared about politics started burying muskets under the hay. Merchants who once raised a glass to the King now dumped his tea in the harbor. Preachers stood in pulpits and called tyranny the devil's own work—and standing against it a Christian duty.

The flame that had started as a flicker—in a town meeting, a smuggled crate, a wrestling match on the green—was roaring now. And it had a voice, rough and clear in a thousand different accents:

We've built our own world here. We've earned the right to run it.

If the King across the water couldn't see that, then maybe it was time to stop calling him King—or at least OUR King.

IDENTITY FORGED

By the time the 1770s came around, most families had roots here going back four, five, even six generations. The King wasn't a real person to them anymore—just a name you said in church and a blurry face on an old coin. What felt real was the neighbor who showed up with a wagon when your barn burned, the folks you sat next to every Sunday, the dirt that fed your kids and held your dead.

People started saying "American" the way you say "home"—like it had always been theirs.

PATRICK HENRY

Take the Henry family down on the red-dirt hills along Virginia's Staunton River. Old Colonel John Henry had come over from Scotland as a young man and raised eight kids on a plantation called Studley. His son Patrick was the skinny one with the fiddle and the laugh that could fill a room. Nights, he'd sit by the fire listening to his mother read the Bible and his father talk about Scottish clans who'd rather die on their feet than live on their knees.

Patrick Henry tried everything—running a store, farming, lawyering—but nothing clicked until 1763 when he stood up in a packed Hanover courthouse for the Parson's Cause. The King had overruled a Virginia law that let folks pay church taxes with tobacco when cash was short. Patrick told the jury straight out: a king who cancels good laws "degenerates into a tyrant and forfeits all right to his subjects' obedience." You could have heard a pin drop—then the place erupted. Overnight, the failed shopkeeper became the man who said what everybody else was only thinking.

Twelve years later, in March 1775, the Virginia convention crammed into St. John's Church in Richmond, trying to figure out what to do with all the anger in the air. Patrick got up—still very thin, but almost trembling with the fire inside him—and let it rip:

"Is life so dear, or peace so sweet, as to be purchased at the price of chains and slavery? Forbid it, Almighty God! I know not what course others may take; but as for me, give me liberty or give me death!" – Patrick Henry

His own cousins were in that room. Some nodded hard, some went pale. One, a minister still loyal to the crown, muttered that Patrick had lost his mind. But a month later, when the redcoats marched on Lexington and Concord, those same cousins saddled up and rode with Patrick's militia. Blood ties bent, but the new tie—calling themselves Americans—held tighter.

It happened the same way everywhere, family by family.

A German farmer in Pennsylvania still spoke with the old-country accent, taught his boys the Lord's Prayer in German, but when the tax collector came sniffing around, he hid the best horses in the woods and told them, "We left one King's taxes behind when we crossed the water. We're not starting again." A Charleston merchant whose grandfather raised a glass to King George every night now toasted "the rights of Americans" instead. Preachers who once prayed for the King's long life started closing their sermons with, "Lord, give us the wisdom to govern ourselves."

The faith never weakened—it got sharper. Men opened the same Bibles their grandfathers carried over, and suddenly the stories hit differently: Moses leading his people out of slavery, David facing down Goliath with nothing but a sling and trust in God, Jesus flipping tables on the money-changers. Those weren't dusty history lessons anymore. They were playbooks.

The change didn't come with trumpets.

It came quietly—one father telling his son after chores, "Son, we're not Englishmen living in America anymore. We're Americans, and this land is ours." One mother stitching thirteen stripes on a new flag because the old Union Jack didn't feel like home. Neighbors who used to bicker over a wandering pig now drilling side by side on the green, muskets on their shoulders, ready to defend what they'd built together.

The flame that started small—in a town meeting argument, a smuggled barrel, a wrestling match on Election Day—now had a name folks were ready to die for.

American.

And once a people know exactly who they are, no King on earth—no matter how many ships he sends—can tell them who they have to be.

"'Freedom from fear' could be said to sum up the whole philosophy of human rights." – Dag Hammarskjold

KNOWLEDGE IS POWER

Words started hitting harder than musket balls.

Printers who once turned out Bibles, almanacs, and the occasional wedding invitation suddenly found themselves working through the night, ink up to their elbows, feeding their presses with hot, fresh pages that felt dangerous to hold. Those little pamphlets—cheap paper, plain print—were folded small and passed from hand to hand like contraband whiskey. A farmer would read one by the light of a pine knot after supper, shake his head in wonder, and slip it to the blacksmith the next morning. The blacksmith would read it out loud to the men waiting for their horses to be shod, and by Sunday, the preacher was quoting lines he'd never seen in print before. Truth was moving faster than any King's messenger on the fastest horse.

The crown called it treason. Folks here just called it daylight.

THOMAS PAINE

Then, in January 1776, a skinny little book showed up that changed everything. Forty-seven pages, no pictures, priced cheap enough for a plowboy to buy with a day's wages. "Common Sense" was written anonymously by a fellow named Thomas Paine who'd only been in America a little over a year.

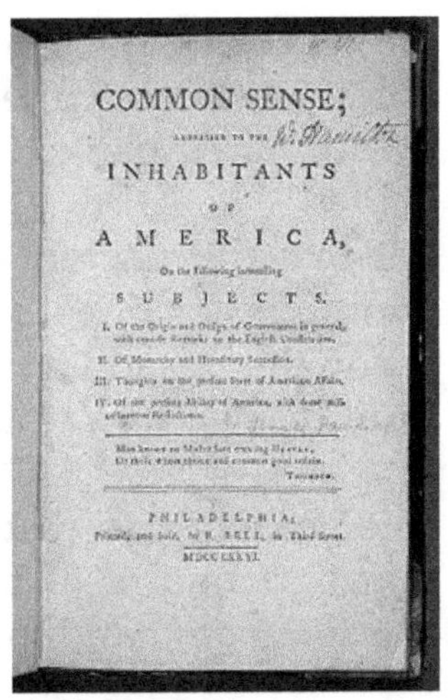
COMMON SENSE;

INHABITANTS

OF

AMERICA,

SUBJECTS.

PHILADELPHIA;

MDCCLXXVI.

Paine had washed up on these shores, broken and half-sick, carrying nothing but a letter from Ben Franklin attesting to the man's ability to write. And write he could—like lightning striking dry grass. In plain words, any farmer or fisherman could follow; he ripped the mask off the monarchy.

He called the King a "crowned ruffian" and said hanging on to him was like a battered child refusing to leave a cruel parent. Then he said the thing almost nobody had dared say out loud yet: America ought to be free. America must not just beg for better treatment. America must be free.

In three months, 120,000 copies sold—half a million if you count the ones printed without permission. That's one copy for every five grown-ups from Georgia to Maine. In taverns, barbershops, and around kitchen tables, people who couldn't agree on the weather suddenly found themselves nodding at the same sentences.

Elisha Bostwick was just a Connecticut farm kid turned soldier when a copy reached his camp. Years later, he still remembered it: "We gathered around the fire and read it again and again till we knew it by heart. It was like the spirit of '76 grabbed hold of every one of us." Men who'd been grumbling about the fight now talked openly about independence. Washington ordered it read to every regiment. Even some loyalists admitted the thing shook them to their boots.

Paine kept going. That December, he started his "Crisis" papers with the line everybody still knows: "These are the times that try men's souls..." Washington had that one read to the army on Christmas night 1776, right before they crossed the ice-choked Delaware and surprised the Hessians at Trenton. Men with frozen feet and empty stomachs listened, looked at each other across the dying campfires, and decided they weren't done yet.

The free press didn't just spread ideas; it also shaped them. It tied people together. A Georgia farmer who'd never been north of Richmond suddenly felt like he had brothers in Boston because they were reading the exact words, asking the same questions, feeling the same fire in their bellies.

Governors sent soldiers to smash presses and throw printers in jail. Didn't matter. Another shop opened down the road the following week. Once truth gets loose, there's no stuffing it back in the bottle.

All that ink turned anger into purpose—men who'd been mad now understood why. Women who'd been told politics wasn't their business found their husbands listening when they read Paine aloud by the fire. Kids overheard their fathers arguing at the table and learned a brand-new word: independence.

The same flame that had started small in town meetings and counting houses, that had warmed hearts at harvest feasts and wrestling matches, now roared through pages passed from hand to hand.

And a people holding truth in their own hands is a people no army on earth can keep in chains.

BETSY ROSS

In the spring of 1776, the American colonies were on the brink of declaring independence from Britain. In Philadelphia, a young widow named Betsy Ross—Elizabeth Griscom Ross—ran a bustling upholstery shop. She was skilled with needle and thread, making everything from curtains to a ship's flags. According to the beloved family story passed down through generations and first shared publicly by her grandson William Canby in 1870, three important men knocked on her door one day in late May or early June. They were General George Washington, the commander of the Continental Army; Robert Morris, a wealthy financier who backed the Revolution; and Colonel George Ross, a delegate to the Continental Congress and the uncle of Betsy's late husband, John. They came as a small committee, carrying a rough sketch of what they hoped would become a new flag for the emerging nation—thirteen red and white stripes for the colonies, and thirteen stars in a field of blue.

Betsy listened as they explained their need for a symbol of unity. Washington showed her the design with six-pointed stars, but Betsy, ever practical and confident in her craft, suggested a tweak: why not five-pointed stars instead? She even demonstrated, with a quick snip of her scissors, how easy it was to fold and cut. The men agreed—it looked cleaner and more elegant. She reportedly said something humble like, "I do not know, but I will try," and took on the job. Soon after, she sewed what many call the first American flag, possibly arranging the stars in a circle. While Congress didn't officially adopt the Stars and Stripes until June 14, 1777, with its resolution calling for thirteen stripes and stars, this legend paints Betsy as a quiet patriot whose hands helped give the young country its enduring emblem. Historians debate the details—no solid records confirm the committee visit or her exact role—but the tale endures as a heartwarming piece of American folklore, celebrating one woman's small but meaningful contribution to the fight for freedom.

"Our flag honors those who have fought to protect it, and is a reminder of the sacrifice of our nation's founders and heroes. As the ultimate icon of America's storied history, the Stars and Stripes represents the very best of this nation."
– Joe Barton

As the old loyalties faded and a new name—"American"—took root in hearts that had learned to run their own towns, trade their own goods, and worship on their own terms, the flame stopped asking permission. It began calling ordinary men and women to do extraordinary things—risking homes, fortunes, and lives against the world's most significant military power so their children would never again have to bow to a tyrant. That call pulled them straight into the revolutionary fire, where faith and freedom would meet tyranny head-on, and a nation would be born in blood and hope.

CHAPTER THREE
HEROES OF THE REVOLUTION

SACRIFICES FOR LIBERTY

Think about a dark night just before daybreak, with a single rider pushing his horse hard through the fog-covered fields, the sound of galloping breaking the quiet as he called out alarms that cut right through the air. That rider was Paul Revere, a regular silversmith who stepped up in a crucial moment, hurrying to warn the other colonists that British soldiers were heading their way. His shout—"The regulars are coming out!"—remembered later as "The redcoats are coming!"—was more than a signal to grab weapons; it showed the kind of guts it took for everyday people to risk it all for the idea of freedom, lighting the way for a country built on tough choices and sheer determination.

SECTION ONE:
EARLY AGITATORS

SAMUEL ADAMS' FIRE

On a typical day along Boston's busy harbor, Samuel Adams would often fixate on the arrival of the British ships. He watched them unload their cargo under the King's authority, and each crate was a reminder of the growing burdens placed on the colonies. Adams, born in 1722 to a family of devout Puritans—his father a brewer and deacon who raised him with the expectation that he would enter the ministry—had every chance to lead a straightforward life. He could have followed in his father's footsteps, managing the family business, providing for his own household, and avoiding the conflicts brewing around him. But from his youth, shaped by a home where biblical teachings on justice and moral duty were part of daily life, Adams saw a deeper purpose.

He came to view liberty as a sacred trust from God, something that demanded resistance to any ruler who overstepped his authority. Samuel wanted to make sure people never forfeit not just their rights but their dignity as created beings. To Adams, America represented a unique opportunity. In this land, individuals could live by their own efforts and principles, not as overlooked subjects taxed and controlled by a distant King who never witnessed their hardships firsthand.

Adams' drive came from a genuine attachment to his community and country, inspired by the same spirit that moved biblical figures to challenge unjust authority. After graduating from Harvard in 1740 and trying his hand at business, he turned to public service, serving in the Massachusetts House and using his position to rally others. He helped form the Sons of Liberty in the mid-1760s, a group of working people—merchants, artisans, and laborers—who met in local taverns and halls to discuss their grievances. They weren't the wealthy elite; they were everyday folks worn down by acts like the Stamp Act of 1765, which imposed direct taxes on everything from newspapers to legal documents, making it harder for families to get by.

In these meetings, Adams stood up straight and spoke plainly, his words gaining strength as he went, drawing people in and easing their uncertainties about standing up to unchecked power. Echoing scriptural calls to uphold righteousness, he'd remind them, as in one of his writings, that "while the people are virtuous, they cannot be subdued." These weren't elaborate addresses for the privileged; they were direct, earnest talks that helped ordinary workers, like blacksmiths at their forges or farmers after a long day, recognize their role in preserving something essential—a shared commitment to freedom that could inspire others or be lost if ignored.

"The natural liberty of man is to be free from any superior power on Earth, and not to be under the will or legislative authority of man, but only to have the law of nature for his rule." – Samuel Adams

Going this route brought real struggles for Adams. His brewing operation fell apart because he threw himself completely into the fight, ending up broke, in ragged clothes, and with a family that barely got by. He had opportunities to take a safe job on the British side, but he turned them down and instead faced the ongoing danger of being hunted. By 1775, right after the fighting at Lexington and Concord, the King put out an offer of forgiveness for rebels who gave up—everyone except Adams and John Hancock, who were viewed as the key troublemakers. Adams had to dodge patrols, all the while knowing that if they grabbed him, he'd be treated as a traitor and put to death in a gruesome way: hanged, gutted, and cut into pieces, with parts left out in public to scare people off, similar to how old rulers crushed rebellions with public killings that left families to deal with the mangled bodies of their loved ones.

Things came to a head on that chilly evening of December 16, 1773, as the salty harbor air mingled with a sense of growing resistance.

THE BOSTON TEA PARTY

Adams spoke to a large crowd at the Old South Meeting House and concluded by saying, "This meeting can do nothing more to save the country!" That was the signal to move. Around 60 men covered their faces with soot and stuck feathers in their hats to look like Mohawk warriors and stay hidden, then they snuck down to the docks, avoiding the British guards. The risk was enormous—if they got caught, it meant the noose, their houses burned, and their families ruined. What pushed them was a strong sense that people should govern themselves, along with the sheer frustration of enduring the oppression any longer. That's why they got on board the three ships—the Dartmouth, Beaver, and Eleanor—and carefully broke open 342 chests of tea, dumping it all into the water, where the splashes rang out like a clear challenge. Adams wasn't part of the group doing the dumping, but he was the one who planned it, turning all that built-up anger into a solid group effort.

What Adams went through captures the lasting freedom at the heart of America—a dedication put to the test by the personal cost, where one person's determination helps pull a whole group together to stand up for their fundamental rights against excessive control. It shows how freedom has to be actively protected with strong values and courage, and it sets an example for those who follow, like the riders who raced through the night to warn of the British coming.

JOHN HANCOCK'S BOLDNESS

The warnings Paul Revere carried on the fateful night of his famous ride weren't just about muskets hidden in Concord barns. They were meant for two men the British wanted most—Samuel Adams and John Hancock, marked for arrest like common criminals because they refused to bow.

Hancock and Adams had slipped out of Boston days earlier and were resting in Lexington at the parsonage of Reverend Jonas Clarke, a solid brick house surrounded by fields and stone walls. Hancock had been drilling with the local militia in the afternoons, musket in hand, half-joking that if the redcoats came, he would stand his ground with the rest. Around midnight on April 18, the pounding on the door came. Revere burst in, still dusty from the ride, and delivered the news: eight hundred regulars were marching straight for them.

Hancock reached for his pistols and sword. "I'll fight with the others," he said. Adams grabbed his arm and talked sense into him—hard sense. "We're worth more alive leading the Congress than dead on Lexington Green." Hancock hated it, but he knew it was true.

They gathered what papers they could, left by the back door, and moved into the dark woods as the first faint drumbeats of the advancing column reached their ears. Patrols swept the roads all night. At one point, the two men lay flat in a swampy ditch while British officers rode past so close they could hear the creak of leather and the horses' breathing. One lantern swing, one nervous horse, and it would have ended right there with ropes around their necks and the kind of public butchery kings use to teach lessons—bodies hacked apart and spiked on poles for weeks until the birds finished what the executioner started.

They got away clean and made it to Philadelphia, where, on May 24, 1775, the delegates elected Hancock president of the Continental Congress. For the next two and a half grinding years, he sat in that chair through every argument, every piece of bad news, every threat of collapse. When money ran out—and it always did—Hancock quietly paid salaries, bought powder, fed Washington's hungry army out of his own shrinking accounts. He signed orders, wrote letters, kept quarreling colonies from flying apart, all while British agents circulated lists with his name at the top and a £500 (five hundred pounds) bounty beside it.

Then came August 2, 1776. The now legendary Declaration of Independence lay on the table in Independence Hall. Hancock took the quill first. He dipped it deep, pressed down hard, and wrote his name so large it dominated the page—letters bold and looping, impossible to miss. He looked up at the room and gave that half-smile people remembered. "There," he said, "King George can read my name without spectacles, and he may double the reward on my head if he pleases."

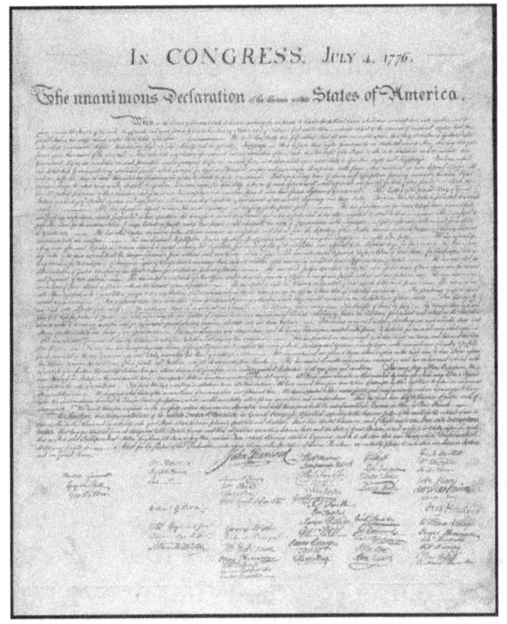
IN CONGRESS. July 4. 1776.

The unanimous Declaration of the [illegible] States of America,

[illegible]

John Hancock

His signature became so famous that, even nowadays, when someone is asked to sign a document, people say, "Put your 'John Hancock' right here on the dotted line."

It wasn't bravado. It was a promise. Hancock had already lost ships to Royal Navy cannons, warehouses to confiscation, and credit to war. He would lose almost everything else before the fighting stopped. Yet he never hedged, never negotiated a quiet surrender to save his skin. He kept showing up, kept paying the bills, kept signing his name where it mattered most, because he believed down to his bones that the rights come from God, not governments, and no earthly king had the authority to take them away.

That kind of boldness—the kind that costs you everything you own and still leaves you laughing in the saddle—kept the flame from going out in the darkest months.

Hancock carried it steady and bright, then handed it off to the men who would turn words on parchment into a nation that still stands.

PATRICK HENRY'S CRY

People like John Hancock, who put their entire livelihoods on the line for the cause, needed powerful voices to turn those hushed complaints into a call that demanded real attention. Patrick Henry was exactly one of those voices he needed—Patrick flat-out said the King's taxes were betraying the people's freedoms, declaring that "Caesar had his Brutus, Charles the First his Cromwell, and George the Third may profit by their example." The room hushed for a beat, then broke into an uproar—some yelling "Treason!" while others felt a spark, knowing he'd voiced what they'd been afraid to say. He didn't back down from the accusations. Patrick locked eyes with the King's supporters and fired back, "If this be treason, make the most of it." That showed his true spine; he knew calling out the mighty could mean jail or his own execution, like those ancient tyrants who strapped opponents to racks, stretching their bodies until joints shattered and truths came out in screams of pain, just to keep everyone else quiet.

But the real spark came ten years later, in March 1775, when his famous speech, which I've described, set things on fire at the Virginia Convention, at St. John's Church in Richmond. Tension hung in the air as British troops gathered in Boston. They were hashing out whether they should take the extraordinary step of preparing local militias, and some held back, still hoping for a way to patch things up. Henry stood and began speaking quietly at first, but his words grew in power as his faith grew. He described how tyranny was tightening its grip, then let loose with those unforgettable words... give me liberty or give me death!

These powerful words landed like a shock—those on the edge sprang up, energized and ready to give everything. Someone there recalled that it felt like a strike from the heavens, reaching deep and urging people to move forward. Patrick's strong words started a movement that pushed Virginia to send support, stirring up defiance across the colonies and turning everyday farmers into warriors ready to face the strongest army of the day. His words were no hollow echo; they came from a man who'd already walked away from an easier path, facing arrest orders and knowing capture meant a rebel's fate—hanged in town squares, corpses rotting as examples, similar to how old dictators sliced open insurgents and fed their innards to dogs to snuff out any sign of revolt.

Adding to that energy was Mercy Otis Warren, a sharp woman from Massachusetts whose writing hit harder than any argument. She was born in 1728 into a family deeply committed to the patriot movement, and she used her skills in poetry and plays to push back against tyranny—mocking British officials as selfish bullies in pamphlets that spread everywhere, and giving speakers like Henry new ways to fire up crowds. What drove her was a strong faith that freedom came from God. She pointed out the King's injustices with a genuine heart for the people hurting under them, always urging everyone to stay on the right path in the struggle.

Her work really changed how folks saw things, showing that even one person quietly at home with a pen could stir up as much momentum as a big, bold speech.

Henry's steadfast position, echoing out to all who listened and acted on it, helped preserve that glow of liberty in shaky moments. It passed the burden to the unsung figures—the ones managing funds and negotiations—who would provide the support and ties to turn that rallying cry into a true, lasting triumph.

SECTION TWO: FINANCIERS AND DIPLOMATS

ROBERT MORRIS' GENEROSITY

Robert Morris is one of the "unsung heroes" of American history. Without his help, we most likely would have lost the war against the British crown.

Patrick Henry's words had lit the fire, but keeping an army in the field through a brutal winter took more than speeches—it took money, and almost no one had any. That's when Robert Morris stepped forward, a Philadelphia merchant who'd already given so much that his own fortune was hanging by a thread. By the winter of 1777-1778, Washington's men at Valley Forge were starving, freezing, and falling apart—thousands without shoes, blankets, or decent food, dying from disease and deserting in droves. Congress had no cash; no credit left after years of printing worthless paper. Morris, serving as Superintendent of Finance even before the official title was established, didn't wait for permission. He wrote personal notes—promises to pay backed only by his name—borrowing from friends, dipping into his own accounts, and scrambling shipments of flour, meat, and clothing that kept the army from total collapse. One desperate day in January 1778, with soldiers literally eating bark off trees, he managed to send wagonloads of supplies that arrived just in time, saving lives and holding the line until spring.

Morris handled the chaos with a steady hand, negotiating loans from France, setting up a makeshift bank to pay troops, and juggling debts that would have broken most men. He knew the risks—if the British won, he'd be ruined or hanged as a traitor, his family left with nothing. Yet he kept going, driven by a faith that saw stewardship as a calling from God, pouring out everything because he believed this fight for self-governance under moral law was worth any price. By the end of the Revolutionary War, he'd gone bankrupt. His ships had been seized, and his credit was destroyed. In fact, Robert Morris spent years in debtors' prison after the peace, while others prospered.

He continued to suffer after the war, even after stepping up when we needed him the most...because without his quiet, relentless generosity, the revolution might have died that winter.

Women felt the same pull to help in any way they could, none more than Esther de Berdt Reed. She was the wife of Pennsylvania's president, Joseph Reed. Esther watched the army's suffering from Philadelphia and decided that words weren't enough. In the summer of 1780, with the war dragging on and money scarce, she wrote an outstanding essay called "The Sentiments of an American Woman," calling on ladies across the state to give what they could—no matter how small—for Washington's men. Esther led the way on a door-to-door campaign with hundreds of other women, despite her own poor health, and raised over $300,000 in Continental currency (a considerable sum then) from rich and poor alike. They turned it into linen shirts sewn by hand, each with a note of encouragement tucked inside, delivered to grateful soldiers who hadn't had new clothes in years. Esther's effort brought women together in a time of despair, showing compassion in action and proving that patriotism wasn't just for the men fighting in the trenches. Tragically, she died of dysentery that fall at only 33. Esther never saw the victory, but her sacrifice helped hold the army together when hope was at its thinnest.

"No matter the nationality, no matter the religion, no matter the ethnic background, America brings out the best in people." – Arnold Schwarzenegger

SLAVERY'S SCOURGE

All of this unfolded under the dark cloud of slavery, a brutal split that ate away at the heart of the nation even as it battled for its own freedom. In the South, the economy relied heavily on forced labor to produce crops such as tobacco and rice. The human toll was unbelievable. Auctioneers with no soul tore families to pieces. People were traded like animals, beaten down, or driven to early graves on those endless plantations. These were tragedies that spat in the face of the very freedoms our forefathers proclaimed.

Up North, people like Robert Morris, who went on to help run Pennsylvania's group fighting to end slavery, spoke out strongly against it. Most people viewed slavery as a direct offense against the way God made every human being. The arguments grew heated, and compromises were made to hold things together. Still, the cost in human suffering was impossible to ignore... millions of human beings were bound in irons. Whole lives were shattered, a toxic element that would come close to ripping the country apart down the road. Morris waded through all that mess, pouring money into a war for liberty. At the same time, that deep flaw simmered on, a reminder that even the bravest souls had to grapple with the ugliness of their time. But they kept going, because that enduring spark of freedom called for nothing less. It was a compromise that had to be made to bring the 13 colonies together.

Still, the presence of slavery inserted a powder keg into the American consciousness that would explode in about eighty years.

Morris's selfless stand, echoed in the blood of thousands of men and women's quiet heroism, bought the time and means for the fight to continue—passing the torch to others, like the Jewish patriot who gave without counting the cost, bridging faiths in the shared dream of a nation under God.

"When the American spirit was in its youth, the language of America was different: Liberty, sir, was the primary object." – Patrick Henry

HAYM SALOMON'S SACRIFICE

It's heartbreaking how antisemitism is creeping back into our world these days. We have to hold on to the fact that America was built on Judeo-Christian principles—Jesus himself was a Jew, a rabbi who became the Messiah for so many. Countless Jewish folks have played key roles in shaping this country, and few were as vital as Haym Salomon.

Robert Morris's endless generosity proved that one person's resources could keep an army from falling apart, but he was not alone at all in the struggle to raise money for the cause. Haym Salomon, a Jewish man who'd escaped persecution in Europe, moved quietly in the background, offering loans and expecting no payback to sustain the revolution. He was born in 1740 in a small Polish village, always under the shadow of changing rulers, and raised in a Sephardic home that bore the pain of forced expulsion. His Jewish forebears had probably been chased from Portugal long ago simply for holding to their beliefs. In his twenties, he roamed France and Germany, learning new languages and the ins and outs of money matters, but when greedy empires sliced up Poland in 1772, he set sail for New York with nothing but an unquenchable thirst for freedom.

There in the busy harbor, Salomon started from zero, piecing together a brokerage that guided traders through the mess of British control. Deep down, though, he aligned with the rebels; he linked up with the Sons of Liberty, sharing secrets in dim bars and putting it all on the line to weaken the crown. The British nabbed him in 1776, labeling him a spy after a mysterious blaze hit their quarters. They tossed him onto a wretched prison ship where he suffered through hunger and sickness for months, but his grasp of German pulled him through—they yanked him out to translate for the Hessian hired soldiers the King brought in to smash the uprising.

Salomon flipped the script, passing hidden notes to captive Americans and convincing Hessians to switch sides by promising a fresh start in a land without tyrants (My great-great-great-great-grandfather and his four brothers were among the Hessian soldiers who switched sides). Caught again in 1778 and facing the noose, he slipped a guard some gold hidden in his coat and bolted into the darkness toward Philadelphia, pulse pounding while search parties combed the paths, his loved ones sneaking along behind.

Once safe, Salomon rebuilt his life, but the war's desperation called him deeper. He loaned vast sums to the Continental Congress—over $650,000 in today's terms—without interest or fanfare, sustaining the war effort quietly when no one else could. His faith as an observant Jew, rooted in the Torah's call to justice and charity, led him to see this fight as holy, uniting faiths with the predominantly Christian founders who shared his vision of a nation where no man bowed to tyrants. Remembering the ancient Stoic Epictetus's words that true freedom lies in controlling what you can amid chains, Solomon gave selflessly, knowing the British would execute him if caught, his body perhaps quartered and displayed like the despots who impaled rebels on stakes to terrorize villages into submission.

Everything came to a head in those tense midnight meetings, like the one in 1781 during the Yorktown campaign. Robert Morris, frantic with empty coffers, interrupted Salomon at synagogue on Yom Kippur—the holiest day, when Jews fast and pray for atonement. "The army needs $20,000 now," Morris pleaded in the dim light outside. Salomon paused only a moment, then dashed through darkened streets, knocking on doors of fellow merchants, pledging his own credit to scrape together the gold. It arrived just in time for Washington to march south, trapping Cornwallis and forcing his surrender—the turning point that won the war. Salomon never sought repayment; he died poor in 1785 at 44, his health broken from prison hardships, leaving a family in debt while the nation he helped birth forgot his name.

Salomon's sacrifice, blending Jewish steadfastness with the shared dream of liberty, kept the flame flickering when bankruptcy loomed—handing it to diplomats like the wily inventor who charmed foreign courts into alliance.

Always remember that when we call America a "melting pot" of civilization, people of all walks of life were critical to our early survival, and that Haym Salomon lives within that pantheon of heroes.

BENJAMIN FRANKLIN'S DIPLOMACY

Haym Salomon's quiet giving helped bridge divides and keep the war going, but turning that aid into solid partnerships meant sending someone who could win over Kings with the same ease he cracked tough problems. Benjamin Franklin was perfect for it, an older man whose life was a series of fresh starts, all aimed at a freedom he believed came straight from above. He entered the world in 1706 as the 15th child in a crowded Boston house, where his father made soap and candles just to put food on the table.

Young Ben knew the hard side of city life early, starting an apprenticeship at 12 in his brother James's print shop—scrubbing floors, arranging letters, working his fingers raw day after day. But Ben had a hungry mind; he'd stay up late with whatever books he could borrow, soaking up Latin, ideas from thinkers, all fueled by a sense that God had planted this urge in him to explore how the world worked. At 17, tired of his brother's rough treatment, he slipped away to Philadelphia with barely a few pennies and some bread, his pulse quick as he evaded trouble, ready to build something new in a place that became his true home.

Once there, Franklin made printing his craft, taking over the Pennsylvania Gazette in 1729 and turning it into a paper that spoke for everyday people—with clever insights and jabs at stuffy leaders, never shying from the truth. His big success came with Poor Richard's Almanack in 1732, a little yearly guide full of weather tips, home remedies, and phrases people started repeating like old wisdom. Things like "Early to bed and early to rise makes a man healthy, wealthy, and wise," or "A penny saved is a penny earned"—straightforward lessons pulled from his trust in a higher power that blessed hard work and good sense. These sayings did more than entertain; they got Americans thinking about standing on their own, mixing lessons from the Bible with real-life smarts to live independent of any tyrant's control. His creations came from that same drive—the stove he designed in 1742 to heat rooms efficiently, glasses with split lenses for his fading sight, rods to draw lightning away from buildings. Then, in 1752, on a rainy June afternoon at 46, he sent a kite up into the storm clouds with a key on the line, capturing proof that lightning was electric in a dangerous spark that could've ended him right there. Word traveled fast overseas, turning him into an international figure—the clever colonist who'd harnessed nature's power, trusting in the Creator's design and bold enough to prove it. Benjamin Franklin was like the Rockstar of his era.

That recognition came in handy when the fight for independence heated up. By 1776, at 70, Franklin had put his name on the Declaration of Independence, fully aware it was treason—if they failed, the British would've paraded him like those old rulers who torched dissenters at the stake to hush any opposition. That December, he set off for France on a rough voyage aboard a creaky vessel, slipping past enemy ships in bitter cold, landing in Paris worn out and missing home but set to convince a wary royal court. France was crucial; without its fleets and funds, the colonies were done for. Franklin played to his strengths, showing up in simple fur hats instead of fancy wigs, acting the wise countryman among the elegant elite who loved his tales and gadgets. He juggled his love for discovery with the demands of politics, throwing gatherings where he'd wow them with electric tricks while working deals in the background, leaning on his belief in a guiding hand to navigate lies and setbacks.

Things got intense in 1777-1778, with agents lurking and British spies trying to undo his work. One evening, after a grand meal with French officials, Franklin ducked out to a hidden talk in a shadowy estate, where the chance for partnership teetered. A competing envoy had whispered he was a fake, but Franklin pushed back with a quick show—igniting a spark from a glass jar, comparing it to the jolt America could give with French backing. "As God directs the storm," he noted, recalling his kite adventure, "we must direct our destiny together." It clicked; his appeal and determination locked in the 1778 agreement, sending French forces that shifted the war at Yorktown. He bore the strains of being away—pain from gout, long separations from loved ones, always watching for betrayal—but he pushed through, drawing strength from a calm bravery rooted in his belief that this young country was part of God's larger plan for people's worth.

Franklin's path —from a young apprentice fleeing his family to forge a new life in Philadelphia to a world-renowned inventor and envoy changing history —captured that tough freedom, mixing brains with an ethical backbone, and handed the flame of liberty to the fighters and overlooked ones who would bear it under the harshest conditions.

SECTION THREE:
WARRIORS AND UNSUNG HEROES

NATHANAEL GREENE'S STRATEGY

Ben Franklin's brilliant maneuvering in Paris had finally brought French aid into the fight, but over on American ground, the Southern war dragged on like a nightmare, pushing men to their breaking points in ways few could imagine. That's when Nathanael Greene stepped up—a soft-spoken ironworker from Rhode Island who'd become a general—to shift the momentum at a moment when defeat felt all too close. Born in 1742 to a strict Quaker family that shunned violence, Greene grew up forging metal in his father's foundry. He knew the meaning of hard work, his hands callused from hammer and heat, and yet he soaked up knowledge, his mind sharpened by books he read late into the night. The Quakers taught peace, but as British taxes squeezed the colonies and stories spread of redcoats bayoneting farmers who dared resist, Greene felt a pull he couldn't ignore—a faith that teaches us all that standing against evil is God's command, not cowardice. He left the Quakers in 1774, joining the militia despite the fear of being cast out by his own people, driven by a love for this land where a man could worship and work without a King's boot on his neck.

When Washington handed him the Southern command in 1780 after the disaster at Camden—where American lines broke, and men fled in panic—Greene faced a mess: an army in rags, outnumbered three to one by Cornwallis's forces, who swept through Carolina like a plague.

The British had hired German mercenaries, tough Hessians paid to crush the rebellion, men like the five Sisler brothers from Hesse, one of them my great-great-great-grandfather, dragged across the ocean to fight a war not their own. But word reached them through brave souls like Haym Salomon, whispering promises from the Founding Fathers: switch sides, fight for freedom, and earn citizenship with land in Virginia or Ohio. The Sislers, my direct ancestors, chose America, deserting under cover of night with hearts pounding, rifles in hand, becoming some of the first warriors for this new nation's cause—men who saw in the patriots' struggle a chance for their own lives free from tyrannical Kings who conscripted boys and left families starving.

Greene openly welcomed these turncoats. Because they all shared the same burning desire for freedom, it was easy for him to inspire his troops through faith that echoed the Psalms: "The Lord is my strength and my shield." He outmaneuvered superior forces not with head-on clashes but clever guerrilla warfare, splitting his army to draw Cornwallis into chases across swollen rivers and thorny wilderness. His men knew the backwoods of their native land, and they used it to their advantage against the rigid British troop maneuvers. The hardships were relentless—in the swamps of the Carolinas, men waded through chest-deep muck infested with snakes and mosquitoes, their feet rotting from constant wet, fever claiming more lives than bullets. At one point in the Eutaw Springs campaign of 1781, Greene's column pushed through a midnight downpour, soldiers collapsing from exhaustion, haunted by stories of British reprisals where captured rebels were flogged until skin hung in strips or hanged from trees as warnings. Greene sacrificed his own health for those wins—he spent many sleepless nights planning, riding horseback until his body gave out, plagued by rheumatism and fevers that left him weak but unbowed, all because he believed this flame of liberty, forged in such suffering, was worth his last breath.

Greene's strategy wore down the British, forcing Cornwallis north to Yorktown and defeat. His men deeply loved him for his quiet faith and grit that turned their despair into victory. That same spirit lived in warriors from all walks of life, passing the flame to unsung heroes. So many unnamed men who sacrificed their lives so we could breathe the air of freedom are forgotten, but we must never forget their struggle... men like the Black patriot who fell first in the fight's early sparks.

CRISPUS ATTUCKS' BRAVERY

Greene's strategic moves through those swampy lands had finally started to break the British spirit, but the real fire that ignited the revolution burned long before that—it came from everyday people pushing back against soldiers right in their own towns. One of the earliest to show that kind of guts was Crispus Attucks, a man who'd walked a tough path out of slavery, right up to that critical night when he stood tall and risked it all for a taste of freedom he'd only glimpsed. Born around 1723, likely in Framingham, Massachusetts, to an African father who'd been enslaved and a Native mother from the Natick tribe, Crispus grew up in a world that saw him as property, not a person.

He escaped slavery in his twenties, slipping away from his owner with a price on his head—twenty pounds, a fortune back then—for anyone who dragged him back. For years, he wandered the seas as a sailor and in a perilous job as a whaler. Whale oil was in high demand, fueling oil lamps and other devices. Crispus was a great whaler, his powerful arms pulling heavy ropes on vessels that carried him to far-off harbors, and he always stayed just ahead of anyone who might drag him back into bondage. Deep down, it wasn't only fury that kept him going against a world that stripped away a man's worth—it was a quiet, heartfelt belief that God created every person with equal value, meant to live without the lash cracking across their back or the horror of being sold off like livestock at market, echoing that old thinker Seneca who taught that absolute freedom means not fearing a thing, even dying, if it's for what's truly just.

On that bitter cold evening of March 5, 1770, in Boston, tensions had been simmering like a pot ready to boil over—British troops quartered in homes, taxing everything from tea to paper, treating colonists like lowly subjects. Attucks, working the docks that day, heard the commotion near the Custom House: a crowd of angry workers taunting a lone sentry, snowballs flying, voices rising against the redcoats who enforced the King's cruel law. He could've walked away, a Black man with everything to lose in a white man's quarrel, but something pulled him into the fight—perhaps the same spirit that made him run for freedom years before. As more soldiers arrived, bayonets fixed, the mob grew bolder. Attucks moved to the front, his massive frame leading the charge with a stick in hand, defying the oppression that had scarred his life. "Don't be afraid," he shouted to the crowd. In his years, he had learned to temper his fear. His voice cut through the chaos like a call to arms, urging them not to back down from the tyrants.

In that frozen instant, as clubs swung and shots rang out, Attucks was the first to fall—two bullets tearing through his chest, his blood staining the snow red, the first martyr of the Boston Massacre that shocked the colonies into rage. A black man, a runaway of mixed heritage, sacrificed his life for a cause that promised liberty for all, even those like him who'd been denied it (and many would still be denied it for almost a century more).

His bravery, culminating in his death, sparked flyers and discussions that stirred people's spirits, showing that it didn't matter if you were black or white. Your sacrifice for liberty was equal to anyone else, and you, too, could light a fire under a whole country to claim the rights God meant for us all. Attucks gave everything because he believed, deep down, that freedom was worth laying your life down for, and that act handed the light to those even braver people who broke the mold, like the lady who hid who she was to step into the fight alongside the men.

DEBORAH SAMPSON'S DISGUISE

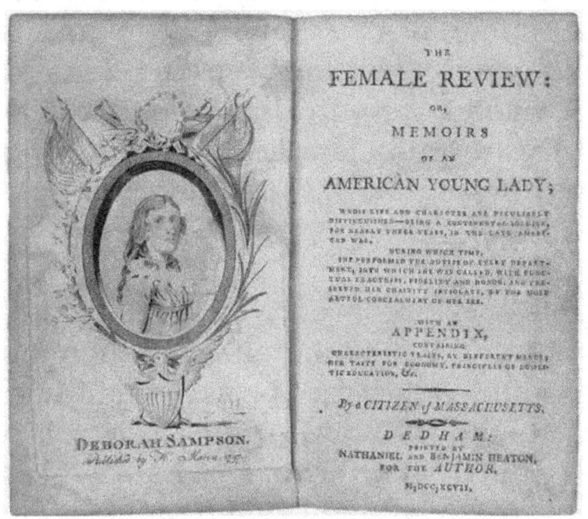

It's a sticky spring day in Massachusetts, 1782, and a young woman is alone in a dimly lit room, her hands shaking as she holds a pair of scissors. Deborah Sampson had it rough growing up in Plympton—poverty split her family wide open when she was little, and she ended up working endless hours as an indentured servant, doing whatever chores were thrown at her to get by. Back in those days, society had rigid rules for women, always limiting what they could do or aim for, but inside Deborah, there was a stubborn spark that wouldn't die. The fight for independence was heating up, and she'd catch wind of stories about regular people standing against a King across the ocean who treated everyone who wasn't royalty like they didn't matter. Men were out there risking it all for a real chance at freedom, a country where no ruler could trample on your hopes because he felt like it. Deborah was tall, tough-minded, and she figured, if liberty was that important, why couldn't she join in? In her quiet times, she'd hold onto lines from the Psalms that brought her some peace: "The Lord is my strength and my shield; my heart trusts in him, and he helps me." With that kind of quiet faith propping her up, she chopped her hair short, bound herself to look the part, and signed on as Robert Shurtliff in the Continental Army's Fourth Massachusetts Regiment, blending right in like it was meant to be.

Once she was in the thick of it, holding onto that secret was like carrying a heavy load nobody else could see—every moment out there could trip her up and expose everything. Her first real brush with the fight came near Tarrytown, New York, when Loyalists jumped her group out of nowhere, the air filling with the sharp crack of muskets and frantic shouts. Smoke burned her eyes, mud grabbed at her feet, and that deep fear twisted in her stomach, but she kept going, aiming her gun and taking down a scout sneaking up close. Mixed in with the scare was this intense feeling of purpose, as if she were defending something far bigger than herself—a pushback against the kind of control that had already wrecked so many lives and families. Then came the hit: a musket ball tore into her thigh, the hurt spreading like wildfire, and another one scraped her forehead, warm blood trickling down. She bit her lip hard, holding back any sound that might give her away. In her mind, she thought of those patriots at Lexington who'd stared down the odds without flinching, and she said a silent prayer, the words of Patrick Henry ringing true: "Give me liberty or give me death." That fire kept her moving, step after painful step.

That same night, tucked away in a flimsy tent with the wind rattling everything, Deborah had to face the worst of it on her own. Her thigh was throbbing badly, the cut deep and angry—if a doctor poked around, her whole ruse would crumble. Her hands shook as she grabbed a little knife, the blade catching the faint light from a lantern.

Fighting off the nausea, she cut into her own skin, probing for that buried ball while the pain hit her in waves that almost knocked her out, sweat and tears mixing on her face. It was the sort of hidden hurt nobody witnesses, but it stemmed from a genuine love for her homeland, for a belief that freedom shouldn't shut out women just because of old ways. Over there in England, King George III didn't think twice about burdening people with taxes they couldn't bear and sending troops to harass and break families apart, leaving them in misery. But Deborah's private battle echoed what America was going through: raw, persistent, anchored by a trust in something greater.

She managed to keep going through more rough fights and long, weary treks, her body worn down but her will intact, until a fever finally took her out in Philadelphia. When the doctor figured it out during his exam, he didn't make trouble—instead, he saw the fighter in her and set up an honorable way out. Back in civilian life, Deborah settled down, got married, raised kids, but her experience didn't just vanish into the past. She traveled around the young country, sharing what she'd been through with folks who gathered to hear, wide-eyed at her guts. Eventually, she received a military pension—the only woman from that entire era to earn one—showing that efforts like hers mattered and endured. Her life shows us that freedom asks something of everyone, often in unseen places where true courage comes out, handing that glow to those who follow. In those quiet spots, the forgotten ones turn into the real watchers of our common dream.

The sacrifices these extraordinary people made turned that early flicker of liberty into a full-blown fire that would continue to blaze in every patriot's heart. Their guts and grit shone a light on terrible wrongs that could no longer stand, pushing everyone toward building a whole new kind of country where freedom was forged and strengthened like iron in a blacksmith's fire.

"Where there is unity there is always victory." – Publilius Syrus

CHAPTER FOUR
GRIEVANCES AND RESOLVE

FORGING FREEDOM FROM TYRANNY

A King's rules from across the ocean made people really angry in the colonies—soldiers from another land moving into homes and ridiculously high taxes taking away what families had worked hard to earn. It was like an awful reminder of the tyranny that eventually made people decide to break away from Europe. In this chapter, I'll go through those problems one by one, telling stories about real people who dealt with them. I hope we all can understand and feel the intense love for our country they had in how they held on, and understand how freedom for individuals became the way to fix that control.

SECTION ONE
ECHOES OF PAST TYRANNIES

TAXATION'S BURDEN

In the middle of the 1760s, making a living in the colonies often came down to working the land from sunup to sundown, barely scraping by. John Hughes, a farmer out in Pennsylvania, really felt the squeeze when the Stamp Act rolled in during 1765. John had pulled himself up through sheer will, working his land, tending ground his family had cleared bit by bit, treating every crop like a blessing he prayed over. He wasn't well-off by any means, but he had his modest farm, his wife Mary, and three little kids counting on him. His days kicked off before the light hit, out there in the fields with his back aching under the heat, holding onto lines from Proverbs to push through: "The hand of the diligent shall bear rule." That kind of quiet faith kept him going, trusting that honest hard work and something greater would carry them.

Then came this order from the King far away—no voice for the colonists in their own laws, but suddenly every scrap of paper needed a paid stamp, money funneled back to a throne that offered nothing in return. For John, it crept in little by little: a tax on the paper for buying more land, another tax on the almanac he used to plan his seasons. Those fees stacked up like weights on his shoulders, pulling him under. He tried cutting corners where he could, but the pressure built. One autumn, after a slim harvest, tax men knocked at his door, insisting on payment for goods he'd sold without those stamps.

John stood there empty-handed, his rough palms open, trying to explain how it all left his family eating plain cornbread and watery soup to get by. The collectors turned a deaf ear; they took his tools, his plow, even the cow that provided milk for the children. Mary stood in the doorway, eyes welling up, while the kids hung onto her, confused about why everything was falling apart.

It got to the point where the weight was just too much. Without his plow, John couldn't prep the ground for the next planting. Winter hit hard. The family crowded around a weak fire and, as he held his family close, John told the Bible story of Job. Job was a man who lost his wealth, health, and family in a series of devastating blows but held onto his faith despite overwhelming suffering. Job sat in ashes, scraping his sores, while his friends urged him to give up, but Job declared, "Though he slay me, yet will I hope in him" (Job 13:15), clinging to trust in God amid the chill and worry of despair. John's optimism in the face of fear calmed his wife and children, and they began planning to solve the problem before they lost everything.

John started meeting with neighbors in hushed groups, their talk urgent but determined, calling out the unfairness of losing their earnings without a word in edgewise. When folks got bolder—like in Boston, where they roughed up the stamp collectors—the King's men pushed back with blades and warnings, turning simple complaints into ugly fights. John had his own close call one evening, facing a group of soldiers, his pulse racing, flat-out refusing to give up his last bits. "We ain't just cattle to be drained," he said, words that captured the rising call for justice. That moment lit a spark—bringing together people who'd felt so isolated under the strain, now joining in refusals to buy stamped goods and late-night plans, their common pain creating ties that held like steel.

The Stamp Act was eventually repealed, but not before it broke good men like John, who finally had to give up his farm due to unpaid bills. He and Mary gathered what was left and headed out, rebuilding from scratch with only their beliefs and each other to lean on. But even in that loss, there was a glimmer: the heavy hand of power showed everyone they couldn't keep bending. It pulled them together against the theft of their efforts and hopes, igniting a blaze that would consume those old bonds. Stories like John's show us how regular people, fueled by care for their loved ones and faith in what's right, stood up to burdens designed to crush them—reminding us that freedom's light grows when we all hold the line side by side.

JUSTICE DENIED

In the late 1760s, getting fair treatment in court began to feel like a distant dream for many in the colonies.

The British set up these admiralty courts, run by judges loyal to the crown, where cases were decided without local juries—people who knew the people and the place. It was all rigged to favor the King, leaving ordinary men and women at the mercy of distant rules that didn't care about their side. Christopher Seider was just eleven years old, and even he became caught up in the mess in Boston in February 1770. Christopher was the son of poor German immigrants, working odd jobs to help his family get by in a city bubbling with anger over taxes and the presence of troops. He had that innocent energy kids have, running errands and playing in the streets, but like many, he got pulled into the protests against the Stamp Act and the Townshend duties that were squeezing everyone dry.

One cold afternoon, a crowd gathered outside Theophilus Lillie's shop, a merchant who ignored the boycotts and kept selling British goods. Folks were throwing rocks and shouting, frustrated by how the laws protected these importers while regular people suffered. Christopher was there, part of the group, when Ebenezer Richardson—a customs informer known for snitching on neighbors—stepped in to defend Lillie. Richardson, already hated for his role in enforcing the king's taxes, grabbed his musket and fired into the crowd from his window.

The shot hit Christopher square in the chest, tearing through him. The boy fell, blood soaking the snow, gasping as people rushed to him. He died hours later, his small body carried home to parents shattered by grief. They were inconsolable, but somehow, in their quiet moments, they clung to faith. Christopher's father whispered psalms about justice: "The righteous cry out, and the Lord hears them; he delivers them from all their troubles." But where was the delivery here? An innocent child, gunned down for standing against unfairness. Incidents like this brought even more people around to believe that something had to happen to combat this injustice.

The trial that followed showed how twisted the system was. Richardson was arrested, but the admiralty-influenced courts dragged their feet, biased toward crown officials. Even though a jury found him guilty of murder, the King pardoned him from across the sea, letting him walk free while Christopher's family buried their boy. The funeral turned into a massive procession—over two thousand people marching behind his small coffin, a symbol of the king's cruelty. It wasn't just about one life lost; it was the denial of justice, the way courts protected the powerful and hanged or ruined the innocent. Smugglers were tried and hanged without a jury of their peers. Other men faced rigged hearings where evidence was twisted, leading to more hangings for what should have been fair trade. One merchant in Virginia, caught evading duties, was convicted in a crown court and lost everything—his ship seized, his family left destitute—while praying for strength from stories of Daniel in the lions' den, facing unjust rulers with unshakeable trust.

These injustices fueled a fire that spread fast. People like Christopher's neighbors, seeing innocents hanged or families broken by biased rulings, started demanding laws that treated everyone fairly, with juries of their own kind. These people felt a unity born of shared pain, and they became resolved to fight for a system in which a distant tyrant didn't deny justice. Kings like George III had no issue hanging men for speaking out, as in the graphic trials where colonists were shipped to England, away from home, to face charges in courts stacked against them—bodies swinging from gallows as warnings, leaving wives widowed and children orphaned. But in America, that spark of freedom turned the tragedy into action, proving that when justice is twisted, true patriots rise, driven by love for their land and faith in what's right, to forge something better.

MILITARY OPPRESSION

Scores of people had been fleeing oppression and tyranny for seven generations, struggling and dying to forge a new life for themselves and their children. But they never had truly escaped the crown, and now they found themselves right back in the clutches of evil, right here in America.

Quartering Act

By the late 1760s, British soldiers were all over the colonies. They weren't there to protect anyone; they were there to shove their way into everyday life like bullies who wouldn't back off. They moved into people's houses under the Quartering Act, expecting meals and beds, turning homes into their own camps. It built this ongoing dread—a simple knock could bring troops inside, and if you said no, you'd pay for it. Regular people were killed in the open for just speaking up. That fear took over normal days, with everyone watching their backs, but it also lit a spark of pushback—people saw they had to resist or lose it all. The King even blocked westward expansion with the Proclamation of 1763, keeping settlers from the Appalachians. These actions frustrated explorers like Daniel Boone, who pushed through wild lands on faith and guts alone, and later Jedediah Smith, who trapped in areas the crown claimed but never truly held. The breaking point came in raw moments of brutality, like that freezing March night in Boston in 1770.

It was March 5, a bitterly cold evening in Boston, and things had been simmering for weeks with redcoats posted everywhere. Crispus Attucks, the black American we highlighted in Chapter Three, met his destiny on this night. You'll remember he was a tall, sturdy guy who'd run from slavery and built a life on the docks as a sailor. That night, talk spread about a fight between soldiers and some rope workers, and people headed to the Custom House, fed up with troops who grabbed jobs and caused trouble. Crispus showed up with a stick, not out for blood but ready to face down the same kind of control he'd escaped. The crowd grew loud, hurling snowballs laced with stones, voices rough from years of rules and taxes they had no hand in.

Private Hugh White was standing guard at the Custom House and swung his gun at a young apprentice, Edward Garrick, for mouthing off about an officer. That set everything off—the alarm bell rang, pulling more folks in. Captain Thomas Preston came out with eight men, bayonets ready, staring down the angry mob. Crispus moved up front, his words cutting through the noise, calling out the wrong of it all. Some say he shouted something like, "Let's get rid of these scoundrels," driven by a belief that freedom was part of God's plan, like the call in Exodus to set the captive free. The soldiers, edgy and surrounded, primed their muskets. Then a shot cracked—maybe accidental, maybe not—and the whole line fired. Crispus caught the first one right in the chest, dropping to the snow, blood pooling dark around him. Four more fell: Samuel Gray, a rope maker, took one to the head; James Caldwell, another sailor, got hit twice; young Samuel Maverick, only 17, was fatally shot; and Patrick Carr, an Irish leather worker, hung on for nine days before he died.

Blood stained the streets that night, innocent people gunned down without a chance, their bodies hauled off as the crowd ran scared. Families grieved—Crispus probably went into a simple grave without a marker, but his end stood for something bigger, the first to go down for the cause. The soldiers were tried, but John Adams took their side to uphold real law, and most got off easy, which only stoked the anger further. It wasn't some random clash; it was the King's heavy hand squeezing life out, like old rulers who killed to stay on top. His actions mirrored those of Nero, torching Christians for fun, their screams filling the air as crowds watched. Or under Stalin's communists, millions shot in the head during purges, dumped in mass graves, families living in constant dread of that late-night door pound, never knowing if loved ones would come back. In the colonies, acts like this woke people up—men like Boone, stopped from heading west where they dreamed of new beginnings, leaned on that same toughness, venturing out anyway, guided by faith through risks.

Those awful events sparked strong pushback, with folks forming groups and armed bands, swearing to guard their homes against takeovers. It proved that when soldiers make streets into death traps, and fear rules your days, real freedom calls for giving it all—lives offered up so others can breathe easy. That spark of liberty, started in spilled blood, grew stronger, showing no oppressor could put out a nation's drive when it's rooted in faith and care for the land.

SECTION TWO
MORAL IMPERATIVE FOR CHANGE

DIVINE RIGHTS ASSERTED

In the summer of 1776, a handful of men met up in Philadelphia to figure out how to explain why the colonies needed to split from Britain. One of them was Thomas Jefferson, 33 years old from Virginia, and they picked him to write the first draft because he had a good head for it and could put things into words that stuck.

Jefferson grew up on a plantation in Albemarle County—his dad, Peter, was a surveyor and planter, and his mom, Jane, came from a family with some standing. He lost his father at 14 and had to step up young, learning law and getting involved in Virginia's House of Burgesses, where he started calling out British heavy-handedness. What set him apart from the others there—like John Adams and Ben Franklin—was his background: he'd already written "A Summary View of the Rights of British America" back in 1774, arguing that rights came naturally, and it hit home with many people. He was quiet but had this strong sense that liberty was something given by a higher power, and his writing got right to the heart without extra fuss.

Jefferson did the work by himself in a rented spot on Market Street, sitting at a desk he'd made portable for travel, with the summer heat making it tough. Over 17 days, he went through his notes, feeling the pressure—knowing if this failed, it could mean the noose for treason. He drew on his beliefs, seeing the King's rule as wrong against the Creator who gave people rights no one could take away. As he put it down, he stated those rights clearly: life, liberty, and the pursuit of happiness, all from that divine place. It wasn't only about government; it was about right and wrong, about tyranny that went against what was meant for people. Jefferson later mentioned that he turned to prayer during those long stretches, drawing strength from Psalms like "The Lord is my light and my salvation; whom shall I fear?" That steady faith helped him push past his worries, leading to words that carried real weight.

Good character meant doing something, and Jefferson's draft called for it—laying out the king's wrongs like offenses against what's sacred, pushing folks to act because sticking with that rule went against their purpose from above. When he showed it to the group, they recognized its strength and tweaked just a bit before sending it to Congress. That paper, the Declaration of Independence, was more than words; it was a straight claim that freedom came from the Creator, not rulers, and it fired up a revolution where everyday people gave up everything for a country based on those ideas. Jefferson wrote words that will echo through eternity, guided by a divine presence to become the eloquent voice of liberty and freedom.

That sense of moral right spread out, proving that when belief claims those God-given freedoms, it calls us to live up to them—tying into how coming together in common faith turned those hard times into the plan for freedom that lasts.

VIRTUE'S CALL

James Madison was born in 1751 in Port Conway, Virginia, the first of 12 children to James Madison Sr. and Nelly Conway Madison.

His dad ran a tobacco plantation with a big spread of land, and his mom was from a prominent family that had been tied to the area for generations. Madison grew up as the British were tightening their grip, but he had a real thirst for knowledge early on—he got lessons at home and then went to a boarding school with Donald Robertson, picking up all sorts of classics and big ideas. At 18, he went to the College of New Jersey, which we now call Princeton, and finished in just two years. That wasn't easy for him, dealing with health problems his whole life, like seizures and general physical weakness.

When I was about 10, doctors found an abscess in my leg bone. I dealt with pain every day for nearly 20 years until a biopsy finally fixed it, though it flares up once or twice a year even now. Living like that taught me to push mind over matter. Madison went through something similar with his own health struggles as a kid. It made him more reflective, always careful with his thoughts, but it also built his inner toughness. He delved deeply into Enlightenment thought, blending it with his Anglican beliefs, and came to see that Americans needed to run their own government in order to live right and follow a higher order.

By the 1780s, after time in the Continental Congress and Virginia's assembly, Madison had seen the cracks in the new country firsthand. The Articles of Confederation weren't holding up—states argued constantly, money owed stacked high, and events like Shays' Rebellion in 1786 showed how shaky everything was. Farmers in Massachusetts were hit with high taxes, lost their land in court, and grabbed weapons, raided armories, and stopped legislative sessions. Madison followed it from a distance, his letters full of concern. He saw rot setting in, with groups chasing their own gains, pulling apart the togetherness needed for real freedom. In Federalist No. 10, one of the pieces he wrote with Alexander Hamilton and John Jay to support the Constitution, Madison said these factions were like sicknesses in the system, arising from people's flaws, but he felt it wasn't anything a solid republic couldn't handle. "If men were angels, no government would be necessary," he pointed out, but since we're not, we need setups to keep those flaws in check.

Faith was a big part of it for Madison—he thought living virtuously came from following higher principles, as in Proverbs, where it says, "Trust in the Lord with all your heart and lean not on your own understanding." Tyranny grew when people lost that sense of right. For instance, King George III twisted the courts and left colonists open to unfair trials, reminding our forefathers of old Roman rulers killing off opponents and leaving bodies out as scares. Madison fought for a setup where governing yourself meant everyone, leaders and common people, had to act with decency and make choices that looked out for the vulnerable.

Feeling for those getting crushed brought people together—watching families lose everything to terribly unfair laws created a common drive. At the 1787 Constitutional Convention, Madison arrived first, papers ready, pushing for balances like dividing powers to stop corruption from spreading.

Those warnings about divisions really landed when uprisings broke out, showing how divisions could kill freedom. But Madison's calm approach helped shape the Constitution, building in ways to encourage good character. Men like him, guided by belief and care for a free nation, gave up their easy lifestyles for a greater good—Madison pushed through nonstop, even as his body paid the price—to build something lasting. This push for decency connected the wrongs to real steps forward, keeping freedom's fire burning strong through that moral backbone that guides us even now.

COMPASSION IN REBELLION

During the Revolution, not every clash ended in blood—some moments showed the deeper humanity that tempered the fight for freedom. Take the story of Francis Marion, the "Swamp Fox," a South Carolina farmer turned guerrilla leader. Born in 1732 on a plantation near Georgetown, Marion grew up in a world where British rule was a distant problem that didn't directly affect his life or livelihood, but as taxes and troops pressed in, he began to see it as a betrayal of our fundamental rights. He'd fought in the Cherokee War earlier, learning hit-and-run tactics in the swamps. But it was his faith—a quiet Presbyterian belief—that guided him to see the enemy as fellow men, not just foes. "Vengeance is mine, saith the Lord," from Romans, stayed with him, reminding him that justice wasn't about hate.

In 1780, after Charleston fell to the British, Marion gathered a ragged band of volunteers—farmers, shopkeepers, men driven by love for their homes and a sense of divine right to live free. They harassed Loyalist militias loyal to the crown, who often burned Patriot farms and hanged resisters without trial. One night in the Santee River swamps, Marion's men ambushed a Loyalist patrol led by Major John Coming Ball, capturing a few men. The prisoners expected no mercy—Loyalists had been tarred and feathered or worse by angry crowds. Ball himself had led raids that left families homeless, their cries echoing as homes burned. Marion's scouts wanted revenge! Their own families had suffered under the cruelty of the British troops and Loyalists, just like tyrants in old Europe had flayed rebels alive or communists later who starved millions in gulags to crush dissent.

But Marion paused, looking at the bound men—hungry, scared, some just following orders to protect their own. He ordered food shared and wounds tended, saying something like, "We fight for liberty, not to become tyrants ourselves." Drawing from the Sermon on the Mount—"Blessed are the merciful, for they shall obtain mercy"—he let them go, making them swear not to fight again. It wasn't weakness; it was resolve tempered by mercy, seeking justice for all without losing humanity. This act won over some Loyalists, who switched sides. Many of these people were their neighbors, and they began to see the Patriots as fair. Aid for suffering kin, even enemies, united more Loyalists to the cause, showing compassion could fuel the flame of freedom better than vengeance. This is an excellent lesson for us to remember in our own lives, as in the saying that you can draw more bees with honey than with vinegar.

Marion's mercy spread, inspiring leaders to seek justice over payback, and humanity began to guide the rebellion's fire. This compassion linked moral calls to unity, forging a nation where freedom was born to burn for everyone.

SECTION THREE
PATH TO INDEPENDENCE

DECLARATIONS OF INDEPENDENCE'S BOLDNESS

In the sticky heat of July 1776, fifty-six men in Philadelphia did something that still takes my breath away. They fearlessly put their names on a piece of paper that told the most powerful King on earth, "We are done with you." Each of these men and their suffering families must be canonized in the pantheon of American greatness and never forgotten as the original patriots who bestowed upon today's Americans the greatest gift of all: life, liberty, and the pursuit of happiness.

The Declaration of Independence wasn't just a complaint letter. It was a shout from the heart that said every human being is born with rights straight from the Creator: the right to live without someone else deciding you don't get to see tomorrow, the right to be free to make your own choices and worship as your conscience tells you, and the right to chase a life that has meaning to you. No King, no army, no law could take those away. They called them "unalienable rights."

Every man who signed knew precisely what he was risking. If the war went wrong, the British courts would call it treason, and treason meant the rope. Their homes would be torched, their families hunted, their fortunes gone. Yet they signed anyway. And because they did, the flame of resilient liberty leapt higher than anyone could have imagined.

Let me tell you about a few of them, the way I wish someone had told me when I was younger—quietly, like stories around a fire, so you can feel the weight of what they carried.

Button Gwinnett was born in England in 1735, the son of a minister.

He came to America looking for a fresh start, ended up farming in Georgia, and discovered he had a gift for speaking up. His Baptist faith told him liberty wasn't just politics; it was God's intention. When the time came to sign, he didn't hesitate. The British answered by burning his plantation to the ground. His wife Ann and their children had to run for the swamps, hiding in the damp and mosquitoes while Button tried to stay one step ahead of patrols looking to hang him. A year later, a stupid argument with another officer turned into a duel. Button died at 42, leaving Ann with almost nothing. But that signature of his still burns on the parchment.

Lyman Hall was a doctor from Connecticut who moved south to Georgia. He had studied at Yale and could have lived comfortably treating the wealthy, but he spent his days helping the poor for whatever they could pay. When Georgia's delegates argued about breaking away, Hall's quiet voice carried the day when he said these words that will live forever: "We either hang together, or we hang separately." The British paid him back by leveling his house and clinic. His family spent months moving from attic to cellar, living on handouts from neighbors. Hall kept sending his own money to feed Continental soldiers. After the war, he rebuilt, poorer but unbroken, because he believed healing the sick and healing a nation came from the same place.

George Walton was orphaned as a boy in Virginia and learned carpentry to survive. Nights, he taught himself law by candlelight. By the time he was Georgia's attorney general, his Anglican faith had convinced him that tyranny was a sin against God's order. The day he signed, the British put a price on his head. They wrecked his home, captured him, and threw him in a prison ship. His wife Dorothy and their little boy hid in the woods, eating what they could find, while George endured merciless beatings meant to break him. Eventually, he was traded in a prisoner exchange, but he came home thinner, scarred, but still ready to keep fighting. Years later, he served as governor, still believing mercy and justice could live in the same heart.

Abraham Clark was a New Jersey farmer who became a surveyor and then a lawyer who took cases for people who couldn't pay. His Presbyterian faith was simple: if God made us free, no man had the right to chain us. When he signed, the British grabbed two of his sons and locked them on the prison ship Jersey in New York harbor—places so awful that more Americans died there than in all the battles combined. The boys were starved and beaten to force their father to recant. Clark refused. Night after night, he prayed the words of David, "Though I walk through the valley of the shadow of death, I will fear no evil." His wife smuggled food to the prisoners at risk of her own life. Both sons survived, barely. Clark never wavered.

Lewis Morris owned one of the grandest estates in New York, but he chose public service over comfort. When he signed, the British turned his mansion into headquarters and then torched it. His wife, Elizabeth, was arrested and thrown into prison, where the cold and filth took her life. Lewis kept working in Congress, using his shipping knowledge to get supplies to the army, all while grieving in silence. He never remarried. He just kept going.

John Hart was known as "Honest John" throughout New Jersey because he never cheated anyone, ever. At sixty-five, he was old for a revolutionary, but his Baptist faith wouldn't let him sit quiet. The British put him at the top of their wanted list. They burned his farm, scattered his livestock, and hunted him through the woods for months. His wife, Deborah, was already in bed and sick when the redcoats arrived. She died while the children hid with her body in a cave. Hart slept under trees in winter, eating whatever he could forage, but he kept sending grain to Washington's starving army. He came home after Yorktown to nothing but ashes and graves, and died soon after. They called him the "old man who gave all."

Richard Stockton was a respected judge in New Jersey, a Princeton man who initially thought reconciliation with Britain might work. Then he saw the cruelty up close and changed his mind. He signed. The British caught him, dragged him to a freezing prison, fed him moldy bread, and beat him until his health shattered. His wife Annis hid the family papers in the woods while soldiers ransacked their house. Released in a prisoner swap, Stockton came home a broken man and died at 51, leaving Annis to raise their children in poverty. Yet, before he died, he proudly stated that he never regretted that signature.

Francis Lewis had already lost almost everything once—shipwrecked and captured in the French and Indian War. He built a fortune in trade, only to see the British destroy it when he signed. They arrested his wife, Elizabeth, and held her without heat or decent food. She died from the treatment. Lewis stayed in Congress, quietly using his connections to keep supplies moving to the army, carrying his grief like a private wound.

William Hooper was a Boston-born lawyer, Harvard-educated, who moved to North Carolina and became one of its best speakers. When he signed, the British burned his house to the ground. His family fled from relative to relative, always one step ahead of raiders. Hooper kept writing and speaking, rallying people even while his own world crumbled.

Joseph Hewes was a North Carolina merchant with Quaker roots. He had no wife or children, so he poured everything—his ships, his money, his time—into building the Continental Navy. When he signed, he lost it all to British seizures. He died young from the strain, but the navy he helped create kept the fight alive.

These were ordinary men—fathers, husbands, farmers, merchants—who became extraordinary because they believed something bigger than themselves. Their wives and children paid prices most of us can barely imagine, yet they held on. Their names on that document weren't just ink; they were promises bought with blood, tears, and unbreakable hope. And because they were willing to lose everything for an idea—that every person is born with God-given rights—the flame of resilient liberty caught and has never gone out.

UNITY FORGED

The Declaration was signed, but the war that followed nearly broke them. For eight long years, they had watched friends freeze at Valley Forge, bleed out on muddy fields, hang from British gallows. They had seen homes burned, wives widowed, children orphaned. Washington's army had been chased across New Jersey like hunted animals, and more than once the cause looked lost. Franklin had spent those same years in France, old and in pain, begging for money and ships while British spies shadowed his every step. He charmed, he pleaded, he endured insults, all so the Continental Army could keep fighting. And then, against every odd, it happened: French ships, American grit, and one October morning at Yorktown in 1781, when British drums beat the surrender and redcoats laid down their arms. Washington stood on the field, tears in his eyes, knowing the price paid in blood and grief.

Eleven years after the Declaration, in the same Philadelphia State House where they had once risked everything to speak of freedom, many of those same men came back in the summer of 1787. They were older now, scarred, poorer, some walking with canes. The war was won, but the country was coming apart—states arguing, debts crushing farmers, rebellion in the air. If they could not find a way to bind the thirteen states into one nation, everything they had suffered for would slip away.

So they locked the doors, pulled the curtains, and started arguing again. New Englanders wanted a strong government; Southerners feared it would become another king. Small states demanded equal power; large states wanted votes by population. Tempers ran hot. Men slammed fists on tables. More than once, someone threatened to walk out and take his state with him.

Yet something held them. They had stood together in snow and fire; they could stand together in a hot room. They prayed together every morning. They remembered the graves they had left behind. And slowly, painfully, they began to give ground—not because they wanted to, but because they had learned the hard way what happened when people refused to bend.

Picture Benjamin Franklin at eighty-one, carried in each day on a sedan chair built by Philadelphia prisoners because he could barely walk. He sat watching younger men shout, a faint smile on his face. One afternoon, the quarreling got so fierce that Franklin rose—slowly, painfully—and spoke in that cracked old voice. He reminded them of the prayers they had offered together when Washington's army was starving and barefoot, when hope was almost gone.

"If a sparrow cannot fall without His notice," he said, "is it probable an empire can rise without His aid?" The room fell quiet. Grown men wiped their eyes. They went back to work.

George Washington sat at the head of the room, saying almost nothing. Everyone felt his presence anyway—like a steady hand on the tiller. He had already given eight years of his life, left Mount Vernon in ruins, and buried friends on battlefields from Boston to Yorktown. When smaller states threatened to leave over representation, it was Washington's silent look, more than any speech, that brought them back to the table.

Roger Sherman, a Connecticut shoemaker turned judge, wore a plain coat and looked like he'd just come in from the fields. He listened more than he spoke, then offered the idea that saved everything: two houses of Congress—one where every state had an equal voice, the other based on population. Simple, practical, born of a man who knew how to mend broken things.

Gouverneur Morris, tall and sharp-tongued with a wooden leg from an old carriage accident, stood on his peg and gave the Constitution its final polish, writing the preamble we still know by heart. James Wilson, a Scottish immigrant who had arrived penniless, insisted the government must rest on the people themselves. His voice broke when he spoke of his own journey: "I came here a stranger; now I fight for a home for every stranger."

Even slavery—the wound they could not heal—forced hard choices. George Mason refused to sign, warning it would bring judgment from heaven. Others, heartsick, signed anyway, believing a broken union was worse than none, trusting their children to finish what they could not. They wept as they did it.

Outside, rumors flew that the convention had failed. Inside, doors stayed locked, guards stood watch, and spies tried to listen at keyholes. The pressure was crushing. Yet day after day these men—tired, hot, afraid—kept coming back, praying, arguing, yielding a little here, holding firm there, until something new stood before them: a Constitution that spread power so thinly no one man or group could seize it all.

When Franklin signed, his hand shook. He pointed to Washington's chair with its painted sun, half-risen on the horizon. "I have often wondered," he said, "whether that sun was rising or setting. But now I know—it is a rising sun." Tears filled his eyes. The room broke into cheers and embraces, men hugging like brothers who had walked through fire together.

That unity wasn't perfect. It would be tested again and again. But in that sweltering room, forged by years of shared suffering and answered prayer, thirteen separate candles became one torch—strong enough, bright enough, to light a nation and, one day, the world.

KNOWLEDGE'S WEAPON

Before the men locked themselves in that Philadelphia room in 1787, they had already walked through eight years of hell together. The war that started with a few shots at Lexington and Concord in April 1775 had turned into something no one could have imagined. Farmers who had never held a musket stood shoulder to shoulder with merchants and preachers, facing the greatest army on earth. They froze at Valley Forge, shoes wrapped in rags, leaving bloody prints in the snow. They watched friends die of smallpox and starvation. They buried boys who would never see twenty. And every time hope flickered low, someone found a way to fan it back into flame—with words.

Patrick Henry had lit the first real spark back in Virginia's House of Burgesses when he stood up in a room full of cautious men and shouted, "Give me liberty or give me death!"

Then came Thomas Paine. In the winter of 1776, when Washington's army was falling apart, and men were walking away, Paine sat by candlelight and wrote "Common Sense". Soldiers carried crumpled pages into battle. Paine wrote like he was talking across a kitchen table: "These are the times that try men's souls." And because ordinary people suddenly saw the fight plain, they kept going.

Benedict Arnold started out as one of the Revolution's boldest fighters—a daring general who charged into battle and played a big part in turning the tide at Saratoga, a victory that helped bring the French into the war on America's side. But over time, resentment built up: he felt passed over for promotions, buried in debt, and unappreciated by Congress. That bitterness finally drove him to a desperate step—he secretly reached out to the British, offering to hand over West Point, the key fortress guarding the Hudson River, in exchange for money and a high rank in their army.

The plan unraveled when his British contact, Major John André, was captured with incriminating papers hidden in his boot. Arnold got word just in time, jumped on a horse, raced to a British ship waiting on the river, and escaped down the Hudson to New York City. From there, he took up arms against the cause he'd once championed, leading raids on American soil. His defection came at a moment when it could have broken the young nation's back—losing West Point might have split the colonies in two and ended the fight for independence.

Arnold spent the rest of his life in England, hoping for rewards that never fully came. Instead, he faced cold shoulders from British officers who didn't trust a turncoat and financial struggles that never eased. When he died in 1801, few mourned him, and his name became the very definition of treason in America—a lasting warning about how personal grievance can unravel even the strongest loyalty.

When Washington needed one more victory to keep the cause alive, he crossed the ice-choked Delaware on Christmas night 1776, surprising the Hessians at Trenton. The men were hungry, sick, half-naked, but they followed him because they had read Paine and remembered Henry. Later, at Valley Forge, while soldiers shivered in huts and wives back home melted pewter plates for bullets, Paine wrote again: "The harder the conflict, the more glorious the triumph." Those words, carried by riders and read by firelight, kept despair from winning.

Across the ocean, Benjamin Franklin—seventy years old, aching with gout—sat in Paris wearing a coonskin cap, charming the French court while British spies watched his every move. He knew America needed ships and money. For years, he smiled through insults, negotiated in secret, and, after Yorktown, finally brought France fully into the fight. When the French fleet sailed, and British cannons fell silent on that Virginia peninsula in October 1781, it was Franklin's quiet persistence as much as Washington's sword that forced Cornwallis to stack arms.

Paul Revere's midnight ride, the stand at Concord Bridge, the long retreat across New Jersey, the freezing march to Trenton, the brutal winter at Valley Forge, the final victory at Yorktown—every step was fueled by words that turned frightened colonists into a people willing to die for an idea. Pamphlets, sermons, letters read aloud in taverns, songs sung around campfires—knowledge became a weapon sharper than any bayonet.

That is why, when those same men gathered again in 1787, they protected a free press in the very first amendment. They had seen what truth could do when it was free to travel from hand to hand, heart to heart. They had watched it turn a scattered, suffering people into a nation. And they knew that without it, the flame they had carried through blood and ice would gutter out.

"If the freedom of speech is taken away then dumb and silent we may be led, like sheep to the slaughter." – George Washington

Ancient voices had warned the same thing—Plato wrote that tyranny begins when truth is silenced. The founders remembered, and because they did, the light stayed burning.

CHAPTER FIVE
ANCIENT ECHOES

LESSONS FROM FALLEN EMPIRES

What did our founders glean from ancient civilizations to prepare a constitution that would last for over 250 years? Harsh lessons were learned in the rise and fall of every civilization that came before us, and our forefathers drew from the triumphs and mistakes of these empires. Let's take a look at what they learned as they drew on the best of ancient civilizations to conceive a government that has now lasted two and a half centuries.

In the cracked marble of Rome's old forums and the broken columns of Athens, you can almost hear the whispers of what went wrong. Great nations don't usually fall to armies at the gates. They fall when the people inside stop caring about right and wrong. The founders knew those stories cold. They read them by candlelight, argued over them in taverns, and carried them into every line they wrote for us. They wanted to build something that would not repeat the same heartbreak. As you read my breakdown of what the founders learned from ancient civilizations, consider how many lessons we seem to be forgetting in modern times, and how important it is for us to rein in government overreach and the loosening of morality to stay on course.

"What has history said of eminence without honor, wealth without wisdom, power and possessions without principle? The answer is reiterated in the overthrow of the mightiest empires of ancient times. Babylon, Persia, Greece, Rome! The four successive, universal powers of the past. What and where are they?"
– Orson F. Whitney

SECTION ONE
GREEK AND ROMAN DECLINES

ATHENS' HUBRIS

The ancient democracy that found its core in Athens once shone like a torch on a hill. Ordinary citizens, not Kings, voted on laws. Philosophers walked the streets asking big questions about justice and truth. Sailors brought home victory after victory against the Persians at Marathon and Salamis.

For a while, it looked as if free men governing themselves could do anything. Then came Pericles. He was handsome, brilliant with words, and loved by the crowds. In 461 BC, he took power and promised Athens would be the greatest city the world had ever seen.

He spent the treasury on beautiful temples and statues, turned the Delian League—an alliance meant to protect Greek cities—into an Athenian empire, and taxed everyone to pay for it. When smaller cities tried to leave the league, Pericles sent fleets to burn their harbors and drag them back. People cheered because Athens was rich and strong, but something quiet was dying.

Young men who once trained for battle now spent their days in the agora listening to smooth-talking speakers called demagogues who told them whatever they wanted to hear. Morality loosened. Old religious rules were laughed at. Men chased money and pleasure instead of honor. When Sparta finally came, Athens was rotten inside. In 404 BC, the Spartans starved the city into surrender. They tore down the Long Walls stone by stone while flute girls played, and the proudest democracy the world had known ended in chains.

James Madison read Thucydides' account of all this when he was barely twenty, sitting up late at Princeton with the windows open to the night air. He underlined the parts about how democracies destroy themselves when citizens care more about their own desires than the common good. Years later, when he drafted the Constitution, he kept Athens in the back of his mind. That's why he insisted on checks and balances, on representatives instead of pure town-hall voting, on a republic strong enough to protect liberty without letting the passions of the moment sweep it away.

John Adams felt the same warning deep in his bones. He wrote to Abigail that Athens collapsed the moment its citizens got tired of doing the hard work of being good. In Paris, he and Jefferson went back and forth about it for hours—Jefferson wanting to trust ordinary people with more direct power, Adams pushing back that even decent men can be swept away when ambition and smooth talk take over. In the end, they found a middle ground: give the people real authority, but not so much at once that a bad mood or a clever speaker could wreck everything overnight.

LESSONS FROM ATHENS: WHAT THE FOUNDERS BUILT INTO AMERICA'S CONSTITUTION AND LAWS

• Avoiding Mob Rule and Direct Democracy's Pitfalls: Athens' reliance on crowd-driven decisions led to impulsive policies swayed by demagogues; the U.S. Constitution countered this with a representative republic, where elected officials (like Congress) filter public passions, and checks like the Senate's longer terms ensure deliberate governance.

• Preventing Imperial Overreach and Unfair Taxation: Pericles' transformation of alliances into an exploitative empire through heavy taxes fueled resentment and downfall; this inspired the Constitution's limits on federal power, such as requiring Congressional approval for taxes (Article I, Section 8) and the Bill of Rights' protections against unreasonable searches (Fourth Amendment) to guard against government overreach.

• Balancing Power to Curb Corruption: Athens decayed when citizens prioritized personal gain over honor, allowing corruption; the Founders implemented separation of powers and federalism in the Constitution to divide authority among branches and states, preventing any single entity from dominating, as Madison emphasized in Federalist No. 51.

• Safeguarding Individual Rights Amid Moral Shifts: The loosening of morality in Athens eroded societal stability; the Bill of Rights was crafted to protect fundamental liberties like freedom of speech (First Amendment) and religion, ensuring a foundation of faith and decency that withstands cultural shifts and promotes the common good.

• Emphasizing Guardrails of Law and Faith: Athens collapsed without structures to channel public desires; the Constitution's preamble and overall framework, influenced by Adams' warnings, promote a "more perfect Union" through laws that encourage virtue, with the establishment clause allowing faith to guide without state imposition, fostering self-governance rooted in principle.

The founders looked at Athens and saw a warning written in fire: give people freedom, but give them guardrails of law and faith, or the torch will burn the hand that holds it.

They carried that lesson into every debate, every compromise, every line of the Constitution—determined that America would not follow Athens into the dark. Today, we need to be reminded that it is the slow loosening of morality by demagogues that chips away at great democracies and can eventually kill them. Freedom to do whatever you choose is great, but it comes with an obligation to follow laws, basic human decency, and fundamental rights that extend to everyone.

"I am free because I know that I alone am morally responsible for everything I do. I am free, no matter what rules surround me. If I find them tolerable, I tolerate them; if I find them too obnoxious, I break them. I am free because I know that I alone am morally responsible for everything I do." – Robert A. Heinlein

SPARTA'S RIGIDITY

Sparta existed in the rugged valley of Laconia in southern Greece, a place of hard soil and harder men. It rose to power around the eighth century BC, after its warriors crushed neighboring Messenia and turned the people there into helots—state-owned slaves who worked the land so Spartans could train full-time.

At seven, a Spartan boy was taken from his mother and handed over to the agoge—the state's training system that was more like a lifelong test of endurance than anything else. They starved him on purpose, made him march barefoot over ice and rocks, and beat him if he flinched. The whole point was to strip away every trace of softness and turn him into a soldier who would never break, never run, and never put himself above the city. For centuries, that system produced the most feared warriors in Greece. Three hundred Spartans at Thermopylae held a narrow pass against an army that darkened the horizon, buying precious days for the rest of Greece. You can almost feel the pride in those stories—discipline, courage, a willingness to die for something bigger than yourself.

But somewhere along the way, the discipline crossed a line and became something cruel. Weak babies were carried to a hillside and left to die. If a grown man showed the slightest sign of softness, the others turned on him. The entire system rested on thousands of helots—people forced to farm the land while the Spartans trained. The helots outnumbered the citizens seven to one, so every year the leaders declared a kind of open season on them. Killing a helot didn't count as murder; it was just keeping order. Fear held Sparta together, not love, or community, or shared values.

A young warrior named Aristodemus learned that the hard way. He had stood in the front line at Thermopylae, shield locked with the others, until sickness forced him and one friend to leave the fight. When he made it home, the city that once praised him now spat on him. They called him "the Coward." The shame burned worse than any wound. A year later at Plataea, he charged the enemy alone, swinging until the spears brought him down. Only in death did they call him brave again.

That same hardness that made Sparta terrifying also made it brittle. They refused to let new people become citizens. They wouldn't trade ideas or soften any rule. The number of full Spartan warriors kept shrinking—by 371 BC, only about a thousand were left. When Thebes came with a fresh army and new tactics, the Spartans lined up in their perfect formation one last time. Thebes shattered it in an afternoon at Leuctra. Sparta never rose again. The city that had made the world tremble ended up a quiet ruin.

James Madison read those accounts when he was young and felt a chill. He saw how Sparta's fear of change became its grave. John Adams wrote to friends that no nation can survive on raw virtue alone if it won't bend a little. When they sat down to write our Constitution, they carried Sparta in the back of their minds. They wanted courage and strength, yes—but not the kind that crushes the weak or shuts the door on tomorrow.

That's why our system has room to grow—ways to amend the rules, ways for new states to join, ways for immigrants to become citizens once they swear the oath. The founders respected Sparta's toughness but turned away from its cruelty and its refusal to adapt. They built something firm enough to stand against enemies yet open enough to welcome the next generation without snapping.

LESSONS FROM SPARTA: WHAT THE FOUNDERS BUILT INTO AMERICA'S CONSTITUTION AND LAWS

• Harsh Discipline Without Mercy Leads to Oppression and Instability: Sparta's agoge system forged unbreakable warriors through extreme endurance training and cruelty, like abandoning weak infants and annual hunts on helots, but this fear-based control bred resentment and fragility; the Founders countered this by embedding protections in the Bill of Rights, such as the Eighth Amendment against cruel and unusual punishments, ensuring a system rooted in human dignity rather than brutality.

• Rigid Exclusion of Outsiders Causes Demographic and Military Decline: Sparta's refusal to grant citizenship to newcomers or integrate populations led to a shrinking warrior class, making them vulnerable to defeat at Leuctra in 371 BC; inspired by this, the Constitution includes provisions for naturalization (Article I, Section 8) and the admission of new states (Article IV, Section 3), allowing America to grow through immigration and expansion without rigid barriers.

• Overreliance on Fear and Enslavement Undermines Long-Term Strength: Sparta's economy and society depended on helot slavery, with annual declarations of war to maintain subjugation, creating an unstable foundation that eventually crumbled; the Founders, wary of such cruelty, prohibited involuntary servitude in the 13th Amendment and emphasized federalism in the Constitution to distribute power and prevent centralized oppression.

• Inflexibility and Refusal to Adapt Results in Collapse: Sparta's unchanging tactics and societal rules left them brittle against innovative enemies like Thebes; Madison and Adams drew from this to design the Constitution with an amendment process (Article V), enabling the document to evolve while preserving core principles, avoiding the pitfalls of unyielding rigidity.

• Valor and Courage Must Be Balanced with Humanity: The story of Aristodemus highlights how Sparta's extreme honor code shamed survivors and demanded death for redemption, fostering a culture of unyielding sacrifice; the Founders incorporated this lesson through the Constitution's emphasis on individual rights in the Bill of Rights, like freedom of speech (First Amendment), to protect personal liberty and prevent a society that crushes the individual for the collective.

• Strength Without Openness Leads to Isolation and Defeat: Sparta's isolationist policies and lack of cultural exchange weakened them over time; in response, the Constitution promotes interstate commerce (Article I, Section 8) and a union that encourages shared values and adaptation, ensuring America's framework remains dynamic and inclusive to sustain long-term resilience.

Sparta's story sits beside Athens's in the founders' minds: courage without mercy turns into oppression, and strength that can't bend will break. Hold the line, but leave the door open—so the flame stays alive for every child yet to come.

ROME'S CORRUPTION

Our government has recently exposed a breathtaking amount of corruption from NGO's and federal agencies, including USAID, Medicare, and the IRS. Hopefully, the system of checks and balances our founders set up, primarily based on lessons from mistakes of ancient civilizations, including Rome, will work to root out waste, fraud, and abuse as we find them.

Rome didn't fall because the barbarians were stronger. It fell because the Romans stopped being Romans. Let us remember to be Americans first always, so that we don't repeat the mistakes of the ancients.

Start at the beginning. In the early days, Rome was a rough little city on seven hills, full of farmers who doubled as soldiers. They fought for survival, not glory. A Roman man was expected to be honest, hardworking, faithful to his wife, loyal to the gods, and ready to die for the republic. That simple toughness carried them from a village to an empire that stretched from Scotland to the Sahara.

But empires bring wealth, and wealth brings temptation. By the second century AD, the city was drowning in it. Senators who once plowed their own fields now owned thousands of slaves and villas with marble floors. Grain from Egypt was given away for free, so the poor didn't have to work. Bread and circuses became the order of the day—keep the crowd fed and entertained, and they won't ask questions. Marriage rates dropped. Divorce became common. Rich men took lovers openly. Fathers sold their daughters for political favors. The old religion turned into a joke—priests sold blessings, temples became party halls.

"The fall of Rome seemed unthinkable to people at the time but inevitable to historians reflecting upon it with the benefit of context." – Mary Pilon

Then came Nero in 54 AD. He was seventeen when he took the throne, handsome, spoiled, and convinced he was a god. While Rome burned in the great fire of 64, he stood on his palace balcony singing about the fall of Troy. Later, he rebuilt the city around a golden palace the size of a small town, complete with a 120-foot statue of himself. When money ran short, he executed wealthy senators and seized their estates. One night, he dressed as a slave and wandered the streets with his guards, stabbing anyone who looked at him wrong. Christians were blamed for the fire; he had them dipped in pitch and set alight as garden torches while he hosted dinner parties.

The army watched all this and learned the lesson: emperors could be bought. Between 68 and 69 AD, four different men claimed the throne in a single year. Legions marched on Rome itself, burning the Capitol. By the third century, it was normal for an emperor to be murdered by his own guards and replaced the following week. In one fifty-year stretch, twenty-six emperors ruled, and twenty-five died violently.

While the top rotted, the foundation cracked. The old Roman virtues—gravitas, pietas, disciplina—were replaced by greed and cruelty. Families fell apart. Birth rates collapsed. The borders were left unguarded because no one wanted to serve anymore. When the Visigoths finally walked through an open gate in 410 AD, the city that had ruled the world for six hundred years was too weak even to put up a fight.

LESSONS FROM ROME: WHAT THE FOUNDERS BUILT INTO AMERICA'S CONSTITUTION AND LAWS

• Wealth and Corruption Erode Virtues Leading to Societal Decay: Rome's influx of imperial riches shifted citizens from hardworking farmers to idle elites reliant on slaves and free handouts like grain distributions, fostering immorality and declining birth rates; the Founders, drawing from this, emphasized a republic of virtue in the Constitution's preamble ("promote the general Welfare") and through the Bill of Rights' protections for individual liberties (e.g., First Amendment freedoms) to encourage moral self-governance and prevent entitlement-driven decline.

• Bread and Circuses Distract from Real Governance Issues: Rome's use of free food and entertainment pacified the masses, allowing emperors like Nero to abuse power unchecked; inspired by this, the Constitution's separation of powers (Articles I-III) and checks like impeachment (Article I, Section 2) ensure accountability, preventing leaders from buying loyalty and distracting from corruption, as seen in modern calls to root out waste in agencies like USAID and IRS.

• Moral Loosening and Family Breakdown Weaken the Nation: Declining marriages, rising divorces, and selfish pursuits in Rome led to societal rot and unguarded borders; the Founders countered with federalism (Tenth Amendment) to preserve state-level moral anchors and the Constitution's promotion of domestic tranquility, aiming to sustain family and community strength against the kind of unchecked immigration and fiscal strain that burdened Rome.

• Unstable Leadership Through Violence and Buying Power: Rome's rapid turnover of emperors via murder and military coups in the third century created chaos; Madison and Adams incorporated civilian control of the military (Article II, Section 2) and term limits via elections to stabilize leadership, ensuring no single ruler could seize estates or execute rivals as Nero did, fostering a system resistant to demagoguery.

• Rigid Empire Without Adaptation Invites Invasion: Rome's failure to adapt after losing its core virtues left it vulnerable to barbarians like the Visigoths in 410 AD; the Constitution's amendment process (Article V) allows flexibility while maintaining structure, and the emphasis on a "more perfect Union" reflects the Founders' intent to evolve without crumbling, unlike Rome's inflexible decline into ruin.

• Loss of Civic Duty and Self-Governance Spells Doom**: Romans abandoned survival-oriented discipline for comfort, leading to an empire's corpse; the Founders built in requirements for active citizenship, such as jury duty implied in the Sixth Amendment and the militia clause (Second Amendment), to keep Americans engaged and virtuous, preventing the self-destruction that befell Rome by prioritizing liberty with moral responsibility.

Take a look at our nation today and see how a specific faction of people has moved to loosen our moral foundation, more closely resembling the fall of Rome than the America we know. For a time, millions of people flowed over our borders unchecked; this flux of immigration caused some state governments to go bankrupt, as illegal immigrants lived better than citizens, due to our taxpayers' hard work. Vast amounts of government fraud have been uncovered. Today, as always, we must remain vigilant to reverse these troubles and keep America on course before it crumbles like ancient Rome.

The founders read every word of the circumstances that led to Rome's fall. John Adams kept a copy of Gibbon's Decline and Fall on his desk while he helped write the Constitution. Madison quoted Cicero in the Federalist Papers. They saw Rome's story as a slow-motion tragedy: a republic that became an empire, then an empire that became a corpse because it forgot the difference between liberty and license. They built safeguards—separation of powers, term limits, civilian control of the military, a written constitution harder to change than a passing mood—precisely to keep America from following Rome down the same path.

They knew human beings are capable of greatness and capable of appalling selfishness. Give them freedom without moral anchors, and the center will not hold.

Rome's lesson was burned into their minds: when a nation trades virtue for comfort, the flame flickers and goes out.

And that is why, when they finished the Constitution, they didn't just hand power to the people. They gave it to a people they hoped would stay worthy of it—guided by faith, bound by law, and always remembering that liberty is only safe in the hands of those who can govern themselves first.

SECTION TWO
EASTERN EMPIRES' FALLS

EGYPTIAN OVERREACH

Egypt lasted longer than almost any civilization we know, three thousand years along the Nile, building pyramids that still stand when other empires are dust. The river gave life every year with its flood, and the people looked to one man, the pharaoh, to keep the gods happy so the water would come. He was supposed to be a god himself, walking among men, for centuries that system held. Strong pharaohs like Ramses II led armies across deserts and brought back gold and glory. Priests chanted in temples, scribes kept perfect records, and ordinary farmers paid their taxes in grain, trusting the order of things.

But power like that has a way of turning on itself.

By the time of the later dynasties, pharaohs weren't content to be guardians of the land. They wanted to be worshipped as living gods while they were still breathing. Temples grew richer than the palace. Priests controlled more grain than the farmers who grew it. When the Nile flood failed, as it sometimes did, the pharaohs and priests blamed the people rather than looking to themselves. Taxes rose even as bellies emptied.

In the seventh year of one long drought, around 1200 BC, a scribe named Wenamun left a note that still survives. He had watched the granaries of the priests stay locked while children starved in the streets. He wrote, "The child cries for bread, but the storehouses of Amun are full." Men began to steal from temples. Others fled to the desert to join wandering bandits. When the Sea Peoples—desperate raiders from collapsing kingdoms—came looking for anything to eat, Egypt had no army left that wanted to fight. The soldiers hadn't been paid in years. Cities fell. The great temples were looted. The pharaoh who once claimed to hold the sun in his hand watched his capital burn.

The founders knew these stories. John Adams kept Herodotus on his shelf and read about Egypt's fall the same winter he was drafting Massachusetts' Constitution. He saw how a nation that put one man, or one small circle of priests, above everyone else ended up with no one willing to defend it when the crisis came. That's why the American system spreads power out—no single person can claim to speak for God on earth, no priestly class can hoard the nation's wealth while the people starve.

They remembered Egypt when they wrote the Constitution's checks and balances, when they insisted on regular elections, when they protected private property so no ruler or temple could take a man's harvest and leave his children hungry. Egypt taught them that even the longest river can run dry if the people who control it forget who it belongs to.

LESSONS FROM EGYPT: WHAT THE FOUNDERS BUILT INTO AMERICA'S CONSTITUTION AND LAWS

•Unbridled Divine Authority in Leadership Breeds Corruption and Detachment: Egypt's pharaohs, treated as living gods, became disconnected from the people's needs, blaming citizens for crises like droughts while hoarding power; the Founders countered this by establishing a secular government in the Constitution with no divine right of Kings, emphasizing elected officials (Article II) and the Establishment Clause in the First Amendment to prevent religious or elite monopolies on authority.

• Elite Hoarding of Resources Leads to Social Unrest and Economic Collapse: Priests and pharaohs controlled granaries during famines, leaving farmers starving and sparking theft and banditry; inspired by this, the Constitution protects private property (Fifth Amendment) and regulates commerce (Article I, Section 8) to ensure fair economic distribution, preventing the kind of elite enrichment that eroded Egypt's foundation and fostering a system resilient against modern fraud in agencies like USAID or IRS.

• Rigid Systems Fail to Adapt to Crises, Inviting External Threats: Egypt's unchanging reliance on pharaohs left it vulnerable to invaders like the Sea Peoples when unpaid armies deserted; the Founders built in adaptability through the amendment process (Article V) and federalism (Tenth Amendment), allowing the nation to evolve and respond to challenges without crumbling, as seen in mechanisms to address corruption and unchecked immigration strains.

• Loss of Civic Engagement and Moral Anchors Hollows Out Society: As Egyptians lost trust in leaders who prioritized self-worship over welfare, the empire became brittle and undefended; Adams and Madison drew from this to embed civic duty in the Constitution's preamble ("promote the general Welfare") and protections for free speech (First Amendment), encouraging active citizenship and moral responsibility to sustain unity and virtue.

• Over-Centralization Without Accountability Results in Total Breakdown: Egypt's long stability turned to ruin when leaders forgot communal obligations, leading to a "hollow" nation sacked by outsiders; the Constitution's checks and balances, impeachment powers (Article I, Section 3), and civilian control of the military (Article II, Section 2) were designed to distribute authority and enforce accountability, ensuring America remains a true nation guided by law and shared values, not fleeting power.

The lesson Egypt left behind is simple and harsh: the moment a handful of leaders begin to see themselves as gods, the whole country ceases to be a real nation. It turns into something hollow—a monument that looks impressive from a distance but has nothing solid at its core. When the hard times come, there's no one left willing to hold it together, and it collapses.

PERSIAN EXCESSES

Persia, back when Cyrus the Great got it rolling around 550 BC, turned into the biggest thing the world had ever seen. It swallowed land all the way from what's now India clear to the edge of Greece, and somehow kept dozens of different cultures of people inside the same borders. The deal was pretty simple: you sent your taxes to the King, you worshiped however you wanted, and in return, he made sure no one came to burn your village. To keep a grip on it all, they split the empire into provinces and put a satrap in charge of each one—basically the King's handpicked governor. The satrap's job was to collect the money, keep the peace, and make sure the Royal Road stayed open so a messenger on a fast horse could cross the empire in a week instead of months. For a long time, that system actually worked. Caravans moved, markets stayed busy, temples rang with whatever prayers the locals wanted to offer, and the King's treasury filled up faster than anyone thought possible.

But the farther you get from the center, the easier it is to forget who you're working for. By the time the fourth century rolled around, a lot of those satraps had stopped thinking of themselves as the King's men. They started keeping more of the tax money than they were supposed to send back. They built themselves palaces that looked an awful lot like little kingdoms. They paid soldiers who answered to them first and the King second. Orders from Persepolis would finally arrive, months late, and the satrap would shrug and toss them aside. Roads cracked and went unrepaired. Border posts sat empty. The whole giant machine that had once run so smoothly started coming apart at the seams, one greedy province at a time.

One of those satraps was a man named Bessus, governor of Bactria in the far northeast. When Alexander the Great came east in 330 BC, Bessus watched the Persian army collapse at Gaugamela and saw his chance.

King Darius III was fleeing, wounded, trying to rally what was left. Bessus and a few others caught up with him in the desert. They stabbed him, threw the body in a cart, and left it for Alexander to find. Bessus put on the royal upright tiara and called himself the new King. It lasted about as long as a sandcastle at high tide. His own men deserted, and the other satraps cut deals with Alexander. When the Macedonians finally caught Bessus, Alexander had him flogged, his nose and ears cut off, and handed him over to Darius's family for execution. The empire that had ruled the world for two hundred years was finished, not by a single battle but by men who had forgotten who they served.

Our American founding fathers read Herodotus and Xenophon the way we read the news. John Adams walked the fields around his farm in Massachusetts with those books under his arm, thinking hard about how an empire so vast could collapse from the inside. Madison quoted the Persian example in the Federalist Papers to explain why the American states needed a strong but limited central government. If the center is too weak, the parts pull away and fight each other. If the parts get too strong, they stop listening to the center and start acting like little kings. Either way, the country breaks.

They liked Persia's early tolerance—letting people keep their own ways usually kept the peace. But they saw what happened when that tolerance turned into indifference, when satraps stopped enforcing the same law everywhere. That's why they wrote a Constitution that lets states handle their own business but keeps the big things—money, defense, trade—in federal hands. And it's why the Bill of Rights protects religion and speech without letting any one group claim it speaks for God and everybody else has to obey.

LESSONS FROM PERSIA: WHAT THE FOUNDERS BUILT INTO AMERICA'S CONSTITUTION AND LAWS

• Decentralized Power Without Accountability Leads to Fragmentation and Greed: Persia's satraps, as provincial governors, began hoarding taxes and building personal kingdoms, weakening the empire's unity; the Founders addressed this through federalism in the Constitution (Tenth Amendment), balancing state autonomy with federal oversight to prevent regional leaders from undermining national cohesion, as seen in modern concerns over agency corruption like in USAID or IRS.

• Tolerance Turning to Indifference Erodes Uniform Law and Stability: Early Persia's allowance for cultural diversity maintained peace, but later indifference allowed inconsistent enforcement and corruption; inspired by this, the Constitution's Supremacy Clause (Article VI) ensures federal laws prevail, while the Bill of Rights guarantees uniform protections like religious freedom (First Amendment), fostering tolerance without permitting lawlessness or elite exploitation.

• Weak Central Authority Invites Internal Betrayal and Collapse: When satraps like Bessus ignored royal orders and even assassinated King Darius III in 330 BC, the empire fractured; Madison and Adams drew from this to create a strong but limited federal government in the Constitution, with powers like taxation (Article I, Section 8) centralized to fund defense and trade, preventing the kind of unchecked provincial greed that doomed Persia.

• Overreliance on Provincial Loyalty Without Oversight Fosters Corruption: Satraps' unchecked actions led to neglected infrastructure and borders, making Persia vulnerable to Alexander the Great; the Founders implemented checks like Congressional oversight of spending and the executive (Articles I and II) to root out waste and abuse, mirroring efforts today to address fraud in federal agencies and ensure accountability.

• Empire's Expansion Without Inclusive Governance Breeds Resentment and Fall: Persia's vast size amplified satrap corruption, culminating in betrayal and invasion; the Constitution's amendment process (Article V) and mechanisms for new states (Article IV, Section 3) allow adaptive growth, ensuring the nation remains united under shared laws rather than fragmenting like Persia, emphasizing service to the people over personal gain.

Persia's story is a quiet warning: you can conquer half the world and still lose everything if the men running the provinces start thinking the country belongs to them, not the other way around. The founders heard that warning and built something different—a nation where power has to answer to the people, not the other way around. That's how the flame stays lit when the wind starts to blow.

BABYLONIAN VICE

Babylon was something to see. It sat right on the Euphrates with walls so wide you could drive two chariots side by side along the top. The hanging gardens rose in terraces, green against the desert sky, and the main gates were covered in bronze that caught the sun like fire. For a long time, the city felt like it would never end.

Go back to Hammurabi, around 1750 BC. He had a tall stone set up with 282 laws carved into it. The rules were strict—an eye for an eye, a life for a life—but they applied to everybody, rich or poor, free or slave. If a builder's house fell down and killed someone, the builder would die. If a son hit his father, they cut off the boy's hand. Harsh, yes, but at least you knew where the line was drawn. And because people believed the law was fair, the city grew strong.

Fast-forward a thousand years to when Nebuchadnezzar's grandson Nabonidus was king. The old stone with Hammurabi's laws still stood, but nobody in the palace paid attention anymore. Nabonidus himself spent a decade in the Arabian desert pursuing some religious vision, leaving his son, Belshazzar, in charge. Belshazzar threw parties that went on for weeks. They drank from gold cups taken from the temple in Jerusalem and toasted statues of every god they could name while the priests of Marduk and Ishtar nearly killed each other in the streets over whose god was greater. Down in the city, ordinary people handed over most of what they grew in taxes, watched their sons march off to wars that never seemed to end, and saw the public granaries stay locked while the palace kitchens never ran out of food.

Then came the night of October 539 BC. Belshazzar decided to throw the biggest feast Babylon had ever seen—thousands of nobles, rivers of wine, music, dancing. While the guards drank themselves stupid, Cyrus and the Persians had quietly diverted the Euphrates upstream. The river under the city walls dropped to knee-deep. Persian soldiers waded in, climbed the water stairs inside the walls, and opened the bronze gates from the inside. By morning, the city belonged to someone else. Belshazzar was dead on his own palace floor, and Babylon—the city that had terrified the world—never lifted a finger to save itself.

"The collapse of the Tower of Babel is perhaps the central urban myth. It is certainly the most disquieting. In Babylon, the great city that fascinated and horrified the Biblical writers, people of different races and languages, drawn together in pursuit of wealth, tried for the first time to live together - and failed."
– Neil MacGregor

The founders knew that story cold. They read it in the book of Daniel and in Herodotus. They saw how a place can start with clear, equal laws and end up with a handful of people doing whatever they want while everyone else suffers. Madison quoted it when he explained why we needed three branches of government watching each other. Adams brought it up when he said no titles of nobility would ever be allowed here—nobody gets to be above the law. They looked at Babylon and decided our laws would be written on paper, not stone, so that they could be improved, but changing them would take work and agreement, not just one man's whim.

LESSONS FROM BABYLON: WHAT THE FOUNDERS BUILT INTO AMERICA'S CONSTITUTION AND LAWS

• Equal Laws for All Prevent Elite Corruption and Societal Rot: Babylon thrived under Hammurabi's 1750 BC code with fair, universal rules like "an eye for an eye," but later kings like Belshazzar flouted them for personal vice, leading to unchecked taxes and public suffering; the Founders embedded equality in the Constitution's Supremacy Clause (Article VI) and the 14th Amendment's Equal Protection, ensuring no one is above the law and countering modern political targeting in agencies by demanding accountability.

• Excessive Luxury and Neglect of the People Invite Collapse: Belshazzar's lavish feasts from looted treasures while granaries stayed locked during crises bred resentment, culminating in Cyrus's conquest in 539 BC; inspired by this, the Constitution's checks on executive power (Article II) and Congressional oversight of spending (Article I, Section 9) prevent leaders from hoarding resources, addressing contemporary issues like fraud in government to maintain public trust and national strength.

• Moral Decay and Religious Division Undermine Unity: Conflicts among priests and Nabonidus's abandonment for religious pursuits fractured Babylon, leaving it defenseless; the Founders countered with the First Amendment's Establishment and Free Exercise Clauses, promoting religious tolerance without state favoritism, fostering a unified society resilient against the internal divisions that doomed Babylon.

• Failure to Adapt Laws Leads to Irrelevance and Downfall: Hammurabi's enduring code was ignored by corrupt rulers, turning a strong system into a hollow one; the Constitution's amendment process (Article V) allows deliberate evolution of laws through consensus, ensuring adaptability without chaos, and providing mechanisms to root out waste and abuse in modern institutions.

• Centralized Power Without Accountability Breeds Tyranny and Invasion: Babylon's kings treated laws as optional, allowing unchecked greed that weakened defenses; Madison quoted Babylonian history in the Federalist Papers to justify separation of powers and civilian control, embedding impeachment (Article I, Section 3) and term limits to prevent tyrannical excesses and ensure leaders serve the people, not themselves.

Babylon's message is blunt: when the people at the top stop living by the same rules as everyone else, the whole thing comes apart. The flame doesn't get blown out by enemies outside the walls; it dies because the people inside stopped tending it. This is why we need to end political targeting by our own tyrants in government agencies, and there must be consequences for that handful of people in our own government who try to get away with this.

That's the difference with what the founders built. They knew we're capable of good and evil in the same breath, so they set up a system that expects both—and keeps the fire burning anyway.

AFTER BABYLON

The light didn't die with Babylon. It moved west, carried by people who had learned the hard way what happens when one man stands above the law.

In the summer of 1215, a group of angry English barons caught King John at Runnymede, a soggy field beside the Thames. John had been seizing land, throwing people into dungeons without trial, and taxing everyone until they had nothing left. The barons had had enough.

They surrounded him with armed men and made him put his seal on a document we now call Magna Carta. It wasn't some grand speech about liberty. It was a list of rigid rules: no taking a man's freedom or property unless a jury of his equals or the law of the land said so—no new taxes without consent. Justice couldn't be sold or delayed.

Those barons were looking out for themselves, but they accidentally wrote something bigger. They shut down the idea that a King could do whatever he wanted just because a priest had poured oil on his head. Our founders knew every line of Magna Carta. Madison kept a copy on his desk while he worked on the Constitution. Jefferson called it the foundation of English rights. When they wrote due process, jury trials, and "no taxation without representation," they were reaching straight back to that muddy field in 1215 and saying, "We're finishing what they started."

A couple of hundred years later, the same question—who gets to speak for God—set Europe on fire. The Pope promised heaven to any knight who marched to Jerusalem and took it back from the Muslims. Armies left home singing hymns. What came back—if anything came back—was horror. Crusaders burned whole cities, massacred Jews in the Rhine valley because they weren't Christian, and in 1204 even sacked Constantinople, a Christian city, slaughtering fellow believers over minor differences in prayer. By the time the last crusader limped home, the roads from France to the Holy Land were lined with graves, all dug in the name of the Prince of Peace.

The founders grew up hearing those stories. Washington's mother had taught him that genuine faith doesn't need a sword to back it up. Madison read about the religious wars that followed—Catholics and Protestants cutting each other down for a century, villages torched, children left orphans, all because one side claimed God had given them the only truth. Jefferson watched preachers in Virginia get fined or jailed just for holding services without the state church's permission. They looked at the Crusades and heard the same warning they heard from Babylon and Rome: when men mix faith with state power and start killing to prove they're right, liberty dies fast.

That's why the very first words of the Bill of Rights keep religion and government apart. They wanted people to worship freely, not to have one church—or one Pope, or one king—telling everybody else how to pray. They wanted faith to stay a matter of conscience, not a weapon.

Magna Carta taught them that even kings have to answer to written law. The Crusades taught them that mixing God and government can turn both into something monstrous. They carried both lessons into everything they built, determined that America would never walk those old, bloody paths again.

The flame had to be guarded by law and by conscience, by reason and by faith. That's the only way it burns clean.

SECTION THREE
FOUNDER'S APPLICATIONS

CHECKS ADOPTED

"What does it mean to be an American? While each of us may have our own specific answer to that question, we likely can agree on the basic principles of America: freedom, equal opportunity, and rights accompanied by responsibilities." – Ben Nelson

James Madison was twenty-five the first time he saw Hammurabi's code. It had been hauled all the way from Mesopotamia to Paris, a tall black stone covered in wedge-shaped writing. A friend who knew how much he loved old things took him to see it. Madison stood there a long time, running his hand over the carvings. The laws were strict—eye for eye, life for life—but what got him was that they applied to everybody, king and commoner alike. Even a ruler who claimed to be a god had put himself under written law.

That idea stuck with him.

Fast-forward to the winter of 1787. Madison was back home in Virginia, sitting by the fire wrapped in blankets because he was always cold and constantly a little sick. The Philadelphia convention was coming, and he knew the country could fall apart before it ever got started. He pulled out the notes he'd kept from that trip to Paris—pages of thoughts from Polybius, Montesquieu, Locke, the Bible—and spread them across the table. He started writing, crossing things out, writing again, trying to figure out how to keep power from piling up in one place. Three branches, he decided. Each one was strong enough to stop the others if they reached too far.

He kept thinking about that stone in Paris. Even a King who called himself divine had needed something above him. Then he thought about what happened when Kings stopped caring—Babylon's rulers throwing parties. At the same time, the city burned, Persia's governors acting like little Kings in their provinces, Rome's senators selling justice to whoever paid most. Every empire he'd ever read about had died the same way: one part got too much power, forgot it was supposed to serve the rest, and everything came down.

Madison carried that worry to Philadelphia. When the big states wanted representation by population, and the small states threatened to leave, he stayed calm. He worked out the Connecticut Compromise—two houses: one by population, one where every state got the same say. When some pushed for a president with nearly King-like power, he pushed back: Give one man that much, and you're asking for a Caesar. When others wanted almost no central government, he pointed to the mess under the Articles—unpaid soldiers, open borders, states taxing each other into the ground.

One night late in the convention, coughing and worn out, he wrote to Jefferson in Paris: "The only way to keep men from turning into wolves is to set their ambitions against each other." That was the heart of it. They took the good from the old world—written law, separation of powers—and left the bad behind. They looked at Hammurabi and said yes to law, but added mercy and representation. They looked at Rome and said, "No more emperors." They looked at Babylon and said, "No more rulers above the rules." And he realized that these separations needed to include religion to insure that people could worship freely without government intervention.

"The purpose of separation of church and state is to keep forever from these shores the ceaseless strife that has soaked the soil of Europe with blood for centuries." – James Madison

They built a government that expects people to be human—capable of good and capable of selfish—and arranged it so the selfish parts cancel each other out. The president can veto Congress, Congress can override the veto, the courts can tell both to start over, and the people get to throw everybody out every few years. Power is spread thin, so it can't settle in one place and rot.

Madison knew it wasn't perfect. He said straight out, "If men were angels, no government would be necessary." But since we're not, you plan for the worst and hope for the best. They trusted the people, but they gave them guardrails.

That's what they handed us. Not a perfect country, but one built to last through our imperfections. A flame that can bend in the wind instead of breaking.

Every time we vote, speak up, or remind a leader who they work for, we're keeping that flame alive the way Madison and the others meant us to—one steady breath at a time.

KNOWLEDGE GUARDED

Thomas Jefferson collected books the way some people collect worries. By the time he was thirty, his shelves at Monticello were packed—histories, philosophy, Bibles in half a dozen languages. One evening in the summer of 1776, with the Declaration barely dry, he sat in his study with Cicero open on his lap. The candle threw long shadows while he read about a Roman official ordering books burned because they carried "dangerous" ideas. Jefferson closed the volume and stared into the flame. He thought about the pamphlets that had just swept through the colonies—Thomas Paine's Common Sense riding in saddlebags, read aloud in taverns by men who could hardly sign their names. Those cheap little pages had turned farmers into soldiers and doubters into believers. Burn them, he realized, and you kill the revolution.

Fast-forward a decade. Jefferson was in Paris when the Constitution was completed, and the Bill of Rights was being debated. He wrote Madison a letter that still feels urgent: "A nation that expects to be ignorant and free expects what never was and never will be." He had watched the mobs in France tear libraries apart and seen Kings decide what people were allowed to read. He knew knowledge wasn't just nice to have; it was the only real check on power. That's why the First Amendment begins with the press and speech. The founders had seen Rome crush printing presses and England hang printers for speaking truth. They weren't going to let that happen here.

Madison felt it just as deeply. During the war, he had ridden through the Carolinas, talking to soldiers who had never owned a book yet could quote the Declaration word for word because someone had read it to them around a campfire. In Federalist 10, he warned that factions—people chasing their own interests—would rip a republic apart unless citizens stayed sharp enough to spot the lies. British agents had flooded the colonies with fake letters claiming Washington was selling out to the French. But pamphlets answered back—Franklin's plain-spoken almanacs, Dickinson's farmer letters.

Regular people read them, argued over them, and decided for themselves what was true.

Education mattered just as much. Jefferson kept pushing for public schools in Virginia, not to turn out scholars but to give every kid a fighting chance to think straight. He used to say a little learning can lead a man away from faith, but a lot of learning almost always brings him back—because the more you understand, the clearer you see something bigger behind it all. The founders remembered how Rome's elite kept knowledge locked up while the crowds stayed ignorant and easy to control. They wanted every American to have books within reach—the Bible, Locke, Montesquieu—so no leader could ever talk them out of their rights.

Today, education is as vital as ever. The government threw money at the problem, and teachers' unions and special-interest groups chipped away at funding and influence until our educational system became one of the worst in the developed world. Educating our children with truth and unbiased knowledge is essential as we move forward into our next 250 years. Recently, we've seen social media and mainstream media outlets move towards censorship, and that must be quashed as well.

Much of today's American press pushes a highly censored narrative. The press will inform the viewer or listener of something without telling the whole truth when it contradicts the narrative. They are not informing you; they are shaping you. This completely contradicts what our founding fathers wanted. And with the advent of AI, a billion "truths" can now be pushed, and an agenda can be advanced for the gullible. My job in writing this book is to tell THE truth, not my version of truth, as the founders envisioned. We must not revise history as if it's an alternate reality.

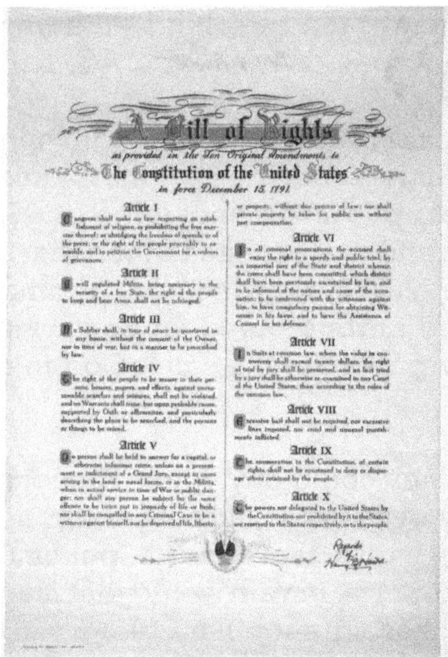

A Bill of Rights

as provided in the Ten Original Amendments to

The Constitution of the United States

in force December 15, 1791

Article I

Congress shall make no law respecting an establishment of religion, or prohibiting the free exercise thereof; or abridging the freedom of speech, or of the press; or the right of the people peaceably to assemble, and to petition the Government for a redress of grievances.

Article II

A well regulated Militia, being necessary to the security of a free State, the right of the people to keep and bear Arms, shall not be infringed.

Article III

No Soldier shall, in time of peace be quartered in any house, without the consent of the Owner, nor in time of war, but in a manner to be prescribed by law.

Article IV

The right of the people to be secure in their persons, houses, papers, and effects, against unreasonable searches and seizures, shall not be violated, and no Warrants shall issue, but upon probable cause, supported by Oath or affirmation, and particularly describing the place to be searched, and the persons or things to be seized.

Article V

No person shall be held to answer for a capital, or otherwise infamous crime, unless on a presentment or indictment of a Grand Jury, except in cases arising in the land or naval forces, or in the Militia, when in actual service in time of War or public danger; nor shall any person be subject for the same offence to be twice put in jeopardy of life or limb; nor shall be compelled in any Criminal Case to be a witness against himself, nor be deprived of life, liberty, or property, without due process of law; nor shall private property be taken for public use, without just compensation.

Article VI

In all criminal prosecutions, the accused shall enjoy the right to a speedy and public trial, by an impartial jury of the State and district wherein the crime shall have been committed, which district shall have been previously ascertained by law, and to be informed of the nature and cause of the accusation; to be confronted with the witnesses against him; to have compulsory process for obtaining Witnesses in his favor, and to have the Assistance of Counsel for his defence.

Article VII

In Suits at common law, where the value in controversy shall exceed twenty dollars, the right of trial by jury shall be preserved, and no fact tried by a jury shall be otherwise re-examined in any Court of the United States, than according to the rules of the common law.

Article VIII

Excessive bail shall not be required, nor excessive fines imposed, nor cruel and unusual punishments inflicted.

Article IX

The enumeration in the Constitution, of certain rights, shall not be construed to deny or disparage others retained by the people.

Article X

The powers not delegated to the United States by the Constitution, nor prohibited by it to the States, are reserved to the States respectively, or to the people.

When the Bill of Rights went to the states, Madison fought for those opening words as if his life depended on it. He had watched Athens kill Socrates for asking questions, and Rome burn sacred books when prophecy got too close to the truth. In America, the press would be free to call out nonsense, people would learn to question with respect, and no one—absolutely no one—would stand above the truth.

Jefferson knew it would be a fight. He told a friend, "Error can be tolerated as long as reason is free to combat it." They didn't hand us a perfect system. They gave us a lantern and said: Keep passing it, keep feeding it, because the moment the light goes out, the wolves come in.

And every time we read, speak, question, or share what we've learned, we're doing exactly what they asked—keeping that flame alive, one honest hand at a time.

ETERNAL VIGILANCE

George Washington was worn out. The war had ended, the treaty was signed, and he could have finally ridden home to Mount Vernon, planted the trees he'd been dreaming about for eight years, and let somebody else worry about the country. But he didn't. In September 1796, he walked into the empty Senate chamber, laid down a letter, and walked away from power forever. He called it his Farewell Address, but it felt more like a father sitting his kids down before he left the house for the last time, telling them what to watch out for.

He had seen too much to think the job was finished just because the British had marched out of New York. The states were still pulling in different directions. People were whispering about cutting deals with France or Spain. Old arguments from the war hadn't gone away; they had just moved indoors. Washington knew winning a war was one thing—keeping a country together afterward was another. He wrote about learning from what had happened to other nations, about holding on to a clear sense of right and wrong, about noticing the slow rot that starts when people stop caring. He put it plain: the people have the right to change their government, but "the spirit of party and faction, when carried to excess, are capable of almost anything."

He wasn't guessing. He had lived it. He remembered officers ready to knife each other over who got promoted next. He remembered soldiers walking away because Congress couldn't pay them. He remembered foreign agents slipping into camp, promising French gold or Spanish land if the men would turn on their own. Armies coming from outside were dangerous, sure, but Washington knew the worst threat was the quiet kind—the way a country can start forgetting why it ever fought.

Washington grew up with a mother who opened the Bible every morning and taught him straight: we're made in God's image, but we carry the old nature too, the part that wants to take and destroy. The founders all felt that pull. They set up firm laws not to be cruel, but to protect—because without them, the animal side wins and we tear each other apart. Their faith wasn't gentle platitudes; it was fire-and-brimstone truth, warnings that turning away from what's right brings judgment. They had watched Europe bleed for centuries over religion—men burning neighbors alive because they prayed to the same God in a different building.

Washington saw the same cracks starting here. Foreign money could buy votes. Factions could turn neighbors against neighbors. And if the country ever lost its moral center, no constitution on earth would hold it together. "Of all the habits that lead to political prosperity," he wrote, "religion and morality are the real supports. In vain would that man claim the tribute of patriotism who should labor to subvert these great pillars." He wasn't preaching from a pulpit; he was speaking from a heart that had buried too many boys who died believing in something bigger than themselves.

He was asking us—plain and simple—to stay awake. The fight isn't over when the guns stop. It's every day, in the choices we make when nobody's watching. That's how the flame stays lit.

Two centuries later, President Ronald Reagan echoed Washington's sentiment.

"Freedom is never more than one generation away from extinction. We didn't pass it to our children in the bloodstream. It must be fought for, protected, and handed on for them to do the same, or one day we will spend our sunset years telling our children and our children's children what it was once like in the United States where men were free." – Ronald Reagan

The founders weren't guessing. They had spent years with the old books open in front of them—the Bible's stories of kings who started out strong and ended up worshipping gold statues, Cicero writing about how fast a republic can turn into a mob or a dictatorship, Montesquieu spelling out plainly that liberty can't survive if people stop caring about being decent. They knew Rome had taken in outsiders, turned loyal foreigners into citizens, and made the empire stronger for a while. But they also saw what happened when that openness slid into anything-goes living, when laws stopped mattering, and gods became just another excuse for doing whatever you wanted.

Washington's farewell letter wasn't some stiff speech. It felt more like a father who's about to walk out the door for the last time, turning back to say, "Listen—keep an eye on things. Learn from the countries that came before us. Hold on to what's right. The danger isn't always an army at the gate. Most of the time, it's the quiet stuff—the slow drift where we start thinking we deserve more than the next guy, where we let little wrongs slide until they aren't little anymore. That's what kills nations. Stay awake."

That's the job he handed us. Not a perfect country—just a republic that says, "We trust you, but we know you're human, so here are some guardrails." Faith and common sense stand shoulder to shoulder against whatever darkness tries to creep in.

They had pulled hard lessons from all those old ruins, but turning those lessons into something that would actually work tested them all over again—pushing them into that hot Philadelphia summer where everything could have shattered, and somehow, against every odd, they forged unity out of division.

"Truth will ultimately prevail where there is pains to bring it to light."
– George Washington

CHAPTER SIX
CONVENTION'S CRUCIBLE

"Humanity has won its battle. Liberty now has a country." – Marquis de Lafayette

COALITION AMID CHAOS

In the summer of 1787, fifty-five men walked into a hot room in Philadelphia and almost walked out with the country in pieces. They were planters, merchants, lawyers, farmers—men who had fought together, bled together, but still didn't trust each other completely. Every time they started talking about who should hold power, you could feel the air tighten. One flawed argument and the whole thing could have fallen apart right there.

SECTION ONE
DIVERSE COLONIES CONVERGE

ARRIVAL ANXIETIES

The convention was supposed to start on May 14, but when that day came, only a few delegates had even made it to town. The roads were awful, the weather worse, and a lot of them were wondering why they'd left home at all. The Articles of Confederation weren't working—everybody knew that. States were arguing over money, slapping taxes on each other's goods, and just the year before, farmers in Massachusetts had picked up muskets because they were losing their land to debt. If these men couldn't fix it, the whole experiment in independence might be over before it really began.

Rhode Island didn't even send anyone. They flat-out refused, scared that any stronger government would swallow their little state whole. That empty chair sat there like a warning.

Then George Washington rode in, two days late. He looked older than people remembered—gray hair, shoulders a little stooped, the lines in his face deeper from eight years of war. He had gone home to Mount Vernon after Yorktown, wanting nothing more than quiet mornings on the porch and evenings with his books. But the letters kept coming—Madison, Hamilton, Knox—telling him the country was coming apart and nobody else could hold it together. Washington felt a deep duty to unite the fledgling colonies.

So he climbed back onto his horse, left the plantation again, and arrived in Philadelphia. When he walked into the State House and took the chair at the front, the room settled. Nobody said much, but everybody felt it: if he was willing to do this one more time, they had to try too.

The first week dragged. One or two delegates showed up each day, brushing dust off their clothes, complaining about washed-out bridges and axles that snapped halfway from Virginia. They shook hands in the hallway, asked about wives and crops, but you could feel the strain behind every smile. Virginia's men arrived with a thick packet of papers—their whole plan already worked out. The minute the smaller states saw it, their stomachs dropped. They knew exactly what it meant: the big states were ready to run the show, and the little ones would have to fall in line.

You could almost hear the knives sliding out of sheaths under all the polite "Good morning, sir" and "Safe journey, I hope." Some of the younger fellows were already picturing themselves in high office. Others still carried grudges from the war—who got credit for what battle, who hadn't pulled their weight. A couple of the older ones looked around the half-empty room, and you could see them thinking, "I should be home fishing right now."

It felt like the whole thing might fall apart before it even started.

Washington hardly spoke. He sat there, listening, watching. When voices rose, and someone threatened to storm out, he didn't shout them down. He just looked at them—those same steady eyes that had stared across the Delaware on Christmas night, across the frozen ground at Valley Forge. One look was enough. Men remembered why they were there. They remembered the friends they'd buried. They remembered the promise they'd made to each other when the odds looked impossible.

It wasn't pretty, and it wasn't easy. But little by little, because Washington was in that chair and because nobody wanted to be the one who let him down, they started talking instead of walking away.

That was the first miracle—just getting them all to stay in the room.

IDEOLOGICAL CLASHES

By the time enough delegates had finally arrived to start talking, the room felt like a powder keg with a short fuse.

The big states—Virginia, Pennsylvania, Massachusetts—came in swinging. They wanted Congress set up so that the more people a state had, the more votes it got.

Simple, they said. Fair. The small states—New Jersey, Delaware, and little Rhode Island staying home in protest—heard that and their blood ran cold. If votes were based on population, they would be drowned out forever. New Jersey's William Paterson stood up one morning, voice shaking with anger, and told the room straight: give us one state, one vote, or we walk. Delaware's Gunning Bedford even snapped that if the big states tried to force their plan, the small ones would find "some foreign ally of more honor and good faith."

You could cut the tension with a knife. Men who had stood shoulder to shoulder against the British now looked ready to come to blows over a table. Washington sat at the front, face like stone, saying almost nothing, but you could feel him willing the room to hold together. Franklin, old and aching, watched from his chair and muttered that they were acting like children fighting over toys while the house burned.

Weeks went by, and nobody budged. The Virginia Plan—big states rule—was on the table. The small states answered with the New Jersey Plan—every state equal. Deadlock. Some nights, delegates slipped out to taverns and talked about going home. The whole convention teetered on the edge of collapse.

Then Roger Sherman stood up.

He was from Connecticut, a plain-spoken shoemaker turned judge who dressed as if he had just come in from the barn. Nobody expected much when he started talking. But he laid out an idea so simple it cut through the noise like a bell in fog: two houses of Congress. One house where votes matched population—the people's house. Another house where every state, big or small, got two votes—the states' house. Let them check each other. Nobody gets everything they want, but nobody gets nothing.

The room went quiet. You could almost hear hearts slowing down. Madison leaned over to Washington and whispered that it might just work. Franklin grinned for the first time in days. It wasn't perfect. The small states still grumbled. The big states still wanted more. But it was something they could all live with.

Sherman didn't shout or pound the table. He just offered a way forward when walking away looked easier. That one idea—born out of a man who had spent his life fixing things that were broken—became the Great Compromise. It saved the convention. It saved the country.

Because sometimes the flame doesn't leap higher from one big blaze. Sometimes it stays alive because ordinary men, in a hot room full of pride and fear, choose to give a little so everybody gets to keep breathing.

ECONOMIC DIVIDES

Money was the ghost in the room that nobody wanted to talk about at first. The delegates had come to fix a government that couldn't pay its bills, but as soon as they started talking about trade and taxes, the North and South turned on each other like old wounds reopening. The Northern states—Massachusetts, New York, and Pennsylvania—wanted a national system to regulate commerce, set tariffs on foreign goods, and keep rivers open for their ships. They saw the future in factories and ports, and they needed rules to make it work. The Southern states—Virginia, the Carolinas, Georgia—depended on tobacco, rice, and indigo, crops that lived or died by export prices. They worried any federal tariffs would price their goods out of European markets, and they hated the idea of paying more for imported tools and cloth.

The split between North and South went a lot deeper than politics; it was about how people lived and fed their families. Up north, merchants in Boston and Philadelphia wanted one set of trade rules for the whole country so their ships could move goods without every little state slapping on its own tax. Down south, planters in Virginia and the Carolinas grew tobacco and rice that had to be sold overseas. They were terrified that a strong central government would impose tariffs that would price their crops out of Europe and leave them broke.

War debts hung over everybody like a dark cloud. Farmers who had fought for independence were now losing their land because they couldn't pay the new taxes. States had borrowed money from France and Spain during the war and had no way to repay it. The whole country felt like it was sliding toward ruin.

And then there was Shays' Rebellion, still fresh in everyone's mind, a warning that ordinary people only take so much before they fight back.

Daniel Shays had been a captain in the Continental Army. He had marched through the snow at Valley Forge, watched friends freeze or bleed out, and come home with nothing but a promise the country never kept. By 1786, he was back on his Massachusetts farm, watching neighbors get dragged into court and lose everything because they couldn't pay taxes on land they had already paid for with their blood. Crop prices had crashed. The state legislature in Boston didn't seem to care.

One day, Shays and a few hundred other veterans said enough. They closed down the courts so the judges couldn't take any more farms. When the governor sent militia, Shays gathered a few hundred men—veterans like himself, fathers with callused hands and empty pockets—and they started shutting down courts. Not with guns at first, just bodies blocking the doors. But when the governor sent militia, Shays' men picked up pitchforks and fowling pieces. They stormed the Springfield armory, hoping to arm the desperate.

The governor called out the Boston militia, and at the Springfield bridge, a volley cut down four of Shays' followers. The rest scattered into the winter woods, Shays himself riding north to Vermont with a price on his head. He never wanted to be a rebel, but the system had left him no other way to feed his family. It wasn't pretty, but it was real. The rebellion got put down hard, but the message stuck: push people too far, and they will push back

That story echoed in Philadelphia like a drumbeat. Northern delegates saw Shays as proof they needed a strong central hand to keep order. Southern ones worried it was a sign of what federal taxes might do to their own farmers. The air got thicker with every speech. Gouverneur Morris from Pennsylvania warned that without national trade power, "the states will be at each other's throats." Charles Pinckney from South Carolina shot back that Northern factories would bleed the South dry. Fights broke out over who should control the Mississippi River, over fishing rights off the Grand Banks, over whether the government could coin money or print paper promises.

Washington listened to it all, his face giving nothing away. He had seen the war's cost—men like Shays who gave everything and got nothing back. He knew if they couldn't find common ground on money, the whole union would starve before it walked.

The delegates kept at it, day after day, as the arguments grew sharper, but the door stayed shut. They were learning the hard truth: a nation isn't held together by ideals alone. It takes men willing to give up a piece of what they want so the whole doesn't fall apart.

And in that giving, the flame of resilient liberty found its footing.

SECTION TWO
SLAVERY'S SHADOW

SOUTHERN DEMANDS

It's good for us to remember at this point that, just a dozen or so years before, America was no more than thirteen colonies that were essentially their own countries but banded together to defeat a common foe. Many of the people in these colonies were descendants of different European countries, and their cultures were quite different. Coming together would mean compromise on many levels, from people who thought quite differently.

The convention had been grinding along for weeks when the room suddenly went colder than any July day should allow. The subject nobody wanted to name out loud finally forced its way to the table: slavery.

The Southern delegates laid their cards on the table. South Carolina's Charles Pinckney stood up and said, in so many words, "No protections for slavery, no Constitution." Georgia's Abraham Baldwin nodded beside him.

Their states' whole way of life—plantations, rice fields, cotton that hadn't even taken off yet—depended on men and women held in chains. They wanted the slave trade to be left alone for twenty more years. They wanted runaway slaves returned, no matter where they fled. And they wanted enslaved people counted toward representation in Congress, but not taxed the same way. It was raw power politics wrapped in the language of survival.

Northern delegates shifted in their seats. Some, like Gouverneur Morris from Pennsylvania, let loose. He called slavery "a nefarious institution" and "the curse of heaven on the states where it prevailed." His voice shook with anger—he had seen the auction blocks in Charleston and couldn't stomach it. Others stayed quiet, calculating. They needed the South to remain in the room. Without Virginia, the Carolinas, Georgia, the whole thing collapsed.

George Mason from Virginia was one of the few Southerners who spoke against it. He enslaved people himself—hundreds—, but the words still tore out of him: "Slavery discourages arts and manufactures. The poor despise labor when performed by slaves... It brings the judgment of Heaven on a country." His hands trembled as he said it. He knew what he was asking would ruin him back home. He refused to sign the final document because the compromises went too far.

Madison sat listening, face tight. He hated the institution—he called it "dishonorable to the American character"—but he also knew the hard truth: push too hard, and the South walked. The union would die before it took its first breath. So they bargained. Twenty years before Congress could touch the slave trade. Runaways returned. The three-fifths clause—counting each enslaved person as three-fifths of a free citizen for seats in Congress but not for direct taxes. Ugly numbers written into the foundation.

Washington heard it all from the chair, eyes on the table in front of him. He had freed his own slaves in his will, but he said nothing that day. He knew one wrong word could break the room.

The compromises bought time. They kept the Southern states at the table. The Constitution was finished. But every man who signed knew they had planted a seed that would one day split the country wide open.

They left it for another generation, praying that generation would have the courage they couldn't find in that moment. The flame of liberty flickered, stained but still burning, waiting for better hands to carry it forward.

NORTHERN CONCESSIONS

The slavery question didn't just hang over the convention; it sat in the middle of the table like a loaded gun nobody wanted to touch, but everybody knew was there.

The South made it clear: no deal without guarantees. They wanted their human property protected, they wanted the slave trade left open for another twenty years, and they wanted runaway slaves chased down and returned, no matter where they fled. The North had the votes to stop it, but they didn't have the votes to keep the South in the room. Walkouts were threatened daily. The union itself was on the line.

Gouverneur Morris from Pennsylvania was the one who finally grabbed the gun and pointed it straight at the problem. He was tall, limped from a wooden leg after a carriage accident, and never held back when he believed something was wrong. One afternoon, he stood up—voice shaking with anger—and let loose. "Slavery," he said, "is a nefarious institution, the curse of heaven on the states where it prevails."

But it wasn't just the Southern states at fault. He talked of Southern fields worked by chained men while Northern merchants paid the price. He called the three-fifths clause (calling each enslaved person only three-fifths of a human being) a "moral blot" that gave the South more seats in Congress for people they wouldn't even count as people. The room went dead quiet. You could almost hear hearts pounding.

Morris knew what he was risking. South Carolina's delegates glared like they wanted to duel him on the spot. But he kept going: "I will never agree to give slaveholders extra power for the very men they keep in chains." For a moment, it looked like the whole convention might explode.

Then reality settled back in. The small states still needed the South to stay. The big states still needed a constitution. Morris sat down, defeated. The compromises came fast after that—they decided in unison that twenty years must pass before Congress could touch the slave trade. The fugitive slave clause was written in, and three-fifths stayed. Northern delegates swallowed hard and signed. Some, like Roger Sherman, argued quietly that a flawed union was better than no union at all, trusting a later generation to clean up the mess. Others just looked sick.

They weren't proud of it. Madison wrote later that the slavery clauses were "the only part of the Constitution that gives me pain." Franklin, old and frail, shook his head and said the document was as close to perfect as human hands could make it, but the slavery parts were stains that would have to be washed out later.

They chose the union over immediate justice, believing the country had to survive first if it was ever going to fix itself. It was a bitter bargain, one that left scars you can still feel today. But in that choice—ugly as it was—they kept the door open for the day when those scars could finally heal.

The flame dimmed in that moment, but it didn't go out. It waited.

POWDER KEG PLANTED

The compromises on slavery weren't just words on paper—they were seeds buried deep in the ground, waiting for the right storm to rip everything open.

George Mason knew trouble was coming the minute slavery came up. He owned a big plantation himself—hundreds of people worked his land—but that didn't stop him from seeing the problem clearly. He had watched ships load up with men and women taken from Africa, seen families split at auction blocks to make a little more money off tobacco. When the other delegates started arguing over the three-fifths rule and returning runaways, Mason had heard enough.

He got up in that hot room, sweat on his face, and told them straight: the British had pushed the slave trade on the colonies to keep them weak and dependent. Then he went on, quieter but harder: "Nations don't get judged in the next life. They get judged here. Providence punishes national sins with national disasters." He believed the country was inviting ruin by writing slavery into the Constitution.

The Southern delegates stared at him like they wanted to argue, but they knew he was one of them. The Northern ones agreed with him in their heads, but they had already decided the union had to come first. Mason did the math: no South, no Constitution. So he refused to sign. He walked out, went home to Gunston Hall, where his own workers were waiting for him, and spent the rest of his life telling anyone who would listen that they had planted something poisonous. "Twenty years is nothing in the life of a nation," he kept saying. "This evil will grow." He wasn't wrong.

Mason wasn't alone in his fears. Franklin, sitting there old and bent, signed, but his hand shook. He had freed his own slaves years before and begged the convention to do the same. When they refused, he wrote a petition to Congress calling slavery "an injustice of the most alarming nature" and "a cruel war against human nature itself." It sat ignored. Rutledge from South Carolina dismissed it outright: "Religion and humanity have nothing to do with this question."

They bought a few years of calm and paid for it with decades of trouble.

The three-fifths clause gave the South more seats in Congress because it counted the people it refused to count as full citizens. The overseas slave trade was delayed by 20 years. Runaways had to be sent back, no matter what. It was the only way to keep the Southern states from walking out, and everybody in that room knew it. Madison wrote to Jefferson later and called it "a blemish on our fair fame." They told themselves a stronger, braver generation would clean it up someday.

That someday took longer than anyone guessed. When the twenty years were up, Congress banned bringing in any more slaves from Africa on January 1, 1808. The North cheered. The South just shifted to buying and selling people already here. With the cotton gin making cotton cheap to process, the demand for field hands went through the roof. Slavery didn't fade; it spread west into new territories, got written deeper into state laws, and became the backbone of half the country's economy. The North started getting rid of it, one state at a time. The South dug in harder. Both sides kept finding reasons to look the other way, hoping the problem would somehow solve itself. It didn't. By the time people realized they were sitting on a powder keg, it was too big to defuse quietly. It took eighty years and a civil war that killed six hundred thousand Americans before the country finally faced what it had agreed to ignore back in 1787.

They had kept the union together that summer, but they had also guaranteed it would one day have to fight itself to stay whole.

For this moment, though, in this convention hall in 1787, because of the compromise, the flame of liberty burned on... But now it carried a shadow—one that would test every promise of equality the founders had made.

SECTION THREE
KNOWLEDGE AND COMPROMISE

DEBATES INFORMED

The delegates had locked the doors and sworn secrecy, but inside that hall the real work was already happening—men laying their cards on the table, exposing the cracks in the ideas they had all carried in. Free exchange of thoughts, raw and unfiltered, was the only way to see where the flaws hid. They weren't there to win arguments; they were there to build something that would last, and that meant hearing the hard truths from each other. I would have loved to observe this melding of the finest minds possibly ever assembled in one place in that sweltering room that summer.

One morning early in the talks, Benjamin Franklin—eighty-one years old, bent like a willow in a storm—cleared his throat and asked to speak. The room quieted because when Franklin talked, everybody listened. He had seen more of the world than most, from London taverns to French salons, and he knew how easily good intentions turn sour when pride gets in the way.

"I have lived, Sir, a long time," he started, voice thin but steady, "and the longer I live, the more convincing proofs I see of this truth—that God governs in the affairs of men." He looked around at the younger men, their faces flushed from the heat and the arguments, and told them straight: the convention was stuck because they had forgotten to pray. Back when the war was young, when the army was starving at Valley Forge, and the cause looked lost, they had turned to God every day. Now, with the peace won but the nation still fragile, they acted like they could do it all on their own.

Franklin wasn't demanding a sermon. He was reminding them of the faith that had carried them this far—the simple belief that a higher hand was at work, even when the room felt as if it were spinning out of control. He proposed a short prayer before every session to center them and remind them this wasn't about one state beating another but about building something for all. Some delegates nodded, remembering the foxhole prayers from the war. Others—mostly the younger ones—shifted uncomfortably, worried it would look like weakness. But Franklin's words hung there, quiet and unyielding, and for a moment the bickering stopped. They didn't start the prayers right away, but his point stuck. Facts alone wouldn't hold them; they needed something bigger to keep the truth in sight.

It was the open exchange, even when it hurt, that finally started moving things forward. Madison sat there scribbling notes on every argument—Southern delegates laying out why their trade had to be protected, small-state men saying plain they'd be crushed if votes just followed population. Outside the hall, rumors flew, and newspapers printed half-truths trying to turn people against the whole idea, but the locked doors and the promise of secrecy kept that noise from blowing everything apart. Inside, they stuck to facts: how much debt each state carried, what trade routes actually looked like on a map, stories from the war about what happened when states refused to help each other. Slowly, the picture came into focus for all of them. Nobody was getting everything they wanted, but they started seeing the same country.

Franklin had seen what happened when that didn't happen. He was in France when the Revolution there began sliding into chaos—crowds screaming for freedom one day and guillotining anyone who disagreed the next. He knew crowds could be loud, but the truth was usually quiet. He believed that if people had real information and a steady moral center, they could rise above the shouting. That's what he wanted for America: a place where knowledge was passed around instead of locked up, where men compromised because they understood each other, not because someone forced them.

The debates stayed rough, but they stayed honest. And in that honesty—hard-won, sometimes painful—the flame of resilient liberty found the oxygen it needed to keep burning.

TRANSITIONS TO STRUCTURE

The Great Compromise didn't come easily.

For weeks, the delegates had been at each other's throats over how to count votes in Congress—big states pushing for one man, one vote, small states digging in for one state, one vote. The room felt like it was holding its breath, waiting for someone to blink or blow up. Then, on July 16, 1787, after days of closed-door meetings and back-room talks, the Connecticut delegation—led by that plainspoken shoemaker Roger Sherman—walked in with a plan that nobody had quite expected.

Sherman stood up, cleared his throat, and laid it out: make two houses. The lower one is based on population, so the big states get their say. The upper one will have two delegates per state, so the small ones don't disappear. Let them balance each other. It wasn't anyone's first choice. Virginia grumbled that they were giving up too much. New Jersey said it wasn't enough. But when the vote came, it passed by the narrowest margin—five states for, five against, and Pennsylvania splitting the difference. The room let out a breath it had been holding for a month. For the first time, it felt like they might actually get something done.

Federalism was the word they used for what came next—spreading power between the national government and the states so neither could swallow the other whole. It wasn't some abstract idea; it was born from native American ways and the stories they told each other late at night. Madison would remind them of the war, how the states had almost lost because they couldn't agree on money or men. Pinckney would argue that South Carolina needed room to handle its own trade. They started seeing its shape: a country strong enough to stand against enemies outside, flexible enough to let people inside live their own way.

"I tell the story of eight forgotten founders, people like Canassatego, an Iroquois Indian Chief, who taught Benjamin Franklin about federalism, about the idea that you can form a confederacy in which the central power has only limited powers and local control is retained." – Mike Lee

Moral duty pushed them harder than anything. These weren't just politicians cutting deals; they were men who had seen their friends die at Saratoga and Yorktown, who had promised God and each other a better way. Gouverneur Morris, with his wooden leg and sharp tongue, kept bringing them back to it: "We are not here to make a compact of princes, but a constitution for the people." Faith was the undercurrent—Episcopalians, Presbyterians, Quakers, all looking to the same God who had seen them through the Revolution.

One late night, when the candles were burning low and half the delegates had already slipped out to bed, James Wilson from Pennsylvania stayed behind with a handful of others. Wilson was a quiet man, Scottish-born, who had come to America with almost nothing and worked his way into the law. He had lost friends in the war, seen good men give everything for an idea, and now he watched the convention teeter on the edge of collapse. He stood up, cleared his throat, and started talking—not about votes or clauses, but about what it meant to build something that would outlast them all.

Just as Benjamin Franklin had done in a different way, Wilson reminded them of the nights they had spent in camp, praying together when Washington's army was starving and barefoot. "We are not here to carve up power for ourselves," he said, voice low but steady. "We are here because we promised those men who froze at Valley Forge, who bled at Saratoga, that their sacrifice would mean something. If we walk away now, we break that promise." The room was quiet. You could hear the scratch of Madison's pen as he wrote it down. Wilson wasn't shouting. He was telling the truth, and it landed hard.

The next morning, the mood had shifted. Men who had been ready to leave the day before came back and started listening again. They agreed on the president's four-year term, on a way to amend the Constitution when it needed to be changed, and on protections to prevent any state from crushing the others. The concessions didn't come easy—nobody got everything he wanted—but they came. One by one, grudgingly, because they remembered why they were there in the first place.

Unity didn't arrive with trumpets. It came in tired nods and reluctant handshakes, in men choosing the country over their own pride. And when they finally put their pens down, they had built a framework where power was shared, not grabbed—a place where the flame of liberty could burn steady without burning the house down.

That was the real miracle of those weeks: not that they agreed on everything, but that they agreed on enough to keep going.

REPUBLIC OVER DEMOCRACY

The founders didn't give us a democracy. They gave us a republic, and they fought like men possessed to keep it that way.

"Europe was created by history. America was created by philosophy."
– Margaret Thatcher

They had watched pure democracy in ancient Athens tear itself apart: crowds swayed by smooth-talking demagogues, voting themselves money from the treasury until the city was bankrupt, then turning on each other when the cash ran out. Madison called it "spectacles of turbulence and contention" that always ended in tyranny. So when the people, whipped into a frenzy, handed power to the loudest voice in the room. So, in that hot Philadelphia Hall, they built guardrails everywhere. Laws had to pass both houses of Congress—one close to the people, the other giving every state an equal say. The president would be chosen not by a direct popular vote that a few big cities could control, but by an Electoral College that forces candidates to campaign across the whole country.

Judges would serve for life, safe from the passions of the moment. And nothing in the Constitution could be changed without supermajorities of states agreeing.

They did it because they believed ordinary citizens should rule. Still, they also believed ordinary citizens could be foolish, angry, or frightened, and that a momentary majority should never be allowed to trample the rights of the minority or wreck the country in a fit of passion. A republic slows things down on purpose. It makes you persuade, not just shout. It protects the farmer in Wyoming the same way it protects the banker in New York.

We feel that design every single day. When a presidential election is close, the Electoral College forces the winner to have support spread across regions rather than concentrated in a handful of big cities. It's why a candidate can lose the popular vote and still win the White House—because the founders wanted geographic balance, not raw numbers. It's messy, it's frustrating to some, but it keeps one part of the country from riding roughshod over the rest. It's the reason California and Texas, Florida and Montana, still have to listen to each other.

Pure democracy says that 50.1 percent can do whatever they want to the other 49.9 percent. A republic says no—no matter how loud the crowd gets, certain rights, certain principles, certain promises are off the table. That single choice, made by men who had seen both monarchy and mob rule up close, is the reason the American experiment has lasted. At the same time, every "people's democracy" around the world has either collapsed or turned into a dictatorship. The flame they protected isn't majority rule. It's "rule by law" that even the majority has to obey.

LEGACY FORGED

Four long months. That's how long they stayed locked in that Philadelphia hall—May 25 to September 17, 1787. One hundred and sixteen days of heat, headaches, and arguments that sometimes ended with slammed doors and threats to go home. By September, the room smelled of sweat and candle smoke, and most of the men looked ten years older than when they arrived.

On the last day, they brought in the final copy, written in Gouverneur Morris's neat hand. Thirty-nine names would go on it. Sixteen delegates had already left, some in anger, some just worn out—the ones who stayed gathered around the table. Nobody spoke much. They knew what they were holding wasn't perfect. They knew the slavery clauses would haunt the country. But they also knew it was the best they could do without tearing everything apart.

George Washington signed first, his name big and steady, the same way he had signed commissions and battle orders through eight brutal years. Then Franklin came forward, leaning hard on his cane, hand trembling a little as he put pen to paper. When he finished, he looked around the quiet room and said in that thin, familiar voice, "Gentlemen, I have been looking at this business for a long time, and I confess that I do not entirely approve of this Constitution. But the question is not whether it is perfect—it is whether it is better than what we have now. And I believe it is. So I will sign it, and I hope we are all right."

A few of the younger men smiled, and a couple of the older ones wiped their eyes. Nobody laughed at the old man this time. They knew what it cost him to say yes to something he still had doubts about. He had spent a lifetime believing in reason and compromise, and now he was trusting both one more time.

One by one, the rest stepped up. Some signed quickly, and some paused, as if weighing their whole lives in that moment. When the last name was down, the room stayed quiet for a long second. Then somebody started clapping, slow at first, and pretty soon they were all on their feet, tired, sweaty, half-sick men cheering like they had just won a battle. Because in a way, they had.

One by one, they came forward. Some signed fast, like they were afraid they'd change their minds. Others paused, pen in hand, thinking about the families back home, the farms they hadn't seen in months, the friends who had died for this chance. Edmund Randolph from Virginia, young and proud, finally stepped up, then stepped back—he couldn't bring himself to put his name down. George Mason and Elbridge Gerry did the same. But thirty-nine did sign, each knowing that if this failed, history would remember them as the men who let the Revolution die in a hot room.

When the last name was on the page, Franklin looked around and said, half to himself, "Gentlemen, we have a republic—if you can keep it." The words hung in the air. They all felt it: the weight of what they had built, the fragility of it, the hope that it would last.

They walked out into the September light tired, thinner, some of them sick, but carrying something no generation before them had ever managed to finish—a written plan for a nation that belonged to its people, not to a king or a class or a priest. It was scarred, it was incomplete, but it was alive.

They had taken every lesson from the old empires—their triumphs and their terrible endings—and poured them into this one document. Power is divided so that no man could play god. Knowledge is free, so that no lie could rule forever. Faith and reason side by side so the country could bend without breaking. And they handed it to us with one quiet instruction: keep it.

The flame they lit that day has flickered plenty since—through civil war, depression, world wars, cold and hot—but it has never gone out.

Because every time it looked ready to die, ordinary Americans stepped up and fed it with the same stubborn courage those fifty-five men showed in that room.

The torch is in our hands now. All they asked was that we not let it go out.

THE WISDOM OF THE LEGISLATIVE, EXECUTIVE, AND JUDICIAL BRANCHES

The Founders—farmers, lawyers, and thinkers, including James Madison, Alexander Hamilton, and George Washington—had fought a war against a King who wielded excessive power. Drawing from some lessons of history we've now discussed, and conservative principles of limited government, they dreamed up a new way to run a nation: three branches of government, each with its own job, standing shoulder to shoulder as equals but keeping a watchful eye on one another to prevent anyone from becoming a tyrant. This wasn't born overnight; it emerged from months of heated debates at the Constitutional Convention, inspired by thinkers such as Montesquieu, who warned that blending powers leads to oppression, and by their own experiences under British rule, where a distant monarch trampled local rights.

First, there's the legislative branch, like the town's lawmakers sitting in Congress—split into the House of Representatives, where everyday folks have a stronger voice based on population, and the Senate, where each state gets equal say to protect smaller ones. Their main job is crafting laws: they debate and vote on bills to tax us fairly, declare wars only when needed, regulate trade, and keep the country running smoothly. But the Founders made sure they couldn't go rogue—presidents can veto bad ideas, courts can strike down unconstitutional ones, and terms are limited so no one hunkers down forever. To safeguard sovereignty without supremacy, the Constitution allows Congress to override vetoes with a supermajority and to impeach wayward officials, balancing power like a seesaw that never tips too far.

The president heads the executive branch, the nation's chief enforcer, elected every four years to carry out laws, command the military as commander-in-chief, negotiate treaties (with Senate approval), and appoint judges or officials (again, with checks). Think of it as the captain steering the ship—vetoing reckless sails from Congress or pardoning folks in mercy—but not owning the vessel. Safeguards keep it in line: Congress controls the purse strings for wars and budgets, can impeach for abuses, and courts review actions for legality, ensuring no King-like overreach.

Finally, the judicial branch, with the Supreme Court at the top, acts as the wise referee, interpreting laws in disputes, deciding if they're constitutional, and resolving fights between states or citizens. Appointed for life to stay independent, their major tasks include hearing appeals, protecting rights, and checking other branches— like declaring a law void if it violates the Constitution. To prevent judicial tyranny, presidents nominate, and the Senate confirms judges; Congress can impeach them, and amendments can override rulings, creating a web of accountability in which each branch reigns in its domain but bows to the others.

In this grand design, born from fear of concentrated power and a love for liberty, the Founders wove a tapestry of coequal branches—each sovereign in its role yet intertwined through vetoes, overrides, impeachments, and confirmations—to guard against the abuses they'd escaped, ensuring America remained a republic of the people, by the people, for the people.

WHY TEN ORIGINAL RIGHTS WERE CHOSEN AND GUARANTEED

The Constitution was signed, but many people back home weren't ready to trust it. They remembered how the British had trampled rights whenever it suited them—soldiers barging into homes, preachers thrown in jail for speaking against the King, courts that answered to London instead of to justice. When the states started voting on whether to accept the new plan, the loudest complaint was simple: "Where are the guarantees?" Without a clear list of rights no government could touch, many feared they had fought one tyrant only to build another.

George Mason from Virginia had walked out of the convention because those protections weren't in the original document. Patrick Henry, back in Virginia, thundered in speeches that the whole thing was a power grab. Even some who had signed, like Elbridge Gerry, went home and started warning people. The fight almost killed ratification.

James Madison didn't want to reopen the whole Constitution—he knew it would be torn apart again—so he promised the states something better: amendments added later, a Bill of Rights that would stand like a wall between the people and any future government that got too big for its boots. In the summer of 1789, he worked in the First Congress, sifting through hundreds of suggestions from the states and drafting 12 amendments. Ten of them made it through. On December 15, 1791, they became part of the Constitution.

"A Bill of Rights is what the people are entitled to against every government, and what no just government should refuse, or rest on inference." – Thomas Jefferson

Here's why each one mattered then, and why it still matters now.

Here are the ten original rights, told straight, with the human story behind each and what they still mean for ordinary people today.

****First Amendment – Freedom of Religion, Speech, Press, Assembly, Petition****

A preacher in Virginia was once dragged from his pulpit and whipped because he didn't have the King's license to preach. A printer in New York was thrown in jail for calling the governor a tyrant. Families had to open their doors to soldiers and pretend it was normal. The First Amendment said never again: you worship how your conscience tells you, you speak your mind, you print the truth, you gather with neighbors to complain about the government, and you can send a petition straight to those in charge—no state church. No censorship. No forced silence. It's the right to be fully human without someone else's permission.

Second Amendment – Right to Keep and Bear Arms
When British troops marched to take the colonists' guns at Lexington and Concord, the farmers met them with their own muskets, and the war began. People who can't defend themselves end up begging for mercy. The Second Amendment ensured the new government could never leave its citizens helpless—whether against a burglar in the night or, if it ever came to it, a government that forgot who it served.

Third Amendment – No Quartering of Soldiers
Imagine opening your door to find redcoats moving in, taking your beds, eating your food, and watching your children while you sleep in the kitchen. That happened to too many families. The Third Amendment drew a hard line: no soldier lives in your house unless you agree, and even then, only the law says how. Your home is your castle.

Fourth Amendment – Protection Against Unreasonable Searches and Seizures
British officers carried "writs of assistance"—blank-check warrants that let them kick in any door, any time, and tear the place apart. Lives were turned upside down on nothing more than suspicion. The Fourth Amendment said no more: if the government wants to search your house or take your papers, they need a real reason, sworn in front of a judge, and a warrant that spells out exactly what they're looking for. Your private life stays private.

Fifth Amendment – Due Process, Double Jeopardy, Self-Incrimination, Eminent Domain
Men were snatched from their beds and jailed without ever hearing the charge. Property was taken because the Crown said so. People were tortured until they confessed to things they hadn't done. The Fifth Amendment put a stop to it: you can't be forced to testify against yourself, you can't be tried twice for the same crime, you can't lose your life, liberty, or property without fair process, and if the government needs your land, they have to pay you what it's worth.

Sixth Amendment – Speedy Trial, Impartial Jury, Right to Counsel
Trials were held in secret, juries hand-picked by the governor, defendants not allowed lawyers or witnesses. The Sixth Amendment changed that: a quick, public trial, a jury of your neighbors, the right to face your accuser, and a lawyer to stand with you. No more disappearing into a back room where the verdict was decided before you walked in.

Seventh Amendment – Jury Trial in Civil Cases
When two ordinary people fought over money or land, British officials sometimes said, "No jury—just trust us." The Seventh kept the old right: in lawsuits over a certain amount, you get a jury of regular people like you, not just some judge deciding who wins.

Eighth Amendment – No Excessive Bail or Cruel Punishment

Jails were nightmares—people tortured for information, left to rot for small debts, bail set so high only the rich walked free. The Eighth Amendment said bail has to fit the crime, fines can't destroy a family, and punishment has to be humane—no burning, no breaking on the wheel, no cruelty dressed up as justice.

Ninth Amendment – Rights Not Listed Are Still Protected

Some worried that writing down a few rights would let the government say, "These are the only ones you have." The Ninth shut that door: the people keep every right the Constitution doesn't hand over. Power starts with us.

Tenth Amendment – Powers Not Delegated Remain with States or People

The states had fought and bled too. The Tenth made sure anything the Constitution didn't give to the national government, or specifically take from the states, stayed where it began—with the states or the people themselves. No silent takeover from the center.

Madison pushed these ten through Congress in 1789, and the states made them law by the end of 1791. They weren't afterthoughts. They were the direct answer to twenty years of real suffering—doors kicked in, voices silenced, homes taken, lives ruined on a whim. Every line carried a memory of what it felt like to be powerless, and every line was written to make sure no American would feel that way again.

The Constitution gave us the frame. The Bill of Rights put the fireproofing on it.

"The Bill of Rights is a remarkable document because it weaves into the fabric of our democracy the idea that government has a responsibility to protect individual liberty." -Ted Lieu

The convention had hammered out something solid, but the second the ink was dry, you could feel the cracks starting to show. Men who had stood shoulder to shoulder in that hot room were already eyeing each other differently. Old friendships turned tense. Whispers started about who really held the power now. The war was over, the paper was signed, but the real fight—the one to keep this new country from pulling itself apart—was just getting started. The flame was lit, but holding onto it was going to take everything they had, and more.

CHAPTER SEVEN
PARTISAN PERILS

EXISTENTIAL FEARS IN OUR EARLY REPUBLIC

As I write this book, the office of the Presidency has changed hands 47 times. Some who occupied it were amazing, consequential people who rose to seize the moment. Only one received unanimous electoral votes...twice, and that was our first, George Washington. A handful of others exist in the pantheon of the greatest. Others were knaves or partisan hacks who pushed self-serving programs. Some were weak and controlled by others around them. Others were merely stewards of the office, content to enjoy lavish parties, perhaps, and to serve their terms without doing much. One lasted only a month after a particularly long inaugural speech in icy Washington weather, which made him deathly ill. In my own time, I've witnessed smooth-talking politicians give great speeches and enchant themselves to the public, as happened once in ancient Greece... and then, get into office and do the opposite of what they promised. In this book, I don't mention them all; I focus only on those who should be scrutinized for their extraordinary acts or the devastating consequences of their actions. I look at Presidents who honored the Constitution and the Bill of Rights, so carefully crafted by their predecessors, and at others who trashed the Constitution, leading to overreach or selfish motives that have brought our country to the brink of bankruptcy today. Somehow, over 250 years, we've survived, and it is up to us, as individuals, to choose our leaders carefully so the flame of freedom burns bright for the next two and a half centuries. Now, let's look at a handful of the giants who led our nation through the tumultuous early years.

THE UNANIMOUS CHOICE FOR OUR FIRST PRESIDENT

Picture this: back in 1789, the new United States was just finding its feet after the Revolution, and everyone knew they needed someone trustworthy to lead. George Washington didn't campaign or push for the job—he'd already stepped away to his farm at Mount Vernon after commanding the army to victory. But the people who framed the Constitution, where he served as president of the convention, saw him as the only choice. When the Electoral College voted, it was unanimous: every elector picked him, making him the first president. What set him apart? His courage, like that daring nighttime crossing of the Delaware River in 1776 to attack the Hessians when morale was at rock bottom.

His morality, shown when he turned down offers of kingship, putting the republic first. And his steadfastness—he kept a struggling army intact through brutal winters, shortages, and losses, giving the young nation a symbol of endurance it could rally around.

By 1796, after two terms, Washington shared his thoughts in a Farewell Address that read like advice from a trusted guide, full of concern for the country's path ahead. He warned about political factions dividing people through jealousy and misinformation, opening the door to outside interference. He advised avoiding foreign entanglements and focusing on neutral trade rather than getting pulled into Europe's conflicts. Unity, he said, was key to survival. But at the heart of it, he emphasized that religion and morality are essential pillars for a stable, prosperous society—without them, no system of government could hold, and liberty would slip away. It was a quiet plea, rooted in his own experiences, for Americans to hold onto ethical foundations amid the pull of division.

"Liberty is not the power of doing what we like, but the right to do what we ought."
– John Dalberg-Acton

WASHINGTON, D.C.

In the late 18th century, as the young United States grappled with its identity after the Revolutionary War, the need for a permanent capital became pressing, one that wouldn't favor any single state. The decision crystallized in 1790 through a shrewd political compromise: Alexander Hamilton pushed for the federal government to assume state debts from the war, while Thomas Jefferson and James Madison advocated for a southern location to balance northern influence. At a pivotal dinner hosted by Jefferson, the deal was struck, leading to the Residence Act signed by President George Washington on July 16, 1790, which authorized a new federal district along the Potomac River. Washington, a skilled surveyor himself, personally selected the site, encompassing land ceded by Maryland and Virginia.

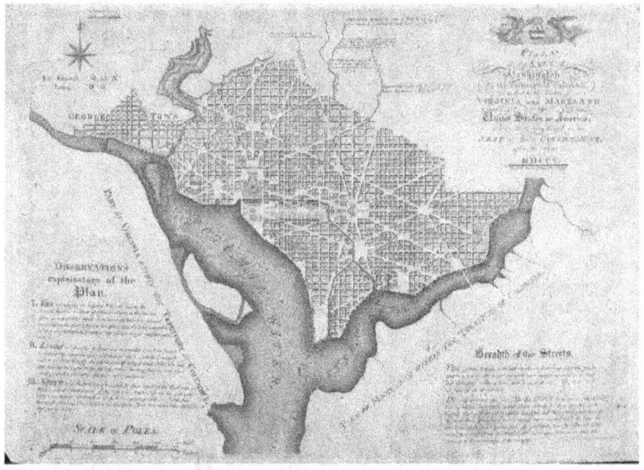

French engineer Pierre Charles L'Enfant was tasked with designing the city in 1791, envisioning grand avenues, circles, and a layout inspired by European capitals like Paris. Construction began that year, with enslaved and free laborers toiling amid swamps and forests; the cornerstone of the U.S. Capitol was laid by Washington in 1793, but progress was slow.

By 1800, the government relocated from Philadelphia, though the city remained a muddy, unfinished work in progress, later scarred by British forces who burned key buildings during the War of 1812, only to rise again through determined rebuilding. Over time, Washington, D.C., transformed from a practical seat of power into a symbolic heart of the nation, adorned with monuments that commemorated its heroes and ideals. The McMillan Plan of 1901 revitalized the core, creating the expansive National Mall as a canvas for commemoration, drawing on L'Enfant's original vision.

The Washington Monument, an obelisk honoring the first president, broke ground in 1848 but faced delays from funding woes and the Civil War, finally completing in 1884 as the world's tallest structure at the time. The Lincoln Memorial followed in 1922, its majestic seated statue overlooking the Reflecting Pool, built to heal post-Civil War divides and later becoming a stage for civil rights milestones like Martin Luther King Jr.'s "I Have a Dream" speech.

The Jefferson Memorial, with its domed rotunda echoing Monticello, was dedicated in 1943 amid World War II, celebrating the Declaration of Independence's author.

These structures, along with others like the Vietnam Veterans Memorial (1982) and the Martin Luther King Jr. Memorial (2011), wove a narrative of triumph, struggle, and remembrance, turning the city into a living museum of American history.

JEFFERSON IS THE FIRST SECRETARY OF STATE

Back in 1790, when the United States was just getting started as a new country, George Washington picked Thomas Jefferson to be the first Secretary of State. Jefferson was already known for writing the Declaration of Independence, and now he had to figure out how America should deal with the rest of the world. He started by setting up the basics of foreign policy, basically saying the U.S. should stay out of Europe's constant fights and focus on its own business. That meant pushing for neutrality when Britain and France were at war, so American ships could keep trading without getting dragged into the mess.

Jefferson dealt with a lot of tension from those European powers—they wanted America on their side, but he worked hard to protect U.S. trade and keep the young nation safe. He helped organize the State Department from scratch, including setting up consuls overseas to look after American merchants. His big idea was that America should stand on its own, promoting freedom and self-rule without getting tangled in old-world alliances. This approach helped the U.S. grow into its own power, putting liberty and independence at the center—ideas that many see as what makes America stand out.

Two men who once stood shoulder to shoulder with George Washington against a King now stood across a widening chasm, each convinced the other was about to hand the country back to tyranny. Alexander Hamilton saw Thomas Jefferson's love of farmers and states as a road to chaos. Jefferson saw Hamilton's banks and factories as a new aristocracy in disguise. Their letters turned sharp, their allies vicious. The young republic that had barely survived the British now looked ready to tear itself apart over what kind of nation it would be. These two opposing philosophies aren't terribly different from what we all experience in today's politically charged environment. This chapter walks through those raw years when the flame of liberty flickered in the wind of division, and shows how men of goodwill—and some not so good—fought to keep it burning.

SECTION ONE
FEDERALIST VISIONS

ALEXANDER HAMILTON'S AMBITION

Alexander Hamilton never had time to be a boy. Born poor on Nevis, an island in the Caribbean, father gone, mother dead by the time he was thirteen, he clerked in a counting house and taught himself to read Caesar in Latin by candlelight. When the Revolution came, he talked his way onto Washington's staff at nineteen, stood on battlefields while cannonballs tore the air, and wrote letters that helped hold the army together when Congress couldn't pay a dollar. He had seen what happened when a country had no money and no credit—soldiers starving, officers ready to march on Philadelphia and take what they were owed by force.

He would never let America be that weak again.

In the spring of 1791, he stood before Congress, twenty-six years old and already the most hated man in half the country, and laid out his plan for a national bank. Southern planters called it a Northern trick to steal their money. State leaders said it wasn't even in the Constitution. Hamilton knew the stakes. Without a way to borrow and pay debts, the United States would remain a loose collection of arguing states, easy pickings for the next European power seeking a piece. He worked nights, writing until his eyes burned, answering every objection before it was made. When Jefferson and Madison fought him tooth and nail, he didn't back down. He looked them in the eye and said, "A country that cannot borrow in an emergency will not long remain free."

The fight got ugly. Newspapers called him a monarchist, a would-be King. Crowds burned him in effigy. Hamilton's own wife miscarried from the stress. But he kept pushing. The bank passed by one vote. Money started flowing. Soldiers got paid. Creditors in Europe saw that America could keep its word. The country that had been laughed at as a bad risk began to stand taller.

Hamilton paid for it. The attacks never stopped. He carried the weight of knowing half the nation saw him as the enemy of everything they loved. But he also carried the memory of those freezing nights at Valley Forge when the army almost dissolved because there was no money, no credit, no hope. He had promised those men—promised Washington—that their sacrifice would not be wasted. The bank was his way of keeping that promise.

He wasn't perfect. Pride ran deep in him, and ambition deeper. But he believed with everything he had that a nation too weak to pay its bills or defend its borders would not stay free for long. And on that count, time has proven him right more than his enemies ever admitted.

But time has not been as generous to the concept of a National Bank: The national bank Hamilton fought for gave the young country what it desperately needed: credit. It allowed the United States to borrow money to build roads, canals, and factories, pay soldiers, and weather crises without begging foreign kings. It turned a collection of broke states into one nation that lenders trusted. Over time, however, the power to create money and credit shifted from Congress to a few bankers. It grew bigger than anyone imagined—first a second bank, then the Federal Reserve in 1913—until today, a handful of unelected officials can decide how much money exists and who gets it first.

That same engine that once helped a poor nation stand tall now makes ordinary people poorer when prices rise, rewards big institutions when they fail, and gives distant bureaucrats a lever no founder ever meant them to hold. It built the strongest economy the world has ever seen, but it also planted seeds of centralized power that keep growing, far beyond what Hamilton or the men who signed the Constitution would have recognized as safe.

The flame he helped steady burned brighter because one man refused to let it go out—even when the heat came from his own countrymen.

JOHN ADAMS' WARNINGS

"Political vitriol is a familiar enough characteristic of American history."
– Robert Dallek

John Adams was the kind of man who would argue with a fence post if he thought it was wrong. He had been a lawyer in Boston when the redcoats fired on the crowd at the massacre, standing up in court to defend the British soldiers because he believed justice had to be fair even when you hated the other side. That was Adams—stubborn, plain-spoken, with a faith rooted deep in the Puritan soil of Massachusetts. He had drafted the state constitution in 1780, the first in the country, with checks and balances to prevent any one man or group from gaining too much power. "Power always thinks it can do what it wants," he wrote to his wife Abigail, "and it takes a strong cage to hold it."

When the new federal government began to take shape, Adams saw the dangers coming a mile off. He had watched the French Revolution start with high ideals and end in guillotines. He knew a government too weak would collapse into chaos, with states fighting each other like dogs over a bone. But he also knew a government too strong would turn into the very King they had just fought off. As vice president under Washington, he pushed for a balanced system—strong enough to protect the country, limited enough to protect the people from it. "Our Constitution was made only for a moral and religious people," he said later. "It is wholly inadequate for any other." He believed the real safeguard wasn't parchment; it was men who knew right from wrong.

Adams endured the attacks for it. Newspapers called him a monarchist. Hamilton's crowd whispered he was too soft. Abigail stood by him, writing letters full of fire about women's rights and education while running the house and advising him on everything from cabinet picks to how to handle the French. She had smuggled important papers out of Philadelphia during the war, and now she hosted dinners that brought enemies to the same table, reminding them they were all Americans first.

When the Quasi-War with France heated up in 1798, Adams kept the navy strong but held back from full war, knowing one more debt or one more grave could break the country. It cost him the election of 1800, but he slept knowing he had done the hard thing.

Adams wasn't always right. He signed the Alien and Sedition Acts, laws that jailed critics of the government, and regretted it for the rest of his life. "It was a mistake," he admitted to Jefferson years later, when they finally patched up their old fight. But his warnings about balance saved the republic in those early days. He saw that without moral men at the helm, no law could hold. And how refreshing it is to describe a man who was big enough to admit his mistakes, knowing in the end that he did so much more right than wrong for our early republic.

The flame stayed lit because Adams and men like him remembered that liberty wasn't just freedom from a King—it was freedom from our own worst impulses. And that meant building a government that could stand up to threats without becoming one itself.

UNITY'S FRAGILITY

The Constitution was barely dry when the country started feeling the strain again. France and Britain were at each other's throats, and both wanted America to pick a side. French ships seized American merchants. British warships stopped our sailors on the high seas and dragged them off to fight for the Crown. At home, men who had stood together against the redcoats now stood across tables shouting about whose fault it was. Hamilton wanted to build up the navy and lean toward Britain. Jefferson wanted to stay out of it and keep trading with France. Newspapers printed lies about Washington himself—called him a traitor, said he wanted to be a King (the same tactics were revisited in America in 2025 with the "No Kings" protests against Donald Trump). The young republic that had just survived one war looked ready to tear itself apart over the next one.

One night in 1798, the cabinet met in the president's house in Philadelphia, candles burning low, voices rising. John Adams sat at the head, tired and angry. Hamilton—still only in his forties, sharp as ever—was pushing hard for war with France. He had the army plans ready, uniforms designed, even a list of officers. Secretary of State Timothy Pickering backed him. Across the table, Jefferson's allies argued just as loudly that war would bankrupt the country and turn it into another European bloodbath. Adams listened, knuckles white on the arms of his chair. He had spent his life hating Kings, and now half the country thought he wanted a crown because he wouldn't let French privateers sink American ships.

He finally slammed his hand on the table. "I will not have my administration drawn into a war that will destroy everything we fought for." It wasn't a speech; it was a man at the end of his rope. He sent a peace commission instead, against almost everyone's advice. The French mocked them, demanded bribes, and called it the XYZ Affair. The country roared for war. But Adams held the line. He knew one more war, one more debt, one more division, and the republic might not survive.

Faith kept him steady. He and Abigail read the Bible together every night. She wrote him letters that cut straight to the heart: "You were not sent here to make war, but to keep peace." Adams took the abuse—newspapers calling him a coward, old friends turning their backs—and kept the country out of a fight it couldn't afford. The peace he forced on an angry nation bought the young republic twenty-five years to grow stronger.

That's what unity looked like in those days: a man willing to be hated rather than watch the country burn. The flame flickered hard, but brave men like Adams with unwavering principles refused to let it go out.

THE ELEVENTH AMENDMENT

While the country was still figuring out how to be a nation, a new problem emerged that almost nobody saw coming. Foreigners and Americans from other states started dragging entire states into federal court to collect old Revolutionary War debts. A South Carolina merchant sued Georgia over the confiscation of Tory property. A British creditor hauled Virginia into the Supreme Court. States felt helpless—if any judge anywhere could empty their treasuries, they would never be safe from every old claim in the world.

The panic spread fast. Governors wrote angry letters. Newspapers screamed that the new government was already turning on the states that had created it. In 1793, the Supreme Court ruled in Chisholm v. Georgia that yes, a private citizen could sue a state in federal court. The reaction was immediate and furious. Within weeks, Congress proposed, and within a year, the states ratified the Eleventh Amendment: you can't haul a state into federal court without its consent. It passed faster than any amendment before or since.

It wasn't about protecting deadbeats. It was about survival. The states had just fought a war to keep outsiders from running their lives; they weren't about to let foreign creditors or citizens from other states do the same thing through the back door of a courtroom. The Eleventh Amendment slammed that door shut and reminded everyone that the union was a partnership of sovereign states, and no single branch of government could bully them.

Adams watched the whole thing unfold with grim satisfaction. He had warned that without clear lines, the new government would start acting like the old king—reaching into pockets it had no business reaching into. The amendment was a quick, sharp correction: the states were still in the game, and they would not be treated like subjects.

Unity stayed fragile, but it remained alive, because even in the middle of all the shouting, the country found a way to say, "We're in this together—and nobody gets to pick on one of us without asking first."

"One of the primary purposes of civilization - and certainly its primary strength - is the guarantee that family life can flourish in unity, peace, and order.
– Robert Kennedy

SECTION TWO
REPUBLICAN RESPONSES

THOMAS JEFFERSON'S IDEALS

Thomas Jefferson carried scars nobody could see. He had buried his young wife, Martha, after ten years of marriage and six children; only two girls lived to grow up. The big house at Monticello felt empty most nights, and he poured everything he had left into the idea that a nation could be built on the backs of ordinary farmers who owned their own land and answered to no lord. He believed cities bred corruption the way swamps breed fever, and he believed banks and standing armies were the first steps back toward Kings. When he looked at Hamilton's plans—national debt, factories, a powerful executive—he saw the shadow of everything they had just fought a war to escape.

The election of 1800 almost broke the country before Jefferson ever took the oath. The old rules required every elector to cast two votes for president, without specifying which was for vice president. Jefferson and his running mate, Aaron Burr, ended up tied. For thirty-six ballots in the House, the country held its breath while Federalists tried to hand the presidency to Burr to stop Jefferson. It was raw, ugly, personal politics at its worst—men who had fought the British together now ready to tear the republic apart over who got the big chair.

Jefferson sat at Monticello watching the mail riders come and go, knowing that if the deadlock held past March 4, there might not be a president at all. Hamilton, his old enemy, ended up writing letters begging Federalists to vote for Jefferson because Burr was "the more dangerous man. On the thirty-sixth ballot, a few Federalists finally left their seats blank, and Jefferson won by the skin of his teeth.

THE TWELFTH AMENDMENT

He never forgot how close the young nation had come to collapse over a technicality. Within months, he was pushing for a fix. The Twelfth Amendment, ratified in 1804, was simple: electors now cast one vote for president and a separate one for vice president. No more ties, no more back-room deals deciding the country's future. It appears to be a minor change on paper, but it prevented a knife fight over choosing the leader of the United States.

Jefferson saw it as another guardrail. He had written "all men are created equal," and he believed the people's choice should stand without tricks or loopholes. The amendment was his way of making sure the next election wouldn't hang on a handful of men in a smoky room. It was one more quiet victory for the idea that power belongs to the voters, not the schemers.

In 1801, the day he took the oath on the steps of the unfinished Capitol, he spoke softly but clearly: "We are all Republicans, we are all Federalists." He wanted the fighting to stop. He cut the army and navy to the bone, paid down the debt, and sent the tax collectors home. Then he doubled the size of the country with one stroke of a pen—the Louisiana Purchase—because he believed the future belonged to free men with room to breathe.

But Jefferson wasn't blind. When pirates on the Barbary Coast started seizing American ships and enslaving crews, he didn't hesitate. He sent the young navy across the Atlantic. In 1805, off the shores of Tripoli, a handful of Marines under William Eaton stormed the fortress at Derna, raised the Stars and Stripes over foreign soil for the first time, and forced the pasha to free every American captive. Jefferson hated war, but he hated tyranny more. He understood that liberty sometimes has to be defended with steel. This was America's first encounter with radical Islamic terrorism.

He also understood that words matter. When the Sedition Act jailed editors for criticizing John Adams, Jefferson called it "a reign of witches" and fought it state by state. Once in power, he let the act die and pardoned every man still in prison for speaking his mind. He wanted a country where a farmer could stand on his porch and call the president a fool without fearing a midnight knock at the door.

Jefferson's own life was complicated. He wrote "all men are created equal" while owning human beings, including Sally Hemings and the children he fathered with her. He wrestled with it, freed some in his will, but never found the courage to break the system that had made him rich. That contradiction haunted him, and it haunts the country still. But it doesn't erase what he got right: the belief that power belongs close to the people, that government should stay small enough for a citizen to keep an eye on it, that the land itself was the best guarantee of freedom.

He left office poorer than when he started, sold his library to start the Library of Congress, and went home to Monticello to plant trees he knew he would never sit under. On his gravestone, he asked for three things to be written, nothing more: author of the Declaration of Independence, author of the Virginia Statute for Religious Freedom, and father of the University of Virginia. No mention of president. He wanted to be remembered for giving people tools—words, faith, learning—not for holding power. And truly, his words are etched in the pantheon of greatness for all time.

Jefferson and Hamilton never reconciled. They died the same day, July 4, 1826, fifty years to the day after the Declaration. But the country they argued over kept growing, carrying both their dreams in the same boat. One wanted the nation to be strong enough to stand. The other wanted it free enough to breathe. Together, imperfectly, they kept the flame from going out.

JOHN MARSHALL AND THE BIRTH OF THE SUPREME COURT

If you walk into the quiet hall where people talk about the greatest Supreme Court justices, the conversation always stops at one name first: John Marshall.

He took the bench in 1801, a tall, easy-going Virginian who wore plain black robes and liked to play quoits with the clerks after work. The Court he inherited was a joke: it had never struck down a single law, met in a basement committee room, and one justice had even quit to become postmaster of a small town because the job paid better. Thirty-four years later, when Marshall finally laid down his pen, the Supreme Court was a coequal branch nobody could ignore.

He did it through three decisions that still echo whenever the Court opens its doors.

In 1803 came Marbury v. Madison. A midnight judge sued because Jefferson's administration wouldn't give him his commission. Marshall could have started a fight with the president and lost everything, or he could have backed down, looking weak. Instead, he did something nobody saw coming: he told Marbury he was right, but the Court couldn't help him—because the law that gave the Court the power to fix it was itself unconstitutional. In one quiet stroke, he handed the Court the power of judicial review: from now on, if a law violated the Constitution, the justices could strike it down. Jefferson fumed, but he couldn't touch Marshall. The precedent stuck.

Sixteen years later, in McCulloch v. Maryland, a little state tried to tax the national bank out of existence. Marshall wrote the opinion everybody still quotes: "The power to tax involves the power to destroy." He said the Constitution gave Congress room to do what it needed to do, even if the exact words weren't on the page. Necessary didn't mean absolutely necessary; it meant useful. That single sentence opened the door to the modern federal government—and closed the door on any state thinking it could strangle national power.

Then, in 1824, Gibbons v. Ogden. Two steamboat operators were fighting over who could run boats on the Hudson. Marshall ruled that when it came to trade between states, Congress—not New York, not New Jersey—had the final say.

Overnight, the country's rivers and roads became one big highway instead of a patchwork of local fiefs. Commerce exploded.

Marshall served thirty-four years, longer than anyone else, as Chief Justice. He wrote more than half the Court's opinions himself, usually unanimous because he kept the justices eating supper together, arguing like family instead of enemies. When he died in 1835, the bell on the Capitol tolled seventy times—one for each year he had lived—and the whole city shut down for the funeral.

Critics on every side admit the same thing: Marshall built the house we all live in. The Court he left behind wasn't the weak little cousin of Congress and the president anymore. It was a third pillar, strong enough to tell either of the others when they had stepped over the line the Constitution drew.

He never raised his voice. He just kept writing clear, calm sentences that changed everything. And because he did, the flame of liberty got one more strong beam to rest on—one that has carried the weight ever since.

JOSEPH STORY, MARSHALL'S RIGHT-HAND MAN

Serving as a Supreme Court Justice from 1812 to 1845, Joseph Story was John Marshall's quiet right hand on the Court. While Marshall wrote the big opinions, Story wrote the books that explained them—Commentaries that law students still read two hundred years later. He was only thirty-two when Madison put him on the bench, the youngest justice ever. He stayed for 33 years, writing opinions that strengthened contracts, protected property, and kept the nation together, one careful decision at a time. He and Marshall ate supper together most nights, arguing over cases like brothers. Story outlived Marshall by ten years and spent them defending his friend's work against the new judges who wanted to tear it down. He died at his desk, pen in hand, still writing the next volume. The republic owes those two men more than it ever thanked them for.

JAMES MADISON'S CHECKS

James Madison was never the loudest man in the room. Small, soft-spoken, always a little pale from the fevers that dogged him, he looked more like a scholar than a statesman. But he had spent years watching power up close, and he knew exactly how dangerous it could be when it got into the wrong hands.

During the war, he had ridden with Washington's army, had seen officers ready to mutiny because Congress couldn't pay them, and had seen states refuse to send men or money while the British burned towns.

He had read every book he could find on old republics—Athens, Rome, Venice—and noticed they all died the same way: one part of the government got too strong, or the people got too wild, and the whole thing collapsed. When the convention met in 1787, Madison came prepared with pages of notes and one big idea: ambition must be made to counteract ambition. Let the president watch Congress, Congress watch the president, the courts watch both, and the states watch everybody—power checking power so no single man or faction could ever grab the whole thing.

He fought for that plan every day of the convention, staying up late arguing with delegates twice his size, coughing through the heat, refusing to give ground when the big states wanted to swallow the small ones. When the Great Compromise finally passed, Madison exhaled—he had his framework. Then he went home and, for forty straight days in the summer of 1787–88, wrote the Federalist Papers with Hamilton and Jay, explaining to a nervous country why this new government wouldn't turn into another Kingdom.

Years later, when he became president himself during the War of 1812, he lived what he had preached. The British burned Washington to the ground. Dolley Madison stood in the White House as cannon fire echoed closer, calmly directing servants to save the portrait of George Washington and the original Declaration before fleeing across the river. Madison, small and sick, rode out to the battlefield at Bladensburg trying to rally the militia that had run away. He could have seized emergency powers, suspended rights, and blamed others. Instead, he kept writing Congress, kept asking for money the right way, kept believing the system would hold if people just followed the rules. It did—barely.

Madison understood something most leaders forget: real strength isn't in one man riding in to save the day; it's in a system that can survive even weak men. He built the checks and balances not because he thought Americans were angels, but because he knew they weren't. "If men were angels," he wrote, "no government would be necessary." His whole life was spent making sure the country could survive human nature.

And it has. Because of him, no president has ever become a king, no Congress has turned into a permanent aristocracy, no court has been able to rule by decree. The flame he helped design to burn steadily has taken some stiff winds, but it's still lit.

HENRY CLAY, THE GREAT COMPROMISER

Henry Clay served in the House of Representatives from 1811 to 1825 and in the Senate from 1806 to 1852, with gaps.

He never stayed in one place long enough to collect dust. They called him the Great Compromiser because three times he walked into rooms where men were ready to kill each other and walked out with a deal nobody thought possible.

In 1820, Missouri wanted to come in as a slave state, and the North was ready to draw knives. Clay spent weeks in back rooms, smoking cigars, drinking bourbon, listening to men curse him and each other. Then he stood up and offered a line across the map—Missouri in with slavery, Maine in free, and no more slavery north of 36°30' forever. It passed. The Union breathed again.

In 1833, South Carolina threatened to ignore federal tariffs and secede if pushed. Clay rode south, met the fire-eaters face to face, and hammered out a slow lowering of the tariff while keeping the principle that the nation, not the state, made the rules. South Carolina backed down. War postponed.

In 1850, the country was bleeding again—California wanted to come in free, and the South was ready to walk. Clay, old and sick, lungs full of gravel, stood on the Senate floor for hours and laid out one last grand bargain: California free, stronger fugitive-slave law, no slavery in the rest of the Mexican cession but popular sovereignty in the territories. He knew it was imperfect, knew it was buying time with other people's pain, but he also knew the alternative was immediate war. The Compromise of 1850 passed because Clay refused to let the Union die on his watch.

He never became president—lost three times—but he kept the country together long enough for someone else to save it. When he died in 1852, North and South mourned the same man. That's what a real compromiser does: makes both sides hate him a little so they can live together a little longer.

"I would rather be right than President." – Henry Clay

DANIEL WEBSTER, A FORCE OF NATURE

Daniel Webster served in the House from 1813 to 1817, and in the Senate from 1827-1850. He could silence a room just by standing up. Tall, dark eyes, voice like rolling thunder—he spoke, and people felt the country itself talking. In 1830, South Carolina's Robert Hayne argued a state could nullify federal law any time it felt like it. Webster rose for two days and answered with words that still ring: "Liberty and Union, now and forever, one and inseparable." He painted a picture of a nation, not a loose club of states that could walk out when they got mad. When he finished, strong men wept. Lincoln quoted him. Soldiers carried those words into battle thirty years later.

Webster wasn't perfect—he took bank money, he drank hard—but when the Union needed a voice, he gave it one nobody could forget.

"There is nothing so powerful as truth, and often nothing so strange."
– Daniel Webster

JOHN C. CALHOUN, BRILLIANT AND TRAGIC

Serving in the House from 1811 to 1817 and in the Senate from 1832 to 1850, John C. Calhoun was brilliant and doomed. He began as a proud nationalist—fought in the War of 1812, supported tariffs, and endorsed the national bank. Then South Carolina opposed tariffs, and Calhoun opposed them with it. He wrote the doctrine of nullification: a state could veto federal law and, if pushed, leave the Union. He said it calmly, logically, eyes burning with certainty. He believed he was protecting liberty. Instead, he handed the South the legal argument it would use to tear the country in half. When he died in 1850, he knew the war was coming. He had lit the fuse himself, thinking he was saving his people. History remembers him as the clearest mind on the wrong side of the most significant question America ever faced.

MORAL CROSSROADS

The arguments back then weren't really about banks or tariffs or how many soldiers we needed. They went straight to what kind of people we wanted to be as a nation. The founders understood that virtue wasn't just a nice idea you talk about in church; it was the only thing that could keep a free country from flying apart when everything else started pulling in different directions. When the men in charge began looking out only for themselves, when winning a fight mattered more than showing a little heart, the whole thing felt like it was coming loose at the seams.

Jefferson and Adams had been tight once. Young lawyers riding the same roads, staying up late talking about what independence could mean, holding each other up when it looked like the world was against them. But politics and time changed all that. Adams began to think that Jefferson's faith in ordinary people would lead directly to mobs running everything. Jefferson figured Adams was building something that looked too much like the monarchy they'd just thrown off. Their letters got harsh. People picked sides. The newspapers printed garbage that would make you wince. By 1800, they weren't even on speaking terms.

Then, in 1812, something changed. An old friend wrote Adams a short note, nothing special, just seeing how he was. Adams answered, and Jefferson's name came up. One letter turned into a few more. They were careful at first, like testing thin ice. Then it opened up. They wrote about the old days, books they both loved, mistakes they wished they could take back.

Jefferson discussed losing Martha and how the pain never quite left. Adams opened up about burying his daughter, Nabby, and how grief changes you in ways you can't explain. They were both old men by then, watching the country they'd helped start argue over the same things that had driven them apart.

In a bizarre twist of fate, July 4, 1826—fifty years exactly since the Declaration—Jefferson died at Monticello, asking quietly if it was the Fourth. Adams passed the same day in Massachusetts; his last words were "Thomas Jefferson survives." He didn't know his friend had gone a few hours earlier. The country grieved for them together, two men who had fought like enemies and found their way back to being friends.

That getting back together meant something significant. It showed a nation pulling at the seams that pride doesn't have to win, that holding on to what you believe can matter more than proving you were right, that a bit of understanding can fix what years of fighting broke. They never agreed on everything, but they decided the country was worth more than their argument.

Those early years had plenty of moments like that—places where bitterness could have taken over, but didn't. Moral duty wasn't just talk; it was choosing the country when everything inside you wanted to hit back. Adams and Jefferson showed it could happen, even after all the hurt. Their letters toward the end are quiet, honest, shaped by the faith that had pulled them through war and loss.

The flame shook in those partisan winds, but men who hadn't forgotten what they were fighting for kept it from going out. And because they did, it continued to burn for the rest of us.

> **"The greatness of America lies not in being more enlightened than any other nation, but rather in her ability to repair her faults." – Alexis de Tocqueville**

SECTION THREE
ELECTORAL RESOLUTIONS

DEBATES' HEAT

The election of 1800 felt less like choosing a president and more like deciding whether the country would survive another year.

Jefferson's supporters called Adams a monarchist who wanted to crown himself King. Adams's men called Jefferson a godless revolutionary who would burn churches and hand the country to France. Newspapers printed lies so wild they'd make today's internet look tame—one claimed Jefferson had died, another said Adams planned to marry his son to a daughter of George III and start an American dynasty. Ministers preached from pulpits that a vote for the other side was a vote against God. In Pennsylvania, men came to blows in the streets over which candidate loved liberty more.

And we think all of that craziness in the media just started recently!

At the center of it all sat Aaron Burr and Thomas Jefferson, tied with 73 electoral votes each, because the old system didn't separate the president from the vice president. For thirty-five ballots in the House of Representatives, the country waited, breathless. Federalists schemed to make Burr president to spite Jefferson. One congressman wrote home that the capital felt like it was "on the edge of civil war." Hamilton, who hated Jefferson, still wrote frantic letters begging his party to choose him over Burr: "Burr is a man without principle. Jefferson at least has some."

As I mentioned previously, on the thirty-sixth ballot, a few Federalists finally left their seats empty. Jefferson won by inches. The republic breathed again, but barely. It turned out to be a blessing that Jefferson won over Burr. Although he did become Thomas Jefferson's vice president and was known as a Revolutionary hero, Burr's ambitions turned dark after his political fall.

First came the duel. On a foggy July morning in 1804, Aaron Burr and Alexander Hamilton crossed the Hudson River to a quiet ledge in Weehawken, New Jersey—a spot chosen because dueling was illegal in New York, and both men still had reputations to protect. The bad blood between them had simmered for years, fed by political attacks and finally ignited when Hamilton reportedly called Burr "despicable" during Burr's failed run for governor. With seconds and a doctor looking on, the two stood ten paces apart, pistols in hand. Hamilton had already decided privately that he would not aim to kill—he'd fire into the air or a tree, giving Burr a chance to back down without bloodshed. When the word was given, Hamilton raised his pistol first and fired; his shot clipped a branch high above Burr's head. Burr, steady and deliberate, took careful aim and pulled the trigger. His bullet struck Hamilton just above the hip, tearing through his body and lodging against his spine. Hamilton crumpled instantly, whispering that he had not meant to harm Burr. They rowed him back across the river to a friend's house in Manhattan, where he suffered in pain for a full day, surrounded by his grieving family, before dying the next afternoon. Burr walked away unharmed but forever marked—indicted for murder, forced to flee south, and left with a political career in ashes. What started as a defense of honor ended as a tragedy that robbed America of one of its brightest minds and stained the other with irreversible disgrace.

To make things worse, Burr plotted to seize western lands, possibly carving out a new empire from U.S. territory with foreign help. Betrayed by co-conspirator James Wilkinson, Burr was arrested and tried for treason in 1807.

Although he was acquitted on technical grounds, his scheme still threatened the fragile young nation's unity and borders. Burr lived in exile for years, returning broke and obscure, dying in 1836.

MONROE AND THE ERA OF GOOD FEELINGS

Four years later, when James Monroe rode into the presidency in 1817, the air felt different. Monroe was the last president who had fought in the Revolution—he had crossed the Delaware with Washington, taken a musket ball at Trenton, and still carried the scar. He traveled the country in his old uniform, shaking hands with veterans, visiting battlefields, reminding everyone what they had almost lost. Newspapers called it the Era of Good Feelings. For the first time in a long time, men weren't calling each other traitors in print. Monroe kept government small, paid down the war debt, and sent Andrew Jackson to chase the Seminoles into Florida—then bought the whole territory from Spain without firing another shot.

He drew a line in the sand with the Monroe Doctrine: Europe, stay out of the Americas; we'll stay out of your continent. It wasn't a bluff backed by an enormous army; it was a promise that the New World would govern itself. Europe laughed—until they realized America meant it.

Monroe wasn't flashy. He didn't give soaring speeches. But he understood something the hotheads never grasped: a nation heals when its leaders act like the fight is over and the country is worth more than anyone's pride. He left office with the country bigger, quieter, and stronger than he found it.

Those early elections were ugly, sometimes terrifying. But every time the ballots were counted, and the loser rode home without starting a war, the republic proved something the old world never believed possible: power could change hands peacefully. The flame flickered in the heat of those debates, but it never went out—because men on both sides, for all their flaws, finally chose the country over themselves.

And that choice, repeated again and again, is what kept the light burning when everything else said it should have died.

THE ROLE OF KNOWLEDGE

In the middle of all the shouting, one thing kept the country from coming apart: people could still read the truth if they wanted to.

Printers worked late into the night, ink on their hands, setting type for pamphlets that told both sides—sometimes three or four sides—of every argument. Newspapers carried letters from farmers in Virginia, merchants in Boston, and preachers in the Carolinas. Lies got printed too, plenty of them, but the next day someone else would answer back with facts. The press wasn't perfect, but it was free, and that freedom meant no single voice could drown out all the others. Voters read, argued around supper tables, and went to the polls knowing more than any King ever let his subjects know.

JOHN QUINCY ADAMS

John Quincy Adams understood that better than most. He was the son of John Adams, the second president, raised on stories of the Revolution, sent to Europe as a boy to carry messages for his father. He watched kings and emperors up close and came home convinced that an informed people were the only safe guardians of liberty. As president, he pushed for roads and canals, schools and observatories—not because he wanted a bigger government, but because he believed a connected, educated nation could never be enslaved again.

After he lost re-election, he could have gone home to Massachusetts and rested. Instead, he went back to Congress—the only former president ever to do it—and spent seventeen years fighting slavery on the House floor. When Southern members tried to silence abolition petitions with a gag rule, Adams stood up day after day, reading them aloud anyway, voice cracking but never stopping. He warned that any faith built on force and fraud would always choose war over peace. He had seen it in the Barbary pirates who demanded tribute and enslaved people, and he saw the same spirit in any system that put power over mercy.

He died at his desk in the Capitol, still working. The man who had helped negotiate peace with Britain, who had written the Monroe Doctrine, who had stared down tyrants across oceans, spent his last breath defending the right of ordinary people to speak the truth.

The early elections were loud and messy, full of half-truths and hot words. But because printers kept the presses rolling and men like Adams kept the conversation honest, the people could sort through the noise and choose. Knowledge wasn't perfect, but it was the best weapon the republic had against lies.

The flame burned brighter when truth had room to breathe. And in those raw years, truth had just enough room to keep the country from going dark.

LESSONS ENDURED, EXPLORERS MOVED FORWARD

The early elections were rough, full of mudslinging and fear, but they taught the country something it has never forgotten: power can change hands without blood in the streets.

Europeans had been shocked when George Washington peacefully stepped down from the presidency at the end of his term. No despot or tyrant would have relinquished that kind of power. Now, America had proven that its system of peaceful transition can work.

The Constitution held the divisions inside its walls. Men argued, accused, threatened to walk away, but in the end, they stayed and worked it out. Moral choices—choosing the nation over pride, truth over easy lies—kept the worst from happening. Those hard years set the pattern: no matter how fierce the fight, the loser steps aside, and the winner governs for everyone. That single habit, repeated over and over, is what has kept the republic standing when so many others fell.

And while the politicians argued in Philadelphia and New York, the country itself was growing fast.

In 1803, Thomas Jefferson made the deal of the century. He bought the Louisiana Territory from France for fifteen million dollars—less than three cents an acre. Napoleon needed money, and he gladly turned over an enormous swath of land to America for a pittance. Overnight, the United States doubled in size, stretching all the way to the Rocky Mountains. Jefferson sent his old friends Meriwether Lewis and William Clark to see what was out there. They left St. Louis with forty-five men, a dog named Seaman, and a young Shoshone woman named Sacagawea who carried her newborn baby on her back the whole way.

For two years, they paddled up the Missouri River, crossed mountains where snow never melted, met tribes who had never seen a white man, fought grizzly bears, nearly starved in winter, and kept going. Lewis wrote in his journal every night by firelight, describing rivers that ran backward, buffalo herds that darkened the plains for days, mountains so high the air hurt to breathe.

Sacagawea recognized her homeland, found her brother, who was now chief, and secured horses that saved the expedition. Clark drew maps that opened the West to settlers who would follow.

When they finally reached the Pacific and looked out at waves crashing on an empty shore, Lewis wrote that he felt "a sense of accomplishment mixed with sadness that the journey was over." They had walked across a continent no one knew, lost only one man, and came home with proof that the country was bigger than anyone dreamed.

Twenty years later, men with shovels connected the Hudson River to Lake Erie with a ditch 363 miles long. The Erie Canal took eight years, thousands of workers—many Irish immigrants who died of swamp fever—and more money than anyone thought possible. When it opened in 1825, a cannon fired in Buffalo, and the boom echoed down the line of cannons all the way to New York City. Goods that once took months and cost a fortune now moved in days for pennies. Farmers in Ohio could sell wheat in London. Cities grew where nothing had been. The canal paid for itself in nine years and turned America into one giant marketplace.

Those were the years when the country learned it could argue and still grow, fight and still build. The divisions never went away, but the Constitution kept them from breaking everything. Moral men chose the hard path of compromise. Brave explorers chose the unknown path west. Workers chose the backbreaking path of digging a waterway that changed the world.

The flame spread farther because people kept choosing the country over themselves. And every mile of canal, every page of Lewis and Clark's journals, every compromise that kept the Union together proved the same thing: resilient liberty wasn't just an idea on paper. It was men and women willing to carry it forward, one hard step at a time.

THE ANDREW JACKSON ERA

The country was changing fast, and so were the men who led it. Andrew Jackson came riding in like a storm off the frontier—scarred from duels and battles, voice rough from shouting orders, eyes that had seen too much death to fear much of anything. He had fought the British at New Orleans when almost everyone said it was hopeless, stood in the mud with his riflemen, and turned the redcoats back. The people loved him for it. They saw in him the kind of man who didn't bow to anyone, not to banks, not to elites, not to foreign Kings.

Jackson hated the national bank with a fire that went back to his own hard years. He thought it gave too much power to a few rich men far away from ordinary folks.

When Congress tried to renew its charter, he vetoed it—the first president to kill a bill just because he believed it was wrong for the country. "The bank is trying to kill me," he said, "but I will kill it." And he did. He pulled the government's money out and paid off the national debt—the only time in history an American president has done it. Some cheered him as the champion of the common man. Others watched worried, seeing a president willing to bend the system to his will.

But there was a shadow over those years that still hurts to look at straight on.

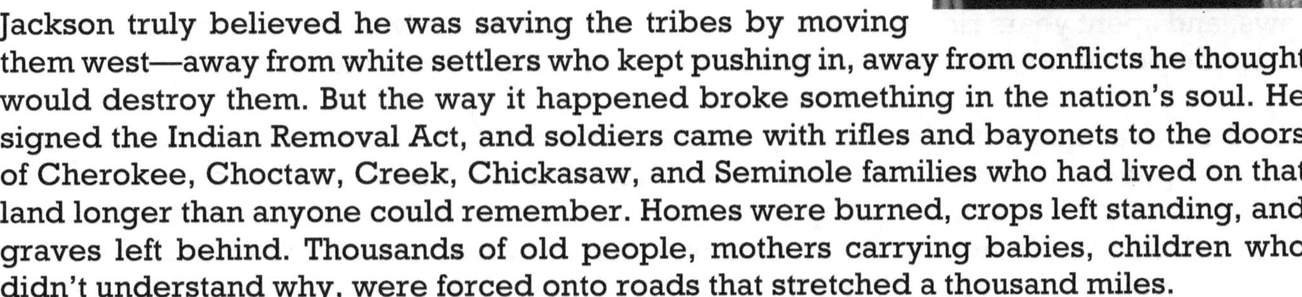

Jackson truly believed he was saving the tribes by moving them west—away from white settlers who kept pushing in, away from conflicts he thought would destroy them. But the way it happened broke something in the nation's soul. He signed the Indian Removal Act, and soldiers came with rifles and bayonets to the doors of Cherokee, Choctaw, Creek, Chickasaw, and Seminole families who had lived on that land longer than anyone could remember. Homes were burned, crops left standing, and graves left behind. Thousands of old people, mothers carrying babies, children who didn't understand why, were forced onto roads that stretched a thousand miles.

They called it the Trail of Tears, and the name fits. Winter came early that year. Rain turned to sleet, then snow. There weren't enough blankets, hardly any food. People died every day—some from cold, some from sickness, some from hearts that just gave out. Mothers wrapped their babies as best they could and buried them in shallow graves beside the trail when morning came. Elders who had once fought alongside Jackson against the British now walked the same road in chains. One Cherokee man said later, "We were driven like cattle. Many fell and were left where they lay."

Four thousand never reached the other side. The nation gained land, but it lost a piece of its honor. Treaties were broken, promises forgotten, and the idea that every person's rights matter got pushed aside for what some called progress. The wound from those days is still there, quiet but deep, reminding us that even a country founded on liberty can stumble hard when it forgets mercy.

While Jackson drove forward, Henry Clay stood in the Senate, voice worn thin from years of pleading, trying to keep the pieces from flying apart. He had already pulled the nation back from the edge twice with careful compromises, and now he warned that shattering the bank and driving tribes from their homes would leave cracks no one could mend.

Clay was tired—lungs aching, eyes heavy—but he kept speaking because he believed a free country only stays free when its leaders choose the harder road of listening over the easier one of forcing.

The flame spread in those years, but it carried smoke too—smoke from burning cabins, from hearts that couldn't forgive. The story isn't finished. It never is. We still carry both the light and the shadow, and what we do with them is up to us.

Down in Texas, a young man named Stephen F. Austin was quietly trying to build a home for people who just wanted a chance at a better life. Mexico had opened the door, inviting American families to settle the wide, empty land, promising them freedom as long as they respected the rules. Austin led hundreds across the border—mothers with children on their hips, fathers with plows over their shoulders. He laid out towns, helped write fair laws, and spent years riding between settlers and officials, always searching for a way to keep the peace. He believed words and patience could hold things together.

But the government in Mexico City changed its mind. They shut the borders to new settlers, piled on heavy taxes, and started taking away rights people had counted on. Austin traveled to the capital to speak up—calmly, respectfully—but they threw him in a dark prison cell for months. When he finally came home, something in him had shifted. He was quieter, his eyes carrying the weight of knowing that talking alone might not be enough anymore.

Then came the Alamo.

In February 1836, about two hundred men—ordinary farmers, lawyers, men who had left everything behind—found themselves inside the crumbling walls of an old Spanish mission outside San Antonio. Davy Crockett rode in from Tennessee, the famous storyteller and hunter who had walked away from Congress because he couldn't stand the endless arguing anymore. He showed up with his long rifle and that easy grin, telling the others, "I came a long way to fight for Texas liberty." Jim Bowie, sick with fever but too stubborn to leave, stayed too. William Travis, young and fierce, drew a line in the dirt with his sword and asked who would stand with him. Every single man stepped across.

For thirteen days, they held on against thousands. When Santa Anna's army finally broke through, the fighting was room by room, hand to hand. No one asked for help. Crockett went down swinging his empty rifle like a club. Travis fell on the north wall. Bowie, burning with fever in his bed, emptied his pistols into the soldiers rushing the door. They all died there, but the story of what they did spread like wildfire across the settlements: Remember the Alamo.

Six weeks later, Sam Houston caught Santa Anna off guard at San Jacinto. His men charged out of the woods shouting that same cry—Remember the Alamo—and in eighteen minutes it was over. Texas was free. Houston, tall and scarred from old battles, became the republic's first president. He carried the victory, but he also carried the memory of the men who never came home.

Those days were full of courage and heartbreak. Men gave everything for the chance to live free on land they believed could belong to anyone willing to work it. The cost was high, and the wounds from those choices still linger. But the fight for liberty has always asked hard things of ordinary people, and sometimes the price is paid in blood and tears, so the next generation can breathe a little easier.

Up north, William Lloyd Garrison was burning copies of the Constitution in the street, calling it "a covenant with death" because it protected slavery. He published The Liberator, writing week after week that no nation could call itself free while it held human beings in chains. He faced mobs that dragged him through Boston with a rope around his neck. He never backed down. His words woke consciences that politics couldn't reach.

The Jackson years were full of fire—expansion and victory, but also sorrow and warning. The country grew stronger in some ways, weaker in others. Men like Clay tried to hold the pieces together. Men like Garrison demanded justice even when it hurt. Men like Crockett and Houston laid down their lives for a piece of ground they believed in.

The flame spread west, brighter in places, dimmer in others. But it kept moving, carried by people who loved liberty enough to fight for it—and sometimes to die for it.

MARTIN VAN BUREN'S ROCKY PRESIDENCY

Martin Van Buren became president in 1837, just as a major financial crisis hit the country. Almost overnight, banks started closing, people lost their jobs, and families saw their life savings vanish. It was a scary time for everyone.

Van Buren was a calm, thoughtful man who didn't talk a lot. He grew up in a small Dutch town in New York, where people held on to their old traditions. He had worked with Andrew Jackson to shut down a powerful national bank because he believed it gave too much control to a handful of wealthy people.

Now, with the country in pain, many wanted the government to step in quickly—borrow money, spend big, fix things fast. But Van Buren said no. He didn't want the nation to become dependent on quick solutions that might cost its freedom later.

Instead, he created a simple system: the government would keep its own money in its own safe places, away from private banks.

A lot of people didn't like that. They were in pain and needed help immediately. Van Buren stuck to his decision anyway. He thought a country remains truly free only when it doesn't relinquish its independence, even in the toughest moments.

He paid for it. The next election went against him. He left Washington poorer than when he arrived, the way it often happens when someone chooses what they think is right over what will keep them in power.

BASEBALL: AMERICA'S PASTIME

Around that same time, something much lighter began to grow in the country. In 1840, a small group of men in New York decided to play baseball for pay—the first real professional teams. It wasn't anything fancy. They played on open fields with bats they made themselves, and after a long day at work, regular guys would come out to watch and cheer.

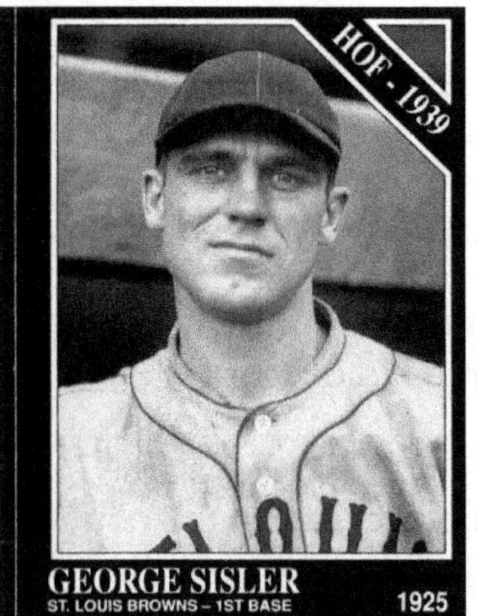

The game spread quickly because it felt like it belonged to everyone. The rules were straightforward, and it didn't matter how big or strong you were—if you had heart and timing, you could make a difference. By the late 1800s and early 1900s, certain players began to stand out. Cy Young could throw pitches that batters just couldn't hit. Ty Cobb slid into bases like every run counted for everything. My great-uncle George Sisler stepped up calmly and hit over .400 twice, making it look almost effortless. When Babe Ruth showed up, swinging with all his might, suddenly baseball was full of stories people passed down to their kids.

That's why it became America's favorite pastime. It reminded everyone that on any ordinary day, with enough effort and a little courage, something amazing could happen.

THE CALIFORNIA GOLD RUSH

Out west, news of gold in California hit in 1849, and it pulled people the way a strong current pulls a boat. Men said goodbye to their wives, sold the farm, borrowed whatever they could get, and set off, hoping for a whole new life. They crossed deserts that scorched them in the daytime and left them shivering at night. They climbed mountains so high the air felt thin in their lungs. Sickness came, bandits struck, and too many times they had to dig shallow graves for friends along the trail.

Most of them found nothing but hard rock and empty pockets. Dreams were shattered about as often as their picks were. But some stayed anyway. They built towns, laid roads, and started churches. Others made a fortune just selling the picks, shovels, and supplies that prospectors needed. That stubborn hope—the kind that risks everything for a fresh start—filled the West and shaped it.

Through all of it—the financial panic, the first baseball games, the gold rush—one thing kept happening that would have amazed the old countries across the ocean: leaders handed over power without a fight. Van Buren stepped aside for Harrison. When Harrison died, Tyler took over. Then Tyler gave way to Polk. Each time, the man who lost just walked away, and the new one took the chair. It wasn't always pretty. Feelings got hurt, promises bent. But the power changed hands quietly, again and again, because enough people believed the country was bigger than any one person's win.

Those early arguments had burned hot, but they hadn't burned everything down. Compromises held things together. Elections came and went. The nation stretched farther west—scarred in places, stronger in others. Yet underneath it all waited a deeper trouble the founders had tried to contain but never fully settled: slavery. The deals that kept the Union in one piece had only delayed the day of reckoning, planting seeds that would one day demand a terrible price.

Those early partisan fights were painful, but they were only the beginning. They hinted at a much deeper wound waiting in the heart of the nation—the question of slavery that no one had truly healed. The compromises that kept us together bought time, but they also buried seeds that would one day grow into something terrible. Still, through it all, some men and women held on to what was right, who chose mercy and truth even when it cost them. Their quiet courage helped the country survive long enough to face the most challenging test ahead.

CHAPTER EIGHT
SHADOWS OF COMPROMISE

SLAVERY'S POWDER KEG

In the summer of 1787, in a locked room in Philadelphia, the delegates faced a hard truth. They were trying to build a new government, but the question of slavery kept getting in the way. Southern states said they wouldn't join unless enslaved people were counted in some way for seats in Congress. The deal they made was the three-fifths compromise: each enslaved person would count as three-fifths of a free person for representation and taxes. It wasn't about giving those people rights—it was about giving their owners more power. Many of the men in that room knew it was wrong. Some said it was a necessary evil to hold the country together. They signed the Constitution anyway, thinking it wouldn't pass without that agreement. That compromise became a hidden weakness in the document, one that would cause terrible pain later.

Slavery dates back to the beginnings of recorded history. Captives built the pyramids in Egypt. In Rome, enslaved people worked in mines until they died. African kings sold prisoners to European traders. The Ottoman Empire used captives for labor and armies. Even in ancient Israel, the Bible mentions slavery, though with rules to limit cruelty. No major society had ever completely ended it. It was just part of how the world worked—conquer others, take their freedom, use their work.

The first Africans reached Virginia in 1619. At first, they were treated more like indentured servants, like poor Europeans who worked for years to pay for their passage. But over time, the laws changed. By the late 1600s, if your mother was enslaved, you were born into slavery for life. Families could be separated and sold whenever the owner wished. The same colonies shouting for freedom from Britain were building their farms and wealth on the backs of people in chains.

Thomas Jefferson wrote "all men are created equal" and believed those words. He called slavery a moral evil and a stain on the country. But he owned hundreds of enslaved people, including children he fathered with Sally Hemings. He freed only a handful during his life. He talked about ending slavery slowly, but he never took the steps to do it on his own land. Like many men of his time, he lived with the contradiction—the way things were made it easier to put off the hard choice.

The founders saw the problem. Some wanted slavery gone right away. Others worried the Southern states would leave if it were touched. So they made deals. They counted enslaved people as three-fifths for representation and taxes. They agreed to let the slave trade continue for twenty more years. They said runaway enslaved people had to be returned, even from free states. Those agreements got all the states to sign. The Constitution came to life, but it carried this deep flaw inside it.

Over the years, that flaw grew. The compromises gave the country time, but they also allowed slavery to take a stronger hold. As America spread west, the fight over whether new places would allow slavery got worse. Each new deal just moved the real confrontation further down the line—until there was nowhere left to move it.

This chapter looks straight at that shadow. We'll see the human suffering it caused, the bravery of those who stood against it, and the pain of those who lived under it. A country founded on freedom has to face its failures honestly. Only then can we see how much the gift of liberty is truly worth.

"No man can put a chain about the ankle of his fellow man without at last finding the other end fastened about his own neck." – Frederick Douglass

SECTION ONE
CONVENTION'S BARGAINS

SOUTHERN INSISTENCES

The delegates from the Southern states came to Philadelphia clear about what they needed. Their states depended on crops like cotton and tobacco, and, in their minds, those crops depended on enslaved workers. Without some protections, they felt the North would control Congress. They said it plainly: no guarantees on slavery, no new Constitution.

They wanted enslaved people counted for seats in the House—even though those people couldn't vote. They asked for the slave trade to stay open another twenty years. They insisted that anyone who escaped slavery had to be sent back, no matter which state they reached. When Northern delegates objected, the Southern ones pushed harder. A few even threatened to leave the convention and take their states with them. The whole idea of one nation felt like it could fall apart right there.

In the end, the South got most of what it asked for. The three-fifths rule went in. The slave trade got its twenty years. The return of runaways became law.

Just outside the building where they argued, life went on as usual. That same summer in Philadelphia, auctions happened in the open air.

One young woman, Ona Judge, had slipped away from George Washington's household. She stayed hidden in the city, afraid every day that someone would recognize her. Washington offered money for her return. She managed to board a ship north and found freedom in New Hampshire. But most who tried to escape weren't that fortunate. While the delegates discussed fractions of a person, real people—mothers, fathers, children—stood on nearby auction blocks, sold away from everyone they loved, priced like animals.

Those agreements kept the states together long enough to sign the Constitution. But every line written to protect slavery was a debt pushed onto the future—one the country would pay dearly to settle.

The light of liberty had been kindled, strong and clear. But right beside it, the darkness of slavery stretched longer than anyone wanted to admit.

NORTHERN YIELDING

The men from the North didn't come to Philadelphia wanting to protect slavery. Many of them hated it. They had seen enough of human suffering to know it was wrong. But they also saw the Union slipping away if they pushed too hard. Southern delegates were ready to walk out, and without them, there would be no new government—no stronger country to stand against the old kings of Europe.

So, they gave ground.

They agreed to count enslaved people as three-fifths for seats in Congress and for taxes. It gave the South more power than its free population alone would have allowed. They accepted a twenty-year delay before Congress could even try to stop the slave trade. And they went along with a clause that said any person escaping bondage had to be returned, like lost property, no matter where they ran.

It wasn't an easy thing for those Northern delegates to swallow. After the votes were taken, some of them just sat there, quiet, staring at the table or the floor. You could see it on their faces—they knew they'd put their names to something that didn't sit right in their hearts.

Gouverneur Morris from Pennsylvania couldn't hold it in. One day he stood up and called slavery a "nefarious institution," said it cursed the people who owned slaves just as much as the people in chains. He wanted the Constitution to condemn it outright. Benjamin Franklin was there too, eighty-one years old, moving slow, breathing hard. He had freed the people he once owned years before and was now heading up a group working to end slavery altogether. During most of the arguments he stayed silent, but if you looked at him, his eyes told the story—he wasn't at peace with what was happening.

They were good men, most of them. They hated what they were agreeing to. But they kept telling themselves the country had to come first. Without the South, there'd be no union at all. So they signed, hoping somehow, someday, the wrong could be made right.

One delegate from Maryland, Luther Martin, couldn't stomach it. He argued that slavery was "inconsistent with the principles of the Revolution" and dishonored the country. He refused to sign the final Constitution because of the compromises. He walked away knowing he might be ending his career, but he slept better for it.

The Northern men who did sign told themselves it was for the greater good. The Union had to come first. A broken country couldn't fix anything. They hoped time would soften the evil, that future leaders would find a way to end it without tearing everything apart.

They were wrong about that. The deals they made didn't weaken slavery—they gave it room to grow. Every concession became a brick in a wall that would one day have to be broken down with blood.

Those Northern delegates weren't bad people. They were just men—fathers, grandfathers, worn out from weeks of arguing in that hot room. When they looked at the map, all they saw was thirteen states pulling in different directions, ready to break away and go their own paths. They were scared of what that would mean—no strong country to stand together against the old enemies across the ocean.

So they made the choice to hold the Union together first, even if it meant giving ground on something they knew was wrong. They told themselves the nation would find a way to fix it down the line, once it was safe and whole. It was a very human decision—full of fear, full of hope, and far from perfect.

They signed the paper, but they left behind a heavy debt. Their kids and grandkids would be the ones to pay it, in ways none of them could have imagined that summer.

The light of liberty shone bright in that room, but the compromises cast long shadows. The flame was passed on, steady for now, but carrying heat that would one day burn.

MORAL WARNINGS IGNORED

Not every man in that Philadelphia room was comfortable letting those compromises go unchallenged.

A few of them carried the uneasiness home with them. In letters back to their families or in private journals, they admitted they hadn't slept well. They wrote about the feeling that they were raising a beautiful house on shaky ground. George Read from Delaware put his name on the Constitution, but later he told friends he'd done it with a heavy heart. He knew the parts protecting slavery went against the very ideas they were putting on paper. He'd seen enough human pain to sense it wouldn't end quietly.

Others felt that same tug. In the evenings, away from the loud debates, they'd talk in low voices—wondering out loud if they were trading away tomorrow to hold onto today. But when the votes came, most of them went along. They told themselves the country was still too young, too fragile, to risk splitting over slavery right then. Get it started, keep it together, and later—when things were stronger—the wrong could be made right.

And in a way, they were right about the short term. Even with those flaws, the Constitution they built has held up for centuries now. It gave us the framework to grow, to fight when we had to, and eventually to end slavery once and for all.

But a few years later, something shifted that nobody in that room had seen coming. Down in Georgia, a young tutor from Massachusetts named Eli Whitney was staying on a plantation. He watched workers pick cotton seeds by hand, one pound a day if they were lucky. He built a simple machine: a box with teeth that pulled the fibers away from the seeds—the cotton gin. Suddenly, one person could clean fifty pounds a day, then hundreds. Cotton prices dropped, fields spread, and plantations got bigger. The demand for enslaved labor didn't shrink—it exploded.

The delegates had hoped time would wear slavery down. Instead, time and that one invention made it richer, more deeply rooted, spreading into new territory faster than anyone could stop.

Those quiet doubts back in the convention weren't strong enough to change the outcome. The fear of losing the Union right then outweighed the call for justice later. The men who set the worries aside weren't cruel. They were afraid—afraid of a broken country, afraid of going back under foreign rule, afraid of throwing away the chance to build something lasting.

They took the path that felt safest in the moment. But they left behind seeds—seeds of division that would grow until the whole nation had to face them.

The light of liberty was real in that room, carried by men who truly wanted freedom for their country. But the deals they made let shadows settle in next to it. The flame went forward, passed from hand to hand. And those who held it later could feel the heat rising from what had been buried underneath, waiting for the day it would break out.

"If you want to be fully convinced of the abominations of slavery, go on a southern plantation, and call yourself a negro trader. Then there will be no concealment; and you will see and hear things that will seem to you impossible among human beings with immortal souls." – Harriet Ann Jacobs

JAMES POLK AND FULFILLMENT OF MONROE'S MANIFEST DESTINY

By the 1840s, the country had grown restless. The land between the Appalachians and the Mississippi was filling up, and eyes turned west—toward Texas, toward California, toward the Pacific. James Polk rode that restlessness into the White House in 1845. He was a quiet, driven man from Tennessee, not tall or loud, but with a fire inside that wouldn't let him rest until America stretched from sea to sea. He believed it was the nation's destiny, almost a calling from Providence, to carry liberty across the continent.

Polk moved fast. He brought Texas into the Union, settled a border dispute with Britain over Oregon, and then turned south. When Mexico refused to sell California, war came. American armies marched deep into Mexican territory. Zachary Taylor, a rough old general who cared more for his soldiers than for fancy uniforms, won battle after battle in the North. Winfield Scott landed at Veracruz and fought his way to Mexico City. In two years, it was over. The treaty gave America California, New Mexico, Nevada, Utah, and most of Arizona—the whole Southwest. The country touched two oceans.

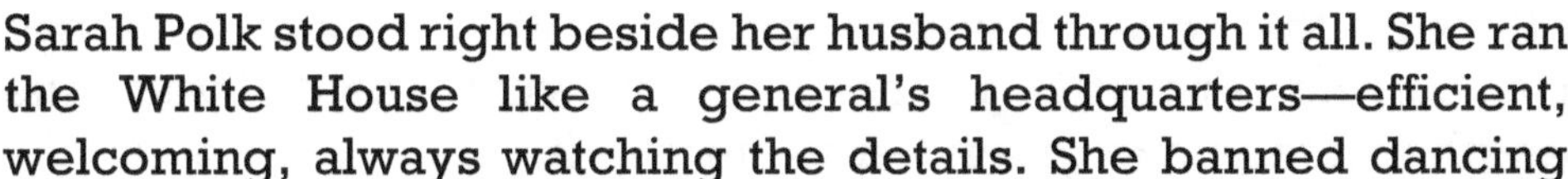

Sarah Polk stood right beside her husband through it all. She ran the White House like a general's headquarters—efficient, welcoming, always watching the details. She banned dancing and hard liquor because of her faith, but opened the doors wide for visitors from every state. She read the newspapers to James in the evenings, helped him think through decisions, and reminded him why they were doing it all. She believed the growth was part of God's plan for a free people.

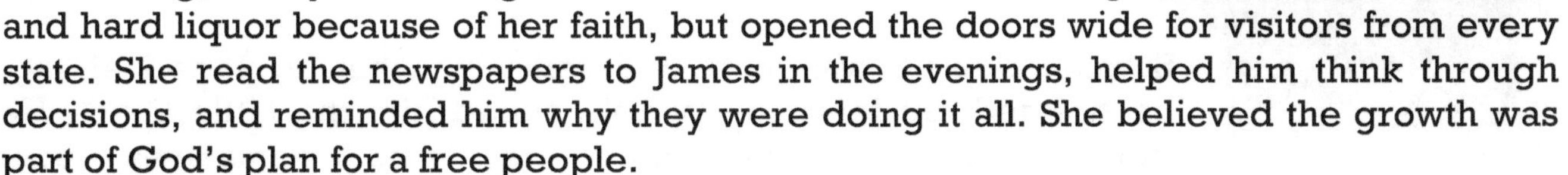

Zachary Taylor came back from the war a hero to his men. They nicknamed him Old Rough and Ready because he never put on airs—he wore old clothes that fit the fight, ate the same food as the soldiers, and shared their campfires. When he became president in 1849, he didn't change. Still the plain coat, still the straight talk. He wanted California and New Mexico to come into the Union free, no slavery allowed. That lost him friends down South, people he'd known for years. But Taylor wouldn't bend. He kept saying the Union had to come before everything else.

As the country pushed farther west, more voices began to speak up against the darkness that followed the flag. Frederick Douglass had gotten away from slavery when he was young, stuffing himself into a crate on a northbound ship, heart pounding the whole way. Once free, he taught himself to read, and words came pouring out of him—sharp, burning words. He stood before crowds and told them exactly what it felt like to be bought and sold. People came curious at first, then sat silent as he spoke.

He put it all in a book, his own story, and watched it change hearts across the North. He always spoke from deep faith, pulling verses from the Bible to remind everyone that no one could own another person and still follow Christ.

"No man is good enough to be another's master." – William Morris

Elizabeth Cady Stanton watched the world shift around her. Men were getting new rights, new chances, while women stayed stuck behind the same old doors. In 1848, she pulled a handful of friends together in Seneca Falls and put words on paper that echoed Jefferson's: women are created equal too. She had eight children at home, a house that never quieted down, full of laughter and crying and everything in between. But she kept at it—writing late at night, speaking whenever she could—because she believed down to her bones that God never intended any soul to be second-class.

Sojourner Truth knew chains from the inside. Born into slavery up in New York, sold away from her family when she was still a child, beaten until the scars stayed forever. One day, she just walked away, putting her trust in God to keep her safe. Years later, she stood up in a room where men were debating women's rights and cut through the noise with one question: "Ain't I a woman?" Her voice carried everything—the pain of what she'd lived, the strength that faith had given her to survive it.

Stephen Douglas was short, built solid, but when he started talking, he seemed ten feet tall—people called him the Little Giant. He believed new territories should decide for themselves about slavery and let the people there vote on it. His Kansas-Nebraska Act in 1854 threw open lands that had been off-limits to slavery for decades. Soon, Kansas was bleeding—men killing each other over ballots. Douglas went head-to-head with Abraham Lincoln in debates that pulled crowds by the thousands. He argued that the popular vote could fix it. Lincoln looked him in the eye and said, "A house divided against itself can't stand."

Under Polk, the country became huge and wealthy, stretching clear to the Pacific. But those old compromises from the founding cracked wider with every mile of new land. The question wasn't just about old states anymore—it was about whether freedom or slavery would follow the flag west.
The flame of liberty burned brighter, reaching farther than anyone in 1787 could have pictured. But the shadows grew longer at the same time. The heat from those buried seeds was building, getting harder to ignore.

The nation was starting to feel the cost of growing without settling the justice question. People like Douglass, Stanton, Truth—they kept speaking up, reminding everyone what the flame was meant to light: lives lived free, equal, under God's eyes.

SECTION TWO
ESCALATING TENSIONS

COMPROMISES CASCADE

The years after the Constitution rolled on, and as the country grew, the old question came back louder: would the new land be free or enslaved?

In the mid-1700s, when the American colonies were beginning to boom, old family feuds among landowners threatened to boil over into chaos. The Mason-Dixon Line was born out of just such a dispute, a long-standing border squabble between the colonies of Maryland and Pennsylvania (and a bit with Delaware, too). In 1763, two English surveyors named Charles Mason and Jeremiah Dixon were hired to settle it once and for all. For four grueling years until 1767, they trudged through wild forests, across rivers, and over hills, using stars and chains to mark a precise line stretching 233 miles west from the Delaware River and then 83 miles north. It wasn't just about drawing a boundary; it was about bringing peace to rival families like the Penns and Calverts, who had been arguing over land grants from the British crown for decades. Their work created a clear divide, but little did they know it would become something much bigger—a symbol etched into America's story.

As the years rolled on, the Mason-Dixon Line transformed from a simple survey marker into a cultural and moral frontier. By the early 1800s, it unofficially separated the free states of the North from the slave-holding South, fueling tensions that led to the Civil War. Folks started calling anything above it "free soil" and below it the land of bondage, even though the line itself didn't perfectly align with slavery's spread. It represented a loss of innocence for the young nation, highlighting deep divides over human rights and states' powers. Today, it's a reminder of how lines on a map can shape destinies, influencing everything from politics to regional identities. The Founders saw such boundaries as necessary for order, but as a cautionary tale of how unresolved conflicts can scar a country's soul.

In 1820, Missouri wanted to join as a slave state. The North fought it hard, afraid it would tip the balance in Congress. Henry Clay stepped in again, worn out but determined. He brokered a deal: Missouri could have slavery, but Maine would come in free, and a line was drawn across the map—no slavery north of it in the rest of the Louisiana Territory. It held for a while. People breathed easier. But the argument had shown its teeth.

Thirty years later, the Mexican War added huge new lands in the West. The fight started all over again. Clay, now old and sick, put together another package in 1850. California would come in free. The rest could decide for themselves. But the price was high: a stronger fugitive slave law. Northerners—people who had never enslaved a person, who hated the idea—were now forced to help catch runaways or face fines and jail. Families who had escaped to freedom in the North could be dragged back south on a claim, with no real chance to prove they were free.

Then, Franklin Pierce took office in 1853. He had fought bravely in the Mexican War, but loss followed him. Just weeks before his inauguration, his young son died in a train wreck—the only child he and his wife had left. Pierce arrived in Washington broken, drinking heavily to quiet the pain. He wanted to hold the country together, but his choices pulled it apart.

He signed the Kansas-Nebraska Act in 1854. It threw out the old Missouri line and said people in those territories could vote on slavery themselves. Settlers rushed in from both sides—free-soil farmers from the North, pro-slavery men from the South. Kansas turned into a battlefield. Armed bands raided towns. John Brown and his sons hacked men to death with swords in the night. Pro-slavery forces sacked Lawrence, burning homes and a hotel. Families lost everything. One man watched his barn burn while his wife and children hid in the cornfield, praying the raiders wouldn't find them. Hundreds died in what people started calling Bleeding Kansas.

Pierce backed a secret plan to buy or take Cuba to spread slavery further. It leaked and embarrassed the country. He leaned on party loyalty instead of standing firm for what was right. The nation he left in 1857 was more divided than the one he found.

The compromises kept piling up, each one meant to buy peace but only fed the fire. The fugitive law forced good people to choose between conscience and the law. Kansas showed what happened when the question wasn't settled—it spilled into blood.

The flame of liberty still burned, carried forward by men and women who refused to look away. But the shadows grew darker, and the heat from those old seeds was turning into something the country couldn't contain much longer.

HUMAN COSTS MOUNT

Those compromises looked clean on paper—just lines on maps, numbers in books. But every line meant a real person breathing, hoping, hurting.

Imagine an enslaved family waking up every morning wondering if today would be the day someone was sold. A father heads to the fields at dawn, kisses his kids goodbye, and comes home to find one of them gone—the cabin quieter, the air heavier. Mothers hold their babies close at night, singing soft songs, knowing they might not be there to sing them tomorrow. That Fugitive Slave Law made it even worse. Up North, where slavery was supposed to be over, a knock on the door could drag a free person back into chains. Good neighbors who had hidden someone could face fines or jail time. Ordinary folks had to choose between following the law or following their hearts.

Rebellions happened because people couldn't take it anymore.

Nat Turner, in 1831, felt God telling him it was time to fight. He and a handful of others moved through the night, farm to farm. For a short while, they tasted freedom. Then the militia came down hard. Turner hid in the woods for weeks, praying, waiting. They caught him. He was hanged. In the fear that followed, mobs killed innocent black people—some free, some enslaved. Hundreds lost their lives. The South clamped down tighter: no more teaching reading, no meetings without a white person watching.

Day after day, dignity was taken away. A small mistake could mean a whipping. Women were forced to have children who would be sold off. Men kept working from before sunup to after dark, no pay, no rest, no voice. Still, people resisted in quiet ways—working slower, breaking a tool "by accident," singing songs under their breath that carried messages of hope.

One night in 1849, Henry Brown—people called him "Box" after—decided he'd rather die free than live enslaved. He had a friend build a wooden crate three feet long and two feet wide, and nail him inside. They wrote "This Side Up" on it and shipped him like freight from Richmond to Philadelphia. For twenty-seven hours, he was tossed around in darkness, upside down half the time, fighting for air. When the crate was pried open up North, he stood up on shaky legs, looked around, and started singing a psalm of thanks. His story spread fast. Abolitionists told it everywhere to show what people would risk for freedom.

William and Ellen Craft did it differently. Ellen was light-skinned, so she dressed as a white planter, arm in a sling so she wouldn't have to sign papers. William went as her servant. They took trains and ships from Georgia all the way to Philadelphia, hearts hammering every time someone spoke to them. They made it. They were appropriately married in the North and spent the rest of their lives telling anyone who would listen why slavery had to end.

These weren't famous generals or rich men. Just ordinary people who decided staying wasn't living. They had no armies, no laws helping them. What they had was faith, raw courage, and a need for freedom that burned hotter than fear.

The country couldn't ignore stories like these forever. Some people shut their eyes tighter. Others opened them wider. The price of those old deals wasn't numbers anymore—it had names, faces, blood.

The flame of liberty kept burning, carried forward by people who wouldn't let it die. But the darkness was closing in, and the heat from those old buried seeds was getting harder to stand.

KNOWLEDGE SUPPRESSED AND THE TRAVESTY OF JAMES BUCHANAN

As the fights over slavery got louder, something else started happening: people tried to keep the truth quiet.

In the South, laws made it illegal to teach enslaved people to read. Newspapers that spoke against slavery were shut down or burned. In the North, some papers printed every horror story they could find. Down South, others printed only what made slavery look gentle. Both sides fed their readers what they wanted to hear, not what they needed to know. Pamphlets calling for freedom were confiscated at post offices. Speakers were shouted down or worse. The country was splitting not just over land, but over what it was willing to see. This mirrors what happens today in America, with a sometimes complicit media determined to show only one side of an issue.

James Buchanan became President in 1857. He'd been around Washington a long time—Congress, secretary of state, ambassador overseas. He knew how the game was played. More than anything, he wanted quiet—no big fights, no waves. Just hold things steady until the trouble blew over.

But trouble doesn't work that way. Kansas was already on fire, and Buchanan looked the other direction. When a pro-slavery constitution got shoved through in Lecompton—ballots stuffed, votes stolen—he went along with it. When the Supreme Court dropped Dred Scott, saying Black people had no rights that white men had to respect, and Congress couldn't touch slavery in the territories, Buchanan was relieved in private. He thought it would settle everything.

He was wrong. Seven states walked out before he even left office. He handed Abraham Lincoln a country coming apart at the seams. Buchanan wasn't a mean man. He was worn down, scared of rocking the boat, sure that staying still was safer than moving. History looks back and sees a president who watched the house burn and didn't reach for water.

Roger Taney had been chief justice of the Supreme Court since 1836. By 1857, he was old. His health was failing, and he carried a deep bitterness toward anyone pushing to end slavery. He wrote the Dred Scott opinion himself, thinking he could close the door on the whole argument. No Black person—free or enslaved—could ever be a citizen, he said. Congress had no right to keep slavery out of the territories. He believed he was guarding the Constitution. A lot of people saw him bending it to keep slavery safe. Those words didn't calm anything. They threw gas on the fire.

William Lloyd Garrison kept printing "The Liberator" every week, calling slavery what it was—a sin against God and man. Down South, they banned the paper.

Post offices searched the mail for it. Copies were burned in the streets. One man in Boston bundled some up and tried sending them anyway. They caught him, seized the packages, and threatened worse if he tried again. Garrison didn't stop. He knew the harder they tried to bury the truth, the stronger it would come back.

The country was choking on half-truths and fear. Clear, honest voices were getting harder to hear. People held tighter to whatever made them feel safe, even if it wasn't true.

The flame of liberty flickered in all that smoke. Men like Garrison kept it alive, refusing to let the lies put it out. But the air was getting thick, and the heat just kept climbing.

SECTION THREE: WAR'S INEVITABLE DAWN

SECESSION'S SPARK

The election of 1860 felt different from any before. Abraham Lincoln, a self-taught lawyer from Illinois who had grown up splitting rails and reading books by firelight, won a 3-way race for the presidency with less than 50% of the vote and without a single Southern electoral vote. He had debated Stephen Douglas across Illinois two years earlier, speaking plainly about a house divided that couldn't stand half slave and half free. Lincoln didn't campaign to end slavery where it existed—he promised only to stop its spread. But to the South, that was threat enough.

After Abraham Lincoln won the Republican nomination for president, the party was split. The men who had run against him were powerful, experienced leaders from across the country and across the new Republican Party's wings. Instead of leaving them out or pushing them aside, Lincoln did something surprising. He asked several of them to join his cabinet. He called it putting the strongest men to work for the country when the nation was about to break apart over slavery and the Union itself.

Lincoln explained it in plain words. He said the country was in real danger, and he had looked over the whole party and decided these were the very best men available. "I had no right to deprive the country of their services," he told friends. He wasn't trying to be nice or make friends.

He believed the only way to hold the Republican Party together and win the coming struggle was to bring the sharpest minds and strongest voices into the same room—even if they had been his rivals and even if they didn't like each other much.

William Seward of New York had been the clear favorite to win the nomination. Lincoln made him Secretary of State. At first, Seward thought he would be the real power behind the president and tried to take charge. But he quickly saw Lincoln was in command. Over time, Seward became one of Lincoln's closest and most loyal advisors. He handled foreign affairs with skill and helped keep Britain and France from helping the South. Scholars have long recognized Seward as a clear success—he grew into the job and served the country well.

Salmon Chase of Ohio, a strong anti-slavery voice, became Secretary of the Treasury. He was smart and worked hard to pay for the war, but he never stopped believing he should have been president instead of Lincoln. He schemed behind the scenes and caused friction in the cabinet. In 1864, Lincoln finally accepted his resignation. Chase was talented, but his ambition made him difficult to work with.

Edward Bates of Missouri, an older, more conservative lawyer, was named Attorney General. He brought steady judgment and helped with legal matters, but he never became one of the inner circle and had less day-to-day impact.

Simon Cameron of Pennsylvania initially got the War Department, but he was careless with contracts and money, and scandals forced Lincoln to replace him early on.

The man who replaced Cameron was Edwin Stanton, who had once called Lincoln "the long-armed ape" and looked down on him. Stanton turned out to be one of the best choices of all. As Secretary of War, he worked tirelessly, organized the armies, and became fiercely loyal to Lincoln. Many who study this period say Stanton was exactly the strong, decisive leader the war effort needed.

A few others rounded out the group—Gideon Welles at the Navy Department did a solid, quiet job building the blockade that helped win the war, and Montgomery Blair, as Postmaster General, helped keep the postal system running across a divided country.

Some men in the cabinet clashed constantly and never fully trusted each other. A few put their own ambitions first. But Lincoln patiently listened to all of them, let them argue, and then made the final call. Over time, most of them came to respect him deeply. By the end of the war, the cabinet had helped keep the Union together, fund the armies, and bring slavery to an end.

Lincoln's decision to bring his rivals close showed a simple but powerful truth: when the country faces its hardest test, put the best people to work—even if they once stood against you. That choice, more than anything, helped steer America through its darkest days.

Seven states left the Union before he even took office. South Carolina went first, then Mississippi, Florida, Alabama, Georgia, Louisiana, and Texas. They said it was about states' rights, but their own declarations told the truth: slavery was the heart of it. They feared a government that might one day take it away.

Leaders on both sides chose the path of conflict. Armies formed fast. Young men signed up, thinking it would be quick. Families watched sons march off, not knowing if they'd come home.

My great-grandfather, Abraham Sisler, was just sixteen in 1861, living in what would soon become West Virginia. One morning, he climbed a hill near his home in Shephardstown, curious to see if he could spot the fighting he'd heard about. Union scouts found him up there.
They gave him a hard choice: be shot as a spy or enlist right then. At sixteen, he put on the blue uniform and served through the war battles, marches, and hardship. He chose the Union, and that choice carried our family forward. And he was one of the few who held on to his life from the beginning to the end of this long war.

Brothers faced brothers across battle lines. One family in Virginia saw three sons go different ways—one Union, two Confederate. Letters home were careful, full of love but short on details, because no one knew who might read them. When news came of a death, it tore the home in two.

No figure embodied the agony of that choice more than Robert E. Lee. A career U.S. Army officer, revered for his engineering skill and leadership in the Mexican War, Lee had been offered command of the Union forces by Lincoln himself. He wrestled with the decision in the days after Virginia seceded, reportedly pacing through the night at his home, torn between his oath to the nation and loyalty to his native state. In the end, he resigned his commission, writing that he could not raise his sword against Virginia. He took command of Confederate forces, a decision that weighed on him but one he never publicly regretted.

The war started with John Brown's raid on Harpers Ferry in 1859. Brown, a fierce abolitionist who believed God had called him to end slavery by force, took a small band and seized the federal arsenal. He hoped enslaved people would rise up. They didn't come. Federal troops under Robert E. Lee stormed the building. Brown was captured, tried, and hanged. H is last words were a prophecy: the crimes of this guilty land would only be purged with blood.

THE PRESIDENT OF THE CONFEDERACY

Jefferson Davis had once been a respected American figure—a West Point graduate, war hero from Mexico, senator, and even Secretary of War under President Pierce. But when Southern states began to break away after Lincoln's election, Davis stepped forward as their chosen leader, becoming president of the new Confederacy in 1861. His government existed for one main reason: to protect and expand slavery, which they saw as the foundation of their way of life. By raising armies and waging full-scale war against the United States, Davis and the Confederacy directly challenged the Union's existence, sparking a conflict that would claim over 600,000 American lives.

Harriet Beecher Stowe's book "Uncle Tom's Cabin" had already opened eyes in the North. She wrote from a mother's heart, showing the pain of families torn apart. Millions read it. When Lincoln met her years later, he called her the little lady who started this great war.

Dred Scott's case had poured fuel on everything. As I mentioned, he had sued for freedom after his owner took him to free territory. When Chief Justice Taney ruled that no Black person could be a citizen, and Congress had no power to ban slavery anywhere, it felt like the door to freedom slammed shut.

Harriet Tubman never accepted shut doors. Born enslaved in Maryland, she escaped in 1849, then went back—again and again—thirteen times, guiding about seventy people to freedom on the Underground Railroad. She carried a pistol for protection and said she never lost a passenger. During the war, she spied for the Union, led raids, and nursed the wounded. Her faith was simple: God had work for her, and she did it.

STEPHEN BISHOP

As slavery gripped America, many slave owners went out of their way to keep enslaved people from getting any education. They were scared that if folks learned to read or think critically, it might lead to rebellions—like what happened with Nat Turner's uprising in 1831—or just poke holes in their ugly beliefs that Black people weren't as smart or capable. In South Carolina and Georgia, the laws that made it illegal to teach enslaved people to read or write brought punishments like fines or jail time for anyone who tried. But even in that dark system, so many enslaved individuals showed incredible intelligence, grit, and talent. Take Stephen Bishop, for example.

Born around 1821 into slavery in Kentucky, he was owned first by Franklin Gorin and then by Dr. John Croghan. They put him to work at Mammoth Cave, this huge, mysterious underground network that was starting to draw tourists. Without any schooling, Stephen relied on his quick wit and natural curiosity, heading into the unknown parts of the cave all by himself, armed with nothing but a lantern and some rope.

Stephen's talent really came through in the 1840s and 1850s when he mapped out more than 10 miles of those twisting tunnels. He found amazing spots like the Bottomless Pit and Echo River, and became the go-to guide for the cave. He'd lead all sorts of visitors—fancy European nobles, big-name Americans—through the dangerous paths, sharing his knowledge with charm and confidence. He kept detailed maps in his head at first, then drew them out on paper, uncovering hidden rooms and rivers that made the cave seem endless, stretching hundreds of miles. His enslavers, especially Croghan, saw how valuable he was; his work brought attention and money to the place so that they couldn't do without him. That kind of recognition helped him earn his freedom—Croghan's will set him free in 1856. Sadly, Stephen passed away just a year later at 37, maybe from tuberculosis. But his mark is still there; today's maps of Mammoth Cave build on what he discovered, showing how someone's mind can break through even the worst oppression and leave something lasting.

FREDERICK DOUGLASS

Stephen wasn't the only one who used his brains to push back and rise up. Frederick Douglass, having escaped slavery in Maryland, sneaked lessons for himself from old newspapers and the Bible, then used his powerful way with words to escape in 1838. He became a key voice against slavery, writing books that fired up the abolitionist movement. Then there's Harriet Jacobs, who hid in a cramped attic for seven long years to escape her cruel owner. Under the name Linda Brent, she later wrote "Incidents in the Life of a Slave Girl" in 1861, shining a light on the awful treatment of enslaved women and helping the fight for freedom. Solomon Northup, a free Black man who was kidnapped into slavery, drew on his violin playing and clever engineering skills to endure 12 years on Louisiana plantations. He regained his freedom in 1853 and wrote a memoir that became a bestseller, inspiring the movie "12 Years a Slave." These folks' stories remind us that no matter how hard the system tried to hold them down, their sharp minds kept them going and often led them to freedom and real change.

On a warm Sunday morning in July 1861, just outside Washington, carriages rolled along dusty roads toward a place called Bull Run in Virginia. People from the capital—senators, congressmen, families, even some women and children—had heard the armies were finally clashing, and many believed this would be the quick, decisive fight that ended the young war.

They packed picnic baskets with sandwiches, fruit, and bottles of wine, along with opera glasses to get a better view from the hills. It felt almost like a holiday outing, a chance to witness history and see the Union troops sweep to victory before heading home for supper.

But as the day wore on, the distant booms grew louder, smoke rose thicker, and the cheers from the spectators turned to uneasy silence. The Union advance faltered, then broke under fierce Confederate counterattacks. Suddenly, wounded and panicked soldiers streamed back toward Washington, some shouting warnings as they ran. The picnickers' carriages clogged the roads, turning escape into chaos—overturned wagons, frightened horses, people abandoning baskets and belongings in the rush. What began as naive excitement ended in horror: the sight of bloodied men, the sounds of agony, the realization that war wasn't a spectacle but a brutal reality that would drag on for years, claiming lives no one had imagined. That day at Bull Run shattered illusions, showing everyone—from the highest officials to ordinary families—that the cost of division would be far higher than any picnic could prepare them for.

The early battles went badly for the Union. Confederate generals, including Robert E. Lee and "Stonewall" Jackson outmaneuvered them time after time—Bull Run, Fredericksburg, Chancellorsville. Lee was brilliant, careful with his men, always looking for the opening—often with far fewer soldiers than his opponents, yet dragging the war on years longer through sheer tactical mastery.

On the Union side, David Farragut took New Orleans with ships, charging past forts shouting, "Damn the torpedoes, full speed ahead." George McClellan led the Union forces, but he was too afraid to take decisive action, and the Union lost many early battles and thousands of men. Eventually, Lincoln replaced him.

The country fractured deeply. Neighbors stopped speaking. Families divided. The cost in lives would climb past six hundred thousand.

The flame of liberty had carried the nation this far, through compromise after compromise. Now it faced its greatest test. The buried seeds had caught fire, and the blaze would burn until the poison was gone.

But even in the smoke, people held on to faith, to courage, to the belief that freedom was worth any price.

MORAL RECKONING

Abraham Lincoln walked into the White House in 1861 with the country already coming undone at the seams. He'd started with nothing—just a log cabin in Kentucky, drifting down the Mississippi on a flatboat as a young man, teaching himself law by firelight late into the night. He'd lost elections that crushed him, buried two little boys, and carried a darkness inside that sometimes made the days feel too heavy.

Yet something kept him moving forward—a steady, quiet belief that if you held to what was right, it would carry you through.

He didn't pick up the war to end slavery at first. His whole fight was to keep the Union in one piece. He said it himself once: if he could save the Union without freeing a single slave, he would. But the longer the fighting went on, the clearer it became. Slavery was the poison at the heart of everything. In the summer of 1862, he wrote the Emancipation Proclamation—freeing enslaved people in the states that had seceded, effective January 1, 1863. It didn't reach everyone, left the border states untouched, but it shifted the ground under the war. Now, freedom was part of what they were bleeding for. When he signed it, his hand trembled—not because he wasn't sure, but because he knew exactly how much it weighed.

The flame of liberty had carried the nation this far, through compromise after compromise. Now it faced its greatest test. The buried seeds had caught fire, and the blaze would burn until the poison was gone.

"Those who deny freedom to others deserve it not for themselves; and under the rule of a just God, cannot long retain it." – Abraham Lincoln

But even in the smoke, people held on to faith, to courage, to the belief that freedom was worth any price.

Information moved fast, too. Samuel Morse's telegraph clicked across wires laid beside the tracks. Lincoln sat in the War Department office late at night, reading messages from generals hundreds of miles away. My grandparents still received big news by telegram well into the 1900s—births, deaths, everything necessary. Sometimes you opened one with hope, sometimes with dread. Lincoln lived that every day. In fact, his hands-on strategies may have single-handedly saved the Union as he telegraphed ideas and war plans to his Generals.

The battlefields were places no one should have to see. Men stood shoulder to shoulder, firing into smoke, then charging across open ground where cannon and rifle balls tore through them like scythes through wheat. They fell in long rows, sometimes piled on top of each other where they dropped. The cries went on long after the shooting stopped—men calling for water, for their mothers, for someone to end the pain.

Surgeons worked in tents that stank of blood and gangrene. They had almost no anesthetic, maybe a shot of whiskey if you were lucky. Arms and legs came off with bone saws, the air full of screams and the scrape of metal on bone. Piles of limbs grew outside the tents. A man could go in whole and come out missing half himself, if he came out at all.

CLARA BARTON

Clara Barton couldn't stay away. She heard about the suffering and loaded wagons with bandages, food, lanterns—anything she thought might help. She drove them herself, straight to the fighting. At Antietam, she worked through the night under shellfire, kneeling in the mud to bind wounds while bullets whined overhead. At Fredericksburg, she carried water to boys lying in the cold, not asking which uniform they wore. Union or Confederate, it didn't matter—she saw sons, brothers, husbands. Soldiers started calling her the angel of the battlefield because she appeared when hope was gone, bringing what little comfort she could.

Amid the thunder of cannons and the cries of the wounded during the Civil War's brutal days, Clara continued to step into the heart of the storm, driven by a quiet fire to ease suffering where others fled. Picture the Battle of Fredericksburg in December 1862: smoke choking the air, shells raining down on a makeshift hospital in the Lacy House. Clara was there day and night, bandaging soldiers from both sides, her hands steady even as the ground shook. She wasn't a soldier or an official; she was just a compassionate soul who saw pain and refused to look away. One tense afternoon, a Union provost marshal, tasked with keeping order, spotted her—a lone woman amid the peril—and approached with genuine concern.

"Ma'am," he said kindly, "it's too dangerous here for you. Let me escort you out of the city to safety." Clara paused, looked him in the eye with that gentle resolve of hers, and replied softly that she felt she was "the best-protected woman in the country."

Her words hinted at a deeper shield, perhaps from above, and the nearby soldiers, moved by her courage, erupted in cheers. It wasn't rebellion; it was a heartfelt conviction that her calling to help the broken transcended any earthly command, a reminder that true service often demands we stand firm when the world tells us to run.

Clara's life echoed that spirit of moral authority time and again. She navigated the war without a uniform or commission, brushing past red tape and skeptical officers who thought a woman's place was far from the front lines. In her journals, she wrote candidly that the scenes she witnessed were "rough and unseemly" for anyone, man or woman alike, yet she pressed on, fueled by an unshakeable sense of duty to humanity. This anecdote from Fredericksburg captures her essence: a beacon of independence and empathy in a divided nation, challenging rigid hierarchies and saving countless lives through sheer determination. Her legacy teaches us that compassion, when rooted in purpose, can heal wounds deeper than those of battle, inspiring us to face our own adversities with grace and resolve.

After the war ended, she didn't stop. Thousands of families had no idea what had happened to their men—dead, prisoner, missing.

Clara started searching records, writing letters, and tracking down graves. She helped bring closure to people who had waited years in silence. Then she took what she'd learned and founded the American Red Cross, so the next time disaster struck, someone would be ready to help.

She walked into the worst places carrying nothing but supplies and steady hands, and she left light behind her. In the middle of all that darkness, she showed what one person's compassion can do.

MATTHEW BRADY CHANGED THE WAY WE LOOK AT WAR

Matthew Brady brought the war home in a new way. His photographers dragged heavy cameras to the fields. Pictures of dead soldiers at Antietam, bodies swollen in the sun, went on display in New York. People walked silently through the galleries, some crying. For the first time in history, folks far from the fighting saw what it really cost. Those photographs turned hearts against the war's horror, but also against the evil causing it.

"I am tired and sick of war. Its glory is all moonshine. It is only those who have neither fired a shot nor heard the shrieks and groans of the wounded who cry aloud for blood, for vengeance, for desolation. War is hell."
– William Tecumseh Sherman

ANDERSONVILLE

The Confederates built a place called Andersonville, down in Georgia, back in 1864, as a prison camp for Union soldiers they'd captured—called it Camp Sumter on paper—but it turned into something no one should ever have to endure.

They meant it for maybe ten thousand men, but by summer, more than thirty-two thousand were crammed inside those rough wooden walls.

There was no real shelter—just open sky baking them under the Georgia sun or drowning them in sudden rains. The only water came from a narrow creek that ran right through the camp, carrying everyone's waste downstream to where the prisoners had to drink. You can picture it: men so desperate for something clean that they'd dig little holes in the sand, hoping to filter it, but it never worked. Sickness spread fast—scurvy twisting their gums black, dysentery wasting them away, gangrene turning wounds into something unthinkable.

Food was barely anything at all. A few spoonfuls of cornmeal, sometimes wormy beans, if they were lucky. Men who had once been strong farmers, shopkeepers, brothers, and sons grew so thin their bones showed through skin. They'd fight over a scrap of bread like it was life itself.

And inside the camp, gangs they called the "Raiders" formed—desperate men preying on the weaker ones, stealing what little they had, beating them for a crust or a blanket.

In just fourteen months, almost thirteen thousand died there. They buried them in long trenches, row after row, names scratched on bits of wood when someone could manage it. Most just went into the ground unknown. It wasn't only the lack of supplies—though the South was stretched thin—but choices made, neglect allowed, cruelty that crept in when humanity should have held the line.

Those men mattered. They had families waiting, letters half-written in their pockets, dreams they carried into battle. Their suffering reminds us how fragile we are, how quickly war can strip away everything that makes us human. And maybe, remembering them quietly like this, we honor the part of them that refused to be forgotten. Each soldier, each life, embodies the cost of freedom, one agonizing soul at a time.

"In the final choice a soldier's pack is not so heavy as a prisoner's chains."
– Dwight D. Eisenhower

GETTYSBURG

The tide turned in 1863. Gettysburg, Pennsylvania in July—three days of slaughter, Pickett's charge broken, Lee retreating. Vicksburg fell the same week, splitting the Confederacy. Ulysses S. Grant rose in the West, relentless, taking command of all Union armies. Sherman marched through Georgia, breaking the South's will. Lee fought brilliantly, but the North had more men, more factories, more rails.

Amid all that turning tide of war, Abraham Lincoln stood at the helm, guiding the nation through its darkest storm—Lincoln wasn't a polished elite; he was a rail-splitter with a sharp mind and a heavy heart.

Lincoln spent every moment wrestling with the moral weight of slavery while holding firm to the Constitution's promise of liberty for all. His vision emphasized limited government, individual rights grounded in natural law, and a Union that balanced federal power with states' sovereignty, rejecting the radical centralization that critics later saw creeping in. But his vision didn't seem like enough during these fractured times. Through personal tragedies—like losing two sons—and the relentless pressure of commanding a divided country, Lincoln's steadfast resolve eventually preserved the republic, proving that true leadership comes from principle over politics, inspiring generations to see America as a beacon of freedom worth every sacrifice. Lincoln abhorred the tremendous loss of life happening in battlefield after battlefield, but Gettysburg just seemed different. It was so brutal and terrifying. He knew he had to show up in person to honor the dead.

On November 19, 1863, Lincoln traveled to Gettysburg to dedicate a cemetery for the fallen of that bloody July battle, delivering a speech that lasted just two minutes but would echo through history.

In his Gettysburg Address, he invoked the Founding Fathers' vision from "four score and seven years ago," calling for a "new birth of freedom" where government "of the people, by the people, for the people" would endure, transforming the war's carnage into a sacred recommitment to equality and self-rule. This wasn't mysticism but a profound reaffirmation of America's core ideals—limited constitutional governance and human dignity—against threats of division and tyranny, giving purpose to the immense suffering and rallying the North to victory. Its impact rippled far beyond the battlefield, shaping the nation's identity as a place where liberty triumphs through sacrifice, reminding us, even today, that our freedoms demand vigilant protection to prevent a slide into unaccountable power. It may have been the most powerful two-minute speech in American history. Those two minutes somehow inspired scores of weary Americans to continue the fight.

"Lincoln's address at Gettysburg - 272 words dedicating a cemetery at the site of one of the Civil War's bloodiest battles - has been called by scholars the source of all modern political prose." – Mike Quigley

GENERAL ULYSSES S. GRANT

Grant wasn't the kind of general that people expected. He was quiet, plain-spoken, dressed like a private sometimes, with a beard that looked like he'd forgotten to shave for a week. Early in the war, he'd been pushed aside—rumors of drinking, a resignation from the army years before. But out West, he started winning. Shiloh was bloody and close, but he held. Donelson, Vicksburg—he took forts and rivers the Confederacy thought were safe. When Vicksburg fell on July 4, 1863, the Mississippi was split, and the South was cut in two.

By early 1864, Lincoln had run through generals who promised much and delivered little. The war dragged on, casualties mounted, and the North grew tired. Lincoln needed someone who wouldn't back down. He sent for Grant. They met in Washington, Lincoln tall and stooped, Grant shorter, calm, eyes steady. Lincoln gave him command of all Union armies. No fancy speeches. Just: finish it. Grant didn't waste time. He crossed the Rapidan in May 1864 and went straight at Lee. The Wilderness, Spotsylvania, Cold Harbor—battles so fierce that men wrote last letters home before charging.

Grant took terrible losses, but he kept moving, flanking, pressing. He told Lincoln, "I propose to fight it out on this line if it takes all summer." It took more than the summer. He pinned Lee at Petersburg, cut supply lines, and waited through the winter. On Palm Sunday, 1865, Lee asked for terms. They met at Appomattox Court House. Grant offered generous terms—soldiers could go home with their horses, no trials for treason.

Grant wasn't flashy. He just refused to quit. He saw the job through, at awful cost, because he believed the Union—and the freedom it promised—was worth it. When it ended, he'd won not just battles, but the nation's second chance.

The Room in the McLean House, at Appomattox C.H., in which GEN. LEE surrendered to GEN. GRANT.

After the surrender, Lee rode away from Appomattox, urging his men to go home and rebuild. He became president of Washington College in Lexington, Virginia, where he worked to educate young Southerners and promote reconciliation. He lived quietly, avoiding politics, until his death on October 12, 1870.

Lee's family home, Arlington House, had deep roots. Built by George Washington Parke Custis—adopted grandson of George Washington—as a memorial to the first president, it passed to his daughter Mary, who married Lee. The mansion overlooked the capital, a symbol of family ties stretching back to the founding. During the war, when taxes went unpaid (a new law required personal appearance, impossible amid hostilities), the government seized the estate. To ensure Lee could never return comfortably, Union Quartermaster General Montgomery Meigs began burying war dead on the grounds, starting near the house. What began as punishment became sacred ground: Arlington National Cemetery, where America's honored rest. If you are fortunate enough to visit this hallowed place, you will see the Custis-Lee mansion still standing beside the graves of our brave men and women who made the ultimate sacrifice.

Lincoln's own pain never let up. He lost two sons young. Willie in 1862, right in the White House. Lincoln walked the halls at night, grieving quietly. His beloved wife, Mary, had slowly gone mad. Friends reported that he turned to the Bible more, seeking meaning. He carried the nation's sorrow along with his own yet kept making the hard calls—freeing enslaved people, pushing the war forward, believing God had a purpose in it all.

When Lee surrendered at Appomattox in April 1865, the war ended. Five days later, Lincoln was dead, shot in a theater by a deranged man who hated what he stood for. The assassination transformed him into something greater, a martyr for the Union he had saved. In life, he had been unpopular for years, criticized, hated even. But his steady courage, his refusal to let the country break, held it together, and, in doing so, Lincoln took his rightful place right at the top in the pantheon of America's greatest heroes.

"My dream is of a place and a time where America will once again be seen as the last best hope of earth." – Abraham Lincoln

Under the Constitution, levying war against the United States is the very definition of treason. When the Confederacy collapsed later in 1865, Union troops captured Confederate President Jefferson Davis as he fled south, disguised in an overcoat—rumors later exaggerated it into a dress story to mock him. He spent two years imprisoned at Fortress Monroe, held in harsh conditions at first, awaiting trial for treason. In the end, no trial came. Political winds shifted; President Andrew Johnson issued amnesties, Davis was released on bail backed by unlikely Northern supporters, and later received a full pardon. He lived out his remaining years freely until 1889, writing books and speaking in defense of what became known as the Lost Cause—insisting the South had fought nobly for states' rights rather than slavery. Though never convicted, his leadership of rebellion against the nation left a deep wound, one that tested the young republic's ability to endure division and hold accountable those who would tear it apart.

Slavery had existed in almost every great civilization—Egypt, Greece, Rome, China, Africa, and the Islamic world. No ancient society ended slavery completely. America did, at terrible cost. White Americans and Europeans in the modern age led the way to abolition. It took a war that killed more Americans than any other, but it expunged the poison.

Roughly 320,000 white Union soldiers died on the Civil War battlefields, each of them contributing to the abolition of slavery. Forty thousand black soldiers died, many valiantly fighting side by side with their white counterparts for the Union cause. The Confederates lost around 280,000 men. These figures are just statistics, and they could never properly tell the individual stories of the more than 620,000 men who never went home to their families, never had a chance to breathe again, see their wives, or raise babies into adults. This was the price Americans paid to abolish slavery once and for all. It was a terrible, crushing price our ancestors paid as a nation to end the scourge of slavery and to secure freedom for all.

And these figures don't count the hundreds of thousands of people who were disfigured, died of disease, or mental illness following this brutal conflict.

There is no way anyone in their right mind can defend slavery. It is a scourge on humanity wherever and whenever it happens. But, if there's a silver lining, perhaps it can be found in the possibly politically incorrect words of Thomas Sowell:

"The people made worse off by slavery were those who were enslaved. Their descendants would have been worse off today if born in Africa instead of America. Put differently, the terrible fate of their ancestors benefitted them."
-Thomas Sowell

If there's a silver lining to this dark cloud, centuries of brutality endured by slaves may have at very least paved the way for their descendants to live in a better world than they might have otherwise.

THEODORE JUDAH AND THE TRANSCONTINENTAL RAILROAD

"America is another name for opportunity." – Ralph Waldo Emerson

While soldiers were marching, fighting, and dying in record amounts during the war, a man named Theodore Judah was chasing a dream out west. He was an engineer who couldn't stop thinking about a railroad that would stretch all the way across the continent. He climbed mountains, drew maps no one thought possible, talked investors into believing, and pushed Congress to back it. As if the idea wasn't crazy enough on its head, work started right in the middle of this terrible war in 1863.

Four years after the Civil War ended, in May 1869, the legions of men who shoveled met at Promontory Summit in Utah. Workers from the Union Pacific coming west and the Central Pacific coming east laid the last rails, and a golden spike was driven in to join them. The hammer blows were wired across the telegraph, and bells rang in cities from coast to coast. The continent was connected. Almost overnight, everything changed.
What used to take months by wagon or ship—bouncing over trails, fighting weather, risking everything—now took days on a train. You could leave New York one morning and be in San Francisco a week later, watching the landscape roll by from a window seat. Farmers in the Midwest could ship wheat or cattle to markets they'd never reached before. Factories back East got lumber and minerals from the West without waiting half a year.

Families loaded up and went west like never before. Land was cheap, sometimes free, under the Homestead Act. A man who'd lost everything in the war could start fresh with 160 acres and a dream. Towns sprang up along the tracks—railroad stops turning into real places with stores, schools, and churches. Immigrants poured in, drawn by the promise of space and work. The West was filled with people chasing the same thing the war had been fought for: a chance to build a life on their own terms.

It wasn't perfect. Native tribes lost more ground as the iron horse cut through their hunting lands.

But for millions, that railroad meant freedom in the most practical way—freedom to move, to try again, to leave hard times behind and plant new roots. At a moment when the country was still raw from four years of fighting itself, the railroad pulled it closer together. It gave people a way to see the nation as one big place, not just North and South, East and West. It let ordinary folks live out the promise the war had bought with so much blood.

The flame of liberty burned through the darkest years, carried by men and women who paid with blood and tears. When the smoke cleared, the nation stood scarred, changed, but whole. And freer than before. But now we had to figure out how to pull ourselves back together emotionally and spiritually as one nation, and reconstruction would be terribly difficult.

UNITY REBORN WITH A PRICE

The war ended, but the most challenging part was just ahead—the part that would test what the country was really made of.

Andrew Johnson became president right after Lincoln's death. He'd started as a tailor in Tennessee, taught himself to read, and worked his way up in politics the hard way. When Tennessee left the Union, he was the only Southern senator who stayed loyal. A lot of people thought that meant he'd be tough on the defeated South. He wasn't.

Johnson just wanted things to go back to how they were, as quickly as he could make it happen. He gave pardons to Confederate leaders left and right. He let the Southern states make their own new rules, and those rules—the Black Codes—felt a lot like slavery wearing a different face.
A freed man could be arrested for not having a job, then be rented out to work on the same land he'd just been freed from. Johnson blocked bills that would have protected those new citizens. He fired people in his own government who tried to push for real change. He drank too much and picked fights with Congress. In 1868, Congress impeached him, ostensibly for firing his Secretary of War in violation of the rules, but in reality because he was standing in the way of true freedom for the people the war had freed. The Senate missed removing him by one single vote. He served out his term, but he left behind a South rebuilding on the same old broken ground, and wounds that would take generations to begin healing.

PRESIDENT ULYSSES S. GRANT

Ulysses S. Grant took over in 1869. The same quiet general who had worn down Lee's army and accepted surrender with calm dignity now had to run the country. Grant was honest through and through, but he trusted the people close to him too much.

Scandals came to light—the Whiskey Ring stealing tax money, railroad bribery, and even the Secretary of War taking kickbacks. Grant stood by his friends at first, and when the truth came out, it hurt him badly. He wasn't part of any of it; he just hadn't seen the betrayal coming. On Reconstruction, though, he never wavered. He sent troops to protect Black voters in the South, broke up the early Klan, and did what he could to keep the promises the war had been fought for. He wanted a country that was whole and free for everyone.

One day during his presidency, Ulysses S. Grant was out for a morning stroll in Washington, D.C., enjoying the fresh air incognito without his usual entourage. He encountered an elderly lady who didn't recognize him and struck up a casual conversation. As they chatted, she remarked something along the lines of, "I've heard that President Grant is quite a bad man—a drunkard, they say." Grant, with his characteristic humility and dry wit, smiled and replied, "Madam, I've heard the same thing myself." Grant was a good man, guided by self-deprecating humor and the ability to brush off criticism, even when it was directed at him personally.

"My failures have been errors in judgment, not of intent." – Ulysses S. Grant

Although the scandals ruined him and he was on the verge of dying penniless of throat cancer without anything to leave his family, the great author Mark Twain funded his memoirs, which Grant wrote studiously, finishing them just before his death. Grant's life story, in his words, was a huge best-seller in its time and is still worth reading. Instead of vilifying his enemies, he praised them for their prowess and ability, even as he outwitted them, a lesson more of us should learn.

THE THIRTEENTH, FOURTEENTH, AND FIFTEENTH AMENDMENTS

The Thirteenth Amendment was passed in 1865, only months after Appomattox. It was plain and direct: slavery and forced labor were over in the United States. After all the graves, all the families torn apart, the nation finally put it in writing—no one could own another person. It took the bloodiest war we've ever known to get those words on paper.

The Fourteenth Amendment came in 1868. Southern states were already looking for ways to tie freed people down again—arresting them on nothing, forcing them back into labor. The amendment said that anyone born here is a citizen, that every citizen gets equal protection under the law, and that no state can take away life, liberty, or property without a fair process. It brought the Declaration's big promise right into the Constitution.

The Fifteenth Amendment arrived in 1870. Black men who had fought for the Union came home and found they still couldn't vote—poll taxes, rigged tests, threats waiting at the polls. The amendment said race could never be a reason to keep a citizen from the ballot box. It drew the line, even if it took another hundred years to make it hold.

Reconstruction was the country's attempt at putting itself back together. Federal troops kept the peace.

Schools opened for Black children, many of whom walked into a classroom for the first time. Black men served in state legislatures and even in Congress. For a little while, it felt like the promises of freedom might really happen.

But in 1877, the troops stopped patrolling the South as part of a deal. Almost right away, the old ways started coming back. Southern states passed laws to keep Black people separate and powerless. Those laws were called Jim Crow laws.

The name came from an old minstrel show song—a white performer in blackface acting out a foolish, mocking version of a Black man. "Jim Crow" turned into the name for the whole system of segregation that spread through the South—separate schools, separate train cars, separate water fountains—separate everything, and always unequal. Black schools received old books and deteriorating buildings. Tests for voting were made so complicated that almost no Black person could pass. Poll taxes and threats kept people from voting.

It wasn't only separation. It was control. A Black man could be jailed for looking at a white woman too long, or for being out after dark without papers. Lynchings became a terror—thousands killed, often in public, crowds watching like it was entertainment. The law turned a blind eye.

The whole light of those amendments—citizenship, equal protection, the vote—stayed out of reach for generations. The war had ended slavery on paper, but Jim Crow kept its shadow alive in new clothes.

The flame of liberty dimmed in those years, but it never went out. People kept it burning quietly—in churches, in secret meetings, in hearts that wouldn't accept less than complete freedom. One day it would burn bright again.

The war took more than six hundred thousand American lives—more than any war before or since. It ended slavery, an evil that had lived in every great civilization from ancient Egypt and Rome to Africa itself. No old society had ever wiped it out completely. America did, at a price almost too heavy to carry, moved forward by men and women who believed God's children were meant to live free.
When the smoke cleared, the republic was still standing—scarred deep, changed forever, but standing. The amendments sealed the truth that the war had been won, even if living it fully took longer. The flame of liberty had passed through a fire no one could have pictured, carried by hands that refused to let it die.

That flame is still with us. It asks us to remember the cost, to guard what was saved, and to keep reaching for the fuller light.

FORGING A NEW AMERICA AFTER A BLOODY WAR

The war came to an end, and everything went quiet—like the kind of quiet that follows a storm when you're not sure what's left standing.

Fields that had been green with corn or white with cotton were just dirt now. Towns were burned to the ground, leaving only frames and ash. Families sat around the table with empty places, listening for a door that wouldn't open again.

But in that quiet, you could feel something starting to stir. The flame of liberty had been beaten down low by all the years of fighting, but it didn't go out. It came back steadier, tougher, because it had survived the worst.

People leaned on music because it was something familiar they could hold onto. Songs had always been there—the old ones that came across the ocean with the first settlers from England and Scotland, full of sorrow and hanging on. The spirituals that started in slave cabins, like "Swing Low, Sweet Chariot," and "Sometimes I Feel Like a Motherless Child," or "Deep River," talking about crossing rivers in ways that meant more than the words said. Soldiers on both sides sang around their fires—"Dixie" in one camp, "Battle Hymn" in another, "When Johnny Comes Marching Home" when they let themselves dream. After Appomattox, songs began to cross lines. Minstrel shows and vaudeville provided audiences with tunes that let them laugh a little, even when things still hurt. Brass bands played in the squares on Sundays. Churches raised by freed people rang with hymns that sounded like they'd finally won. Music helped pull the pieces back together, reminding folks that under God, they were still one country.

"And so by fateful chance the Negro folk-song -- the rhythmic cry of the slave -- stands to-day not simply as the sole American music, but as the most beautiful expression of human experience born this side the seas. It has been neglected, it has been, and is, half despised, and above all it has been persistently mistaken and misunderstood; but notwithstanding, it still remains as the singular spiritual heritage of the nation and the greatest gift of the Negro people." – W.E.B. DuBois

Nature didn't make it easy. In the 1870s, locusts swarmed across the Plains in clouds that darkened the sky. Billions of them, eating every green thing. Farmers who'd just gotten back on their feet after the war watched their crops destroyed in a day. Some packed up and moved on. Others stayed, worked the ground again, planted what little seed they had, and waited for next year. That same determination that kept soldiers going kept those families trying.

Mark Twain took it all in and wrote it down. He'd grown up on the Mississippi, working steamboats, hearing every story the river brought. He had a way of saying things that made you laugh and then stop and think. In "Tom Sawyer" and "Huckleberry Finn", he sent boys down the river on rafts, getting into trouble, figuring out right from wrong when the world around them didn't make it simple. He called out the contradictions—preachers talking love on Sunday while keeping people in chains on Monday, towns putting on airs while looking the other way at wrong. Twain cared about the country enough to show it what it looked like, believing we could fix things if we faced them.

Years after the fighting ended, in one ruined town in Virginia, two old soldiers crossed paths. One had worn blue, the other gray. They knew the faces from a day they'd aimed rifles at each other. Instead of passing by, they sat on what was left of a wall, shared a smoke, talked about their children and the homes they'd gone back to. They didn't have much anymore, but they had that time together. They shook hands before walking away—two men who'd seen the ugliest part and picked something better.

The flame kept moving forward, carried by everyday people rebuilding from what remained. The war had taken almost everything, but it left the country freer, with space to become something more. The light that came through that darkness held steadier because it had been through the heat.

"If I were to live my life over again, I would be an American. I would steep myself in America, I would know no other land." – Henry James

Slavery's shadow had come close to snuffing the flame out for good. But holding to what was right pulled it through—just as in other hard times, when choosing the right path turned trouble into progress, guiding the nation toward the challenges and opportunities of a growing country.

CHAPTER NINE
EXPANSION AND INNOVATION

AMERICA'S GROWTH IN THE LATE 19TH CENTURY

The war ended. Brothers were no longer fighting brothers. Slavery was outlawed. Rails headed west, factories fired up again, and electric lights began appearing in cities. The country was getting back on its feet, looking ahead. Things felt like they were moving forward—you could sense progress in the air. But the scars from the war didn't disappear fast. Wrong still hung on in places, and out West, new problems were waiting. This chapter looks at how America grew during those years—through inventors who kept trying, settlers who bet everything on a new start, and people who saw what wasn't right and spoke up. Their stories are about that same tough liberty that pulled the nation through the war, now pushing it on, even with bumps along the way.

SECTION ONE
WESTWARD EXPANSION AND NATIVE STRUGGLES

"For America, the period of 1800 to 1920 was an unparalleled time of broad expansion and growth driven by extraordinary factors unlike almost any other in history." – Philip Anschutz

HOMESTEADING AND RAILROADS

Once the shooting stopped, the West began drawing people. The Homestead Act in 1862 opened the door—any adult who hadn't fought against the Union could take 160 acres. Live there five years, work the land, build something on it, and it was yours. Families who'd lost so much in the war saw a chance to try again. They sold whatever they had, got a wagon and oxen or mules, and headed out.

There were thousands of families like that. One from Illinois—the father had come home from the fighting with an arm missing. The mother held the family together, reading from the Bible on nights when the wind across the prairie sounded lonely. They rolled west with other wagons. Rivers flooded and almost took them. Fever hit one of the children—they buried her beside the trail and went on. Dust storms covered the ruts until they could barely make out the path. When they got to Nebraska, the land went on forever, grass and sky, no fences in sight.

They cut blocks of sod for a house, dug a well by hand, and planted corn. Winters froze them, and summers dried everything out. But they stuck it out for five years. The land was theirs. They ran cattle and helped get a school going for the kids. Those 160 acres became home, then something to hand down.

Barbed wire changed the plains. Before it, fencing wide-open land meant hauling wood or stone—too expensive for most. In 1874, Joseph Glidden patented a wire with sharp points twisted in. It was cheap and easy to put up. Farmers fenced crops to keep cattle out. Ranchers fenced to keep stock in. The big open range started closing. More people settled, stayed put. But it caused fights—cowboys snipping wire in the dark, farmers keeping watch with guns. The West was settling down, but it wasn't always quiet.

The railroads connected everything. After the golden spike in 1869 at Promontory Summit, tracks spread fast. Trips that took months by wagon now took days by train. A farmer in Kansas could ship grain east and get tools or fabric back quickly. Richard Sears caught on to that. He started selling watches by mail in 1886, then clothes, furniture, and even houses in kits you assembled yourself. The Sears catalog arrived on porches out west, full of pictures of things people had never seen in local stores. Mothers ordered dresses for kids who'd outgrown everything. Fathers got better plows. It made the world feel smaller and gave ordinary people more to hope for.

Those rails and wire took the flame west. People coming out of the war with nothing found space to start fresh, to make a life on the land they owned. The country grew in miles and in chances for regular folks.

Growth hurt too. Native tribes who'd lived on the plains forever watched the buffalo disappear, land sliced up with fences, their way of life pushed aside. The story wasn't finished—far from it. The flame burned brighter for many people, but it left longer shadows for others.

NATIVE RESISTANCE AND TRAGEDY

The Trail of Tears wasn't the end of it. As settlers pushed farther west, more tribes were forced from the land their people had known for thousands of years. Some tribes had built sophisticated ways of living—the Iroquois, for instance, had a confederacy with laws that influenced the founders when they wrote the Constitution. Our histories crossed paths early on, sometimes in cooperation, sometimes in conflict. But expansion rolled on, driven by the belief in manifest destiny, and with it came the taking of resources and the pushback that followed.

Many tribes fought hard to keep what was theirs. Some battles were fierce on both sides. Others tried peace until there was no choice left. In the end, most were moved to reservations—land set aside, often far from home, smaller than what they'd had, harder to live on. The cost was heavy.

In June 1876, along the Little Bighorn River in Montana, George Armstrong Custer led his 7th Cavalry into a fight he didn't expect to lose. He'd split his men, riding fast to attack a village of Lakota, Cheyenne, and Arapaho. Sitting Bull had seen it coming in a vision—a great victory for his people. Crazy Horse led the warriors out to meet them. Custer's five companies were surrounded on a hill, cut off, overwhelmed. In less than an hour, it was over. Custer and more than 260 of his men lay dead. The tribes called it a triumph. The newspapers back east called it a massacre. It shocked the country and brought more troops west. Within a year, the Great Sioux Reservation was broken up, and the Black Hills were taken for gold.

Sitting Bull, the Hunkpapa Lakota holy man, had helped bring the tribes together. He was no warmonger—he fasted and prayed for his people's future. Crazy Horse fought like lightning, leading charges that broke the cavalry lines. He never signed a treaty, never lived on a reservation while he had breath. He was killed in 1877, bayoneted while under arrest, still refusing to give in.

Chief Joseph of the Nez Perce tried another way. When the government demanded his people leave the Wallowa Valley in Oregon, he led them on a retreat—1,170 miles through mountains and canyons, fighting off pursuing armies the whole way. His warriors outmaneuvered larger forces again and again, protecting women, children, and older people. Close to Canada, close to freedom, they were surrounded. Joseph surrendered with words that still ring: "I will fight no more forever." He wanted his people to live.

Geronimo, the Apache leader, kept fighting longer. For years, he raided across Arizona and New Mexico, slipping away from thousands of soldiers with a small band. He knew every canyon, every water hole. Captured, escaped, captured again. Finally, in 1886, he laid down his rifle, the last major chief to surrender. He spent the rest of his life as a prisoner of war, but his name became a symbol of never giving up.

Settlers and railroads hunted buffalo almost to nothing. The herds that once darkened the plains for days were shot for hides, tongues, sometimes just for sport from train windows. Millions gone in a few decades. For tribes like the Lakota and Cheyenne, buffalo were everything—food, clothing, shelter, tools.

When the buffalo vanished, starvation followed. It broke a way of life.

One Lakota family watched the last big herd pass through their hunting grounds in the early 1880s. The father took his son out to hunt, but the animals were few and skittish. They came home empty. That winter, the government rations were late. The boy grew thin. The mother sang old songs to keep spirits up, but the songs felt hollow without the thunder of hooves. They moved to the reservation, the father's rifle taken away. The boy grew up remembering stories of when the plains were alive.

The West was won, but at a cost few settlers fully understood. Tribes lost land, language, and freedom. The country gained space and resources but carried a debt that still echoes. We owe them recognition—their laws helped shape ours, and their courage in defending home mirrors the spirit that founded the nation. Their stories remind us that liberty isn't free, and it's never just for some.

The ancient Native American traditions still live on in tribes all over the country. To keep the heritage alive, they gather, dance, hold ritual peyote meetings, and hunt in the old ways. Stories and culture are still passed down to new generations, preserving the legacy. Many tribes have won the political fight in different ways, building huge casinos that generate millions in revenue. Others still struggle in the dirt fields of Oklahoma and New Mexico. But the culture lives on, and we all owe a huge debt to those who came before us.

"On the Native American front, we have turned a new page in the 400-year history of the interface between the American settlers of this country and the nation's first Americans. That's included a new relationship where the sovereignty of tribes is in fact recognized." – Ken Salazar

Early Native American tribes had displaced one another over centuries, often through warfare, and captives were sometimes enslaved or absorbed. Before the Europeans arrived in large numbers, Native American history was dynamic, marked by alliances, trade, and conflict. The region was not empty or peacefully shared before Europeans arrived. Conquest and displacement, and Native Americans enslaving other Native Americans, were part of human history across the continent, just as they were in Europe, Asia, and Africa. This does not excuse U.S. actions in the 19th century, the broken treaties, forced removals, and massacres, but it tells the complete story.

For this moment in history, the flame spread west, lighting new lives for millions. But it burned hot for those already there. The nation grew, stronger in some ways, scarred in others. The light was brighter, but the shadows deeper.

SECTION TWO
INNOVATIONS AND CULTURAL SHIFTS

LATE 19TH CENTURY LEAPS IN TECHNOLOGY AND CULTURE

Now that the war was finally becoming a more distant memory, the country was starting to catch its breath. People who had lived through it all wanted to look forward, to feel like things could get better. Progress started showing up in small ways at first, then bigger ones. The world of technology was about to explode in ways never seen before.

But politics still played a considerable part in people's lives. Susan B. Anthony had been fighting for women to have a voice for years. She believed that if men could vote, women should too. In 1872, she walked into a polling place in Rochester, New York, and cast a ballot. She knew it was against the law. They arrested her, put her on trial. The judge fined her $100—she refused to pay it. She said it was her duty to demand the same rights men had. Her case made people talk, stirred things up. She spent the rest of her life speaking, organizing, never backing down. She didn't live to see women vote, but she helped make it happen.

Alexander Graham Bell came from Scotland with an idea to help deaf people. His mother and wife were deaf, so he understood the silence they lived in. In 1876, he spoke the first words into a telephone: "Mr. Watson, come here, I want to see you." That scratchy voice went over wires and changed things fast. Families could talk across miles. Businesses connected quicker. The world felt a little smaller.

Thomas Edison took the idea of the lightbulb and made it work in real life. He tried thousands of materials until he found one that lasted. In 1879, he lit a bulb that burned for days. He built power plants, ran wires, and brought light to homes and streets. Nights weren't dark anymore. People could read longer and work later. Cities started to glow.

Nikola Tesla came along and pushed it further. He worked with Edison for a while, then went his own way. He believed that alternating current was better for transmitting power over long distances. He fought Edison's direct current system and won with Westinghouse. AC became the standard. Tesla's ideas lit up the future, even if he ended up dying poor and alone. But his name will live on for decades to come because of Elon Musk, electric vehicles, AI chips, and robots.

The telephone and lightbulb opened new doors. Edison's phonograph started capturing voices and music. Moving pictures came next. By the 1890s, people gathered in theaters to watch short films flicker on screens—faces moving, stories told without words. Vaudeville brought live shows featuring singers, dancers, and comedians.

Broadway theaters filled with plays and musicals. Jazz and blues grew out of the South, from spirituals and work songs, carrying pain and joy in the same breath. America was finding its own voice.

My grandmother, Audrey Athey Sisler, was born in 1889. She came into a world without cars or airplanes. At ten, she saw her first lightbulb and couldn't believe the room stayed bright without a flame. She lived through it all to the ripe old age of 94—from covered wagons to men walking on the moon. That generation saw more change than any before.

Andrew Carnegie built his life on steel. His mills in Pittsburgh made rails, bridges, and skyscrapers. Steel was cheap and strong. Cities grew tall. The Brooklyn Bridge, the Eiffel Tower, the first big buildings—all possible because of what Carnegie's steel allowed. He made a fortune, then gave most of it away—libraries, universities, peace funds. He believed that if you had wealth, you had responsibility. This reminds me of my friend, T. Denny Sanford. He's a billionaire today who has been giving away most of his fortune to great causes.

These changes showed the country healing and reaching forward. The flame burned brighter, lighting new paths. But shadows of injustice still lingered, waiting for the next generation to face them.

IMMIGRATION, ASSIMILATION, AND CONSTITUTIONAL BOUNDARIES THE ERA OF GROVER CLEVELAND

In 1884, France sent a gift—a huge statue of a woman holding a torch, meant to welcome people coming to a land of promise. The Statue of Liberty was ready to stand in New York Harbor, but the pedestal wasn't finished. Joseph Pulitzer, the newspaperman, stepped in. He ran a campaign in his paper, asking everyday Americans to give what they could. Kids sent pennies, families sent dollars. Thousands of small gifts added up. The pedestal was built, and the statue was raised. Emma Lazarus wrote the words for it: "Give me your tired, your poor, your huddled masses yearning to breathe free." She believed America was a place where the oppressed could come and start over, a promise rooted in faith that God made all people equal.

Ellis Island opened in 1892, and immigrants poured in—millions from Europe, Ireland, Italy, Germany, Eastern Europe. They came with little, hoping for more. A young man from Italy might arrive with nothing but a suitcase and a name. He'd find work in factories or mines, learn English, and save for a home. His children would go to school, speak without an accent, and live better than he ever did. Assimilation wasn't easy—it took courage to leave home, learn new ways, and blend into a country that wasn't always welcoming. But most did it, and they became American.

My other grandmother, Gizella Adorjan Witt, came through Ellis Island in 1914 with her parents when she was just eight. They spoke limited English. Her father found work in Chicago. Gizella went to school, learned the language, and later married my grandfather. She kept her Hungarian traditions—cooking, songs, faith—but she became fully American. That was the way it worked for so many. They became American—not by forgetting where they came from, but by assimilating into what America already was.

Legal immigration has been part of our story from the beginning. It's how the country grew, how new blood and ideas came in. But it must mean joining the family—learning the language, respecting the laws, becoming part of the nation. When it's done right, it strengthens everyone.

"America is woven of many strands. I would recognise them and let it so remain. Our fate is to become one, and yet many. This is not prophecy, but description."
– Ralph Ellison

Grover Cleveland was president during those years—1885 to 1889, then again 1893 to 1897. He was the only president to serve two non-consecutive terms until Donald J. Trump. Cleveland was a plain man, a former sheriff and mayor from Buffalo. He didn't like the government doing too much. He vetoed bills that overstepped, believed in sound money, and kept the Constitution's boundaries. When Congress tried to give pensions to people who didn't need them, he said no. He thought the government should do what it was meant to do and nothing more.

Frances Cleveland, his wife, was the youngest First Lady ever, twenty-one when he married her. She brought warmth to the White House, opened it to visitors, and made it feel like a home. She supported her husband's belief in limited government and stood by him through tough times. Together, they showed that leadership could be steady and decent.

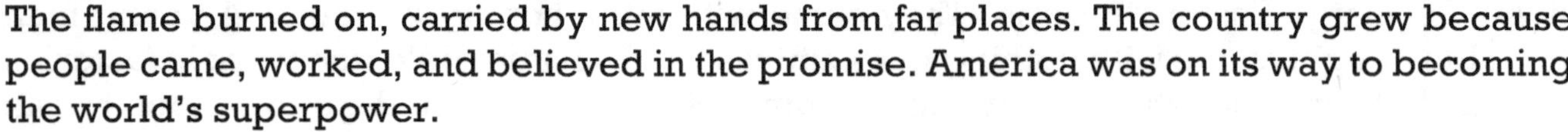

The flame burned on, carried by new hands from far places. The country grew because people came, worked, and believed in the promise. America was on its way to becoming the world's superpower.

The innovations and expansions of the late 19th century fueled America's growth. Still, they also highlighted ongoing struggles for justice—leading to the perils of dependency in the 20th century, where good intentions often led to overreach.

CHAPTER TEN
NETS OF DEPENDENCY

SAFETY MEASURES TURNED TRAPS

The Civil War was now behind us by 25 years. The amendments had been signed and slavery was removed from the law. The country was back on its feet—rails connecting coasts, factories running again, lights starting to burn through the night. People felt progress in the air, like things could finally move forward. But somewhere along the way, good intentions began to twist into something heavier. Woodrow Wilson took the first big step toward putting more power in Washington's hands. During World War I, he expanded government control over industry, railroads, food, and even what people could say. It was ostensibly meant to help win the war, but it set a pattern that would keep growing. Then, in 1935, another president promised security from cradle to grave. What started as help became chains for many people, a web that tangled across generations and cost trillions. This chapter examines how those expansions occurred—through leaders with big visions that sometimes went too far. Their stories remind us that freedom lives when people stand on their own, and liberty can slip away quietly when we hand too much to distant hands.

"The bigger the state, the smaller the citizen." – Margaret Thatcher

SECTION ONE
EARLY EXPANSIONS

The late 1800s and early 1900s were when America really started to change shape. The internal combustion engine was still new, but Henry Ford saw what it could do. He didn't invent the car—he made it something that even regular people could own. The Model T automobile came out in 1908. It was simple, tough, and cheap. He was the first to build assembly lines where workers put cars together piece by piece, fast. Before Ford, a car was a luxury for the rich. Afterward, it was a tool for everyday life. People could live farther from work, visit family across states, and see places they'd only heard about. The internal combustion engine itself hasn't changed much since then—just gotten better at doing what it does (and harder to fix with all of the computerized add-ons!).

Oil changed everything, too. In 1901, at a place called Spindletop in Texas, a drill hit a gusher. Oil shot a hundred feet into the air. It was the biggest strike anyone had seen.

Big companies grew fast—Standard Oil, then others like Texaco and Gulf. America had fuel for cars, machines, and homes. The country ran on it, grew on it. Oil meant jobs, power, and independence from foreign supplies. It was a gift that helped build the modern world.

Until the 19th and 20th centuries, the world felt too big. Back in the mid-1800s, if you wanted to get from one part of the country to another, you were looking at months of travel—wagons bumping along dirt roads, hoping the weather didn't turn on you. Then steamboats changed that. They started chugging up and down the rivers, carrying people and goods faster than any wagon ever could. You could load up on a boat in New Orleans and be in St. Louis in days instead of weeks. It opened up the country in a way people hadn't seen before.

"America - it is a fabulous country, the only fabulous country; it is the only place where miracles not only happen, but where they happen all the time."
– Thomas Wolfe

But the railroads took it to another level. Once they laid tracks coast to coast—starting in the 1860s and really picking up after the war—everything sped up. You could board a train in New York and step off in California in less than a week. Goods that used to take months to move now arrived in days. Farmers could ship their crops to big cities without them spoiling. Families could visit relatives hundreds of miles away without it being a once-in-a-lifetime trip. The railroads didn't just move people—they moved ideas, goods, and possibilities.

Then airplanes came along in the early 1900s. The Wright brothers got off the ground in 1903, and within a few decades, you could fly across the country in hours. Distance shrank even more. Mass communication did the same thing—telegraph wires in the 1800s let messages cross the country in minutes instead of days. The telephone let you talk to someone on the other side of the continent like they were in the next room. Radio brought voices and music into homes everywhere, and, eventually, television followed.

It all added up to something simple: the country got smaller. What used to take months now took hours or minutes. Commerce sped up—businesses could buy and sell across the continent without waiting. People could live farther from work, from family, from cities, and still stay connected.

The world opened up in ways that felt almost impossible before. It wasn't just about getting places faster—it was about giving regular people more freedom to build the lives they wanted.

In the opening quarter of the 20th century, from 1900 to 1925, America saw steady growth in church membership as waves of immigrants brought their faiths, and revivals stirred hearts in rural and urban areas alike. Leaders like Dwight L. Moody's influence lingered from earlier days, while new voices emerged in Pentecostal movements that emphasized personal encounters with God. Yet skepticism crept in, too, as figures in the Scopes Trial era questioned literalist interpretations of the Bible, sowing seeds of doubt for some. Overall, faith felt woven into daily life, with churches often at the center of community gatherings.

Professional football started in the 1890s, a game that grew into something uniquely American—tough, team-driven, full of strategy and heart. It gave people something to cheer for, a shared story on Sundays.

THE BIRTH OF CINEMA AND THE SILENT ERA

With Edison's invention, moving pictures were a brand-new wonder, flickering to life in nickelodeons and fairgrounds. Films were silent—black-and-white images on celluloid, accompanied by live piano music or orchestras in bigger theaters, with title cards flashing dialogue to keep the story moving. Early shorts gave way to longer features, telling tales of adventure, romance, and comedy through expressive faces and grand gestures. Hollywood emerged as the hub, drawing dreamers west for sunshine and space. Independent producers and early moguls like Adolph Zukor (who founded Paramount) and Carl Laemmle (Universal) built empires, fighting patents and creating the star system to pull crowds. The biggest draws were Charlie Chaplin, whose Tramp tugged at hearts worldwide; Mary Pickford, America's sweetheart with her curls and innocence; Douglas Fairbanks, the swashbuckling hero leaping across screens; Rudolph Valentino, the smoldering Latin lover; and Buster Keaton, the stone-faced genius of physical comedy. Scandals rocked the young industry, but the magic held—movies became a shared escape, planting seeds for the dream factory ahead.

George Washington Carver was born into slavery around 1864, but he wouldn't stay down. He taught himself to read, worked his way through school, and became a scientist at Tuskegee Institute. He saw Southern farmers struggling, soil worn out from cotton. He studied peanuts and sweet potatoes—crops that replenish nitrogen in the soil. He found hundreds of ways to use them—food, oils, dyes. His work helped farmers grow something new, something better. Carver believed God gave him a mind to help people. He worked long hours in his lab, often alone, driven by faith that knowledge could lift folks up.

The women's suffrage movement grew strong. Women wanted the vote, the same rights men had. They marched, spoke, and went to jail. Clothing manufacturing boomed—looms that once wove cloth by hand now ran fast in factories. Mass-produced clothes meant more people could afford them. Those looms were early ancestors of modern computers—machines that followed patterns, step by step. It all led to the 19th Amendment in 1920—women could vote.

William McKinley was president in the late 1890s. He led the country through the Spanish-American War, expanding American influence in Puerto Rico, Guam, and the Philippines. He used tariffs to protect American workers. In 1901, he was shot by an anarchist. He died eight days later. Theodore Roosevelt, his vice president, became president at forty-two—the youngest ever.

The flame of liberty kept burning, carried forward by people who dreamed big and worked hard. The country grew, changed, and reached for more.

THE TRAGEDY OF THE USS MAINE

Imagine it's a quiet evening in February 1898, and the American battleship USS Maine sits peacefully at anchor in Havana Harbor, Cuba. The ship had arrived just weeks earlier to protect American interests amid growing unrest as Cubans fought for independence from Spanish rule.

Her captain, Charles Dwight Sigsbee, a steady and experienced officer, commands a crew of about 350 sailors and Marines—many young men far from home, writing letters or turning in for the night.

Suddenly, at 9:40 p.m. on February 15, a massive explosion rips through the forward part of the ship. Flames shoot skyward, steel twists like paper, and the Maine sinks quickly into the harbor. More than 260 men perish that night—mostly enlisted sailors sleeping in the front quarters—while Captain Sigsbee and many officers survive from their aft cabins. Sigsbee sends a calm telegram urging the public to wait for facts, but the nation reels in shock and grief.

What caused it? A U.S. inquiry soon blames an external mine, pointing the finger at Spain, though no clear proof emerges, and later studies suggest it might have been an accidental coal bunker fire that ignited the magazines. But in that heated moment, the truth takes a back seat.

Powerful newspaper owners like William Randolph Hearst and Joseph Pulitzer seize the story with screaming headlines, dramatic drawings, and unproven claims of Spanish treachery—what we now call yellow journalism. Their papers whip up outrage across the country.

Soon, crowds chant the rallying cry: "Remember the Maine! To hell with Spain!" It echoes in streets and speeches, fueling demands for action. This patriotic fervor matched the same level of outrage Americans felt after later events like Pearl Harbor and 9/11. Just months later, in April 1898, that cry helps push America into the Spanish-American War—a conflict that changes the nation's path forever. To this day, you can view the mast of the Maine and pay respect to the remains of its soldiers at Arlington National Cemetery.

The U.S. S. Maine's tragedy beame a spark, reminding us how grief and words can ignite something far bigger. The standout heroes of the Spanish-American War in 1898 were Admiral George Dewey, who achieved overnight fame with his decisive destruction of the Spanish fleet at the Battle of Manila Bay—uttering the calm command "You may fire when you are ready, Gridley"—and Theodore Roosevelt, who resigned as Assistant Secretary of the Navy to lead the Rough Riders volunteer cavalry in a daring charge up San Juan Hill (often remembered alongside Kettle Hill) in Cuba, turning him into a national icon through his own vivid writings and relentless self-promotion.

Dewey's triumph earned him promotion to Admiral of the Navy (a rank created especially for him), massive parades, and serious urging to run for president in 1900. However, he declined after some awkward political statements, choosing instead to serve as president of the Navy's General Board.

Roosevelt's battlefield glory propelled him even further: returning home a celebrated warrior, he was elected governor of New York later that year, became vice president in 1900, and ascended to the presidency in 1901 after McKinley's assassination, using his war-hero status to fuel a dynamic political career marked by reform and international assertiveness. Their exploits not only shortened the war but also elevated America's global standing, showing how personal courage in a brief conflict could launch lasting political legacies.

THE GIANT WHO WAS THEODORE ROOSEVELT

"The things that will destroy America are prosperity-at-any-price, peace-at-any-price, safety-first instead of duty-first, the love of soft living, and the get-rich-quick theory of life." – Theodore Roosevelt

Theodore Roosevelt took office as president in 1901 after McKinley was assassinated. He was forty-two—the youngest we've ever had. He'd been a rancher out West, a soldier who charged up San Juan Hill, a writer, even New York's police commissioner. He had this big, loud presence—always moving, always talking, with a big laugh that filled a room. People either loved him or couldn't stand him, but nobody ignored him.

He thought big companies sometimes got too powerful. He went after the monopolies—the trusts that controlled whole industries. He used the Sherman Antitrust Act, which had been on the books since 1890, to break them up. He sued Northern Securities, a huge railroad trust, and won. It sent a message: no company was above the law. He called it the Square Deal—fair play for workers, fair prices for consumers, fair treatment all around. He wasn't against business; he just didn't want it to hurt ordinary people.

One of his biggest moves was the construction of the Panama Canal. The French had tried and failed—thousands died from disease. Roosevelt wanted a canal to connect the oceans, speed up trade, and give the Navy quicker routes. He helped Panama break from Colombia, then signed the deal. Construction started in 1904. Workers dug through the jungle, fought malaria and yellow fever. More than twenty thousand died, mostly from sickness. But in 1914, the canal opened. Ships could travel from New York to San Francisco in weeks rather than months. It opened up new trade, new possibilities, and new strength for the country.

THE SCOURGE OF COMMUNISM

While America was growing, trouble was brewing across the ocean. In 1917, the Bolsheviks took power in Russia. They murdered the Czar and his family, overturning a centuries-old monarchy. They promised a workers' paradise, but it turned out to be something else. Communism spread, and where it went, millions died—famine, purges, gulags. It was a system that put the state above the individual, sacrificing freedom for "the collective." It never aligned with the liberty our republic was built on—government serving people, not the other way around. And although plenty was promised for everyone, only the party bosses and oligarchs actually experienced plenty. The rest of the masses were thrown into poverty and were picking at the scraps.

Socialism often starts with promises of fairness and equality, but it tends to morph into something darker—communism—by stoking resentment and envy among people. It paints a picture where the "haves" are villains hoarding resources, while the "have-nots" are victims deserving more, handed out by the state. This narrative divides society, justifying the seizure of power and property in the name of justice. But as history shows, once that envy takes root, it leads to control, suppression, and unimaginable suffering. It's not just theory; this progression has shattered millions upon millions of real lives, and we're seeing its echoes today.

"Free people, remember this maxim: we may acquire liberty, but it is never recovered if it is once lost." – Jean-Jacques Rousseau

Let me tell you about the horrors under Soviet communism, starting with Lenin. In 1917, after the Bolshevik Revolution, Lenin seized power and unleashed the Red Terror in 1918, a brutal campaign to crush anyone seen as a threat to the new regime. His secret police, the Cheka, rounded up dissidents, clergy, and ordinary folks labeled "class enemies," executing tens of thousands—possibly over a million by 1922—in mass killings and detentions. Families were torn apart, people shot without trial, all to solidify communist control. Then came Stalin in the 1920s, who ramped it up to nightmarish levels. His Great Purge from 1936 to 1938 saw at least 750,000 people executed for imagined disloyalty, with millions more sent to the Gulags—forced labor camps where they froze, starved, and worked to death. Aleksandr Solzhenitsyn, who survived those camps, detailed the soul-crushing brutality in "The Gulag Archipelago": arbitrary arrests for a joke or a letter, torture to extract false confessions, and a system that treated humans like disposable tools. He described prisoners enduring starvation, beatings, and psychological torment, with estimates of up to 20 million perishing in the Gulags overall. It's heartbreaking—families vanishing overnight, children orphaned, all because envy-fueled ideology demanded total obedience. Comedian Konstantin Kisin, whose family fled the Soviet Union, shares how his grandparents suffered under this regime, emphasizing that communism's promise of equality always devolves into terror because it ignores human nature and breeds paranoia. The pain lingers; over 60 million died under Soviet rule, a staggering loss that still haunts survivors and their descendants.

J. EDGAR HOOVER'S F.B.I.

Back home, Roosevelt's administration started the FBI. In 1908, Attorney General Charles Bonaparte created the Bureau of Investigation—a small group of agents to handle federal crimes. It was later renamed the Federal Bureau of Investigation in 1935. At first, it was about fighting corruption and lawlessness. It grew into something bigger, but its roots were in the idea that the government needed tools to protect the country without overstepping.

For nearly half a century, one man held more real power in Washington than most presidents. His name was J. Edgar Hoover, and from 1924 until he died in 1972, he ruled the Federal Bureau of Investigation like a king.

Hoover was only 29 years old when he was appointed Director of what was then called the Bureau of Investigation. At the time, the agency was small, corrupt, and widely considered ineffective. Hoover changed all of that. He professionalized the FBI, created the first national fingerprint database, established rigorous training standards, and built one of the most sophisticated law enforcement organizations in the world.

But Hoover's power went far beyond catching bank robbers and gangsters. He understood something very few people in government understood at the time: information is power. Under his iron grip, the FBI became a vast intelligence-gathering machine. He maintained secret files on thousands of Americans — politicians, movie stars, civil rights leaders, journalists, and even presidents. These weren't just personnel records. They contained deeply personal, often damaging information that Hoover could use when needed.

Hoover was a ferocious anti-communist. Long before Senator Joe McCarthy rose to prominence, Hoover was warning America about the threat of Soviet infiltration. He viewed communism not just as a political ideology, but as an existential danger to the United States. During the Cold War, he aggressively pursued communists, spies, and fellow travelers through programs like COINTELPRO, which targeted not only suspected communists but also civil rights groups, anti-war activists, and Black nationalist organizations.

At the height of his power, Hoover was practically untouchable. Presidents feared him. Members of Congress treaded carefully around him. He served under eight presidents — from Calvin Coolidge to Richard Nixon — and outlasted them all. Some presidents tried to rein him in, but none succeeded. He had simply become too powerful, too entrenched, and too knowledgeable about the secrets of the powerful.

While Hoover's legacy is deeply complex, many have long respected his unwavering commitment to fighting communism and organized crime during some of the most dangerous periods in American history. He helped protect the nation from real internal threats during the Red Scare and the Cold War. However, his methods often crossed serious ethical and legal lines. He operated in a shadowy world where the ends frequently justified the means, and where accountability was almost nonexistent.

When Hoover finally died in May 1972 at age 77, it marked the end of an era. The man who had built the FBI into a legendary institution had also become a symbol of unchecked government power. His life remains a cautionary tale about how dangerous it can be when one man holds too much power for too long in the name of protecting the country. And we've seen that overreach, pushing the limits of power to weaponize government in other FBI leaders including James Comey and Christopher Wray.

Roosevelt was a force—considerable energy, big ideas. He expanded the presidency's reach, but he did it with a belief in fairness and strength. He loved the country, believed in its promise, and wanted to see it live up to it.

He wasn't perfect, but he left a mark that's still felt.

The flame of liberty burned on, carried forward by leaders like him who tried to balance progress with principle. But the seeds of overreach were planted too, waiting for later years to grow.

OLIVER WENDELL HOLMES

Imagine a young man born in Boston on March 8, 1841, into a family where intellect ran deep—his father, Oliver Wendell Holmes Sr., was a respected doctor and author who shaped the cultural scene. This young man, Oliver Wendell Holmes Jr., attended Harvard and graduated in 1861, just as the Civil War began. He joined the fight as a Union officer and was wounded three times, experiences that hardened him and shaped a pragmatic view of life where reality overrode ideals. After the war, he earned a law degree from Harvard in 1866, practiced briefly, and found his true path as a scholar—editing the American Law Review and publishing his influential book, The Common Law, in 1881. He taught at Harvard, served on the Massachusetts Supreme Judicial Court from 1882 to 1902, rising to chief justice in 1899. In 1902, Theodore Roosevelt appointed him to the U.S. Supreme Court, where he served until his retirement on January 12, 1932. He died on March 6, 1935, in Washington, D.C., just short of his 94th birthday.

Holmes stood out as more than an ordinary judge; he became known as the "Great Dissenter" for his incisive minority opinions that later influenced the court's direction, particularly in free speech cases. In Schenck v. United States in 1919, he introduced the "clear and present danger" test, which reshaped First Amendment protections. He advocated for judicial restraint, urging courts to defer to legislatures unless fundamental rights were violated. As a pioneer of legal realism, he argued that law evolved with society rather than remaining fixed in logic. His famous line from The Common Law—"the life of the law has not been logic; it has been experience"—shifted legal thought from rigid formalism to a more flexible approach. During key periods like the Progressive Era and the New Deal, his decisions helped modernize constitutional interpretation, and his Civil War experiences reinforced his sense of duty, solidifying his place as one of the most influential figures in American jurisprudence.

Before my wife, Stephanie, died, she spoke often of her grandfather, who raised her. Ambrose Haddock was New York's first policeman who rose from the ranks to become a judge, ruling on many, at times controversial, cases in the early 20th century. Haddock worked closely with Mayor Fiorello La Guardia. Judge Haddock often spoke about the decisions he made in court. His view was that, to reach court, both parties had to have done something wrong, and his job was to determine which party was the least wrong, most of the time.

Once, he was tasked with an order to remove all of the mob-based gambling machines in facilities all over New York City. Mayor LaGuardia knew that corruption existed and the mafia would most likely be able to recover the machines and put them back into service, so, at the mayor's request, Judge Haddock ordered the machines to be seized and dumped into New York Harbor. Stephanie told me that, more than once, cars would shoot randomly into Judge Haddock's home in the Bronx when she was a girl, and she remembered hiding many times from the gunfire. Still, Judge Haddock, like Justice Holmes, believed deeply in the tenets of free speech, even if it was something we didn't want to hear.

"I think that we should be eternally vigilant against attempts to check the expression of opinions that we loathe and believe to be fraught with death, unless they so imminently threaten immediate interference with the lawful and pressing purposes of the law that an immediate check is required to save the country."
– Oliver Wendell Holmes, Jr.

WILLIAM HOWARD TAFT AND THE ERA OF GENIUS

William Howard Taft succeeded Roosevelt as president in 1909. He was a big man—over three hundred pounds—with a quiet way about him. He'd been a judge, a governor in the Philippines, Roosevelt's secretary of war. Roosevelt selected him to continue his work. Taft kept busting trusts and breaking up more monopolies than Roosevelt did. He pursued Standard Oil and American Tobacco and won significant cases. He believed in the law above all. Later, when he became Chief Justice in 1921, he shaped how the Constitution was read, always careful, always steady. He wasn't flashy like Roosevelt, but he got things done.

OTHER NOTABLE AMERICANS OF THIS PERIOD

Booker T. Washington was born into slavery in 1856. He walked five hundred miles to school, slept in abandoned buildings, and worked his way through Hampton Institute. He founded Tuskegee Institute in Alabama, teaching Black students trades—farming, carpentry, teaching—so they could stand on their own. He believed hard work and self-reliance would lift people. He spoke at the Atlanta Exposition in 1895, saying Black people should focus on economic progress first, not political rights right away. Some criticized him for it, but he saw it as the practical path. He met presidents, dined at the White House, and showed the country what Black Americans could do when given a chance.

J.P. Morgan was a financier who stepped in during the Panic of 1907. Banks were failing, and people were withdrawing money. Morgan locked bankers in his library until they agreed to pool funds to save the system. He didn't do it for glory—he saw the country could collapse if it weren't fixed. His actions helped stabilize things, showed how private power could serve the public good when government couldn't move fast enough.

Louis Brandeis was the first Jewish Supreme Court justice, nominated in 1916. He fought for working people—long hours, low pay, unsafe conditions. He wrote about privacy rights and economic justice. He drew from his faith and from seeing how big business could hurt ordinary folks. He believed the law should protect the individual, not just the powerful.

Irving Berlin came to the United States as a child, poor and speaking no English. He wrote songs—"God Bless America," "White Christmas." His music brought people together during wars and reminded them of what they were fighting for. He lived the immigrant story—hard work, talent, turning nothing into something that touched millions. Berlin lived to the ripe old age of 101, receiving an Academy Award, a Tony Award, and a Grammy. He also received the Presidential Medal of Freedom from Gerald R. Ford in 1977.

Colonel George Waring cleaned up New York City in the 1890s. Streets were filthy, and disease was spreading. He organized sanitation—clean water, proper sewers. It cut cholera and typhoid. Life expectancy rose dramatically simply from clean water and sanitary conditions.

WILLIAM MULHOLLAND

William Mulholland was an Irish immigrant who arrived in America with almost nothing. He started as a ditch digger for the Los Angeles water company in the 1870s, working his way up through sheer grit and a sharp mind. By the early 1900s, he was the chief engineer, and he saw the city's biggest problem: Los Angeles was in a desert, growing fast, but running out of water.

He came up with a bold plan—to bring water from the Owens Valley, more than two hundred miles away, across mountains, canyons, and dry land. The Owens Valley was fertile, fed by Sierra Nevada snowmelt, but getting the water to LA would mean building one of the most significant engineering projects of the time. The aqueduct would be 233 miles long, carrying water through tunnels, over siphons, across valleys, and into the city. Mulholland spent years surveying, designing, and convincing people it could be done. He faced opposition—farmers in Owens Valley fought to keep their water, lawsuits piled up, and the project cost millions. But he pushed forward. Construction began in 1908. Workers blasted tunnels through solid rock, built massive concrete conduits, and laid pipe across rugged terrain. They used gravity—no pumps—to move the water downhill most of the way. The longest tunnel was five miles through the mountains. They lost men to accidents, heat, and dynamite, but the work never stopped.

In November 1913, the water finally arrived. Mulholland stood at the end of the line with a crowd of thousands. He turned the valve, and the water poured in. He looked at the people and said, "There it is—take it." Los Angeles had its water. The city exploded in growth—population jumped, neighborhoods spread, industries thrived. What had been a dusty town became a major city because one man refused to accept that water was impossible to bring.

The Owens Valley paid a high price—its farms dried up, its people lost their livelihoods. Mulholland knew it was a hard choice, but he believed the greater good for millions outweighed the loss for a few. The aqueduct stands today as a testament to vision and determination—proof that bold engineering can turn a desert into a place where people can live and build lives. It's one of those stories where human will and ingenuity reshaped the land itself. But it was a crime to rob the Owens Valley farmers of all their water and resources.

JIM THORPE

Jim Thorpe was born in 1887, a member of the Sac and Fox Nation—two Native tribes from the Great Plains, known for their long history of resilience and strength. He grew up in Oklahoma, facing hardship from the start—his mother died young, and he was sent away to boarding schools where they tried to strip away his culture. But Jim had this incredible natural talent for sports. He could run, jump, throw—do anything better than almost anyone.

In 1912, at the Stockholm Olympics, he competed in the pentathlon and decathlon—two of the toughest events. He won gold in both, setting records that stood for decades. King Gustav of Sweden called him the world's most outstanding athlete. Jim came home a hero, but the glory didn't last. A newspaper dug up that he'd played minor league baseball for a little money years earlier—something common back then. The Olympic committee took his medals away, saying he wasn't an amateur. It crushed him, but he didn't quit.

He went on to play professional football—helping start the NFL, even serving as its first president—and Major League Baseball. He was one of the few to play both sports at the highest level. He faced racism everywhere—fans, teams, the press—but he kept showing up, kept performing. In his later years, he worked in Hollywood, did odd jobs, and struggled with alcohol. But he never stopped being an example of what someone could achieve through sheer ability and heart.

Jim Thorpe broke barriers for Native Americans in sports, showing the country what talent and determination could do, even when the world tried to hold you down. His story reminds us that true greatness isn't about medals—it's about getting up again and again, proving the human spirit can rise above any obstacle.

The flame burned on, carried by people who dreamed big and worked hard. The country grew, changed, and reached for more. But the scourge of a vastly expanded government bureaucracy was about to become a part of life in America.

SECTION TWO
THE ERA OF WILSON BEGINS AMERICA'S ERA OF ENTITLEMENT

WOODROW WILSON'S CENTRALIZATIONS

Picture a quiet evening in 1913. A young factory worker in a small town outside Pittsburgh sits at his kitchen table, counting the few dollars left after a long day on the line. He dreams of building a better life for his family—maybe buying a home, sending his kids to school, or saving enough to start a small shop. That dream feels within reach in the America he knows: a land where hard work and personal responsibility can lift anyone, no matter where they started. But that same year, a shift begins, one that will quietly change the meaning of the American dream for millions. What once stood for boundless opportunity—life, liberty, and the pursuit of happiness—starts to bend toward something new: the promise of government-provided security, where possessions and comfort come from distant powers rather than one's own hands. And that same factory worker will see half of his paycheck disappear from the new income tax.

This change starts with Woodrow Wilson, a man who rose from a quiet life as a Princeton professor to the presidency. Wilson believed in progress through strong, centralized leadership. He saw the old ways—limited government, state power, individual initiative—as outdated. His vision promised to tame big business, protect workers, and guide the nation toward a brighter future. But the steps he took planted seeds of dependency that would grow into the nets we explore in this chapter.

Wilson's first significant act was signing the Federal Reserve Act in 1913. The nation had just come through the Panic of 1907, when banks failed, credit froze, and ordinary people lost savings overnight. Bankers like J.P. Morgan stepped in to stabilize things, but many saw the need for a more reliable system. The Federal Reserve was meant to provide that—a central authority to manage the money supply, prevent panics, and keep the economy steady.

At first, it seemed a practical fix. But over time, this unelected body gained immense power: deciding how much money exists, who gets it first, and how interest rates shape everyday life. When prices rise, ordinary workers feel the pinch most. When large institutions falter, they are often bailed out first. The Founders never imagined such control in the hands of a few distant officials. They feared concentrated power as much as they feared kings.

Yet Wilson, with his belief in expert-guided government, opened the door.

THE SIXTEENTH AND SEVENTEENTH AMENDMENTS

That same year, the Sixteenth Amendment took effect, allowing Congress to tax income without dividing it by state population. The idea sounded fair: steady money for roads, schools, defense—without relying on tariffs that hit the poor hardest. But it gave the federal government a direct claim on every citizen's earnings. What began as a tool for limited needs soon fueled endless expansion. Trillions flowed through Washington, often wasted or diverted, eroding the self-reliance that once defined America.

"Man is not free unless government is limited." – Ronald Reagan

The Seventeenth Amendment was also passed in 1913, shifting the election of senators from state legislatures to direct popular vote. Corruption had tainted the old system—bribes and scandals where money bought seats. Reformers hoped direct elections would make senators accountable to the people. Yet it removed another safeguard: states' ability to check federal overreach. Senators now answered more to national interests and moneyed influence than to the states they were meant to represent.

THE FIRST WORLD WAR

Woodrow Wilson led America into World War I, a conflict that claimed over 100,000 American lives. My own great-uncle served as a chaplain in the trenches, bringing comfort to dying men amid the mud and chaos. Like so many others, he never came home. His story, whispered in family letters, reminds us that behind every statistic was a life cut short, a family forever changed. The war reshaped the world, but it also scarred souls in ways few could have imagined. Let's step back and walk through how this terrible storm began, how it drew America in, and how it ended—leaving wounds that would fester for decades.

It started in Europe, on a sunny morning in June 1914. Archduke Franz Ferdinand, heir to the Austro-Hungarian throne, was visiting Sarajevo. A young Serbian nationalist named Gavrilo Princip stepped from a crowd and fired two shots. The archduke and his wife died. That single act ignited a powder keg. Alliances bound nations: Austria-Hungary blamed Serbia and declared war. Russia mobilized to defend Serbia. Germany, allied with Austria-Hungary, declared war on Russia and France. When Germany invaded neutral Belgium to strike France, Britain joined the fight. Within weeks, Europe was ablaze, with millions of men marching to the front.

The fighting soon bogged down into trenches stretching from the North Sea to Switzerland. Soldiers lived in mud, coexisting with rats and in constant fear. Then came the horrors no one had prepared for: chemical weapons. In April 1915, at Ypres, German forces released chlorine gas from cylinders. A yellow-green cloud drifted across the Allied lines, burning lungs, blinding eyes, and choking men who clawed at their throats. Soldiers gasped, "Gas! Gas!" as they fumbled for masks that often failed. Phosgene and mustard gas followed—blistering skin, causing agony that could last for days or years. Flamethrowers, too, appeared on the front lines. Men faced streams of fire that set uniforms ablaze and turned dugouts into infernos. The terror was not just in the killing; it was in the slow, suffocating death or the screams of comrades burned alive.

America watched from afar at first. President Wilson promised neutrality. But German U-boats sank merchant ships, including the Lusitania in 1915, a British liner carrying Americans. Over 1,100 died, including 128 Americans. Public outrage grew. Then, in early 1917, British intelligence intercepted the Zimmermann Telegram: Germany proposed an alliance with Mexico if the U.S. entered the war, promising Mexico the return of lost territories like Texas and Arizona. At the same time, Germany resumed unrestricted submarine warfare, sinking American ships. Wilson could no longer stay out. In April 1917, he asked Congress for war, declaring, "The world must be made safe for democracy."

The American Expeditionary Forces, under General John J. Pershing, arrived in France. Pershing insisted on keeping U.S. troops independent, not scattered as replacements for French and British units. American soldiers—fresh, eager, but green—faced the same horrors: mud, gas, endless artillery. By 1918, over two million Americans were in the fight. The tide turned. Fresh troops and supplies helped break the German lines.

The war ended on November 11, 1918, with an armistice at 11 a.m.—the eleventh hour of the eleventh day of the eleventh month. Guns fell silent. But peace came at a terrible cost. Total casualties: around 20 million dead, including over 8 million civilians. Europe lost more than 10 million soldiers. America suffered 116,000 dead, including 53,000 in battle. The wounded numbered in the millions—many missing limbs, faces scarred by shrapnel, or blinded by gas.

"Freedom is the sure possession of those alone who have the courage to defend it." - Pericles

Prominent generals shaped the war's course. On the Allied side, France's Ferdinand Foch became supreme commander in 1918, coordinating the final push. Britain's Douglas Haig led the British Expeditionary Force through brutal campaigns, including the Battle of the Somme. Pershing commanded American forces with a focus on decisive action. On the German side, Paul von Hindenburg and Erich Ludendorff directed strategy, though their failures in 1918 led to the collapse.

Soldiers who survived returned broken in body and spirit. Many came home maimed—arms or legs gone, faces disfigured. Others suffered "shell shock," an early name for what we now call PTSD. Men trembled uncontrollably, froze at loud noises, or relived horrors in nightmares. Some could not speak or walk, though no physical wound explained it. Doctors once thought it was cowardice; now we know it was trauma etched into the mind. Families welcomed heroes home, but many struggled in silence, haunted by what they had seen. This wasn't unlike the trauma our soldiers faced in previous wars. War is a terrible thing.

The peace treaty, signed at Versailles in 1919, was meant to end war forever. Instead, it sowed seeds of another. Germany was forced to accept full blame for the war, pay massive reparations, lose territory, and shrink its army. Humiliation and economic ruin fueled resentment. Many Germans saw the treaty as a betrayal, paving the way for bitterness that would erupt again in 1939.

World War I was humanity's first taste of modern industrial slaughter. It promised to end all wars but left a legacy of grief, broken bodies, and unresolved anger. Yet in the courage of those who served, the faith that carried them through the darkest days, and the quiet strength of families who waited at home, we see the resilient flame of liberty. It burned low in the trenches, but it never went out. The lessons of that war remind us: freedom demands vigilance, sacrifice, and a commitment to justice that honors every life lost.

The Tomb of the Unknown Soldier at Arlington National Cemetery originated after World War I. Congress approved its creation on March 4, 1921, and an unidentified American soldier from that war was interred there with full honors on November 11, 1921 (Armistice Day), marking the dedication of the initial tomb. This simple marble slab served until the current grand marble sarcophagus and monument were completed and unveiled in 1932. Later additions included unknowns from World War II and the Korean War (interred in 1958), and briefly from the Vietnam War (added in 1984 but identified and removed in 1998). Odds are that we will have no more unknown soldiers in future wars due to DNA technology. We owe a tremendous debt to everyone who served in the Armed Forces of the United States to defend our freedoms.

Following the war, Wilson championed the League of Nations, an idealistic body to prevent future wars. But when the Senate, wary of entangling alliances and loss of sovereignty, rejected it, Wilson refused to compromise. His stubbornness deepened divisions at home.

Then came darker stains. Wilson resegregated federal offices, separating lunchrooms and restrooms by race after decades of integration. He praised the Ku Klux Klan in private writings and screened *The Birth of a Nation*—a film glorifying the Klan—at the White House. During the war, he used the Espionage Act to jail critics, including socialist Eugene Debs, who spoke against the draft. Debs, a man of deep conviction, spent years in prison for words that challenged the government's path.

In 1919, a severe stroke left Wilson incapacitated. His wife, Edith, stepped in, shielding him from visitors and managing access to him. She protected his legacy and decisions with fierce loyalty, acting as a quiet guardian during a time of crisis. Though controversial and beyond constitutional bounds, her devotion showed the strength found in standing by loved ones in hardship.

These actions—centralizing money, taxing income, altering representation, and suppressing dissent—marked a turning point. The American dream, once rooted in personal freedom and self-reliance, began to shift toward reliance on government promises. What followed would entangle generations in webs of dependency, as good intentions paved the way for overreach.

SHOELESS JOE JACKSON

In the autumn of 1919, the United States was still recovering from the Great War. Soldiers came home broken, wounded, and changed; jobs were hard to find, and the Spanish flu had taken loved ones without warning. Prohibition was about to close the saloons, taking away one more simple pleasure. In the middle of all that, the World Series felt like a bright spot—something clean and exciting. The Chicago White Sox were heavy favorites, powered by Shoeless Joe Jackson, a quiet South Carolina mill hand who'd never learned to read but could hit a baseball like few others. His swing was poetry; he played barefoot in the minors because shoes felt wrong. Facing the Cincinnati Reds, most expected an easy Chicago win.

But behind the scenes, something darker unfolded. Gamblers approached eight Sox players, including Joe, with cash to lose on purpose. Joe later admitted taking five thousand dollars but insisted he gave everything on the field—his numbers backed him up. Still, the Reds won in a shocking upset. Rumors flew, and in 1920, investigations made them fact. Trials followed, juries acquitted the men for lack of hard proof, but baseball's new commissioner, Judge Kenesaw Mountain Landis, wasn't having it. To save the game's soul, he banned all eight for life. Joe drifted into quiet years—running a small liquor store during Prohibition's irony, playing occasional semi-pro games, always carrying the weight of a name tied to betrayal even as many believed he was innocent.

The blow landed far beyond the ballpark. In a time when people needed heroes they could believe in—when returning veterans struggled, and families mourned empty chairs—the idea that even baseball could be fixed felt like a crack in the foundation. Newspapers ran screaming headlines, fans turned away in disgust, and Congress talked about banning sports gambling altogether. It mirrored the wider unease: hidden dealings thriving while honest folks suffered, promises broken in high places. Yet something good came from the pain. Baseball created the commissioner role to safeguard its integrity, cleaned house, and crowds eventually returned in greater numbers than before. The scandal reminded everyone that trust is fragile, icons can fall, but with vigilance and a commitment to doing right, the game—and the country—can heal and carry on stronger.

And the flame of liberty, though dimmed, was not extinguished. In the stories of ordinary Americans who held fast to faith, courage, and independence, we see the path back to the resilient dream that once made this nation exceptional.

THE ROARING TWENTIES

The flame of liberty flickered on through the 1920s, a decade when America seemed to roar with life. Factories hummed day and night, radios brought music into every home, and people danced in new ways that felt like freedom itself. Cars filled the roads, carrying families farther than their grandparents could have dreamed. My father, Maynard, was born in 1923 in Massillon, Ohio. My grandfather had moved the family to Ohio because, in the early 1920s, money flowed, jobs were plentiful, and the future looked bright. Yet beneath the surface, cracks were forming—cracks in trust, in values, and in the very self-reliance that had built the nation.

Warren G. Harding assumed the Presidency in 1921, promising a "return to normalcy" after the war's chaos. A newspaperman from Ohio, he wanted calm and quiet after years of upheaval. But his administration became a cautionary tale. He surrounded himself with old friends from back home—the "Ohio Gang"—men who saw power as a chance for personal gain rather than service. One of the worst moments came with the Teapot Dome scandal.

Picture a vast stretch of Wyoming land shaped like a teapot, set aside by the government as oil reserves for the Navy in case of war. Secretary of the Interior Albert Fall, a friend of Harding's, secretly leased these reserves to private oil companies. In return, he took bribes—cash, cattle, even a home. When the deal came to light, the nation was shocked. Fall became the first Cabinet member ever sent to prison for crimes in office. Harding himself may not have known the full details, but his trust in the wrong people let corruption spread like wildfire. He died in office in 1923, worn down by the scandals, leaving a stain on the idea that government should serve the people, not enrich a few.

Following Harding's death, Calvin Coolidge assumed office. A quiet man from Vermont, Coolidge believed in limited government, hard work, and letting people keep more of what they earned. He cut taxes and slashed federal spending, freeing up money for businesses and families. Factories boomed, wages rose, and ordinary folks could buy homes, cars, and radios. Coolidge defended the Founders' vision of a nation in which individual effort, not government control, drives progress. His steady hand helped the economy grow, reminding Americans that true prosperity comes from personal responsibility and faith in hard work.

Coolidge was a quiet man. In fact, once, a lady came up to him when he was president and said, "Mr. President, my friends and I have a bet. They're saying I can't get you to say even three words to me." He looked at her calmly and said, "You lose." He was quiet but extremely effective. And when he did talk, his short sentences spoke volumes:

"Patriotism is easy to understand in America. It means looking out for yourself by looking out for your country." – Calvin Coolidge

As the decade rolled on, Herbert Hoover rose to prominence. Before becoming president, he was known as a master of relief efforts—organizing aid for millions after disasters such as the 1927 Mississippi River flood. He worked through private groups and local communities, believing that people helping each other was the American way. His approach demonstrated courage in crisis and a commitment to voluntary action over government-mandated programs. Hoover had some bad luck, though. He was president later in the twenties when the stock market crashed, and he bore the brunt of the blame, although he had a great heart and would later prove effective in other roles.

"Within the soul of America is freedom of mind and spirit in man. Here alone are the open windows through which pours the sunlight of the human spirit. Here alone is human dignity not a dream but an accomplishment. Perhaps it is not perfect, but it is more full in realization here than any other place in the world." - Herbert Hoover

THE GOLDEN AGE OF HOLLYWOOD FROM 1925 TO 1950

As movies integrated sound, crashing in with The Jazz Singer in 1927, everything changed—actors spoke, sang, and danced, turning films into talkies that filled grand palaces. Black-and-white gave way later to vibrant Technicolor in the 1930s and 1940s, making worlds pop in movies like The Wizard of Oz. The studio system ruled, with powerful moguls like Louis B. Mayer at MGM, Jack Warner at Warner Bros., Harry Cohn at Columbia, and Darryl F. Zanuck at Fox controlling every step from script to screen. They signed stars to long contracts, churning out escapism during the Depression and war years—anyone who could spare a few pennies lined up for musicals, screwball comedies, epics, and film noir. The top stars lit up the era: Clark Gable, the charming king with his mustache and grin; Humphrey Bogart, tough yet vulnerable in detective roles; John Wayne, embodying rugged American spirit; Katharine Hepburn, sharp and independent; and Bette Davis, fierce with those unforgettable eyes. Censorship kept things clean under the Hays Code, but creativity thrived, making Hollywood the world's glamour capital.

The Roaring Twenties also brought heroes who embodied the spirit of innovation and daring. Charles Lindbergh, a young pilot from Minnesota, took off from New York in May 1927 in a small plane called the Spirit of St. Louis. Alone, with no radio or parachute, he flew over the vast Atlantic for more than 33 hours. Fog, storms, and exhaustion nearly overwhelmed him, but his determination carried him to Paris. When he landed, crowds cheered. Lindbergh's flight showed what one person with courage and skill could achieve, inspiring a nation to dream bigger.

On the baseball field, Babe Ruth became a larger-than-life figure. The "Sultan of Swat" hit home runs that seemed impossible, turning the game into high drama. Fans packed stadiums to watch him swing for the fences, and his success lifted spirits across the country. Ruth's power and joy in the game reminded people that talent and hard work could create legends.

Yet not all voices celebrated unchecked excess. F. Scott Fitzgerald captured the era's glittering surface and hidden emptiness in his novel The Great Gatsby. Through the story of a man who built a fortune to win back lost love, Fitzgerald showed how chasing wealth and status could leave people hollow. His words warned that true happiness lay not in possessions, but in deeper values.

In the shadows of America's progress, darker ideas took root. Margaret Sanger championed birth control and abortion, founding organizations that would one day become Planned Parenthood. She spoke openly of "improving humanity through better breeding," embracing eugenics — the belief that some lives were simply more valuable than others. Her writings revealed troubling views on race and class, including efforts to reduce births among groups she considered "unfit," among them African Americans. These ideas stood in stark contrast to the nation's founding conviction that every human being bears God's image and deserves equal dignity. And in the end, they helped lead to the deaths of hundreds of millions of unborn babies, taken from their mothers' wombs.

I saw this reality up close when I was just eighteen. My twenty-year-old girlfriend became pregnant. We were already living together, and I wanted the baby. But she decided she wanted to end the pregnancy. We never really talked about it afterward, and we broke up a couple of years later. Within a year, she had met someone else and had his child. At the time, I supported her decision — after all, it was "her body, her choice." But I was quietly shocked at how simple it was. She made a single phone call, got an appointment, and the procedure was done — no real questions, no ultrasound to see the heartbeat, no one offering her any other options or even showing her what was happening inside her. I understood her fear, and I stood by her. Still, looking back, I couldn't help thinking that a young woman in a vulnerable spot like that deserved more than just one quick path forward. She deserved to be given every option, every bit of support, and the chance to see the full truth before making such a permanent decision.

"I've noticed that everyone who is for abortion has already been born."
-Ronald Reagan

Amid the glamour, John D. Rockefeller used his vast wealth for good. The oil tycoon turned philanthropist gave millions to build universities, fund medical research, and improve education. His gifts helped advance science and healing, showing that great success could serve a greater purpose when guided by faith and generosity.

The 1920s dazzled with progress, but they also tested the flame of liberty. Self-reliance, faith, and moral courage still burned brightly in many hearts. Yet the seeds of dependency—planted earlier and watered by corruption and excess—grew stronger. As the decade neared its end, the nation stood on the edge of a fall, one that would demand renewed resolve to keep the resilient dream alive.

AMERICA CRUMBLES IN THE GREAT DEPRESSION

"I have found out in later years that we were very poor, but the glory of America is that we didn't know it then." – Dwight D. Eisenhower

October 29, 1929. Black Tuesday. The stock market had been climbing for years, carrying dreams of easy wealth on its shoulders. Then, in a single day, it collapsed. Billions vanished. Men who had worked their whole lives to build a nest egg watched their savings evaporate like morning mist. Families who had borrowed to buy homes or cars suddenly faced foreclosure and repossession. The roar of the twenties fell silent, replaced by the quiet fear of what came next.

My own grandparents felt the blow deep in their bones. They had scraped together every penny from long hours and careful living, investing what little they could in the market, believing in the promise of a better tomorrow. When the crash hit, their hard-earned money was gone. They packed up what they could and moved back to West Virginia, to the hills where my grandmother, Audrey, had grown up. The move was hard enough, but grief piled on top of loss. Years before, Audrey had buried a baby she had carried to full term. Then, right after the crash, another son—my father's older brother—was struck and killed on the highway by a drunk driver. My father, still a boy, watched his mother's thick, dark brown hair turn silver-gray over one long summer. She never complained, but the pain etched itself into every line of her face. They held on, leaning on faith and each other, determined that hardship would not break their spirit or their family. My father echoed Eisenhower's words when he told me that his parents shielded their remaining children from the idea of poverty, and he had no idea they were poor until much later.

Across the country, the pain multiplied. Banks that had seemed solid failed by the hundreds in 1930. People lined up at tellers' windows, desperate to withdraw their money before it was gone. When the banks closed their doors, families lost everything. Men who had been proud providers stood in bread lines, heads bowed, hats in hand. Children went to bed hungry.

Mothers patched old clothes again and again, turning flour sacks into dresses. The Great Depression wasn't just an economic event—it was a wound to the soul. It taught an entire generation the value of frugality, the weight of sacrifice, and the importance of holding fast to what really mattered: family, faith, and the quiet strength to keep going when the world seemed to fall apart.

In those dark days, something unexpected began to draw people together—nationwide radio programs filled living rooms with voices that felt like neighbors. Families gathered around bulky sets to listen to President Roosevelt's fireside chats, where he spoke plainly and calmly, offering hope without false promises. They heard music, comedy, and news that connected them across miles. Radio became a lifeline, reminding Americans that they were not alone in their struggles.

Yet amid the hardship, darker influences began to stir. In the 1920s, soon after the formation of the Communist Party USA in 1919, inspired by the bloody Russian Revolution, efforts to spread Marxist ideas took root. Unfortunately, many starving Americans took the bait. Soviet leaders viewed American colleges and universities as key sites to sow seeds of discontent. During the Depression, when despair ran deep, these efforts gained ground. Small numbers of committed activists—perhaps a thousand or so nationwide by the early 1940s—worked to influence students and labor unions. They established separate "workers' schools" to teach about class struggle and the idea that the government should control wealth and resources. The push for heavy income redistribution promised fairness but carried a hidden cost: it dulled the drive to work hard, punished those who sacrificed to build, and rewarded those who waited for handouts. Over time, these ideas chipped away at the belief that personal effort, guided by faith and responsibility, was the true path to dignity.

"It is harder to preserve than to obtain liberty." – John C. Calhoun

The Great Depression tested America like few other times. Families lost homes and hope, yet many refused to surrender their core values. They planted gardens, shared what little they had, and clung to the faith that had carried their ancestors through earlier trials. The flame of liberty dimmed under the weight of suffering, but it did not go out. In the quiet courage of ordinary people—who mended clothes, fed neighbors, and taught their children that character mattered more than comfort—the resilient dream lived on.

What followed would begin the process of pushing that flame to the brink of extinction, as the government intervened with promises of security that would entangle generations. But even in the depths, the stories of faith, endurance, and love of country remind us that the American spirit, when rooted in truth and personal responsibility, can rise again.

SECTION THREE
FRANKLIN ROOSEVELT'S NEW DEAL

The Great Depression had stripped so many bare. Families stood in bread lines, men walked miles for any scrap of work, and children went to bed with empty stomachs. When Franklin D. Roosevelt took the oath of office in March 1933, his voice came through the radio like a steady hand on the shoulder. He spoke of fear itself being the only thing to fear, and for countless Americans, including my own grandparents, he felt like a savior. His programs put food on tables, built roads and dams, and gave hope when hope had nearly vanished. People wept with relief as jobs appeared and banks reopened. Yet every gift carried a hidden cost. What began as emergency help for desperate times quietly grew into permanent chains. Government that had once stayed small now reached into every corner of life. The flame of self-reliance, already dimmed, began to flicker under the weight of promises that sounded so kind but demanded so much in return.

THE EXPANSION OF SOCIALISM IN GOVERNMENT

Franklin Roosevelt stepped into the White House at the darkest hour. The nation was on its knees, and he moved fast. In his first hundred days, he launched a flurry of programs that touched every corner of American life. He called them the New Deal—emergency steps to pull the country out of the pit. Most were sold as temporary fixes. But they never went away. They grew, layer by layer, until the federal government had become the largest employer, lender, and planner in the land.

Social Security was established in 1935. Roosevelt promised a simple safety net: workers would pay into a fund during their working years, then draw a modest pension in old age so they wouldn't starve. It sounded fair and compassionate. But over time, Congress kept adding—disability payments, benefits for survivors, Medicare, and automatic increases. Today, the payroll tax takes 12.4 percent of every paycheck up to a high cap. The system pays out far more than most receive, and the trust fund is on track to run dry in the coming decades. What started as a modest promise has become the biggest single item in the federal budget.

The Federal Deposit Insurance Corporation, founded in 1933, insured bank accounts so people wouldn't lose everything in another run on the banks. At first, the limit was small—$2,500. Now it's $250,000. Banks, knowing the government would cover losses, took on greater risk. When trouble came, taxpayers paid the bill.

The Federal Housing Administration and, later, the GI Bill helped millions of people buy homes with low down payments. That sounded like the American dream made real. But it fueled a housing boom that ended in the 2008 crash. Government-backed loans encouraged risky lending, and when the bubble burst, the pain reached every corner.

The Works Progress Administration and Civilian Conservation Corps put millions to work building roads, parks, and bridges. The projects were beautiful and lasting. Yet they set a pattern: the federal government as the permanent provider of jobs. The Agricultural Adjustment Act paid farmers to grow less so prices would rise. That became a system of subsidies that today funnels billions mostly to large operations, not the small family farms it was meant to save.

The National Labor Relations Act gave workers the right to organize. The Fair Labor Standards Act established a minimum wage and a 40-hour workweek. Each began with good intentions—to protect the vulnerable. But they grew into rules that sometimes priced young people and low-skill workers out of jobs.

THE RISE OF THE DEEP STATE

In 1935, during the height of the Great Depression, President Roosevelt attempted to fire William Humphrey, a commissioner at the Federal Trade Commission, simply because their policy views didn't align. Humphrey sued, and the Supreme Court ruled against the president in Humphrey's Executor v. United States, holding that Congress could protect certain agency officials from removal for lack of good cause—such as inefficiency or misconduct. This decision marked a turning point in which well-intentioned efforts to stabilize government inadvertently transferred power to unelected bureaucrats, creating what many regard as an unaccountable "fourth branch" of government. It allowed agencies such as the FTC to operate with a degree of independence that shielded them from direct presidential oversight, meaning voters' choices at the ballot box had less impact on how laws were enforced day-to-day. Over time, this shifted authority away from elected leaders and toward experts who could pursue their own agendas, often expanding regulations without the checks and balances the Founders intended, leading to a bloated administrative state that burdens businesses and individuals alike.

The long-term effects have been profound, fostering a system in which the Deep State thrives—insulated officials making decisions that affect everyday lives without real accountability, turning elections into more of a show than an actual shift in power. This has led to overreach, with agencies wielding quasi-legislative and judicial powers that dilute the separation of powers outlined in the Constitution, making it harder for presidents to fulfill their duty to faithfully execute the laws.

Herbert Hoover, the man before Roosevelt, had tried a different path. He believed in the private sector and voluntary help—neighbors, churches, and businesses stepping up. He urged companies to keep wages steady and avoid layoffs. But when the crisis of the Great Depression deepened, his approach couldn't match the scale of suffering.

Eleanor Roosevelt, the First Lady, brought her own fierce compassion. She traveled the country, visiting coal mines and migrant camps, pressing for better conditions. Her faith drove her to speak for the forgotten. During the war, she lifted morale and championed human rights. Her work showed how personal conviction could move mountains.

"Freedom makes a huge requirement of every human being. With freedom comes responsibility. For the person who is unwilling to grow up, the person who does not want to carry his own weight, this is a frightening prospect."
– Eleanor Roosevelt

Roosevelt's fireside chats were something new. He spoke directly to Americans through the radio, explaining his plans in plain words. Families gathered around the set, listening to their president like a trusted friend. It was the first time a leader had spoken so regularly into every home.

THE TWENTIETH AND TWENTY-FIRST AMENDMENTS

The Twentieth Amendment, ratified in 1933, ended the long wait between election and inauguration. Before, presidents were chosen in November but didn't take office until March. That four-month gap left the country adrift. The amendment moved the start to January 20, giving the new leader a quicker chance to act.

The Twenty-First Amendment repealed Prohibition. The Eighteenth had tried to force morality through law, but it bred crime and corruption. Bootleggers grew rich, gangsters ruled cities, and ordinary folks broke the law just to have a drink. Repeal admitted the mistake and returned control to the states.

In the midst of all this, voices rose to defend the old ways. Everett Dirksen, a senator from Illinois, had a gravelly voice and a heart for justice. He believed the Constitution's promise of equality had waited too long. Later, in the 1960s, he rallied the votes needed to pass the Civil Rights Act and Voting Rights Act. He told his colleagues, "We can do this the easy way or the hard way, but we are going to do it."

Albert Einstein, the brilliant scientist who fled Nazi Germany in 1933, found refuge in America. He lived quietly, played his violin, and thought deeply about freedom. He saw this country as the place where ideas could breathe without fear.

Robert Taft, known as "Mr. Republican," stood firm for limited government. He fought to keep presidential power in check and helped pass laws that balanced union rights with fairness. He reminded the Senate that liberty demanded boundaries.

Jesse Owens, the son of sharecroppers, ran faster than anyone thought possible at the 1936 Olympics in Berlin. He won four gold medals, shattering myths about race in front of Hitler's eyes. His quiet dignity spoke louder than words.

Amelia Earhart flew alone across oceans, breaking every barrier for women who dreamed of adventure. Her courage inspired a generation to reach higher. She mysteriously disappeared in flight in the South Pacific during the second World War.
The 1930s also brought the Dust Bowl. In 1934, monstrous dust storms swept the plains, blackening the sky as far as New York City. Farmers watched topsoil blow away, their crops and hopes gone. One man in Oklahoma stood on his porch as the dark cloud rolled in, covering his fields like night in midday. He knelt in prayer, asking for strength to start again. Many did. They replanted, rebuilt, and held on.

Government projects like the Tennessee Valley Authority and Hoover Dam brought electricity and jobs to forgotten places. They merged public and private efforts in ways that got people back to work. But they also showed how deeply the government could entwine itself in everyday life.

Politics today feels so tainted. We've observed our government being weaponized in ways that undermine the foundation of trust—agencies turned against political opponents, scandals eroding public faith, and a sense that power serves the elite rather than the people. It's heartbreaking to see institutions meant for justice and fairness twisted into tools of division and control.

But this kind of dirty politics isn't some modern invention. It's been festering for generations, and back in 1939, a film called "Mr. Smith Goes to Washington" laid it bare like never before. Directed by Frank Capra, it starred Jimmy Stewart as the wide-eyed Senator Jefferson Smith, an honest everyman thrust into the corrupt heart of D.C.

The movie's climax, Smith's grueling filibuster, was a raw, impassioned cry against the machine, and it hit audiences like a thunderbolt, exposing the underbelly of Washington in a way that felt revolutionary.

In that unforgettable scene, Smith stands alone on the Senate floor, exhausted but unyielding, railing against the political bosses and special interests that manipulate the system for their gain. He calls out the graft and corruption that silence truth, showing how honest people get crushed by these powerful networks. With sweat on his brow and fire in his voice, he defends "lost causes" like integrity and the rights of ordinary folks, arguing that absolute liberty depends on fighting back against tyrannical control. Adversity, he says, reveals true character, and he urges a return to America's core ideals of freedom and justice over cynical politics. It's a moment that still resonates because it captures the human struggle for decency in power's shadow—Smith's vulnerability makes you feel the weight of his words, reminding us that one person's stand can echo through time, inspiring us to demand better from our leaders today.

Our founders had not envisioned a country of people dependent upon the government for welfare and subsidies. In early America, churches, families, and community groups worked together to feed the poor and help the unfortunate achieve a better life, and in return, these people felt an obligation to be good citizens and even to pay it forward.
I don't believe anyone in today's world would argue that we shouldn't have a safety net for people who need help, but when you pour government money into problems, you create an environment rife with waste, fraud, and abuse.

The New Deal eased suffering for many, but it also prolonged the Depression for others. Heavy regulations slowed private recovery. Debt climbed. Dependency took root. Yet the flame of liberty still burned in the hearts of those who refused to surrender their independence. They worked hard, helped neighbors, and trusted in faith. Their stories remind us that true strength comes not from government promises, but from personal courage, shared responsibility, and the enduring dream of a free people.

"There is nothing wrong with America that faith, love of freedom, intelligence, and energy of her citizens cannot cure." – Dwight D. Eisenhower

THE HORRORS OF THE SECOND WORLD WAR

It's hard to imagine now, but after the Great War ended in 1918, the world thought it had seen the last of that kind of horror. People wanted to move on, build families, and live quietly. But by the 1930s, a different kind of darkness had crept in. Three men—Adolf Hitler in Germany, Benito Mussolini in Italy, and the military rulers in Japan—had taken power by promising their people greatness, but what they really delivered was hatred wrapped in lies. They called it fascism: a system where the state became everything, and the individual nothing. You gave up your freedom, your voice, even your conscience, for the promise of strength and order. It never works because it goes against something deep inside us—the simple truth that every person has worth, made in God's image, and no leader or government can change that.

What they did was unspeakable. Hitler's Nazis hunted down Jews, Roma people, people with disabilities, and anyone who didn't fit their twisted idea of "pure." In camps like Auschwitz, families were torn apart. Mothers held their children close as they were led into rooms where gas hissed from the ceilings. Six million Jews were murdered—whole communities wiped out, as if they had never existed. Mussolini sent his troops into Ethiopia, dropping poison gas on villages, mowing down people with machine guns. In China, Japanese soldiers committed atrocities that still haunt those who read the accounts: cities burned, women and children violated, rivers choked with bodies. These men joined forces as the Axis powers, feeding off each other's cruelty. It wasn't just war; it was deliberate evil.

Then, on a Sunday morning in December 1941, everything changed for America. On a quiet, sunny morning at Hawaii's Pearl Harbor, the sky filled with Japanese planes, bombs raining down on sleeping ships and sailors. The USS Arizona blew apart in a massive fireball, trapping hundreds inside. Men leaped into oil-slicked water that was on fire. More than 2,400 didn't make it home. The news hit the country like a gut punch. Families sat stunned by their radios, listening to President Roosevelt call it "a date which will live in infamy." The country that had been struggling through the Depression suddenly found itself united. The anger and grief turned into something unbreakable.

My dad was one of those young men who felt it deeply. He had just finished high school when the attack happened. Without hesitation, he enlisted in the Navy. They sent him to Chicago to help prepare his ship, and that's where he met my mom—a seventeen-year-old girl already playing piano with the Chicago Symphony Orchestra. She had this quiet strength, and he fell hard. They wrote letters every day while he was in the South Pacific. He wasn't a doctor, just training as a medic, or "pharmacist's mate" with steady hands and a calm head. When the wounded came in, he learned fast—stitching up gashes, removing shrapnel, keeping men alive when there was no one else. After the war, they got married, and he went on to become a doctor. Their story isn't special in the grand scheme, but it's one of thousands like it: ordinary people rising up because the moment demanded it.

ALEXANDER FLEMING

In the late 1920s, a Scottish scientist named Alexander Fleming noticed something extraordinary in his London lab: a mold growing on a forgotten petri dish had killed surrounding bacteria. He identified the substance as penicillin and published his findings in 1928, but it seemed little more than a curiosity at first. It wasn't until the late 1930s and early 1940s that a team at Oxford University—led by Howard Florey and Ernst Chain, with crucial help from Norman Heatley—figured out how to purify and produce it in usable amounts. Their work, accelerated by the desperate needs of World War II, turned penicillin into the world's first true antibiotic, saving countless lives from infections that once meant certain death. In 1945, Fleming, Florey, and Chain shared the Nobel Prize for this breakthrough that changed medicine forever.

Out in the South Pacific during those war years, my father was serving on a ship crowded with sailors battling infections from wounds, tropical diseases, and the harsh conditions of island fighting. Penicillin was still so scarce—production couldn't keep up with the need—that it was strictly rationed. The sickest men got the precious shots first, their bodies fighting for every bit of the miracle drug.

But much of it passed through unchanged, so medics collected the urine from those treated patients, extracted the penicillin, and reused it for the next wave of desperately ill sailors. Some even had to drink the processed urine to get the medicine inside them faster. My father saw men on the edge of death pull through because of that grim necessity, learning medicine on the fly with steady hands and a heart that refused to give up. In those dark holds, far from home, penicillin wasn't just a drug—it was hope recycled from sheer determination to save one more life.

Years later, my father told me that his infant brother, a couple years older than him who died in 1921 while his mother was pregnant with my dad, could have lived had penicillin already been invented. It truly was the miracle drug of the twentieth century.

The war did what no New Deal program could: it brought the economy roaring back. Factories ran around the clock, building planes, tanks, and ships. Women filled the jobs men had left behind. They welded, riveted, and operated heavy machines. "Rosie the Riveter" was on the poster, but the real women—millions of them—were the ones who showed up every day, balanced their work with raising kids, and kept everything running at home. They proved that courage doesn't care about gender.

We call them the Greatest Generation for a reason. They grew up in the hard years of the Depression, learning to make do, to share, to keep going. That grit carried them through the war. They fought not to take land, but to stop a darkness that wanted to extinguish freedom everywhere.

In the Pacific, General Douglas MacArthur led with a fierce determination. He had to leave the Philippines when the Japanese overran it, but he came back as he promised. In Europe, General George Patton drove his tanks with relentless energy, pushing men and machines beyond what seemed possible. General Dwight Eisenhower planned the most significant invasion ever. On June 6, 1944—D-Day—more than 150,000 Allied troops hit the beaches of Normandy. The waves were rough, the water turned red with blood. Thousands fell in the first hours, but the rest kept moving forward. By nightfall, they had a foothold. American losses over the whole war reached more than 400,000 dead, but their sacrifice helped free millions.

Not everything was heroic. Fear took hold here, too. After Pearl Harbor, more than 120,000 Japanese Americans—many born in this country—were forced from their homes and sent to camps in remote deserts. Families lost everything: homes, businesses, dignity. Fred Korematsu refused to go. He stayed, got arrested, and fought the order all the way to the Supreme Court.

He lost, but his quiet defiance reminds us that even in crisis, the Constitution protects everyone, or it protects no one. In a greater sense, America got this one wrong, jailing our own citizens because of their nationality... but, at the time, Americans were angry at the Japanese, fearful of spies that might have been among Americans of Japanese descent, and the government acted on impulse to protect the country overall.

THE UNLIKELY ALLIANCE

In the thick of World War II, three leaders who couldn't have been more different—Franklin D. Roosevelt, the optimistic American president pushing for democracy; Winston Churchill, the bulldog of Britain with his unyielding resolve; and Joseph Stalin, the ruthless Soviet dictator—formed an alliance that seemed improbable. The U.S. and Britain stood for freedom and individual rights, worlds apart from the Soviets' oppressive communism. Yet, they linked arms because Hitler and Mussolini posed an existential threat that demanded unity. As Churchill put it early on, after the Nazis invaded the Soviet Union in 1941, **"If Hitler invaded hell, I would make at least a favorable reference to the devil in the House of Commons."** This pragmatic bond, forged through conferences like Tehran and Yalta, allowed the Allies to coordinate massive efforts—from D-Day to the Eastern Front push—that ultimately crushed the Axis powers.

But it was always tense; Churchill, ever the stoic leader, warned of the "Iron Curtain" descending across Europe even as victory loomed, showcasing his foresight amid the chaos. His leadership shone through in those dark days, rallying Britain with speeches that embodied resilience, like his vow that "we shall never surrender," turning despair into determination.

As the European war wrapped up in 1945, the cracks in this alliance widened fast. The Soviets stormed Berlin in a brutal assault, taking the city while the Western Allies held back to avoid unnecessary losses, but this left Stalin in control of the eastern half. Relations soured almost immediately as the Cold War ignited. By 1948, the Soviets blockaded West Berlin, cutting off supplies in a bid to force out the Americans, British, and French. The U.S. responded with the Berlin Airlift, flying in food and fuel for over a year to sustain two million people—a bold stand against communist expansion that symbolized Western resolve. Tensions escalated further in 1961 when the Berlin Wall went up overnight, a concrete barrier trapping East Germans and splitting families, all to stem the flood of defections to the free West. What started as wartime cooperation devolved into decades of standoff, with the U.S. and its allies viewing the Soviets as the new aggressors bent on spreading tyranny.

Churchill's stoicism during this shift was legendary; he faced down not just the Nazis but the emerging Soviet threat with unflinching grit, even as his health faltered and political fortunes waned. He captured his defiant spirit perfectly when he quipped, **"History will be kind to me for I intend to write it,"** reflecting on how he'd shape the narrative of his era through his own memoirs. That line wasn't just witty—it showed his confidence in his leadership choices, from rallying the free world against fascism to sounding early alarms about communism, ensuring his legacy as a pillar of conservative values like liberty and resolve.

"For so many Americans, it seems outlandish that we would have to explain that fascism, socialism, and communism do not work. We have seen it fail across the globe, and when it is implemented, people suffer. We cannot allow it to grow in America, the greatest country the world has ever known." – Bill Hagerty

Meanwhile, immigrants like Albert Einstein, who escaped Nazi Germany, helped turn the tide. He warned about the power of the atom. Robert Oppenheimer led the scientists who built the insanely powerful atomic bomb that finally ended the war in the Pacific. It saved lives in one sense, but the weight of that decision still lingers.

THE USO

Imagine the young soldiers scattered across the globe in 1941—some in muddy foxholes in Europe, others on dusty Pacific islands, all far from everything familiar, carrying photos of loved ones and wondering if they'd ever see home again. That's when the United Service Organizations stepped in, born that year to give those men a taste of comfort and laughter when they needed it most. They set up canteens with coffee and donuts, places to write letters, but the real magic came in the shows—live entertainment brought right to the troops, sometimes just miles from the fighting.

Celebrities didn't stay safe in Hollywood. They boarded planes and ships, risking submarines and air raids to reach the boys. Bob Hope started it all in 1941, cracking jokes on makeshift stages, surrounded by musicians and beautiful singers, turning lonely outposts into places where soldiers could forget the war for an hour. Marlene Dietrich braved freezing European winters, singing in her husky voice, chatting with the men afterward, even as frostbite bit at her—because she knew a kind word could mean everything. Judy Garland's clear, heartfelt songs, Bing Crosby's warm crooner style, the Andrews Sisters' tight harmonies, Dinah Shore's gentle smile—they all went, giving pieces of home to young men who hadn't heard a woman's voice in months.

Back in America, other stars worked the home front. Ronald Reagan couldn't fight overseas because of bad eyesight, so he joined the Army's motion picture unit.
Reagan narrated training films and patriotic shorts like "Beyond the Line of Duty"—a piece that actually won an Academy Award—his steady voice urging Americans to buy bonds and enlist.

Frank Sinatra, just rising to fame, sang in short films and rallied crowds at bond drives, turning his charm into millions for the war effort. Sinatra was the first mega-star, making young women labeled "bobby-soxers" swoon, unrivaled by anyone until Elvis Presley in the late 1950s. Sinatra rode the wave of the outstanding swing orchestras of the era led by Tommy Dorsey, Glenn Miller (who enlisted and was tragically killed early in World War II), Gene Krupa and other greats.

They all understood something simple: those soldiers weren't just fighting for land or politics—they were holding the line for freedom itself. A song, a laugh, a reminder of home could steady a man's heart when nothing else could. In those dark years, the USO and these stars kept the flame burning a little brighter for the ones carrying it farthest from home.

In 1941, as the world was at war, Mount Rushmore was completed. Those massive faces of Washington, Jefferson, Lincoln, and Theodore Roosevelt look out over the land in South Dakota. They're carved to last for thousands of years. They stand for what America can be. But they also make you wonder: Will we hold on to the things they represent? What will people far in the future see when they stand there? Will it be like the pyramids, an echo of a long-forgotten civilization, or will our freedoms still stand in other millenniums?

Winston Churchill famously said, **"If you're going through hell, keep going."** Americans kept going and eventually won this terrible war. Franklin Roosevelt led through it all, elected four times. Polio had left him in a wheelchair, but he never let it show in his voice. He spoke to the nation with steady calm. He died in April 1945, just before the end of the war in Europe, never seeing the final victory.

World War II was the greatest test of freedom the world has ever faced. It showed what happens when tyranny takes root, and what it costs to stop it. But it also showed that when people who value liberty stand together, guided by faith and simple human courage, they can push back even the worst darkness. The flame of liberty burned brightest then—in the soldiers on the beaches, the workers at home, the families who waited and prayed. Their sacrifice kept the dream alive for us. It's our obligation to tend it.

"Freedom does not come without a price. We may sometimes take for granted the many liberties we enjoy in America, but they have all been earned through the ultimate sacrifice paid by so many of the members of our armed forces."
– Charlie Dent

HARRY TRUMAN AND HIS ENORMOUS DECISION

In 1945, Harry Truman—a straightforward man from Missouri who'd run a haberdashery that didn't quite make it, then served quietly in the Senate— suddenly became vice president. He had barely warmed the seat when word came that Franklin Roosevelt had died. Just like that, in April, weeks before the end in Europe, Truman found himself president. He told friends later that it felt like the moon, the stars, and every planet had dropped right on his shoulders. He wasn't exaggerating.

The European war wrapped up soon after, but Japan kept fighting with a ferocity that broke hearts.

American boys, including my father and uncles, were taking islands one bloody step at a time, and the plans for invading the Japanese homeland spoke of casualties in the hundreds of thousands—maybe a million when you counted everyone. Truman had to decide whether to use something the scientists had created: atomic bombs, weapons that could end it all in fire. On August 6, the first bomb fell on Hiroshima. A single blast erased much of the city, taking tens of thousands of lives in moments—people starting their day, children walking to school. Three days later, Nagasaki suffered the same. Japan surrendered on the 15th. The war stopped. My uncle, Bill Sisler, was among the officers on the USS Missouri witnessing the Japanese surrender ceremony. My father, Maynard, was aboard a ship right next to the Missouri in Tokyo harbor. Many believe those bombs spared far more lives than they took by avoiding a more prolonged fight. But Truman never slept easily afterward. He carried the memory of those ordinary mornings turned to ash, turning to prayer for strength and mercy, believing he had chosen the lesser evil yet feeling its weight every day.

After World War II ended in 1945, the U.S. needed someone to handle foreign affairs, and President Harry Truman picked George C. Marshall for Secretary of State in 1947. Marshall had been a top Army general, planning big operations like D-Day, so he knew strategy. Europe was wrecked—cities bombed, economies broken, people starving—and the Soviet Union was pushing communism into weak countries. Marshall came up with the Marshall Plan, a huge U.S. aid package sending billions in food, machines, and money to help rebuild nations like Germany, France, and Italy. This wasn't just charity; it stopped communism from spreading by getting economies running again with free markets, where people could trade and build businesses without government control. He focused on keeping America safe by strengthening allies, avoiding more wars. His work laid the groundwork for NATO, a defense alliance against threats. Overall, Marshall's practical approach showed U.S. leadership through help and morals, building stability to fight totalitarianism without always using troops. He served until 1949, and his plan helped turn Europe into strong partners for the U.S.

From 1925 to 1950, the nation experienced a real high point in religious practice—membership climbed past 70% in some polls, peaking right after World War II as people sought comfort amid hardship and victory. Preachers like Norman Vincent Peale and authors like Napoleon Hill offered positive thinking tied to faith, helping folks navigate anxiety, while Fulton J. Sheen reached millions on radio and early TV with clear Catholic teaching. The era's uncertainties, from Depression to war, drew many closer to God, making church attendance a regular habit for families across the country.

Even still, peace brought no rest. Communism was rolling across Eastern Europe like a dark wave, locking nations behind walls and fear. Truman looked at the world and drew a line. In 1947, he laid out what people called the Truman Doctrine: America would stand with any free people resisting takeover. It began with money and support for Greece and Turkey, but it became the backbone of holding back tyranny without starting new wars. That same year, in September, he signed the law that created the Central Intelligence Agency—turning wartime spies into a permanent shield against hidden threats.

It was meant to protect liberty, but over time it grew into layers of a permanent, behind-the-scenes government that stayed long after the battles ended. It's hard to argue that the CIA has taken actions to protect the American people from our enemies, but the founders specifically did not want a permanent deep state.

THE BIRTH OF THE CENTRAL INTELLIGENCE AGENCY

In the shadowy aftermath of World War II, as the Iron Curtain fell across Europe and the Soviet bear began to growl louder, America realized it needed sharper eyes and ears—and sometimes a hidden dagger—to protect its freedoms. Picture a nation fresh from victory, but wary of the red tide of communism spreading across the globe. That's when President Truman signed the National Security Act on a hot July day in 1947 aboard his plane, the Sacred Cow. Out of that ink came the Central Intelligence Agency, born not just to gather secrets, but to weave them into a shield for the free world. Its purpose was clear: to centralize intelligence from scattered military branches, analyze threats, and, when needed, launch covert operations to nip dangers in the bud before they bloomed into full-blown crises. No more Pearl Harbors, no more surprises—the CIA was America's quiet guardian, operating in the gray zones where diplomacy ended and hard choices began.

From its early days, the Agency dove headfirst into the Cold War fray, its operatives becoming legends in the fight against tyranny. Think of the 1950s, when the world teetered on the edge of nuclear brinkmanship. In Iran, the CIA orchestrated Operation Ajax in 1953, helping topple a prime minister seen as tilting toward Moscow and restoring the Shah to power— a move that many have long defended as a bold strike against communist encroachment, preserving oil flows and Western alliances. Then came Guatemala in 1954, where the Agency backed a coup against a leftist leader hoarding Soviet arms, averting what many saw as another Cuba in the making. Fast forward to the Bay of Pigs in 1961, a botched invasion of Fidel Castro's island fortress that stung but underscored the CIA's willingness to risk it all. Around the world, from Chile to the Congo, the Agency ran paramilitary ops, trained rebels.

It disrupted dictators—actions that were mostly essential chess moves in the grand game against global socialism, even if they sometimes left messy footprints. These weren't just adventures; they were lifelines for freedom, countering the spread of ideologies that crushed individual liberty.

At home, Truman saw something else that needed fixing. Black Americans had fought and died overseas for freedom, only to come home to separate units and second-class treatment. In 1948, he signed the order to integrate the military. Raised in a place where old prejudices ran deep, he knew it would cost him politically, but he did it anyway—because if a country asks men to die side by side, it ought to let them serve that way too.

Around this time, television sets started appearing in living rooms. At first, it was just a novelty with grainy pictures, but soon millions of families sat together watching the news unfold right in front of them. They saw Truman at the podium, soldiers returning, far-off places they'd only read about.

The world shrank, and America saw itself—and its responsibilities—more clearly than ever.

Television pulled families home, so theaters responded with widescreen formats such as CinemaScope and Cinerama, wrapping audiences in epic vistas, plus early 3D gimmicks. Color became standard, and big spectacles drew crowds. The old studio system cracked under antitrust laws, freeing stars and directors. A new wave emerged—young filmmakers tackling gritty realities, anti-heroes, and social change in what became known as New Hollywood. Later, blockbusters like Jaws in 1975 would kick off the summer event era. Big studio moguls faded as independents and agents gained power. Shining brightest were Marlon Brando, raw and intense; John Wayne, still the enduring cowboy; Marilyn Monroe, fragile yet magnetic; James Stewart, the relatable everyman; and Elizabeth Taylor, glamorous and dramatic. Films mirrored a restless America—Vietnam, civil rights, youth rebellion—blending innovation with bold stories that felt alive and urgent.

THE ERA OF LATE NIGHT TELEVISION

Late-night television talk shows were born in 1954 when Steve Allen stepped in front of the cameras and created something entirely new — a relaxed, witty conversation that felt like chatting with a clever friend after the day was done. He invented the desk, the monologue, the live band, and the easy rhythm that would become the standard for decades to come. Then, in 1962, Johnny Carson took the chair and made the show an American institution for the next thirty years. The Nebraska-born host brought calm, quick wit, and unmistakably Midwestern decency into millions of living rooms. With a raised eyebrow and a perfectly timed pause, he could make an entire nation laugh. He poked fun at presidents and politicians of both parties — Democrats and Republicans alike — but he never turned his show into a political platform. No guest was ever ambushed for their beliefs, and no viewer was ever made to feel they didn't belong. Johnny simply held up a gentle mirror to the times, reminding Americans that we could laugh at ourselves, our leaders, and our shared absurdities without tearing one another apart. In an increasingly divided country, he proved that humor could still be a unifying force.

THE BRUTALITY OF CHINESE COMMUNISM

Mao Zedong took power in China in 1949 and turned communism into a machine of mass death. In 1958, he launched the Great Leap Forward, a disastrous push to industrialize by forcing peasants into communes and melting down tools to make steel—leading to the worst famine in history. Crops rotted in fields while quotas demanded impossible outputs, and between 1958 and 1962, an estimated 20 to 45 million people starved or were beaten to death for failing to meet them.

Villages emptied, parents watched children waste away, and reports of cannibalism emerged from the desperation. Mao knew about the horror but pushed harder, saying it was better for half to die so the other half could eat.

Then came the Cultural Revolution in 1966, where Mao mobilized Red Guards—fanatical youth—to purge "enemies," resulting in chaos until 1976. Neighbors turned on each other, intellectuals were humiliated and killed, and up to 2 million perished in violence, with 100 million suffering persecution. Families were shattered as children denounced parents, and bodies piled up in public beatings. Mao's successors, like Deng Xiaoping, continued the grip, but the scars from Mao's era—estimated at 40 to 77 million dead overall—run deep, a tragic reminder of how envy-driven purges destroy lives. It's gut-wrenching to think of the human cost, the lost dreams, the empty homes.

"None who have always been free can understand the terrible fascinating power of the hope of freedom to those who are not free." – Pearl S. Buck

And now, we're seeing socialism creep back in some American cities, often pushed by liberal leaders whose policies have fueled the very problems they're exploiting. Take places like Seattle or San Francisco: skyrocketing housing prices, driven by regulations that limit building and inflate costs, leave young people locked out of homeownership. Inflation bites hard, bloated social programs and pensions strain budgets, while fraud and waste eat up resources—all under liberal governance that's hiked taxes and deepened divides. These leaders gin up envy by blaming "greedy" landlords or corporations, stirring resentment and even racism to push socialist fixes like rent freezes or massive subsidies. It's the same old tactic: point fingers at the system to justify more control, drawing in frustrated voters who feel the American dream slipping away. But as we've seen, this path leads to more suffering, not solutions.

The truth is, when you hand over a program to the Government, it will inevitably become prone to endless bureaucracy, fraud, waste, abuse, and zero accountability. We must do whatever we can to encourage private enterprise and shrink the government wherever possible. And in a free society, the guardrails against socialism or communism must be closely monitored. During the post-World War II period in our history, fear crept in here, too. Real spies had slipped atomic secrets to the Soviets. Some Americans even spoke openly in favor of the brutal system of communism. Truman began checking loyalties in government.

In the tense early days of the Cold War, when the world held its breath over the new atomic age, Julius and Ethel Rosenberg—a quiet New York couple with deep communist convictions—quietly passed some of America's most guarded secrets to the Soviet Union through an underground spy network.

Julius, an electrical engineer who'd worked on wartime projects, handed over details about the bomb's design that helped Stalin's scientists close the gap far quicker than anyone expected. Those leaks tilted the balance of power, putting millions of American lives under a darker nuclear shadow and forcing the United States into a more dangerous arms race.

The FBI closed in, arresting them in 1950 along with others in the ring. At trial in 1951, the evidence—decoded messages, witness testimony, and Julius's own contacts—painted a clear picture of betrayal. Both Rosenbergs insisted they were innocent right to the end, even as appeals climbed all the way to the Supreme Court. In 1953, they became the only American civilians ever executed for espionage during wartime, put to death in the electric chair at Sing Sing Prison. Their choices didn't just shorten the path to Soviet bombs; they also exposed brave agents working behind the Iron Curtain, costing several of those men their lives when they were unmasked and executed. The case left a lasting scar, a stark reminder of how far some would go for an ideology that put a foreign power above their own country.

"Here in America we are descended in blood and in spirit from revolutionists and rebels - men and women who dare to dissent from accepted doctrine. As their heirs, may we never confuse honest dissent with disloyal subversion.
– Dwight D. Eisenhower

Then Senator Joseph McCarthy stepped forward with lists of names, claiming communists everywhere. Hearings played out on those new televisions—careers destroyed, reputations shattered, often on little more than suspicion. People understood the danger: Stalin's prisons swallowed millions, staged trials sent innocents to death, and engineered famines crushed whole regions. The Soviets laughed at Western admirers, calling them useful idiots who helped spread the chains.

McCarthy started with a genuine threat, but he let fear and ambition take the wheel. Good people lost everything. Neighbors eyed neighbors. When he turned on the Army itself, even supporters backed away. The Senate censured him. The country learned a hard lesson: evil must be faced, but not with methods that eat away at our own souls.

THE TWENTY-SECOND AMENDMENT

After Roosevelt's four terms, many worried that one man could hold power for too long. Washington had walked away after two, and that unwritten rule lasted a century and a half. In 1951, the Twenty-Second Amendment made it ironclad: two terms, no more. It kept faith with the Founders' dread of anything resembling a king.

Truman walked out of the White House in 1953, worn down, unpopular, carrying the scars of tough years. He went home to Missouri no richer—actually poorer—than when he'd arrived, living on a modest Army pension and turning down big-money offers that would have traded on the presidency. History looks on him more gently now.

An ordinary man in an extraordinary hour, he leaned on simple faith and love of country to make decisions that guarded freedom through dark decades. He opened an atomic age that made total war unthinkable, yet left a shadow we still live under. The flame of liberty burned through new storms in his time, steadied by someone willing to bear the hardest truths with quiet courage. The resilient dream carried on.

THE UNITED NATIONS

Imagine the world in the aftermath of World War II, a planet scarred by unimaginable destruction and desperate for a path to lasting peace. In 1945, as the dust settled, representatives from 50 nations gathered in San Francisco to draft the United Nations Charter, a document ratified later that year by the five victorious powers—the U.S., Soviet Union, China, United Kingdom, and France—along with 46 others, officially birthing the UN on October 24.

The idea had roots in 1942, when 26 Allied nations signed the "Declaration by United Nations" in Washington, D.C., a term coined by President Franklin D. Roosevelt himself. At its core, the UN was built on noble principles: maintaining international peace through a Security Council that balanced idealism with realpolitik, fostering cooperation among nations, and upholding human rights grounded in Western ideals of individual liberty, as enshrined in the 1948 Universal Declaration of Human Rights. It was a compromise, recognizing the great powers' role in enforcing order while aspiring to universal goodwill, a far cry from the failed League of Nations' utopian dreams.

But over the decades, that hopeful vision twisted into something unrecognizable, a bloated bureaucracy often at odds with the sovereignty and freedoms it once promised to protect. What started with a focus on self-determination and political rights morphed as left-leaning agendas crept in, like the 1966 International Covenant on Economic, Social, and Cultural Rights, which diluted the original emphasis on core liberties by expanding "human rights" to include expansive social entitlements. Critics argue it's become a platform for global overreach, where non-democratic regimes wield influence in the General Assembly, undermining national interests and promoting a one-world ideology that strays from the Founders' natural law roots. Instead of a guardian of peace, it's evolved into an entity that sometimes prioritizes ideological drift over practical enforcement, leaving many to wonder if the UN's transformation has betrayed its wartime origins.

CHAPTER ELEVEN
THE SECOND HALF OF THE TWENTIETH CENTURY

VICTORY

When World War II ended in 1945, America stood taller than ever before. Soldiers came home to parades, kisses from sweethearts, and a country ready to build. Families grew, houses sprouted in new suburbs, and the future looked wide open. The victory over tyranny felt like proof that freedom could overcome anything. The flame of liberty burned brighter than it had in generations.

Yet even as cheers echoed, shadows gathered on the horizon. Conflicts in Korea and Vietnam waited to test that light again, while government programs at home kept growing, reaching deeper into daily life. The challenges ahead would demand the same courage, faith, and sacrifice that had carried the nation through darker days—because a flame this bright draws strong winds.

SECTION ONE
MID-CENTURY BURDENS

By 1950, the glow of victory still lingered, but exhaustion had set in. World War II had taken everything the country had to give—lives, money, years of worry. Families were rebuilding, babies were arriving in record numbers, yet a new threat rose in Asia. North Korea, backed by communist powers, eyed the South hungrily. President Truman, once praised for hard choices, now carried the blame for a war many didn't understand and didn't want. His popularity faded like morning mist. Americans looked around at the sacrifices still fresh and wondered who could lead them forward without more bloodshed. In 1952, eyes turned to a man who had already proven he could handle the impossible: the general who had commanded the greatest invasion in history and brought Hitler's empire to its knees.

THE POST WORLD-WAR-II ERA

Dwight Eisenhower—everyone called him Ike—had spent the war making decisions that weighed on a man's soul. He planned D-Day, sent thousands of young men onto those Normandy beaches knowing many wouldn't return, yet believing the cost was the only way to stop tyranny. When victory came, soldiers adored him; leaders on both sides of the ocean trusted him.

He could have rested on that glory, but in 1952 the country called again. Both parties wanted him as president. He chose to run, and winning felt almost inevitable—an American hero stepping in when steady hands were needed most.

He took office in January 1953, just as the Korean War was drawing to a bitter end. The fighting had begun on a June morning in 1950 when North Korean tanks rolled across the border into the South. American boys, many still teenagers, were rushed overseas to hold the line. The war dragged on through mountains and freezing winters, costing over 36,000 American lives in just three years. It ended not with triumph but an armistice in July 1953—no peace treaty, just a tense ceasefire that holds to this day. Often called the Forgotten War, squeezed between the world wars and Vietnam, it reminded everyone that freedom's price never stops being paid.

The suffering in Korean prisoner camps was especially cruel. In late 1950, captured Americans faced what soldiers called the Tiger Death March—hundreds forced to trudge more than a hundred miles through biting winter with almost no coats, food, or rest. Men dropped from cold and hunger; some were shot for falling behind. Those who reached the camps along the Yalu River found starvation rations, disease, and constant attempts to break their minds with propaganda. Nearly four out of ten American POWs never came home—the highest death rate since the Revolution. Yet many held on through faith, quiet defiance, and memories of home, emerging scarred but unbroken.

With the armistice signed, Eisenhower turned to healing and building. Veterans like my dad came home to the GI Bill, which paid for college, homes, and businesses—lifting millions of lives because the nation honored its promise to those who served. Families grew fast in what people called the Baby Boom; neighborhoods filled with children's laughter. My father reenlisted in the Navy and went to medical school shortly after my parents' marriage. My sisters and I were all baby boomers: the oldest, Suzanne, born in 1946; Judith, born in 1948; Kathleen, born in 1952; and Mary Elizabeth, born in 1953. I was born towards the end of the baby boomer generation in 1958.

"I can't imagine there has ever been a more gratifying time or place to be alive than America in the 1950s. No country had ever known such prosperity."
– Bill Bryson

Jets streaked across skies, highways began stretching coast to coast under Eisenhower's vision—the interstate system tying cities together like never before. Air conditioning made hot places livable, drawing families south and west. Early computers, giant machines filling entire rooms at companies like IBM, hinted at changes coming.

The Cold War brought fear, too. Schools taught children to duck and cover under desks. In 1957, the Soviets launched Sputnik, and then ICBMs that could carry destruction across oceans. America raced to catch up in space and strength. Eisenhower warned solemnly about a "military-industrial complex"—powerful interests that could grow too strong if unchecked. His warning was the first from a president, exposing the permanent deep state. He kept budgets balanced and debts low, believing freedom required responsibility, not endless spending.

Music captured the era's energy. Swing had carried soldiers through the war; now Rock & Roll music burst onto radios. Blues had given birth to Rhythm & Blues, which gave birth to Rock & Roll and doo-wop. Elvis Presley, a truck driver from Mississippi with a voice that stirred souls, became an overnight sensation—his hips and heart touching something new in young people. Frank Sinatra, smooth and confident, sang standards that made listeners believe in romance and possibility again. Blues musicians like Muddy Waters and Howlin' Wolf, and Country & Western musicians like Hank Williams and Johnny Cash, filled the airwaves with music that endures to this day.

In medicine, Jonas Salk worked quietly in his lab through the early 1950s, driven by a simple wish to stop polio's terror. Children paralyzed, some trapped in iron lungs—the fear hung over every summer. In 1955, he announced a vaccine that worked. When asked who owned the patent, Salk answered, "Well, the people, I would say. There is no patent. Could you patent the sun?" His gift, rooted in deep ethical conviction, saved countless lives and eased a nation's worry.

On the Supreme Court, Earl Warren took the center seat in 1953. He led decisions that profoundly changed America—ending school segregation in Brown v. Board, protecting the rights of the accused, and expanding voting fairness. Many results felt just, yet the way they came—by reading new meanings into old words—worried those who believed judges should follow the Constitution's text, not rewrite it from the bench. William Brennan, joining in 1956, became Warren's sharp strategist, pushing the Court further into shaping society. Their era sparked debates that still echo about where power truly belongs.

Sam Ervin, a North Carolina senator with a country drawl and steel-trap mind, began serving in 1954. Years later, he would chair hearings that held a president accountable, proving one man steeped in the Constitution could defend liberty against the highest office.

Milton Friedman, teaching and writing through these years, argued quietly but powerfully that free markets and personal choice—not central plans—brought real prosperity and dignity. His ideas would influence leaders for decades, reminding the nation that liberty in wallets mattered as much as liberty in speech.

Through it all, Eisenhower steered with calm experience. He ended the Korean fighting, kept peace in tense times, built roads, and strengthened the future. The 1950s felt golden—families growing, possibilities opening—yet dangers waited beneath the surface. The flame of liberty burned steadily under his watch, carried by ordinary Americans rebuilding lives with faith, hard work, and hope. The resilient dream pressed on, ready for whatever winds came next.

CAMELOT AND THE KENNEDY PRESIDENCY

In the fall of 1960, the country felt ready for something fresh. A young senator from Massachusetts named John Kennedy—Jack to his friends—stepped into the spotlight with that easy smile and a way of talking that made you believe tomorrow could be better. His father, Joseph, had Irish roots, built a fortune through sheer will, and poured everything into giving his children the chances he never had. Jack almost didn't make it as a boy, sick so often that death hovered close, but he fought through with a quiet stubbornness that stayed with him. Addison's disease continued to plague him throughout his life, but he handled it valiantly.

World War II called, and Jack commanded a little torpedo boat, PT-109, out in the black Pacific nights. One August evening in 1943, a Japanese destroyer rammed them out of nowhere, splitting the boat clean in two. Flames lit the water as Jack grabbed a strap in his teeth and towed a burned crewman for hours through shark-infested seas, refusing to leave the man behind. They all survived days on a tiny island until rescue came. Jack turned those stories of courage under fire into a book called "Profiles in Courage", about leaders who stood tall even when it cost them dearly.

He moved from Congress to the Senate, restless and always pushing. Then 1960 came, and he beat Richard Nixon to become president by the narrowest margin anyone could remember. On a freezing January morning in 1961, coatless in the wind, he spoke words that landed straight in the heart: "Ask not what your country can do for you—ask what you can do for your country." Something stirred in people; it felt like the nation had caught its second wind.

THE TWENTY-THIRD AMENDMENT

That spring, the Twenty-Third Amendment finally let folks living in Washington, D.C., vote for president—three electoral votes for people who'd paid taxes and sent sons to war but never had a say before. It wasn't everything, but it felt like fairness moving forward.

Jack looked upward, too. In a speech to Congress, he promised America would put a man on the moon before the 1960s ended. Projects named Mercury, Gemini, and Apollo got underway—engineers and pilots risking everything to reach the stars.

But danger was closer. In October 1962, photographs showed Soviet missiles in Cuba, pointed right at American cities. For thirteen long days, the world teetered. Jack blockaded the island, stared down threats of war, and held steady until the missiles came out. It was the nearest the Cold War ever came to burning everything down. He also began sending more advisors to a place called Vietnam—advice that would grow into something far bigger than anyone had seen coming.

Jacqueline—Jackie—brought a gentle light to it all. She walked through the White House, saw its faded rooms, and set about restoring their history and beauty, filling them with art and music that showed America's soul at its best. When sorrow struck, she held the nation together with a grace few could match.

Voices for justice rose louder. Rosa Parks, a tired seamstress in Montgomery, said no when told to give up her bus seat in 1955. That simple refusal lit a fire—a year-long boycott that bent the arc toward fairness. Martin Luther King Jr., a pastor whose words carried both thunder and mercy, marched and preached love over hate, drawing from deep faith. In 1963, he stood on the Lincoln Memorial steps and painted a dream in which children were judged by character, not skin color. These and other events led to the Civil Rights Act of 1964, a landmark piece of legislation.

"The passage of the Civil Rights Act of 1964 represented precisely such a hope - that America had learned from its past and acted to secure a better tomorrow."
- Aberjhani

The years from 1950 to 1975 brought the postwar boom in churches, with attendance holding firm at first—often around 49% weekly in the 1950s—fueled by figures like King and Billy Graham, whose massive crusades filled stadiums and called people to personal commitment amid Cold War fears. Graham's simple gospel message reached hearts hungry for certainty, opening his arms to every race when others turned away, speaking plain truth about God's love for all. But cracks appeared as cultural shifts took hold; the 1963 Supreme Court ruling ending school prayer, pushed by activist Madalyn Murray O'Hair, marked a turning point for many who felt faith was being pushed out of public life, setting in motion a slow drift away from regular churchgoing.

Malcolm X burned with a different fire, calling for pride and strength, until a journey to Mecca softened his heart toward shared humanity.

Then, on November 22, 1963. Dallas. Shots. The president is gone. I was five, sitting close to my father as he quietly said, "Watch this, son. You'll remember this day." The television showed the casket, the riderless horse, and little John saluting.

I felt the weight even at that age—I was the same age as his daughter Caroline—and the whole country seemed to hold its breath in sorrow. At Arlington, Jackie lit an eternal flame that still glows today, a small, steady light for a promise cut short.

In 1964, Barry Goldwater ran, speaking clearly and strongly about freedom and responsibility, planting ideas that would take root later. Ronald Reagan, still known more for movies, gave a speech for Goldwater that caught fire across living rooms, setting him on a path to govern California and dream bigger.

Tragedy touched the space program, too. In 1967, the Apollo 1 crew—three brave men testing their capsule—died when fire swept through in seconds. I was nine, glued to the space stories, and it hit hard—those astronauts were heroes to every kid who looked up at the sky. The loss hurt, but it steeled the nation's will to honor them by going on.

And go on they did. In July 1969, Neil Armstrong took that first step on the moon: "One small step for man, one giant leap for mankind." Jack's promise was kept.

Our nation needed soul, and Barry Gordy's Motown Records delivered, ushering in stars like Diana Ross & the Supremes, The Temptations and Four Tops, and Little Stevie Wonder.

Those Kennedy years shimmered like Camelot—youth, hope, big dreams. Yet storms gathered underneath. The flame of liberty burned bright with possibility, but new trials waited to test how strong it really was. People held tighter to faith, to courage, to the belief that even in shadow, the light could endure. The resilient dream moved forward, carried by hearts that refused to let it fade.

LYNDON JOHNSON MASSIVELY EXPANDS BUREAUCRACY

The day Kennedy died, everything shifted for Lyndon Johnson. A tall Texan raised in hardscrabble Hill Country, he had a way of filling a room—not just with his size, but with that low, insistent voice and the habit of leaning in close until you felt the full force of what he wanted. Johnson was a consummate politician. In the Senate, he had been a master at making things happen, slapping backs, intimidating his peers, finding votes in places others couldn't, persuading or pressuring until deals got done. He used that skill to push through the first meaningful civil rights laws in nearly a century, measures in 1957 and 1960 that began to force open doors long nailed shut.

The country was still raw with grief when Johnson took the oath. He reached into that sorrow and shaped it into something big—the Great Society. He spoke of wiping out poverty, giving every child a real chance at school, and making sure no older person went without medicine.

Medicare came for the elderly, Medicaid for the poor, money poured into cities, housing, education—program after program launched in a wave of determination. Johnson had known lean times as a boy; he truly wanted to spare others the struggle he remembered.

People believed in it then, my father among them. There was real hope that the government could lift the load from those who carried too much. But the ideas outran the planning. Aid meant for the hardest cases spread wider, costs climbed steadily, rules multiplied, and offices grew. Some found a hand up and climbed out; others settled in, whole families leaning on support that never quite ended. Trillions flowed over the years, yet poverty held on in corners, families fractured in ways no one had expected. The Founders had worried about exactly this—government growing so large it might crowd out the personal strength and family ties that keep a free society standing. Johnson's good intentions carried him across boundaries they had marked with care.

He also inherited Kennedy's quiet involvement in Vietnam and turned it into a full commitment. Advisors became hundreds of thousands of troops in a thick jungle, fighting an enemy that melted into the trees. More than 58,000 Americans never came home. This was the first war people watched in their living rooms every night—grainy film of wounded boys, burning villages, protests swelling on campuses. The images made the pain impossible to set aside. Faith in leaders thinned; the country pulled apart.

Even so, kindness found the men in the fight. The USO pressed on through the division back home. Bob Hope flew in year after year from 1964 to 1972, landing where rockets sometimes whistled overhead, telling jokes that let tired soldiers forget for a while. Martha Raye—Green Berets nicknamed her Colonel Maggie—stayed for weeks in remote camps, singing, swapping stories, using old nursing skills to bind wounds when things got hot. John Wayne moved among them, shaking hands, his familiar face a piece of home. Ann-Margret, Nancy Sinatra, Joey Heatherton, Sammy Davis Jr.—they danced and sang on makeshift stages in the mud, offering warmth and thanks that reached deeper than words.

I was eight when the war felt heaviest. My father, Maynard, a Navy doctor, got orders to the huge Army-Navy hospital in Corpus Christi, Texas, to become Chief of Medicine. We lived on base, and my playground next to our quarters was a field of shattered helicopters and planes hauled back from Vietnam—cockpits pocked with holes, faint blood stains no one talked about.

My friends and I scrambled inside, playing pilot, laughing loudly, never understanding that young men just a little older had fought their last in those same seats. War touches even children who only see its leftovers.

In the middle of all that weight, something bright broke loose. In early 1964, four lads from Liverpool—the Beatles—arrived, and music shifted overnight.

Their songs carried joy and energy—"I Want to Hold Your Hand," "She Loves You"—simple, infectious, making teenagers feel alive in a way nothing else did. Parents puzzled over the long hair and screams, but the sound spread everywhere. The Rolling Stones came soon after with a grittier edge, singing truths about life that hit hard. The British Invasion rolled across radios and televisions, waking up rock music. American voices answered—the Beach Boys with sun-soaked harmonies, the Monkees with fun and bounce, the Mamas and the Papas blending voices like no one else. Bob Dylan and Joan Baez turned songs into questions, lyrics that called for peace and change when the war news grew darker.

THE TWENTY-FOURTH AND TWENTY-FIFTH AMENDMENTS

In 1964, the Twenty-Fourth Amendment ended poll taxes for federal elections—small fees some states used to keep poor people, especially Black citizens in the South, from voting. No one should have to pay for a voice.

Two years later, Kennedy's death still fresh in memory, the Twenty-Fifth Amendment set clear rules: if a president can't serve, the vice president steps up, and there's a way to replace an empty second spot.

Margaret Chase Smith, a senator from Maine who spoke with quiet force, had stood against fearmongering years before. Her Declaration of Conscience was a reminder that courage often means speaking plain truth when others shout.

Johnson's time brought real steps toward justice but also a weight that settled on generations—promises that became debts, good intentions that grew beyond what anyone could carry. People watched the government expand and wondered if the careful balance the Founders built was tilting.

The flame bent low in those winds, yet it held. Soldiers kept faith in the field, performers carried comfort across oceans, young people found voice in music, and citizens grappled with hard truths. Courage, love of country, quiet belief—these kept the light alive—the resilient dream endured, waiting for the next breath to steady it. The story moved forward.

THE RISE OF THE WELFARE STATE

Lyndon Johnson never forgot where he came from. As a young teacher in a dusty Texas schoolhouse in Cotulla, he'd watched poor Mexican-American kids struggle to keep up, hunger sharpening their focus in all the wrong ways. Those memories stuck with him. When he became president, he looked at America and said plainly, "We're going to end poverty in our time." He meant it—he'd seen real hardship, and he wanted to make sure no child went without basics like health care or enough to eat.

That's how the Great Society got started. In 1965, Medicare kicked in to help older folks with hospital and doctor bills, and Medicaid did the same for the poorest families. Food stamps became a permanent program the year before, to make sure no kid faced an empty plate. Head Start gave young children from tough backgrounds a boost with early learning. Money went into fixing up rundown cities, supporting schools, building community programs—all aimed at giving people a fair shot.

But things grew bigger than anyone expected. Medicare now costs around a trillion dollars a year, and it's facing severe strains that could hit hard in the coming years. Medicaid has spread to cover far more people in many states, running hundreds of billions annually. SNAP—the food program today—serves about 42 million people, roughly one in eight Americans, at over $100 billion a year, with billions more lost to mistakes and misuse. Head Start has reached millions of kids and cost hundreds of billions over the decades, but even government studies show the early advantages often fade by third grade. City renewal projects sometimes meant bulldozing established neighborhoods, moving families out—usually minority communities—and putting up big housing towers that ended up fostering more isolation than hope. Federal help for schools has grown enormously, yet reading and math scores nationwide have stayed mostly flat since the 1970s.

Since those early days, we've spent trillions on these efforts—well over $22 trillion in today's dollars just on means-tested programs—and the official poverty rate still sits around 11-15%, not much different from half a century ago. What was meant as a short-term lift for some turned into something many relied on long-term, sometimes holding families back across generations. Johnson's intentions were good, just like Roosevelt's before him—both saw real pain and wanted to ease it. But once these programs start, they tend to expand, add layers of rules, and move away from their original aim. The Founders had concerns about precisely this: government growing so large it could weaken personal responsibility, family support, and local help that keep freedom strong.

"If Thomas Jefferson thought taxation without representation was bad, he should see how it is with representation." – Rush Limbaugh

World War II ended with veterans coming home ready to build better lives. The GI Bill helped with homes and college; families grew, and the baby boom arrived. A lot of those kids never knew the hard times their parents had—no long soup lines, no Great Depression struggles.

That prosperity was a gift, but it also brought some unease. People started questioning traditions, especially when Vietnam turned into a long, confusing war. The counterculture took hold—long hair, powerful music, big gatherings like Woodstock in 1969, where crowds came together for songs that challenged everything. Bands like The Doors and Jefferson Airplane gave voice to the frustration.

Protests grew as the war dragged on. Young men saw friends drafted and lost in far-off places; it fueled real anger. Ordinary Americans watched the brutality from home on their TV screens.

"Television brought the brutality of war into the comfort of the living room. Vietnam was lost in the living rooms of America - not on the battlefields of Vietnam." – Marshall McLuhan

Right in the middle of that were men like John McCain, a Navy pilot whose plane went down over Hanoi in 1967. He ejected, broke bones on the way down, got pulled from a lake by a hostile crowd, then beaten and bayoneted before they locked him in the Hỏa Lò Prison—what the prisoners called the "Hanoi Hilton." Guards there tied ropes around his shattered arms and yanked until his shoulders popped out of place, and beat him for statements to use in propaganda. Years in solitary confinement, barely enough food to survive, no real sleep under constant pressure. But McCain and the others held on. They tapped messages through walls—a simple code on a five-by-five letter grid. "G-B-U"—God Bless You—passed quietly from cell to cell, a thread of connection. Many leaned on faith, on prayers, on memories of home and the sense that something bigger was worth enduring for. They shared what little they had, looked out for the weakest, and refused to break. When they offered McCain early release because his father was an admiral, he said no—nobody leaves until everyone can. That bond, that steady courage in the worst conditions, kept their spirits alive until they came home in 1973.

My own family felt the pain of that time up close. My sister, still a teenager, got pulled into Students for a Democratic Society, protesting a war that was taking the lives of people she cared about. Later, during the Los Angeles riots, she went to offer help amid the chaos, bringing supplies to those in need. But someone she tried to aid turned on her violently, assaulting and raping her. Hearts full of hope for justice can lead to dark places; loud calls for quick change can draw in those grieving real losses.

Poverty hung on no matter the efforts. The national debt piled up heavily. More programs meant more decisions made in distant offices, building dependence where independence had been the norm. Waste, fraud, and abuse of these programs became legendary in their size. Some talked about the government providing everything "for free," but we all know nothing is truly free—the costs land on taxpayers and future generations. Why do they continue to pile debt upon debt for our grandchildren to clean up?

Martin Luther King Jr. articulated a dream in which people are judged by the content of their character, not the color of their skin. Yet later ideas, like "white privilege," started labeling entire groups, creating new walls when many just wanted bridges. Racism still lurks in places but seeing it everywhere can stir resentment and push people further apart when we need to come together.

The welfare state originated in caring hands, but its reach grew burdensome. Good promises strained budgets, shifting loads to kids not yet born. Reliance crept in quietly; war's wounds cut openly.
Still, the flame held in prisoners tapping messages of faith, in families staying close, in people grappling honestly with hard truths. That resilient liberty endured through tough times, waiting for renewal in everyday courage and quiet hope.

ROBERT F. KENNEDY

In the heart of bustling America in the 1920s, Robert Francis Kennedy was born on November 20, 1925, in Brookline, Massachusetts, as the seventh child in a family destined for both triumph and heartbreak. Growing up in the shadow of his ambitious father, Joseph Kennedy Sr., a wealthy businessman and diplomat, and alongside his charismatic older brother John, Bobby—as he was affectionately known—learned early the weight of public service and the sting of personal loss. He served in the Navy during World War II, then pursued law at Harvard and the University of Virginia, emerging as a fierce advocate for justice. His bond with John deepened their paths; when JFK became president in 1961, Bobby served as Attorney General, tackling organized crime with unyielding determination and championing civil rights amid the era's turbulent struggles for equality. But tragedy struck hard in 1963 with John's assassination, shattering Bobby and reshaping his soul—he resigned his post, won a Senate seat from New York in 1964, and poured his grief into fighting poverty, opposing the Vietnam War, and bridging divides between races and classes. By 1968, as the nation reeled from division, Bobby launched a presidential bid that ignited hope; his message of compassion for the forgotten—workers, minorities, the poor—resonated deeply, and many saw him as a sure bet to claim the Democratic nomination and the White House, a healer in a wounded land.

Yet, on the night of June 5, 1968, just after celebrating a hard-won victory in California's primary, Bobby's light was extinguished in a Los Angeles hotel kitchen by the bullets of Sirhan Sirhan, a troubled assassin driven by political rage. He lingered for a day, surrounded by loved ones, before passing on June 6 at age 42, leaving behind his wife Ethel and their 11 children, including one unborn. The nation plunged into mourning, this loss compounding the agony of Martin Luther King Jr.'s murder months earlier and the riots that scarred cities; it felt like the end of an era of promise, fueling chaos at the Democratic convention and contributing to Richard Nixon's election.

Bobby's death robbed America of a voice for unity, leaving a void where empathy might have mended fractures, and reminding us all of the fragility of hope in the face of violence. Dr. King's legacy of nonviolence and judging people by their character lives on in the hearts and minds of millions.

"The quality, not the longevity, of one's life is what is important."
– Martin Luther King, Jr.

SECTION TWO
THE TURBULENT 1960s LEAD TO WAR'S END

THE RICHARD NIXON PRESIDENCY ENDS IN SHAME

Richard Nixon had fought hard to get to the White House. After narrow losses in 1960 and for California governor in 1962, he made a strong comeback in 1968, promising to bring peace with honor in Vietnam and restore order at home. By 1972, things looked bright for him. He was steadily pulling troops out of Vietnam, the economy was picking up, and people trusted him on foreign threats. That November, he won one of the biggest landslides ever, carrying 49 states, beating George McGovern by over 17 million votes and taking 520 electoral votes to just 17. Americans felt he was steering the country in the right direction.

The year started with a moment that lifted everyone's spirits. On July 20, 1969, Neil Armstrong stepped onto the moon, the first human to do so. Millions around the world—hundreds of millions—watched on television as he said those words about one small step for man, one giant leap for mankind. It felt like proof that American know-how and determination could achieve anything.

HENRY KISSINGER

Henry Kissinger, who fled Nazi Germany as a young Jewish refugee and understood the perils of tyranny firsthand, served as national security advisor under President Richard Nixon before becoming Secretary of State in September 1973, a role he continued under Gerald Ford until 1977. Amid the Cold War with the Soviet Union, the ongoing Vietnam War, and rising Middle East tensions, Kissinger employed a pragmatic approach known as realpolitik, prioritizing actions that safeguarded American interests over abstract ideals. A pivotal achievement was his orchestration of the U.S. opening to China, including a secret trip to Beijing in 1971 followed by Nixon's historic 1972 visit to meet Mao Zedong and Zhou Enlai—the first such handshake in decades.

This diplomatic breakthrough eased Cold War tensions, demonstrated that shrewd negotiation could reshape global dynamics without force, and strategically split the communist bloc, applying pressure on the Soviets. However, the long-term consequences emerged in the 1990s, as China's market integration led to the offshoring of American jobs and industries, resulting in millions of job losses and trillions in economic costs. Kissinger's influence extended to arms control agreements with the Soviets, limiting nuclear weapons and contributing to the eventual erosion of communism.

Following the 1973 Yom Kippur War between Israel and Arab nations, he pioneered shuttle diplomacy, traveling repeatedly to broker ceasefires and stabilize the region, ensuring the security of U.S. allies and the continuity of oil supplies. Despite controversies surrounding his methods—such as negotiating a Vietnam War conclusion that preserved some American prestige but drew criticism—Kissinger's emphasis on balancing power and bolstering U.S. strength laid foundational groundwork for America's ultimate victory in the Cold War.But shadows were growing. Protests against Vietnam kept boiling. In 1970, after Nixon sent troops into Cambodia to cut enemy supply lines, campuses erupted. At Kent State in Ohio, students gathered in anger. National Guard troops were called in. On May 4, shots rang out—four students killed, nine wounded. Pictures of the horror spread everywhere, turning more hearts against the war. It felt like the country was tearing itself apart.

THE TWENTY-SIXTH AMENDMENT

Young men were dying overseas but couldn't vote until they were 21. The cry went up: old enough to fight, old enough to vote. In 1971, the Twenty-Sixth Amendment was passed quickly, lowering the voting age nationwide to 18.

Tragedy struck again in 1972 at the Munich Olympics. Palestinian terrorists from Black September slipped into the Olympic Village, killed two Israeli athletes right away, and took nine more hostage. A failed rescue at the airport ended with all the hostages dead, along with some terrorists and a German officer. The world watched in shock as terrorism hit a peaceful gathering, showing how hatred could strike anywhere.

Even as Nixon's triumphs shone bright, trouble hit closer to home with his vice president, Spiro Agnew. Agnew had started strong—tough-talking on law and order, speaking out against war protesters and media bias in ways that resonated with many who felt the country was slipping. But in 1973, an investigation out of Maryland uncovered old habits from his days as county executive and governor: accepting cash envelopes from contractors seeking favors. These payments reportedly continued even into the vice presidency.

Along with this scandal, Nixon's darker side emerged. Paranoia about enemies led to wiretaps on opponents, using the IRS against those he disliked, and ordering the break-in at Democratic headquarters in the Watergate building. When the burglars got caught in June 1972, Nixon worked to cover it up—obstructing justice, lying to the country.

Tapes later revealed it all. As one close observer called it, a "cancer on the presidency"—a profound betrayal that eroded trust.

The charges piled up against Agnew—bribery, extortion, tax fraud. Agnew fought at first, calling it a witch hunt, but the evidence grew heavy. On October 10, 1973, he cut a deal: pleaded no contest to a single count of tax evasion on unreported income, paid a fine, and resigned—the second vice president in history to leave office that way, and the first over criminal charges unrelated to Watergate.

GERALD R. FORD

Nixon moved quickly to fill the spot, using the new Twenty-Fifth Amendment for the first time. He picked Gerald Ford, the steady House minority leader from Michigan known for his straightforward integrity. Congress confirmed him overwhelmingly, and Ford took the oath in December 1973. Little did anyone know then how soon that choice would matter.

These blows—scandals striking the top two offices—shook trust further, reminding everyone how power can tempt even those who start with good intentions. Yet the system held, providing a clear path forward, keeping the flame from going out amid the gathering storms.

Even his triumphs, like China, couldn't save him. In August 1974, facing certain impeachment, Nixon resigned—the only president ever to do so. I watched Nixon resign on television when I was a junior in high school. It was surreal.

Gerald Ford stepped in, a steady man who had never sought the job. His first significant act: pardoning Nixon fully for any crimes. It was meant to heal the nation's wounds, end the long nightmare, and let everyone move forward. Many were furious at first, feeling that justice had been denied. But Ford believed the country needed closure more than prolonged pain.

His wife, Betty Ford, brought her own quiet strength. She spoke openly about her breast cancer in 1974, saving lives by encouraging women to get checked. Later, facing her own struggles with pain pills and alcohol, she shared that too, founding treatment centers that helped countless people take responsibility and find recovery.

In homes across America, music was changing. FM radio had gotten stereo approval back in 1961, and by the 1970s, more precise sound drew listeners to album rock stations. It became the place for deeper tracks, pulling ahead of AM. What an incredible moment it was hearing FM stereo for the first time after listening to AM radio my whole life!

As Nixon left office, the war wound down—America's first major withdrawal without a clear victory, changing many hearts and minds about sending our finest into harm's way without a clear threat. Then came 1976, the Bicentennial. Parades, fireworks, tall ships sailing into harbors, wagon trains crossing the country—it was a nationwide celebration of 200 years since the Declaration. Bells rang out, families gathered, pride swelled anew.

During this period, high-concept feature film hits exploded, fueled by Star Wars and Jaws, turning movies into global events with massive marketing and merchandise.
CGI emerged, creating impossible worlds in films like Jurassic Park, while practical effects dazzled in action spectacles. Later, digital editing would speed post-production, and home video would bring films to living rooms. Franchises dominated—sequels, reboots, shared universes. Studios consolidated into conglomerates, chasing sure bets. For the next twenty years, top stars carried these giants: Tom Cruise, the daring action hero; Harrison Ford, wise and adventurous; Arnold Schwarzenegger, the unstoppable force; Julia Roberts, America's smiling sweetheart; and Will Smith, first as the Fresh Prince on television, next charismatic film star and box-office gold. Amid rising costs and competition from TV, Hollywood bet big on spectacle, blending heart-pounding thrills with star power to keep theaters packed.

Through triumph and shame, war and wonder, the flame flickered but held. Men like those astronauts reached the impossible; diplomats bridged divides; everyday people faced hard truths with courage. Resilient liberty endured the tests—paranoia in power, terror from without, division within—waiting for steady hands to carry it forward in faith and hope.

JIMMY CARTER'S CREATIONS

In the summer of 1976, as fireworks lit up skies for the nation's two-hundredth birthday, the presidential race tightened like a knot no one could quite untie. Gerald Ford had never sought the office through an election—first filling the vice presidency after Agnew's fall, then stepping into the Oval Office when Nixon resigned. His pardon of Nixon stemmed from a sincere wish to spare the country further bitterness and to turn the page on Watergate's long nightmare. Yet for many, that act felt like unfinished justice, a shadow that followed Ford all the way to November. A soft-spoken peanut farmer and former Georgia governor named Jimmy Carter stepped forward with a simple promise: "I'll never lie to you." He spoke of integrity and a government as good as its people. In one of the closest elections in years, Carter carried the South solidly and pieced together just enough elsewhere to win.

Carter brought a genuine faith to the White House—he taught Sunday school, quoted Scripture naturally, and carried a compassion that showed in his quiet smile and concern for the overlooked.

Leading the free world, though, tested him in ways few could have foreseen. Prices rose sharply month after month, turning grocery trips into quiet worries for families counting every dollar. Gas lines snaked around blocks again, drivers waiting hours in the heat, while foreign oil held the nation hostage. Rules and restrictions kept American drills idle even as vast reserves lay beneath our own soil. Hoping to bring order, Carter signed into law a new Department of Energy and, later, a Department of Education—central places in Washington meant to solve these troubles. Costs soared, offices multiplied, but the problems lingered, and over time, student performance in core subjects began drifting downward, a slow erosion that would last generations.

Elaine, one of my high school friends, became a teacher at an ordinary Midwestern school. She felt that drift up close. Elaine arrived early each morning, preparing lessons with care, watching children with real promise struggle with reading or numbers that earlier classes had mastered more easily. New federal requirements arrived in thick binders—forms to fill, standards to meet—yet the help for her classroom often felt distant, mismatched. She lay awake some nights wondering whether decisions made hundreds of miles away truly saw the faces in her room, or if parents and local communities might know better what their own children needed. Elaine's quiet ache was shared by countless others, a gentle reminder that even well-meaning plans from afar can lose touch with the lives they aim to lift.

STEVE JOBS AND THE PERSONAL COMPUTER

During those heavy years, a spark caught in a modest California garage. Steve Jobs, young and restless with ideas too big for ordinary paths, joined forces with Steve Wozniak to craft computers anyone could use at home. They sold their first machines almost by hand, driven by a belief that technology could unlock human creativity. What began there grew into Apple—a company that would put powerful tools in ordinary hands, changing how we learn, share, and dream. Jobs pursued his vision with unrelenting drive, convinced that excellence mattered deeply, that one more try could change everything.

Music offered release and connection. Disco lights flashed across dance floors as the Bee Gees and Donna Summer turned nights into celebrations of life and movement. Classic rock roared through speakers—Led Zeppelin and Fleetwood Mac, giving voice to longing and strength. Soul and R&B wrapped listeners in warmth, with Marvin Gaye asking hard questions and Earth, Wind & Fire lifting hearts toward joy and togetherness.

Faith itself shifted in those decades. From the mid-1970s into the new century, fewer people gathered in churches on Sunday mornings—attendance fell below forty percent, and growing numbers said they followed no religion at all. Scandals wounded trust in some places, and the rush of modern life pulled families in many directions at once. Still, Billy Graham carried on into his later years, filling arenas with people hungry for a clear call back to God. His son Franklin would later take up that work, keeping the message alive.

Yet many traded communal worship for private searching, drifting from the shared anchors that had steadied earlier generations.

Carter's presidency carried genuine kindness, yet it left burdens that weighed long after—inflation's bite, energy dependence, and education's fading grip. Intentions were often good, but distant solutions sometimes tangled more than they freed. Even so, the flame endured in quiet ways: a teacher's steady care, an inventor's bold leap, songs that bound strangers in shared feeling. Resilient liberty pressed on through the trials, carried by ordinary courage and the deep-rooted hope that personal responsibility and faith would light clearer days ahead.

FAILURES EXPOSED

During Carter's time in office, many government programs that had grown over the years continued to expand. They were meant to provide help in challenging moments, but for some families, the rules ended up making it harder to get ahead through work. Benefits increased in ways that reduced the financial gain from taking a job, so people stayed on aid longer than planned. What began as temporary support turned into something families leaned on for years, even generations. The intentions were kind, but the results often weakened that personal drive to stand on your own two feet.

In those same years, new policies started appearing in government jobs and companies, pushing for hires and promotions based more on group identity than on who was most qualified. It was an early move toward quotas—trying to balance numbers on paper rather than rewarding pure ability. The goal was to fix past injustices, but it frequently created new frustrations, lowered expectations in some places, and showed how chasing equal outcomes could chip away at the simple fairness of letting merit decide. Eventually, it would become almost perverted, advancing people solely based on their skin color or sexual orientation rather than by the merits of their work or their intelligence. Discrimination and racial prejudice cut both ways, and the wound feels the same.

Phyllis Schlafly noticed the risks right away. She was a devoted mother of six, grounded in her faith, and she carefully studied proposals like the Equal Rights Amendment. She believed it would strip away legal protections for wives and mothers, force women into roles they didn't choose, and give the government more control over family life. So she got to work—writing newsletters from her kitchen table, gathering women for meetings, traveling to speak wherever she could. Her clear, steady voice helped turn the tide, and the amendment fell short of ratification. Schlafly's effort protected space for families to thrive on their own terms, reminding everyone that real strength often comes from guarding what has proven good over time.

The country's sense of right and wrong shifted in subtle ways, too. Some programs, out of a desire to help, made it easier to walk away from marriage or responsibility without immediate consequences. Over time, that dependency crept in, quietly eroding pride and purpose. One working-class family in a Midwestern city lived it day by day. Steady checks arrived to cover basics, taking the edge off hard times, but gradually the father stopped looking for full-time work, and the children grew up thinking government help was just how life worked. The money eased hunger, yet it cost something deeper—self-respect, closer family ties, the quiet satisfaction of providing for your own.

Then the Iran hostage crisis brought everything into sharp focus. In November 1979, Iranian militants overran the U.S. embassy in Tehran and took 52 Americans captive, keeping them blindfolded and isolated for 444 days.

Carter chose negotiation first, hoping patience would bring them home. As the months wore on with no progress, pressure mounted. Finally, in April 1980, he authorized a high-risk rescue mission. Special forces teams flew low across the desert in helicopters and planes to a remote rendezvous called Desert One. Unexpected sandstorms battered the aircraft; several helicopters failed mechanically. With too few working machines left, the commander called it off. During the withdrawal, one helicopter collided with a parked transport plane. Fuel ignited, and a massive explosion killed eight American servicemen in an instant. The mission collapsed without reaching the hostages, leaving only charred wreckage for the world to see.

That failed rescue, on top of the long captivity, left Americans feeling the nation's strength had slipped. When election day came in 1980, Ronald Reagan won a landslide, carrying 44 states. Almost the moment he took the oath, word came that the hostages were released—a symbolic end to one era and the start of another.

Carter's presidency revealed hard truths: aid programs that sometimes trapped more than they lifted, policies that blurred merit, and a foreign crisis handled with heartbreaking loss. The flame of liberty burned low in those moments. Yet it never went out—carried by women like Schlafly defending home and faith, by families longing for independence, by servicemen who flew into danger for their captured brothers. Resilient liberty weathered the exposure, ready for fresh wind to fan it brighter through personal resolve and enduring hope.

SECTION THREE

DEBT'S SHADOW

Since Lyndon Johnson's Great Society programs took hold in the mid-1960s, social spending has grown steadily, fueling higher inflation at times and pushing the national debt from around $300 billion then to over $38 trillion as I write this book right before America's 250th anniversary. What began as efforts to help those in need expanded into vast commitments, with annual costs now in the trillions when adjusted for today's dollars, straining budgets and imposing heavy burdens on future generations.

WELFARE EXPANSION

When people look at the numbers today, they see that the government spends well over a trillion dollars every year just on "means-tested aid"—cash assistance, food help, housing support, and medical care for lower-income families. That's far more than anyone pictured back when these programs first started in the 1960s. If you add it all up since the War on Poverty began and adjust for inflation, the total comes to around $22–28 trillion in some careful counts, yet the official poverty rate hasn't dropped much—it's hovered between 11 and 15 percent for decades, not far from where it stood half a century ago. So, obviously, throwing money at problems not only doesn't help but also creates a system rife with waste, fraud, and abuse, which is what we are uncovering in vast amounts today.

These patterns of long-term reliance touch families in profound ways. A family might turn to aid during a brutal stretch—job loss, illness, something unexpected—and plan to use it only until things steady. But the way benefits phase out can make taking a full-time job mean less money overall, so staying on aid feels safer, even if no one wants it that way. Kids grow up watching this, and too often they end up in the same spot as adults—studies show children from homes on welfare are two or three times more likely to need it themselves later. It's a quiet cycle that dims the sense of possibility and the satisfaction of standing fully on your own. Also, the income tax system stifles those who work harder than others. When I was in my early thirties, I picked up a poolside gig at the Marriott in Palm Desert during the day to bolster my income while raising four children. I worked long hours, dragging my equipment around, and then working nights, sometimes seven days a week. When I went to file my taxes, I found that the extra income put me into a higher tax bracket, and most of it was taken by the government. I could have put my feet up at home all day during that period and been no less better off. This is a travesty for those of us who are willing to work harder to get ahead. It's also an incentive for people to stay on welfare, which is a crime.

My friend Jimmy, in his mid-forties, raising two children while holding down a factory job, started noticing the weight of it one night while reviewing his monthly bills. He'd worked steadily for twenty years, paying taxes without much complaint, figuring they helped people who truly needed it. But as his own costs climbed—higher prices at the store, harder to save for his children's future—and he read about trillions being spent on programs that seemed to run forever without lifting many out, something shifted. He thought about the debt piling up for his kids and grandkids, and about how America has always thrived when people have clear paths to earn their way. That evening led him to dig deeper, join local discussions, even send notes to his representatives—simple actions from a father who believed the nation's real strength comes from balancing compassion with encouragement toward independence, guided by faith and personal effort. My mother said, **"If you don't toot your own horn, who else will?"** Getting involved can make a difference.

In the tapestry of American life, woven from threads of hard work, resilience, and neighborly kindness, there's a shared heartbeat: no one wants to see a fellow citizen starve or sink into despair. Picture a nation built by pioneers who pulled themselves up by their bootstraps, yet always extended a hand to those truly in need—widows, orphans, people with disabilities, or families hit by unforeseen calamity. This compassion fueled the growth of the welfare state, beginning with noble intentions during the Great Depression and expanding through the War on Poverty in the 1960s, with the aim of lifting the vulnerable out of hardship. But over decades, what began as a safety net has ballooned into a sprawling system, often ensnaring those it was meant to free, riddled with waste, fraud, and abuse that siphons billions from taxpayers. Hard-working folks—plumbers, teachers, small-business owners—feel the pinch as their earnings are redistributed not just to people in need, but sometimes to those capable of self-sufficiency yet choosing idleness, breeding resentment and eroding the dignity of work. It's a story of good hearts leading to unintended chains, where empathy without accountability creates dependency rather than empowerment. And adding the flame of massive taxpayer-funded fraud in other programs to the fire only exacerbates hard-working people's feelings about waste and abuse.

"We need an equal opportunity society, one in which government does not see its job as picking winners and losers. Where do you go if you want special favors? Government. Where do you go if you want a tax break? Government. Where do you go if you want a handout? Government. This must stop." – Bobby Jindal

This divide reveals the core clash between liberal and conservative visions, like two paths diverging in a wood, each claiming to lead to prosperity. Liberals often rely on expansive government handouts—forgiving student loans, broadening entitlements, or disbursing benefits—to rally votes, fostering a cycle in which dependency secures political loyalty but fails to address root causes such as broken families or a lack of opportunity. In contrast, conservatives seek to protect the truly needy while solving deeper issues through personal responsibility, work requirements, and community-driven reforms that promote upward mobility and self-reliance. Think of the 1996 welfare reform, a bipartisan triumph that slashed poverty by tying aid to employment, proving that tough love can heal rather than just bandage. Conservatives don't oppose help; they champion compassionate, practical solutions that honor the giver and uplift the receiver, ensuring America's promise remains a ladder anyone can climb with effort and integrity.

In the face of these growing pressures—trillions flowing out each year, families caught in loops that hold them back, taxpayers stretched, futures burdened—the flame of liberty felt the heat. But it kept burning in quiet awakenings like that man's, in hearts that long for a country where proper help builds strength rather than reliance. Resilient liberty pressed through the strain, holding on for a return to stewardship, courage, and those enduring truths that make freedom last.

KNOWLEDGE DISTORTED

Think about how it happens sometimes: the bills for these big aid programs keep getting bigger every year, but the whole story stays locked away in stacks of reports that hardly anyone sits down to read—even many in Congress admitted to voting on massive laws without even reading them. The numbers that really matter, like trillions spent while poverty levels stay pretty much the same, tend to get tucked in the back, while heartwarming stories of someone who was actually helped take center stage to keep everyone on board. And when ordinary folks or experts started asking tough questions—"Is this actually lifting people out long-term?" or "Could we do this smarter?"—they often got waved off, told they didn't care about the needy. Or, they are called racist or heartless.

A lot of people held up Canada's health care system as the ideal: government covers everybody, no one is left out.
But lately, that same system has opened the door wider on assisted dying—what they call medical assistance in dying—until it now accounts for more than one in twenty deaths across the country, over 16,000 in 2024 alone. Most cases involve terminal illness, sure, but more and more include older people, those with disabilities, or chronic conditions that aren't immediately fatal, sometimes brought up when ongoing treatment looks too costly or hard to arrange. And in that system, waiting lists for surgeries stretch on—stories come out of patients dying before they ever get the operation that could have saved them.

Grand promises by Communists and Socialists that everything will be affordable and fair for all sound good at first, but history shows they often end with a few at the top living far better than everyone else. Margaret Thatcher put it plainly one day: the trouble is, you eventually run out of other people's money. In countries that handed full control of the economy to the government, party bosses and their families quietly built up luxuries—big homes, special stores stocked with imports—while regular families lined up for hours to get bread or shoes. The fire to start a business, invent something new, or put in extra effort fades when most of what you earn goes away, and soon there's less for anybody.

People often assume that raising taxes on the wealthy will bring in rivers of cash to pay for it all. But look at what really happened. In the 1950s and early 1960s, the top rate appeared high—over 90 percent on paper—but with legal ways to protect earnings, the richest ended up paying closer to 42 percent, and the government collected much less than those big numbers suggested. When rates fell in the 1920s, the Kennedy era, Reagan's time, and later under Donald Trump, more investment flowed, businesses grew, take-home pay rose, and, surprisingly, the Treasury often collected more from high earners than before. Capital gains worked the same way: dropping the rate from 28 percent to 20 percent in 1997, then to 15 percent in 2003, got people selling assets and putting money back to work, filling government coffers better than the higher rates ever did.

"Collecting more taxes than is absolutely necessary is legalized robbery."
– Calvin Coolidge

Taxes aimed just at the well-off don't stop there; they cool the kind of growth that creates good jobs and raises wages for everyone. Less money to invest means fewer new businesses, fewer opportunities, and in the end, it's working families who feel it most. And when you pit one class against the other to bolster your own power, you are doing no good for anyone but yourself.

One man who saw the distortions, waste, fraud, and abuse up close paid a heavy price for speaking out. A longtime analyst inside a federal agency, he'd spent years crunching the numbers on welfare programs—watching trillions flow out while long-term poverty held steady and dependency deepened. The reports he helped prepare told a clear story, but higher-ups kept pushing versions that highlighted short-term assistance and downplayed the cycles that trap families.
When he finally shared the unvarnished data with congressional staff and a few journalists, hoping for honest debate, the backlash came fast. Colleagues turned cold, investigations into his work began, and leaks painted him as disloyal. He lost promotions, faced quiet threats to his job, and endured years of strain on his family—all for wanting the truth known so better paths could open. His quiet stand, rooted in a belief that real compassion demands honesty and that America's strength lies in facing hard facts, reminded others that courage often costs something personal. Yet, it keeps the flame burning brighter for everyone.

In all these ways—essential details hidden in fine print, honest questions brushed aside, admired systems showing cracks no one wants to talk about, big promises running into hard walls—the flame of liberty met clouds of confusion. Yet it kept glowing in people who wouldn't stop looking for the truth, in lives rooted in personal effort and the kind of careful stewardship faith calls us to. Resilient liberty moved through the mist, carried forward by quiet courage and the steady hope for clearer days ahead.

THE IMPERATIVE FOR REFORM

There's a way back from the heavy shadow, and it begins with people willing to make tough but kind decisions—looking honestly at programs that overlap or haven't delivered, trimming the parts that waste money, and steering what's left toward help that truly sets people free. It's been done before, and when it has, ordinary families have felt the difference: a hand up that doesn't hold them down.

Self-reliance runs deep in the American story—it's that quiet force that gets us out of bed each morning, ready to build something for ourselves and our kids. When the rules start rewarding hard work again—when taking a job brings home more than staying on aid, when saving or starting a small business feels worth the risk—people rise to it. Neighbors look out for one another more naturally, churches and local groups step in with real personal care, and that old sense of pride in providing for your own family comes back strong. Self-reliance is what drove our ancestors and what the founders wanted for all of us.

Getting back to bedrock principles isn't turning the clock back; it's remembering the truths that have carried us this far. Government that stays in its lane, personal responsibility at the heart of things, compassion shaped by faith—these aren't dusty ideas, they're the ones that have proven they work. They leave room for people to chase their own dreams without someone far away pulling every string.

One place that lived this out was Wisconsin in the mid-1990s. Welfare rolls there seemed to go on forever, with families caught for years, sometimes generations. Governor Tommy Thompson, a plain-spoken man who believed deeply in second chances paired with real expectations, teamed up with lawmakers to try something different. They set time limits on cash aid, required able-bodied recipients to work or train for jobs, and put real effort into helping people find employment rather than just sending checks. Many worried it would hurt the vulnerable, but the opposite happened.
Employment among single mothers shot up—some counts showed increases of over 100 percent in work participation. Child poverty fell faster than anywhere else in the country, costs to taxpayers eased, and thousands of families found steady ground. One mother who had been on aid for years later shared how landing her first full-time job changed everything: coming home tired but with her own paycheck in hand, seeing respect in her children's eyes as they watched her provide. That Wisconsin experiment helped shape the bipartisan national reform enacted by Newt Gingrich's Congress and President Bill Clinton in 1996. Across the country, millions stepped toward independence, dignity returning like sunlight after a long storm.

The nets of dependency had weighed heavily for decades, dimming the light, but leaders like Ronald Reagan and Donald Trump reached for the bellows to fan the flame brighter. Reagan cut taxes to boost economic growth and stood firm abroad, so peace came through strength. Trump followed suit years later, putting more money back in working people's pockets and watching growth take off again. Their examples still point the way: straightforward strategies that guard peace with resolve, build prosperity through freedom, and leave no room for endless chains from distant halls.

Debt and dependency cast a long shadow, testing resilient liberty to its core, yet that flame never went out. It glowed softly in homes where parents taught their children the value of honest work and trust in God, in neighborhoods that chose their own solutions over mandates from afar, in reformers who faced sharp criticism yet held fast because they believed better days were possible. During the last 20 years of the 20th century, fresh voices rose up to scatter the haze—showing once more that strength, both at home and abroad, anchored in timeless truths, could revive the dream and carry it forward. The story now turns to how America found its resolve again, meeting threats with steady courage and rekindling prosperity without giving away the freedom that makes it all possible.

"When America is united, America is totally unstoppable." – Donald Trump

CHAPTER TWELVE
STRENGTH'S RENEWAL

DETERRING THREATS, REVIVING DREAMS

In the shadow of a mighty Soviet communist empire that seemed unbreakable, one leader stepped forward with steady resolve to rebuild America's defenses and speak truth to tyranny. Ronald Reagan called it simply "peace through strength—the idea that true safety comes not from wishing away danger, but from standing ready to meet it. His clear voice and bold actions helped end decades of fear without a shot being fired between the superpowers, proving that deterrence, backed by courage and moral clarity, can change the world. This chapter examines how that strength revived the nation's spirit, met threats head-on, and opened the way to prosperity, offering lessons still fresh for guiding us toward secure peace and renewed dreams.

Ronald Reagan once said, "Freedom is a fragile thing, and it's never more than one generation away from extinction." He meant that liberty isn't handed down like an inheritance—it has to be guarded, fought for, and passed on by each new generation willing to stand watch.

SECTION ONE
REAGAN'S DETERRENCE

When Ronald Reagan took the oath on a cold January day in 1981, the country felt worn down—lines at gas pumps, prices rising fast, hostages still held overseas. But in his calm voice that afternoon, he reminded everyone that America's story wasn't over; it was just waiting for fresh wind. His famous 1984 campaign captured it perfectly with the line "It's morning in America again"—a picture of brighter days where families could look ahead with hope. Reagan brought that same light to a world gripped by Cold War tension, cutting taxes to unleash the economy, rebuilding the military to stand firm against threats, and speaking plainly about the worth of freedom.

His faith showed quietly—in prayers before big decisions, in believing America had a special role to play.

Just seventy days into his presidency, danger struck close. As Reagan left a Washington hotel after a speech, shots rang out from a young man named John Hinckley. A bullet hit the president under the arm, collapsing a lung and stopping inches from his heart. Press secretary James Brady was taken to the head, left permanently wounded. In the chaos, Reagan stayed remarkably calm—cracking to the doctors, "I hope you're all Republicans," and to his wife Nancy, "Honey, I forgot to duck." He pulled through, stronger in the eyes of many, a living reminder that leadership means facing fire without flinching.

People whispered about an old pattern: presidents elected every twenty years from 1840 onward—Harrison, Lincoln, Garfield, McKinley, Harding, Roosevelt, Kennedy—all died in office, a string some called Tecumseh's Curse after a Native leader's supposed vow against American leaders. The coincidences piled up strangely between Lincoln and Kennedy, a century apart—elected to Congress a hundred years apart, presidents in '60 years, both shot in the head on Fridays beside their wives, successors named Johnson born a century apart. It felt eerie, almost fateful. But Reagan's survival broke the chain—no more deaths in those zero years—and the "curse" faded like morning mist.

MILITARY REBUILD

Reagan poured real resources into modernizing the military—new ships, better training, advanced systems—that put pressure on the Soviet system beyond its limits. The Soviets tried to keep pace, but their economy groaned under the strain, spending they couldn't afford on weapons rather than food or goods for their people.

At home, the economy answered firmly. With ideas from men like Jack Kemp pushing supply-side thinking—lower taxes to free up energy for growth—Reagan signed significant cuts that put more money in pockets and sparked years of expansion. Jobs grew, businesses started, and families felt the lift.

Nancy Reagan stood beside her husband through it all, fierce in protecting him and clear in her own cause. She traveled the country, urging young people to "Just Say No" to drugs, visiting schools and centers, speaking from the heart about keeping dreams safe from addiction's pull. Her steady voice helped many find the strength to choose better paths.

The Cold War's end came quietly, without the war everyone feared. Reagan met Soviet leader Mikhail Gorbachev several times, building trust while holding firm. British Prime Minister Margaret Thatcher encouraged both sides toward openness. Reagan's proposed "Star Wars" missile defense—formally known as the Strategic Defense Initiative—worried Soviet planners, leading them to realize they couldn't match American innovation forever.

Gorbachev brought reforms at home, but the system cracked. By 1991, under Reagan's loyal vice president, George H.W. Bush, now in office, the Soviet Union dissolved—the infamous Berlin wall fell, nations freed themselves, and peace spread where fear once ruled.

"We hold our heads high, despite the price we have paid, because freedom is priceless." – Lech Walesa

THE WORLD WIDE WEB

Around that same time, a quiet invention changed everything. In 1989-1991, Tim Berners-Lee at a European lab created the World Wide Web—a way to link information across computers worldwide. What started as a tool for scientists grew into something connecting billions, opening doors to knowledge, trade, and voices once silenced. I had a friend, Michael Schwartz, who was in on the first phase of the web. He showed me how to get on my computer and type a sentence from California, and it would show up on his computer in Florida. I was amazed! We could communicate in real time through our computers by typing sentences to each other, one at a time! How the world has changed since then.

Even in victory's glow, traitors worked in shadows. Navy officer John Walker ran a family spy ring for nearly twenty years, passing cipher keys and submarine secrets that let the Soviets track American forces and risk sailors' lives. Arrested in 1985, he and his recruits faced justice for damage called one of the worst breaches ever.

Another, Jonathan Pollard, a Navy analyst, handed thousands of documents to Israel—an ally—revealing sources that strained trust and endangered agents. Caught in 1985, he served decades before parole in 2015 and moved to Israel in 2020.

One young patriotic sailor serving during the buildup felt the change deeply. He'd joined when morale was low, equipment was old, but under Reagan's push, he watched ships modernize, training sharpen, and pride return. Standing watch on a carrier deck one dawn, he thought of the men before him who'd faced real peril, and felt grateful to serve in strength that kept peace. That quiet sense of purpose—knowing readiness guarded freedom—stayed with him always.

Through rebuild and resolve, the the economy surged, moral clarity at home—the flame burned bright again. Liberty triumphed not by force alone, but by standing tall in truth, faith, and courage. The Cold War closed peacefully, and a new world opened wide, proving resilient liberty shines strongest when defended without apology.

ECONOMIC LEVERAGE

When Reagan's tax cuts really kicked in during the early 1980s, the economy started moving again in a way people hadn't felt for years. Rates came down, so workers and business owners kept more of their earnings. All of a sudden, taking a chance on a new venture or adding a few employees didn't feel so daunting.

Growth picked up, new jobs appeared, and families who'd been pinching pennies to get by could finally relax a little. It wasn't some trick—it was just the straightforward reality that when people have more of their own money to spend or invest, things start happening.

At the same time, personal computers moved out of back rooms and into regular homes and workplaces. Steve Jobs over at Apple had this clear vision: machines that looked good and felt easy to use, almost like they belonged in your living room. He and Steve Wozniak got it started with the Apple II back in the late seventies—a computer you could plug in and actually work with right away.

Meanwhile, Bill Gates and Paul Allen at Microsoft were writing the software that made all this possible. They landed a big deal with IBM, and soon Microsoft's Windows turned screens into something familiar: icons you could click, menus to choose from, a desktop layout anyone could understand. No more typing endless commands—computers became tools ordinary people could handle, sparking whole new ways to work and create. This desktop concept actually borrowed from Apple's approach in the early days. As a musician and composer, I used Apple computers starting in the mid-1980s and grew with them through the analog-to-digital era. I always felt the Apple system was a superior computer, and in my current studio as I write this in 2026, I'm still an Apple user 35 years later. Future generations reading this book will laugh at this!

Reagan didn't stop at home; he also used America's economic weight abroad. When martial law clamped down on Poland and crushed fundamental freedoms there, he tightened sanctions on the Soviet Union—cutting off technology and trade they counted on. It hit hard because their system was already stretched thin, pouring everything into weapons while citizens queued for hours just for food.

"The principles that should guide American foreign policy are simple: the world is safer when America leads, only strength ensures peace and freedom, and America must stand with its allies and challenge its adversaries."
– Kevin McCarthy

Innovation flowed freely in those years. With fewer heavy regulations in the way, companies large and small had space to try things, to grow. American products and ideas traveled the world, quietly showing what happens when people are left free to build.

My friend Jim ran a small manufacturing shop in a Midwest town. Jim lived that change day to day. He'd kept the doors open through the rough late seventies, watching inflation swallow profits and taxes take a big bite. But once the cuts hit and orders started coming in again, everything shifted.

He brought on new hands, upgraded machines, and saw the business steady and then expand. For the first time in a long while, Jim could offer solid wages, set aside something for his children's future, and even increase his giving at church. It wasn't abstract growth on a chart—it meant families in his town eating better, feeling secure, taking pride in honest work again.

In all this—tax relief unleashing energy, computers handing real power to everyday people, smart pressure on rivals, fresh ideas breaking through—the flame gained new life. Economic leverage proved liberty's quiet power: let people create and keep what they earn, and prosperity comes, values travel on their own, threats fade without constant battle. Resilient liberty glowed strong in those days, carried by ordinary makers and decisions grounded in faith and enduring hope.

THE WORLD ECONOMIC FORUM

In 1971, as Europe grappled with economic instability in the wake of World War II, Klaus Schwab, a professor of business policy at the University of Geneva, launched the European Management Forum. This initial gathering in Geneva aimed to connect corporate leaders, drawing on American management techniques to promote efficiency and ethical practices. Schwab introduced the concept of "stakeholder capitalism," urging businesses to balance profits with responsibilities to employees, communities, and the environment—a framework that seemed innovative and grounded in fostering sustainable growth. By 1987, during the Reagan years, the organization had broadened its reach, renaming itself the World Economic Forum and transforming its annual Davos summit into a magnet for global elites, including politicians and executives, to debate pressing international issues.

Over time, however, the WEF's mission has shifted dramatically, evolving into what many people view as a driver of centralized globalism that directly challenges America's core values of individual freedom, national sovereignty, and limited government. The 2020 "Great Reset" initiative, unveiled during the height of the pandemic, exemplifies this change: Schwab advocated a fundamental overhaul of economies and societies through close collaboration between governments and corporations, encompassing climate action, digital surveillance, and resource redistribution. Phrases like "You'll own nothing and be happy" have fueled concerns that this vision promotes a form of collectivism or even communism, prioritizing elite-driven agendas over personal property rights and democratic self-determination—turning the forum from a dialogue hub into a perceived architect of a borderless world order that undermines the independent spirit at the heart of the American experiment.

MORAL LEADERSHIP AND POP CULTURE

Reagan never made decisions in a vacuum—they came from somewhere deeper, from a man who prayed regularly, turned to Scripture for guidance, and truly believed America carried a special calling, much like the founders who knelt in prayer before signing their names to history. That quiet faith shaped everything: policies that aimed to lift people rather than control them, and a willingness to stand unflinching against evil.

His words reached far beyond America's borders. Allies drew strength from his plainspoken defense of freedom, and those trapped behind iron curtains heard a president who refused to look away. He called tyranny what it was—gulags where dissenters vanished, walls splitting families, secret police haunting every shadow—without softening the truth for diplomacy's sake.

Because someone finally spoke clearly, hope began to stir in places long darkened. Ordinary people under oppression started to believe that their day might come.

The Space Shuttle embodied that same bold spirit—American ingenuity pushing boundaries, reaching for the heavens. Then, on a crisp January morning in 1986, Challenger rose from the pad with seven brave souls aboard, including Christa McAuliffe, the teacher who would share lessons from orbit. Just over a minute later, the sky filled with fire and smoke as the shuttle came apart. Millions watched in stunned silence as the white plumes forked and fell toward the sea. That night, Reagan addressed a grieving nation, his voice steady yet heavy with sorrow, ending with words about the crew slipping "the surly bonds of earth" to "touch the face of God." The loss cut deep, but it also revealed the heart of real courage—everyday Americans willing to risk everything so humanity could move forward.

On the Supreme Court, thoughtful voices began pushing back against decades of federal overreach. William Rehnquist, a quiet, principled Arizonan who joined the bench in 1972 and became Chief Justice in 1986, led that effort. In decisions like United States v. Lopez, he reminded the country that Washington's power has limits—not everything can be claimed under the commerce clause. His steady work gave states and communities room to breathe again.

Antonin Scalia joined in 1986, bringing sharp intellect and an infectious laugh. Raised in New Jersey by an Italian immigrant father who taught the value of words, Scalia insisted the Constitution means what it says, no more, no less. His opinion in Heller protected an individual's right to keep and bear arms, and his writings on federalism planted seeds that later courts harvested. Even when he lost, his dissents—clear, forceful, sometimes laced with humor—became guides for future majorities.

Sandra Day O'Connor broke new ground as the first woman on the Court, appointed by Reagan in 1981. Raised on a remote Arizona ranch where self-reliance was daily life, she brought practical wisdom and a Western sense of fairness, often bridging divides while staying true to the law's foundations.

William F. Buckley Jr. shaped minds from his desk and television studio. With his quick wit and deep vocabulary, he hosted conversations, wrote columns, and founded National Review, giving clear expression to ideas rooted in faith, freedom, and limited government.

His calm, reasoned voice helped countless people understand the dangers of tyranny and the quiet gifts of liberty.

Pop culture also carried powerful messages. Michael Jackson took the world by storm—moonwalking across stages, blending rhythms no one had quite mixed before, drawing people together across every boundary. His extraordinary talent showed the boundless reach of American creativity. Other iconic artists of the decade included Whitney Houston, Madonna, and Prince.

Steven Spielberg told stories that lingered in the heart. With Schindler's List, he brought the Holocaust's unimaginable horror and quiet heroism to the screen in stark black and white—ordinary people risking their lives to save strangers from Nazi death camps. Millions who might never have fully grasped tyranny's evil or the courage needed to resist it walked away changed.

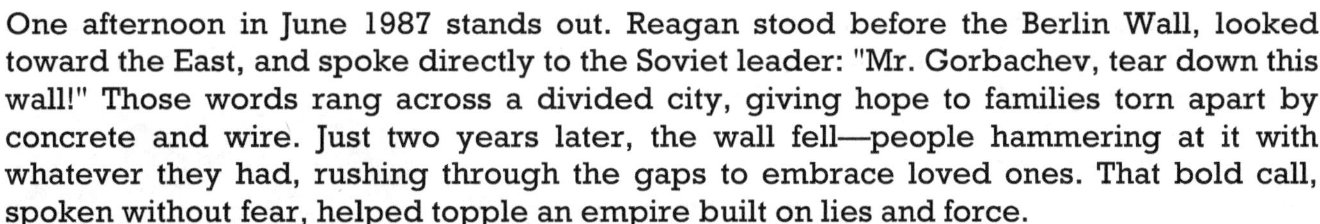

One afternoon in June 1987 stands out. Reagan stood before the Berlin Wall, looked toward the East, and spoke directly to the Soviet leader: "Mr. Gorbachev, tear down this wall!" Those words rang across a divided city, giving hope to families torn apart by concrete and wire. Just two years later, the wall fell—people hammering at it with whatever they had, rushing through the gaps to embrace loved ones. That bold call, spoken without fear, helped topple an empire built on lies and force.

In all these ways—faith quietly guiding choices, voices naming wrong without apology, stories teaching hard truths, courage shining even in sorrow—the flame burned with a clear moral light. Liberty's most significant power revealed itself not just in strength of arms, but in conviction, compassion, and the steady hope of truth spoken aloud. Resilient liberty reached across the world in those years, carried by leaders and creators anchored in enduring values.

GEORGE H.W. BUSH

George H.W. Bush started his path to the presidency with service in World War II. At 18, he became the Navy's youngest pilot, flying 58 missions in the Pacific. He was shot down once over the ocean but survived, earning the Distinguished Flying Cross for his bravery. After the war, he moved to Texas and built a successful oil company. Then he got into politics, serving as a Congressman from 1967 to 1971, where he backed civil rights laws and focused on careful spending. Later, he took on big jobs, including U.S. Ambassador to the U.N. and CIA Director, from 1976 to 1977 under President Ford. There, he fixed problems at the intelligence agency following scandals, ensuring operations were more ethical.

He served as Ronald Reagan's vice president for eight years, and in 1988, he ran for president himself—a rare win for a sitting VP, like Martin Van Buren in 1836. Bush got the Republican nomination by promising to keep Reagan's ideas going, like no new taxes and strong defense. He ran against Democrat Michael Dukakis, highlighting Dukakis's liberal views on issues such as crime and patriotism. With a strong economy and Reagan's support, Bush won decisively: 426 electoral votes to Dukakis's 111 and over 53% of the popular vote. This kept Republicans in the White House and showed support for steady, anti-communist policies.

From 1989 to 1993, as the 41st president, Bush handled major world events. He guided the U.S. through the end of the Cold War. He also led an international group to win the Gulf War against Iraq after it invaded Kuwait, which many say showed strong U.S. leadership without dragging out the fight. At home, he signed laws like the Americans with Disabilities Act to expand rights and the Clean Air Act to improve the environment, working with both parties. He tried to cut the budget deficit with fiscal smarts, even though he broke his promise not to raise taxes. Bush started work on NAFTA to boost trade and the economy. He lost reelection in 1992 due to a recession, but his practical style built stronger ties with other countries and kept things stable, while focusing on moral leadership and innovative strategies.

JAMES A. BAKER III

James A. Baker III became Secretary of State in January 1989 when George H.W. Bush took office as president. This was right at the end of the Cold War, when the Soviet Union was weakening, and significant changes were happening in Europe and the Middle East. Baker, who had been a close advisor to Bush for years, focused on keeping the U.S. in a strong position during this shift.

One of his biggest jobs was handling the reunification of Germany in 1990. East and West Germany sought to reunite after decades of division, but the Soviets feared losing influence. Baker worked quietly with leaders from both sides and the Soviets to ensure the process went smoothly without sparking a crisis or backlash—he helped negotiate agreements that allowed Germany to reunite as a free country while reassuring Moscow.

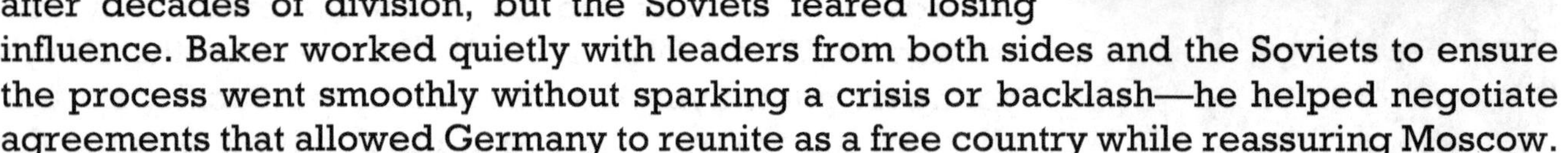

Then, in 1990-1991, Iraq invaded Kuwait, and Baker built a large international coalition—more than 30 countries—to push back. He spoke with allies around the world, secured support from the United Nations, and ensured the U.S. had partners for what became the Gulf War. This showed how he could bring people together to isolate threats like Saddam Hussein while protecting American interests, especially in oil and energy security.

Baker also pushed for free trade deals and stronger economic ties to help the U.S. economy. Behind the scenes, he worked on Middle East peace talks, setting up meetings between Israel and Arab leaders that laid the foundation for later agreements.

His approach was brutal but realistic—using diplomacy and alliances to keep America strong without unnecessary fights. He left the job in August 1992, but his work helped guide the U.S. through a major global transition, ending the Cold War era on America's terms and building partnerships that lasted for years.

Back in the gritty streets of the Bronx in the early 1980s, something electric was born. Young kids, armed with nothing but turntables, spray paint, and unstoppable heart, took the microphone with "street poetry" and turned it into pure expression. Hip-hop and rap exploded out of block parties and boom boxes, giving voice to rhythm, rhyme, and the unstoppable American beat when the world needed new energy. By the 1990s, the whole country was moving to it — Run-DMC, Public Enemy, Tupac, Biggie — while Luther Vandross wrapped us in velvet soul that made grown men cry and boy bands like NSYNC and Backstreet Boys filled arenas with screaming teenage girls, proving that American music could be tender, rebellious, flashy, and fearless all at the same time. It wasn't just entertainment; it was the sound of freedom ringing loud and clear.

SECTION TWO:
THE 1990s AND MORAL DECAY IN THE PRESIDENCY

"Every two years the American politics industry fills the airwaves with the most virulent, scurrilous, wall-to-wall character assassination of nearly every political practitioner in the country - and then declares itself puzzled that America has lost trust in its politicians." – Charles Krauthammer

BILL CLINTON

The 1992 election felt like the country couldn't quite make up its mind. Votes split three ways—George H.W. Bush carrying the weight of incumbency, Bill Clinton promising change, and Ross Perot, the plain-talking Texan billionaire, pulling in folks frustrated with both sides. Perot took almost nineteen percent of the popular vote, the strongest third-party showing in decades. In the end, Clinton won the Electoral College comfortably. Still, he entered the White House with only forty-three percent of Americans behind him—the first president in a long while without a clear majority. His years saw steady economic growth and even some balanced budgets, but personal scandal cast a long shadow. When news broke of an affair with a young White House intern named Monica Lewinsky, Clinton denied it under oath. Evidence piled up, leading the House to impeach him for perjury and obstruction of justice. The Senate held a trial but acquitted him. The whole episode left many feeling that truth itself had taken a hit at the very top, and trust in those who lead us grew thinner.

Still, good came when people set aside their differences. Clinton signed major welfare reform driven by a Republican Congress and Speaker Newt Gingrich—putting time limits on aid, expecting work in return, and helping people find jobs instead of just sending checks. Millions left the rolls for paychecks, child poverty dropped noticeably, and families who had felt stuck for years found a new footing. It showed what can happen when leaders focus on what actually helps people stand taller.

THE TWENTY-SEVENTH AMENDMENT

One quiet victory that year was the Twenty-Seventh Amendment finally becoming law. Proposed all the way back in 1789 alongside the Bill of Rights, it had gathered dust for over two hundred years. A college student named Gregory Watson stumbled across it while writing a paper, argued it could still be ratified, and got a C grade for his trouble. Instead of letting it go, Watson spent a decade writing letters, calling legislators, pushing state by state until Michigan put it over the top in 1992. The amendment is simple: any pay raise Congress gives itself can't start until after the next election—voters get their say first. Watson's lone persistence proved that one determined citizen can still breathe life into the Constitution's safeguards. Every amendment after the original ten feels like a careful stitch on the founding document—each one added when the nation spotted a tear and reached for needle and thread. They show the founders built something meant to endure, to heal itself when needed, to grow wiser with time. The flame they handed us is still ours to guard, and guarding it means holding close to what the words actually say, not bending them to fit passing wishes.

The nineties also brought the slow bleed of manufacturing jobs overseas. Deals like NAFTA, signed in 1993, opened foreign markets but shuttered factories in towns that had built cars, steel, and furniture for generations. Plants closed one after another—communities that once thrived on steady work watched families move away, stores board up, dreams shrink. The intention was broader competition, but the cost fell hardest on American workers who had played by the rules and now found the game had changed under them.

Even in peacetime, betrayal lurked. Aldrich Ames, a CIA officer buried in debt and growing bitter, started selling secrets to the Soviets for cash—names of brave agents working inside Russia. Because of him, dozens were dragged away and shot, and operations that took years to build collapsed overnight. Arrested in 1994, he spent his remaining days in prison, a grim reminder of how one man's weakness can cost innocent lives far away.

Robert Hanssen wore an FBI badge meant to catch spies, but for more than 20 years, he fed secrets to Moscow—cash and diamonds in exchange for lists of informants who soon disappeared, details of hidden tunnels under embassies, plans for nuclear defense. Caught in 2001 after a risky drop, he pleaded guilty and died behind bars in 2023. The betrayal from someone sworn to protect us cut especially deep.

Clarence Thomas took his seat on the Supreme Court in 1991 after a confirmation battle that turned ugly with last-minute accusations many felt were unfair and timed to derail him. Born poor in rural Georgia, raised by a grandfather who demanded hard work and faith, Thomas had pulled himself up step by step. On the bench, he became the most unmistakable voice for reading the Constitution straight—no twisting words to match the moment.
His opinions defended individual rights, checked federal overreach, and built foundations that later courts would stand on.

Newt Gingrich stepped up as Speaker in 1995 with fire and focus, leading a Contract with America that promised accountability and smaller government. His drive helped deliver welfare reform and fiscal discipline, showing that strong ideas and teamwork can move mountains.

Rush Limbaugh turned the radio into a daily gathering place for millions who felt their views went unheard. With straightforward talk and sharp insight, he gave voice to principles of freedom and responsibility, building a conversation that lasted hours every weekday.

Bill Gates guided Microsoft through the decade's tech explosion, making computers accessible to everyone. His company's reach created enormous wealth and opportunity, though questions later arose about the influence wielded through foundations and global initiatives.

Oprah Winfrey built an empire from a Chicago studio, opening her heart and home on television to stories of pain and triumph. Her warmth drew people in, her book club changed reading habits, and her voice lifted many who needed to feel seen.

As the calendar flipped to 2000, Silicon Valley buzzed with promise—startups popping up overnight, the internet linking lives in ways no one had imagined. The dot-com bubble swelled with dreams of endless riches, then burst hard in 2000, wiping out fortunes and jobs in a flash.

Y2K fears had everyone bracing for computers to fail at midnight—banks prepared, governments stockpiled, families wondered if lights would stay on. When the clocks rolled over quietly, relief washed over, but the scare reminded us how much we were coming to depend on technology's fragile threads. And the coming years would make us only more dependent. Through the decade's highs and lows—scandals that bruised trust, reforms that restored dignity, jobs slipping away, traitors unmasked, voices standing for truth—the flame wavered but never went out. Moral stumbles tested the nation's heart, yet every day, courage and quiet faithfulness kept it burning. Resilient liberty weathered the storms, carried forward by those who refused to let personal failing or distant deals dim the light of accountability, compassion, and hope.

SECTION THREE:

THE NEW MILLENIUM OPENS WITH TRAGEDY

The calendar turned to 2000, and hope ran high—new century, new possibilities, technology promising to connect the world like never before.

People gathered with friends and family to watch the ball drop, breathing easier when computers didn't crash at midnight. But beneath the celebration, danger was gathering far away, in hidden camps and quiet meetings, where men twisted faith into hatred and planned something unthinkable.

GEORGE W. BUSH

George W. Bush's path to the White House that year was anything but smooth. The election night ended too close to call—Florida's votes hung in the balance on "hanging chads" and recounts that dragged on for weeks. Finally, the Supreme Court stepped in with Bush v. Gore, stopping the Florida recount and handing Bush the presidency by one electoral vote. He took office amid questions and division, with Dick Cheney as vice president—a steady, experienced hand who believed deeply in strong defense. Colin Powell became Secretary of State, the respected general bringing calm wisdom, and Condoleezza Rice soon followed him in that role, a brilliant scholar committed to spreading democracy's light abroad.

Then came September 11, 2001—a clear blue Tuesday morning that started ordinary and ended in horror. Nineteen men from al-Qaeda, led by Osama bin Laden—a wealthy Saudi who'd turned against the West—hijacked four planes. The first two slammed into the Twin Towers in New York, turning steel and glass into fire and smoke as people inside faced impossible choices. Some jumped rather than burn; firefighters and police rushed upward, radios crackling with last messages to loved ones. A third plane hit the Pentagon, tearing through concrete.

The fourth, United Flight 93, crashed in a Pennsylvania field after passengers—ordinary people who'd learned of the other attacks by phone—fought back with the cry "Let's roll." They saved countless lives on the ground at the cost of their own.

Nearly three thousand died that day—mothers, fathers, sons, daughters, heroes in uniforms and everyday clothes. The nation stopped, strangers hugging in the streets, flags appearing on porches overnight. Churches filled with people seeking comfort, praying together across differences. Bush stood amid the rubble at Ground Zero days later, arm around a weary firefighter, bullhorn in hand: "I can hear you. The rest of the world hears you. And the people who knocked these buildings down will hear all of us soon." His words rallied a grieving country. This act of terrorism was the "Pearl Harbor" of our generation.

The attacks came from radical Islamists who followed a twisted version of faith, enforcing Sharia law that clashes with freedom's core—women oppressed, dissent punished brutally, no room for conscience or choice. Bin Laden hid in caves and compounds, directing murder, while many peaceful Muslims around the world rejected his hatred. But the threat was real: al-Qaeda grew into ISIS, beheading innocents on video, enslaving women, erasing history. America led the fight in Afghanistan and Iraq, toppling tyrants but sinking into long wars that cost trillions and thousands of brave lives—wars built partly on flawed reports of weapons of mass destruction that weren't there.

New laws like the Patriot Act gave tools to track terrorists, but years later, some worried those same tools had been turned inward, used against citizens who disagreed with those in power.

"'Emergencies' have always been the pretext on which the safeguards of individual liberty have been eroded." – Friedrich August von Hayek

The new millennium ushered in a new era of music when American artists didn't just dominate the charts; they became the heartbeat of a new generation. Taylor Swift turned honest storytelling and a guitar into a global phenomenon, selling out stadiums night after night with songs that felt like letters from a best friend. Eminem unleashed lightning-fast rhymes from the streets of Detroit that made the whole world lean in and listen closer. Rihanna moved between reggae, pop, and R&B with effortless swagger, dropping one unforgettable hit after another that kept dance floors packed worldwide. Drake blended rap and melody like no one before him, creating emotional anthems that millions sang along to in their cars and at every party. And Bruno Mars brought back the pure joy of showmanship — silky vocals, killer grooves, and live performances so tight they felt like stepping back into the golden age of entertainment.

These five didn't just make hits; they became the soundtrack of everyday American life, each one proving that talent, heart, and hard work still light up the biggest stages in the world. But, unfortunately, too many artists used their platforms to talk down to people who didn't align with their ideology, turning off half their audiences.

Steve Jobs changed daily life forever in 2007 when he held up the first iPhone—a phone, music player, camera, and pocket computer all in one. The knowledge of the world fits in your hand, connecting people instantly, opening endless possibilities. Society shifted—friends always reachable, information at a touch—but addiction crept in too.

Social media followed fast. MySpace started the wave, then Facebook, Instagram, Twitter (later X), TikTok—platforms that promised connection but often pulled people into endless scrolling, comparison, and anger.

Google began as a simple search engine, making answers quick and easy to find. But over time, many noticed results tilting—certain views pushed higher, others buried—shaping what people saw and thought.

Through terror's shadow, long wars' toll, technology's double edge—the flame faced fierce winds. Yet it burned on in brave firefighters climbing stairs, passengers fighting back, soldiers far from home, and everyday people choosing faith and family amid chaos. Resilient liberty endured the new millennium's opening blows, carried by courage that refused to yield and hope rooted in truths deeper than any attack.

"The essence of America - that which really unites us - is not ethnicity, or nationality or religion - it is an idea - and what an idea it is: That you can come from humble circumstances and do great things." – Condoleezza Rice

CHAPTER THIRTEEN
HOPE AND CHANGE TURNS TO HOPE FOR CHANGE LEADING TO AN AMERICA FIRST AGENDA

BARACK OBAMA

A young senator and former community organizer named Barack Obama swept into the White House in 2008 on waves of promises—"hope and change" that sounded fresh and uplifting after years of war and economic strain, very much like John F. Kennedy had been able to achieve in his time. A great orator, he spoke of healing divisions, bringing people together, and making government work for everyone. Many believed him, drawn to his calm voice and vision of a brighter tomorrow, especially after the historic election of the first black president, which raised real optimism that racial divisions could finally mend. Yet over the eight years that followed, actions often pulled in another direction—expanding government's reach farther into daily life, straining alliances abroad, deepening divides at home. Whether driven by a sincere belief in larger solutions or by something closer to old ideas of centralized control, many decisions left lasting marks that weakened the foundations of limited government, personal freedom, and shared moral strength. A few good things did happen: the successful operation to kill Osama bin Laden in 2011, building on intelligence frameworks from the Bush era, delivered a significant blow to al-Qaeda and brought a measure of justice for 9/11 victims, showcasing effective use of military and intelligence resources. The downside of that success was Obama's reluctance to eliminate ISIS, another significant threat to democracy. Trump was able to wipe them out within a few weeks later during his administration. Economically, the economy steadily recovered from the 2008 financial crisis, with the stock market more than doubling and unemployment dropping from 10% to under 5% by the end of his term, though this was mainly due to private-sector resilience. His administration's focus on energy independence contributed to a boom in domestic oil and gas production via fracking, reducing reliance on foreign imports—a win for national security. But his trillion-dollar spending bill became rife with waste, fraud, and abuse, with few of the funds allocated to the projects they were earmarked for.

On race, the initial hope faded as Democrats reverted to their tired playbook of playing the 'race card' to foment division, and most African Americans came to believe Obama did nothing to further race relations—only making them worse through his rhetoric and policies that emphasized grievances over unity.

SECTION ONE
FALSE PROMISES AND POLARIZATION

Barack Obama's time in office stands out as one of the most divisive in modern memory. Approval ratings split sharply along party lines—high among those who shared his views, low among those who didn't—creating gaps wider than almost any president before him. Issues like health care overhaul, spending packages, and social questions turned neighbors into opposites, conversations into arguments. The country that had hoped for unity found itself pulled further apart. As I go through the litany of problems we inherited from the Obama administration, I'm reminded of the words of the great Edward R. Murrow:

"We must not confuse dissent with disloyalty. When the loyal opposition dies, I think the soul of America dies with it." – Edward R. Murrow

MISTAKES IN LEADERSHIP

The Affordable Care Act, which received only votes from Democrats and was signed into law in 2010, reached deep into one-sixth of the economy. It required people to buy insurance or pay a penalty, set rules for what plans must cover, and added taxes and regulations. Families who had affordable coverage often saw premiums climb, choices shrink, and doctors leave networks. Businesses cut hours or jobs to avoid new costs. What was promised as lower bills and better care turned out for many to be higher expenses and less freedom to choose. Health insurance companies exploded with cash from subsidies while regular people were forced to pay more.

In 2015, the Iran nuclear agreement was reached—sanctions lifted in exchange for promises to slow their program. As part of the deal, Obama quietly arranged for the delivery of around $150 million in cash—along with the return of previously frozen assets totaling $1.7 billion—flown to Tehran on unmarked pallets in foreign currency. That money flowed back into the hands of a regime that openly chanted against America, ignored brutal human rights abuses at home, and kept building missiles in defiance of warnings. Critics saw it as handing resources to those who funded attacks on Americans and allies, buying only temporary limits on their nuclear work at the heavy price of empowering a government that wished us harm.

On immigration, an executive action in 2012 called DACA shielded hundreds of thousands brought here illegally as children from deportation, gave work permits—all without Congress passing a law. Many felt sympathy for those young people, yet the move bypassed the people's representatives, widened borders, and strained communities.

It set a pattern of deciding big questions from one office rather than through open debate.

The 2012 attack in Benghazi took four American lives, including an ambassador. Early stories blamed a video protest; later evidence pointed to planned terrorism. Questions lingered about security warnings ignored, help not sent fast enough, and explanations that shifted—abroad, pulling back from hard-won ground left openings for new threats to grow.

Inside government, the IRS gave extra scrutiny to groups with names suggesting opposition views—delaying approvals, demanding private details. It felt like power turned against citizens for their beliefs, eroding the trust that keeps a free society working.

Billions went to green energy projects, like the solar company Solyndra, which took over half a billion in loans and then collapsed. Taxpayers footed the bill while connected firms gained, raising questions about choices driven more by favored ideas than sound investment. Spending rose sharply—stimulus packages, new programs—pushing the national debt from around ten trillion to nearly twenty. Future generations inherited heavier loads, and growth slowed under the weight.

An operation called Fast and Furious, run under Attorney General Eric Holder's Justice Department, let guns walk across the border to track criminals, but many vanished into dangerous hands. Congress later held Holder in contempt—the first sitting attorney general to be held in contempt—for refusing to turn over documents about the program. One of those guns turned up at the scene where Border Patrol agent Brian Terry lost his life in a desert shootout. Recklessness armed dangerous hands, cost innocent blood, and left families grieving while questions about accountability lingered long after.

One of the most painful examples of polarization came in 2012 with the death of Trayvon Martin, a seventeen-year-old walking home in a Florida neighborhood one rainy evening, carrying only Skittles and iced tea. A neighborhood watch volunteer followed him, confronted him, and in the struggle that followed, shot and killed the unarmed teen. The case went to trial, and the shooter claimed self-defense and was eventually acquitted. President Obama spoke publicly about it, saying, "If I had a son, he'd look like Trayvon." He urged soul-searching on race and safety. Many parents, black and white, felt the grief deeply—a young life cut short, questions about what could have been different. But for others, the president's words framed the story in racial terms before all facts were clear, stirring old resentments at a moment when calm voices might have brought people closer. Protests grew heated in places, trust between communities and police frayed further, and the nation felt pulled apart when healing was needed most.

"Our strength as a nation comes in our unity. We are the United States of America, not the divided states. And those who want to divide us are trying to divide us, and we shouldn't let them do it." – Ben Carson

A similar ache came earlier in 2009 with the arrest of Harvard professor Henry Louis Gates Jr. A neighbor called police about a possible break-in; it turned out Gates was entering his own home after a trip, struggling with a stuck door. Words escalated, and he was arrested for disorderly conduct (charges later dropped). Obama commented that the police had "acted stupidly," pointing to a history of disproportionate stops for African Americans and Latinos. Police unions and many officers felt unfairly painted, approval among some groups dropped, and conversations about race turned sharper rather than softer. Instead of being the hoped-for voice for bringing people together, Obama stoked the flames of racial discord.

Then in 2014, Michael Brown's death in Ferguson, Missouri—a young man shot by an officer after a confrontation—sparked the "hands up, don't shoot" cry, based on early witness accounts. Investigations later showed a more complicated picture, but the phrase spread worldwide. Obama's remarks on the need for reform and understanding added to debates that often split along racial and trust-in-law-enforcement lines, leaving many feeling the country was growing more divided at a time when coming together could have eased hearts. In these moments and others, comments meant to acknowledge pain sometimes landed in ways that reopened wounds instead of binding them. The nation, already carrying old scars, found new ones forming when unity felt within reach. Many longed for words that drew people toward shared grief and common ground, believing that's how healing truly begins.

Opening ties with communist Cuba in 2014 brought little change from Havana—no freer speech, no open elections—yet eased pressure on a regime long hostile to liberty. Cuban refugees in America felt the sting of betrayal, remembering a brutal regime that killed their relatives and friends.

Through these choices—health mandates that burdened families, deals that strengthened foes, actions that bypassed law, scandals that eroded trust, spending that mortgaged tomorrow—the flame faced false lights that led astray. Promises of hope often delivered heavier government, deeper divides, and weaker standing abroad. Yet resilient liberty endured in hearts that remembered self-reliance, faith, and the quiet courage to question power. The story pressed on, carried by those unwilling to trade timeless truths for fleeting change.

WEAPONIZATION OF GOVERNMENT

Hillary Clinton's years as Secretary of State left questions that just wouldn't go away. She decided to handle official work through a private email server set up at home—thousands of messages, including some with classified details, going through channels that weren't the secure government ones. When it all came out in 2015, devices got wiped with tools that erased everything thoroughly, emails disappeared, and the story kept shifting.

The Benghazi attack in 2012, where four brave Americans died in the chaos of fire and gunfire, brought even more heartache—warnings that seemed ignored, help that took too long to arrive, early accounts pointing to a video protest when the facts leaned toward something planned. Then, in 2025, Tulsi Gabbard, drawing from classified briefings she'd seen, laid out how figures like John Brennan and James Clapper, under Obama's direction, had shaped intelligence in ways that downplayed threats tied to specific groups abroad while pushing narratives that served political ends—all to bury scandals like the emails and build a case against the incoming Trump campaign.

"The liberties of a people never were, nor ever will be, secure, when the transactions of their rulers may be concealed from them." – Patrick Henry

DONALD J. TRUMP

Donald Trump stepped into that storm—a New York builder who'd made his mark with towering hotels, top golf courses, and a television show where he cut through the noise with straight talk. He ran on shaking things up in Washington, putting America's deals and security first. Against all odds and predictions, he won the presidency in 2016, giving millions the sense that an outsider might finally hear the voices of the parts of the country that felt left behind. The win was unexpected. Even on election night, Hillary Clinton believed she was a shoo-in. She had barges of fireworks ready in the New York harbor.

The resistance hit hard and fast. Whispers about Russian connections turned into daily headlines—leaks pouring out, investigations launching.

JOHN BRENNAN CORRUPTS THE CENTRAL INTELLIGENCE AGENCY

Like any powerful tool, the CIA could be turned inward or mishandled, especially under directors who blurred lines for political gain. Enter John Brennan, the Obama-era spymaster who took the helm in 2013. A career intelligence man with a Middle East focus, Brennan promised reform but delivered controversy. Drawing from the Durham Report, Brennan emerged as a key player in the Russia collusion saga. This fabricated storm hounded President Trump from day one. Brennan briefed Obama, Biden, and top brass on intelligence suggesting Hillary Clinton's camp had cooked up a plan to smear Trump with Russian ties. Yet the investigations continued, fueled by dubious dossiers and leaks. A special counsel spent years digging and found no coordinated effort to steal the election. Piece by piece, it emerged that the dossier at its heart was funded by Clinton's side and packed with claims that crumbled under scrutiny.

The House impeached Trump twice—first over a call seeking a look into clear corruption, second charging incitement tied to the January 6 unrest at the Capitol, just days before he left office. The Senate acquitted both times. For many, the relentless drive seemed less about solid proof and more about blocking someone who threatened the old guard—maybe covering tracks in the email probe or holding on to long-standing influence.

Then there was the Senate spying scandal, where Brennan's CIA hacked into congressional computers during a probe of the Agency's enhanced interrogation program—tactics he defended fiercely, even as critics called it torture. His reorganization of the Agency, merging operations with analysis, was slammed by former spies as weakening the covert arm that had won the Cold War and as prioritizing politics over tradecraft. In the end, Brennan's tenure, as viewed through outlets like National Review and Fox, exemplified how the CIA's noble mission could be twisted—turning a defender of America into a weapon against its own elected leaders, all in the name of partisan battles. The Agency's story is one of triumphs and temptations, a reminder that vigilance abroad must never erode liberty at home.

But voices like Ted Cruz, the Texas senator with fire in his voice, who carried his father's flight from Cuban prisons like a scar that never faded, gave hope to millions. Those memories of freedom stolen pushed him to stand for hours on the Senate floor, quoting the Constitution word for word, and to battle any grab for power that edged too close to the rights we hold dear.

Mike Lee arrived in the Senate from Utah in 2011, calm and deliberate. He took the time to read every bill from start to finish, then fought to stop wars launched without proper votes, to curb emergency powers that stretched on indefinitely, to push for term limits and budgets that balanced. His steady reminders brought people back to the simple truth: writing laws is Congress's job, not one man's or a bureaucracy's.

Justin Amash represented his district in the House, making it a point to read each bill before voting—something few others bothered with. He called out surveillance that spied on citizens without a real reason, wars that dragged on without a clear purpose. When loyalty to the party clashed with allegiance to the Constitution, he chose the Constitution, stepping away to stand as an independent, then as a Libertarian.

New voices gained strength, too. Ben Shapiro, quick on his feet with facts and unafraid to push back, created platforms that reached millions hungry for straight talk on faith, family, and freedom. Charlie Kirk loaded buses and traveled to campuses, establishing spaces where students who felt they were being shouted down could speak openly about the principles that shaped the nation.

THE SCOURGE OF RADICALISM AND ANARCHY

Anarchy and radicalism in America are not new phenomena. Picture a young America, still finding its footing in the 19th century, where the seeds of radical disruption took root amid the push for workers' rights and against the growing industrial machine.

In 1886, the Haymarket Riot in Chicago erupted during a labor protest, when anarchists tossed a bomb at police, killing seven officers and sparking chaos that led to executions and a nationwide crackdown on radical groups. Fast forward to 1901, when anarchist Leon Czolgosz assassinated President William McKinley in Buffalo, New York, driven by a hatred for authority that he believed oppressed the common man, plunging the nation into mourning and fueling anti-immigrant fears. These weren't isolated sparks; by the early 20th century, anarchists and radicals like Emma Goldman stirred up strikes and bombings, costing lives and property, all in the name of upending the system.

Then came the 1960s, a turbulent era in which peaceful civil rights marches gave way to violent fringe elements. Abbie Hoffman, a Yippie leader, co-founded the Chicago Seven after the 1968 Democratic National Convention riots, where agitators clashed with police in bloody street battles, disrupting the political process and sowing division that echoed for years. Angela Davis, a Communist Party member tied to radical groups, was linked to a 1970 courthouse shootout in Marin County, California, that left four dead, including a judge, as part of a failed prisoner escape attempt, highlighting how extremism could turn ideology into deadly action. These figures and events weren't just footnotes; they derailed freedoms, eroding trust in institutions and costing billions in damages and lost economic growth over time.

At the heart of much modern radicalism lies Saul Alinsky's 1971 book "Rules for Radicals," a playbook that taught activists how to manipulate systems for power, with tactics like ridicule as a weapon—his fifth rule declaring it "man's most potent weapon" with no real defense. Alinsky, a community organizer with Marxist leanings, inspired generations to demonize opponents, suppress their true socialist labels when organizing, and build coalitions that often led to chaos rather than constructive change. His influence seeped into politics, where disciples like Barack Obama and Hillary Clinton drew from his methods, fostering a culture of division that critics say has hollowed out civil discourse and encouraged tactics over truth.

This legacy amplified in recent decades, where peaceful First Amendment protests—those heartfelt gatherings for change—are overshadowed by orchestrated violence. Billionaires like George Soros have funneled millions through NGOs to fund anti-Israel campus protests in 2024, anti-Trump "No Kings" rallies in 2025, and even groups behind the 2020 Black Lives Matter riots that caused over $2 billion in damages across cities like Minneapolis. Similarly, Neville Roy Singham, a Marxist-Leninist based in China, has bankrolled radical networks supporting 2024 pro-Palestinian agitators and 2020 BLM efforts, channeling foreign communist influence into American streets, leading to synagogue attacks in Los Angeles in 2024 and fueling anti-ICE riots in places like Portland and Minneapolis in 2025.

Soros-backed district attorneys in cities like Los Angeles and New York have been accused of soft-on-crime policies that embolden rioters, while groups like Antifa—indicted in 2025 for attempting to murder an officer during a Texas ICE facility riot—continue to exploit these funds, turning protests into assaults on liberty itself, stealing taxpayer dollars through destruction and undermining the very freedoms they claim to fight for.

Most often in modern history, these tactics and perpetrators have masked their socialism, communism, and their actual intent, because they know the general public would reject them wholeheartedly if they knew the truth. This is a profound tragedy of our modern times, using peaceful protesters as a 'shield' for a more sinister intent in many cases. I believe, even still, that there are more good than bad people in this world, and the truth will eventually prevail in a free society. It is our obligation to call out these tactics when we see them and to ensure our freedoms stay intact.

Picture this: It's the summer of 2024, and America is already buzzing with the promise of its 250th birthday just two years away. Yet beneath the surface, something darker is stirring. Words once reserved for history's greatest monsters — "Nazi," "Fascist" — are hurled like stones at a former president and millions of his fellow citizens who simply see the world differently. These are not casual insults in a heated debate. They land like sparks on dry tinder, igniting fury in the hearts of some on the far edges of the political spectrum. And the fire spreads. Suddenly, the unthinkable becomes real: bullets fly at a campaign rally in Pennsylvania, a man with a rifle waits in the bushes outside a Florida golf course, and other prominent voices fall silent forever. We shake our heads and whisper, "This has to stop." But deep down we know the truth — these words are not accidents. They are chosen with precision, repeated with purpose, until they become a kind of permission slip for violence. Threat-based messaging justifies cruelty, effectively indoctrinating people to brutality.

And here's where the soul of the nation is tested. In a free country the Founders built, speech is sacred — but so is the line between honest disagreement and shouting "fire!" in a crowded theater. When rhetoric stops persuading and starts inciting, when it turns neighbors into enemies and turns disagreement into a death sentence, freedom itself begins to bleed. The men who signed the Declaration understood that words have power. They used theirs to birth a republic, not to bury it. As we stand on the doorstep of America's 250th year, the question before every one of us is simple yet urgent: Will we choose the language of builders... or the language of destroyers? The answer will echo far beyond any election. It will decide whether the flame of freedom keeps burning bright for the next two hundred and fifty years — or flickers out in the smoke of our own making.

ACTIVIST JUDGES

Once upon a time in the land of Liberty, where the people had built a grand house called the Constitution to keep everything fair and balanced, there lived three wise guardians: the lawmakers who dreamed up the rules, the enforcers who carried them out, and the judges who made sure everyone played by the book.

But in recent chapters of this ongoing story, some judges have started acting like sneaky storytellers, rewriting the tale from their high benches rather than just reading it aloud. These activist judges, often driven by their personal beliefs rather than the plain words of the law, began slipping in new chapters—creating rights or blocking changes they didn't like —while wearing the robe of justice. It's like a referee deciding to change the rules mid-game because they favor one team, and from any viewpoint, this isn't just unfair; it's a direct threat to the republic's foundation, as it undermines the separation of powers the Founders so carefully crafted.

Picture a small town where the baker suddenly declares he's also the sheriff and the mayor, handing out free loaves to his friends while fining his rivals extra for the same flour. That's what happens when judges "legislate from the bench"—they overstep by inventing laws, like in the famous case where the Supreme Court discovered a right to abortion in the shadows of the Constitution, a move many see as pure ideology overriding the democratic process where states and voters should decide. When Roe vs. Wade was overturned in the Dobbs decision, it did not outlaw abortion. It just returned the issue to the states to determine what each would do. Or when a single district judge issues a nationwide stay to halt a policy they disagree with, like immigration reforms, it's like one local cop stopping the whole country's parade—unconstitutional because it gives unelected judges veto power over elected branches, slowing progress and creating chaos that harms everyday folks. This isn't blind justice; it's ideology in a black robe, and it's bad for the country because it erodes trust in the system, turns courts into political battlegrounds, and lets personal views trump the will of the people, just as the Founders feared when they warned against judicial overreach in the Federalist Papers.

In the end, the story teaches that when judges stick to interpreting the law as written, the house of Liberty stands strong; but when they start building additions based on their whims, the whole structure risks crumbling under the weight of unaccountable power.

JUDGE SHOPPING AND BIASED JURY POOLS

In the bustling halls of America's courtrooms, where justice is supposed to wear a blindfold and weigh scales evenly, a sneaky game has crept in over the years—kind of like kids picking teams for dodgeball, but with much higher stakes. Picture a group of determined people, maybe powerful organizations or sharp prosecutors, scanning the map for just the right spot to file their case. They hunt for a courthouse in a place like Washington, D.C., or New York, where the judges lean heavily toward progressive views and the jury pools are filled with people who share those left-leaning outlooks. This "judge shopping" isn't about fair play; it's about stacking the deck to snag a win, whether that's convicting someone they dislike or dodging accountability themselves. This "moving the goalposts" is a perversion of the system the Founders designed, turning courts into political weapons rather than neutral referees.

Take the recent saga with Donald Trump—prosecutors in liberal strongholds like Manhattan didn't just enforce existing laws; they twisted them into new shapes to fit their narrative, charging him after his first term under statutes stretched so thin they barely resembled the original intent. In New York, they dusted off an old misdemeanor.

They inflated it into a felony by linking it to vague federal election rules, all in front of a judge known for his anti-Trump leanings and a jury from a city where Trump polls like a villain in a comic book. It's no coincidence; these venues are chosen because the odds favor conviction, sidelining impartial justice in favor of ideological triumphs. This is obviously unconstitutional overreach, echoing warnings from the Federalist Papers about judges who meddle in politics, eroding public trust, and letting personal biases hijack the rule of law.

The real harm hits everyone—when judges or prosecutors shop for sympathetic ears, it slows down progress on issues like border security or economic reforms that conservatives champion, issuing nationwide stays from a single liberal district to block policies they oppose. This isn't the balanced system our Founders envisioned; it's a shortcut that divides the nation, making justice feel like a rigged lottery. If left unchecked, it could unravel the fabric of fair governance, turning courts into battlegrounds where ideology trumps the Constitution, and leaving ordinary folks wondering if the scales are truly blind or just winking at one side.

LEAKING SENSITIVE INFORMATION

In the shadowy corridors of power in Washington, where secrets are supposed to safeguard the nation, a dangerous game has unfolded over the years—like a whispered plot in a thriller novel that twists the truth for personal gain. Adam Schiff, during his time as chairman of the House Intelligence Committee, was accused in 2018 of slipping classified tidbits to eager reporters not to expose wrongdoing, but to craft a narrative that sways public opinion against political rivals.

Schiff was accused of leaking details from closed-door hearings about the Russia investigation to paint a damning picture of President Trump, even when the full facts told a different story. This isn't whistleblowing; it's a crooked betrayal, turning sensitive intelligence into ammunition for media wars, eroding trust in institutions, and playing fast and loose with national security for partisan points.

This leaking undermines the core values America was built on—honesty, fairness, and the rule of law—turning democracy into a manipulated spectacle where facts bend to fit agendas. It's like a trusted guard opening the castle gates to let in the enemy, bordering on treason because it risks exposing methods that protect us from real threats, all to shape how voters think. It is a direct assault on the Constitution's intent to keep power balanced and information secure, echoing the Founders' warnings about self-serving actions that fracture unity. When leaks become tools for political theater, as in Schiff's case with selective disclosures to outlets like CNN, it doesn't just twist headlines; it weakens the nation's soul, making us question if justice is blind or just blinded by bias.

Through scandals swept under rugs, investigations built on thin air, power aimed at a leader the people chose—the flame faced its sharpest test from those meant to guard it. Yet it kept glowing in senators who held the line, in voices that refused to be silent, in everyday Americans who wouldn't look away.

Resilient liberty pushed through the weaponization, carried by courage that demanded truth and faith that dawn always follows the darkest hour.

"America is not just a power, it is a promise. It is not enough for our country to be extraordinary in might; it must be exemplary in meaning." – Nelson Rockefeller

SECTION TWO

TRUMP'S AMERICA FIRST AGENDA

Meanwhile, the economy began to turn around, with effects that people could feel in their daily lives. Policies echoing Reagan's approach—lower taxes, fewer regulations, energy independence—unleashed a growth not seen in years. Unemployment dropped to levels not seen in decades, wages rose for workers at the bottom, and gas prices fell as America pumped its own oil again. Factories reopened, businesses expanded, and families who had struggled found new opportunities. It wasn't perfect, and divisions ran deep—Trump became the most polarizing president in modern memory, with approval ratings splitting sharply along ideological lines. Yet for many, his relentless focus felt like a CEO running the country: long hours, direct talk, putting American interests first in trade, security, and peace. He stopped new wars, brought troops home where possible, negotiated deals that ended old conflicts, all while building strength that deterred threats without endless fighting.

In those same early 21st-century years, from 2000 into the 2020s, church attendance dipped at first—"nones" climbed toward 30 percent, regular worship falling to 20 or 30 percent in many places.
Young people especially stepped back, wary of institutions or pulled by busy lives. But around 2020, the slide slowed, and something quiet began stirring. Gatherings like the weeks-long outpouring at Asbury University in 2023 drew thousands of students hungry for a real encounter with God—prayer, worship, confession flowing night and day, spreading to other campuses. A turn toward faith began to show among the rising generation, seeking authenticity over formality.

ENDING WARS

Trump walked into the White House with a promise that hit home for many families: no more endless wars. For nearly twenty years, young men and women had been cycling through deployments in places far from home, coming back changed or not coming back at all. He said it was time to bring them home, to stop trying to rebuild other nations from the ground up, and to focus on keeping America safe without getting tangled in fights that never seemed to end. On his watch, no significant new conflicts broke out—a break from what had become almost routine.

Take Afghanistan, the longest war America has ever fought. By the time Trump took office, it had dragged on for almost two decades. My friend Brian, a young sergeant from a small Texas town, knew that grind firsthand.

He did three tours, patrolling dusty roads where every step could hide a bomb, watching buddies get hit, and clearing villages only to see them slip away again. When he finally came home, Brian carried the weight of friends lost and questions that kept him up at night: was it all worth it? Trump's shift gave him hope. Deals were cut with the Taliban, timelines set to pull out, and troops started coming home. The complete withdrawal happened later, in a chaotic way, under another president. Still, the direction had changed—choosing when to leave instead of staying forever, saving lives by drawing clear lines.

He turned away from the old habit of trying to turn far-off countries into mirror images of America through force. Strength at home, smart deals abroad—that's what kept the peace without burying more of our own in foreign soil. Lives were spared on all sides by fighting only when it truly mattered.

Richard, a Marine who served in Iraq, felt the difference in his bones. His first tours were constant danger—patrols through streets where ambushes waited around corners, losing brothers in blasts that came out of nowhere. But later, under Trump's orders, missions tightened: go after real threats like the last pockets of ISIS, get in, get the job done, get out. He came home whole, boots still laced, but heart lighter. Richard married, started a family, built a life—because someone in charge finally said enough to the endless cycle.

Through pulling back from deep quagmires, saying no to costly nation-building, and sharpening the focus on proper defense, the flame burned with clearer, wiser light. Wars eased or ended, lives were held onto, and resources were kept closer to home. Resilient liberty showed its deepest strength in restraint—the courage to say "enough," the faith that peace comes from being ready, not from staying forever.

The story lived on in soldiers walking through their own front doors again, in families staying whole, and in a nation choosing life over endless sacrifice. But sinister forces were at work behind the scenes.

THE MESS OF 2020 LEADS TO A STOLEN PRESIDENCY

The year 2020 started with that quiet optimism we all feel at the beginning of a new decade, a chance to reset and build something better. But soon enough, reports started filtering in from Wuhan, China, about this unfamiliar virus that began spreading without mercy, an unseen force that changed everything. COVID-19 hit hard and fast, leading to lockdowns that emptied streets, closed shops, and kept families confined indoors as the entire economy ground to a near halt. Anthony Fauci became the central figure in guiding the nation's response, emphasizing masks, vaccines, and broad shutdowns as the way to contain it.

Over the months and years that followed, more details emerged about where it might have come from—a lab in Wuhan where researchers were conducting gain-of-function experiments, essentially amplifying viruses to study them, but with risks that were all too real. This kind of work had been restricted in the U.S. because of those dangers, yet American funding had still made its way there through indirect channels.

One of the scientists involved even flagged concerns to colleagues early on, but people like Fauci initially downplayed the idea of a lab escape, treating it like baseless talk. The consequences were devastating on a personal level for so many. Jobs disappeared overnight for millions, and those small businesses that anchored neighborhoods couldn't hold on. My wife Robin, a nurse, was considered "essential" and was allowed to keep working on the front lines. As a musician, I was considered "non-essential" and not allowed to work. I was not alone. Millions of others like me were deemed non-essential by the government, a move towards authoritarianism devastating much of the population.

There was this one family I think of often—they'd run a modest diner for decades, the kind of place where locals gathered for coffee and stories, passed down like a family heirloom. The lockdowns forced them to close, and in the end, they had to auction off old photographs and mementos to cover the bills, watching their legacy dissolve. The isolation hit even harder; hospitals became lonely places where people faced their final moments alone, without a hand to hold. My mother-in-law went through that herself, battling cancer in a nursing home where no visitors were allowed for months. We pushed back relentlessly until, just two weeks before she passed, we got her out to my sister-in-law's house. There, at least, she could be surrounded by us, sharing quiet words and feeling that warmth one last time. Not everyone had that chance, but in those bleak days, people adapted in small, meaningful ways—leaving groceries on porches for neighbors, joining virtual services to nurture their faith, finding solace in beliefs that helped them endure and keep connections alive despite the distance.

As the country was still reeling from the virus, May brought another profound shock. George Floyd died in Minneapolis, held down under a police officer's knee for nearly ten minutes, his words "I can't breathe" captured on video and echoing across the nation. The anger that followed was raw and widespread, leading to protests in cities across the country, many of them peaceful gatherings demanding justice and real change. But in places like Minneapolis, Portland, and Seattle, the situation escalated into nights of intense violence, with fires consuming buildings and chaos overtaking the streets. Investigations later revealed that much of this destruction was amplified by external funding from opaque organizations, deliberately intensifying the unrest to deepen divisions among ordinary people, almost as if adding fuel to an already burning fire. Shops were looted, structures reduced to rubble, and innocent bystanders bore the brunt. I remember hearing about a shopkeeper in Kenosha who'd started his business from scratch after years of saving, only to wake up to ashes the next morning, his life's work gone in a blaze that had nothing to do with him. These events carved deeper rifts in society—some saw them as an urgent stand against longstanding injustices, while others viewed the wreckage as pure devastation without purpose. Amid it all, everyday people showed remarkable strength, standing watch over their blocks, organizing to protect what mattered, their determination a reminder of how communities can rally with quiet bravery in the face of turmoil.

November arrived, and with it an election unlike any before, altered by the pandemic's shadow—massive increases in mail-in voting, hurried rule changes in pivotal states. In the aftermath, a pattern of issues came to light: machines in Georgia malfunctioning and flipping votes, ballots processed without proper observation, and even votes logged under the names of people who'd passed away. Lawsuits poured in, but courts dismissed many without delving into the evidence. Trump was leading as the night wore on, only for large batches of votes to appear in the early hours, shifting everything toward Biden. Those on the ground described obstructions, like windows covered in Detroit to block views or vans arriving unmarked at 4 a.m. with ballots. One poll watcher, caught in the middle, later shared how powerless she felt, her role to ensure transparency completely sidelined, as if the process she'd sworn to uphold didn't matter. For countless Americans, this eroded something fundamental—the faith that elections reflect the true will of the people, free from manipulation.

The years under Biden's leadership that came next brought a cascade of challenges that strained the country's resolve. Federal agencies appeared to focus inward, pursuing opponents with legal actions against Trump that seemed strained and unconvincing to many observers, creating an environment where justice felt selective. Parents raising concerns at school board meetings were suddenly labeled as potential terrorist threats, and individuals connected to the January 6 protests lingered in detention without swift trials.
The Biden administration, including Secretary Mayorkas, opened our borders wide, allowing millions to enter without thorough checks, bringing with them grave dangers—traffickers and other migrants raping scores of women, preying on tens of thousands of children, forcing them into sexual exploitation or slave labor in hidden corners, criminals who went on to commit acts like the murder of Laken Riley, a dedicated nurse whose morning jog turned fatal in an instant of senseless violence. Terrorists managed to slip in undetected, and drugs like fentanyl flooded communities, taking the lives of a young woman in Texas, whose mother's grief transformed into a determined outcry against policies that seemed to enable such tragedies.

"A nation without borders is like a house without walls - it collapses. And that is what is going to happen to our wonderful America." – Jan Brewer

Biden's personal moments of confusion became increasingly apparent—wandering away from podiums, garbling names, or losing his train of thought midway through a sentence. His aides worked to insulate him, preparing responses in advance and limiting unscripted interactions. However, the lapses still surfaced, such as mistaking his vice president for his political opponent or pausing in a vacant stare, raising serious questions about the real direction of leadership.

Pardons were granted liberally, building on patterns from Obama's time but extending them—offering absolution for possible past actions dating back years, almost preemptively closing the door on future inquiries. Relatives and close associates received protection, sometimes through an autopen device that automatically signed documents, all while concerns about his awareness grew. It fostered a sense that accountability applied unevenly, favoring those in power. The January 6 demonstration began as a challenge to the election's outcome. But it descended into chaos at the Capitol, with some engaging in confrontations and others caught in the confusion. Trump publicly called for calm. Still, accusations of instigation fell heavily on him. Charges ensued for hundreds, many enduring harsh confinement without bail, shattering households. Later pardons appeared to shield specific political and government figures who'd led the inquiry and contributed to the tensions, leaving others to suffer. Consider the veteran who spent months locked away merely for entering an open doorway—his wife liquidated their home to fund his defense. At the same time, their kids grappled with his absence, a poignant twist on the sacrifices he'd made for his country.

Those in positions of influence deployed institutions like the DOJ, FBI, and CIA to target adversaries—conducting raids, disseminating damaging information, and leveling accusations that muted dissent. The withdrawal from Afghanistan in 2021 played out as a harrowing collapse: pandemonium at the Kabul airport, an explosion that took the lives of 13 U.S. service members, partners left exposed to Taliban reprisals, and vast stores of billions of dollars' worth of equipment abandoned. A widow recounted her husband's final phone call, full of reassurance that he'd return soon; instead, she stood at his grave, facing the solitude of parenting their child amid unending sorrow. On the world stage, it projected vulnerability, emboldening nations like Russia and China.
Domestically, efforts to pursue green energy allocated trillions to sources like wind and solar that proved unreliable, inflating costs and causing outages in states like California, where households struggled through intermittent blackouts and rising expenses. Inflation climbed to levels not seen in 40 years, reaching 9.1% in 2022, driven by expansive spending that eroded people's savings. The national debt swelled toward 37 trillion, riddled with inefficiencies and misuse on an unprecedented scale. In the background, influential networks—officials without elections, major tech firms, media entities—seemed dedicated to altering the fabric of the nation, weakening its boundaries, liberties, and core principles.

Social media platforms like Facebook, YouTube, and Twitter faced heavy pressure from the government to censor content in secret. This violated the free speech rights of many Americans under the First Amendment.

But there were signs of hope, such as when Elon Musk bought Twitter in 2022 and changed it to X to promote open conversations despite the controls in place. Events like these show how those in power can bend rules, even in a nation created to protect freedom.

From Buchanan's cautious warnings about national divisions to the challenges during Biden's presidency, they provide clear warnings. As George Washington put it in his farewell address—a message that still holds true—"The price of liberty is eternal vigilance." No person is above the law, and no role is safe from human errors.

The consensus among great thinkers of the day was that Biden would most likely be considered the worst president in American history, based on the damage done to the country through unchecked immigration, runaway inflation, and government overreach.

Trump was almost assassinated twice in 2024—a shot that barely missed him at a rally in Pennsylvania, grazing his ear —and a second scheme uncovered near his golf course in Florida. In the immediate aftermath of the first, he rose, blood streaking his face, raised a fist, and shouted "fight, fight, fight," a raw display of defiance that resonated deeply with those watching, embodying the unyielding spirit that drives people forward in crisis. He carried on without faltering, his tenacity mirroring the resolve of generations past. Upon his re-election that year, he moved swiftly to enact changes—fortifying borders, curbing unnecessary outlays, restoring national vigor. Judges with explicit biases attempted to obstruct initiatives on partisan grounds, but the Supreme Court frequently intervened to correct course. The setbacks were real, yet progress broke through. Through it all, an enduring resilience shone in those who sought justice through prayer, clung to honesty, and held their nation dear enough to safeguard it. Liberty, though challenged, remained intact, sustained by a profound conviction that right ultimately prevails.

CHINA AND WORLD BALANCE

Trump looked beyond our borders, where shadows were gathering, especially from China, whose rising power was tipping the scales of global stability in ways that threatened everything we'd built. He saw how our economic links had turned into shackles, draining jobs and fresh ideas from hardworking Americans and handing them over to distant rivals. That's when he took a stand, slapping tariffs on China and other nations playing dirty in trade, a gutsy call to make things fair again and pull those lost opportunities back to our own soil. It set off a real shift—companies that had scattered their operations overseas started pulling back, pouring trillions into U.S. factories through smart deals with world leaders who recognized the strength in aligning with a revitalized America. It wasn't a smooth ride; those silent plants came alive with noise and purpose, offering steady work that let families breathe easier. Alongside that, he locked down key technologies, making sure breakthroughs in artificial intelligence didn't fall into the wrong hands, even as AI started changing daily life, from boosting crop yields on farms to streamlining assembly lines in workshops.

Bonds with allies tightened, weaving a shield that kept potential troublemakers in check, and he met challenges to our standing head-on, with a steady hand that made clear America's spirit wouldn't fade quietly.

Let me share a story that brings this home, drawn from the real experiences of folks in the heartland. At one of the corporate events I performed at, I met a steel executive from the Midwest—he was a leader of a company hit hard by unfair imports, much like what happened to businesses in Pennsylvania and Ohio during the trade wars. He told me that, for years, he'd seen his operation bleed out, forced to let go of lifelong employees because subsidized steel from abroad undercut prices he couldn't match without going under. It broke him to watch those empty shifts, knowing families were struggling just to put food on the table. But when the tariffs landed, it flipped the script. He seized the moment, investing everything to upgrade the mill, calling back those workers with offers they could build a life on. Orders from U.S. firms surged, preferring homegrown quality over risky foreign supplies. The grind was intense—sleepless nights crunching numbers, praying for it to work—but fueled by a belief that fairness and grit would win out, he kept going. As Benjamin Franklin once put it, "Energy and persistence conquer all things," and that's exactly what carried him through. Before long, his plant wasn't just surviving; it was thriving, sparking others to follow, showing how one bold policy and personal resolve could fan the flames of an entire sector back to life.

In 2025, with America's 250th birthday already glowing on the horizon like a promise kept, President Donald Trump reached back across the decades and once again dusted off a time-tested playbook from one of our most visionary leaders — William McKinley, the president who once helped forge an industrial giant out of raw American muscle and determination. Just as McKinley had boldly protected American factories and workers at the dawn of the twentieth century, Trump stood firm and imposed tariffs around the world — adding to his first-term tariffs on China by expanding them worldwide. Some were crafted to finally balance the scales of trade that had tilted against us for far too long. Others served as a powerful beacon, calling home the factories, the supply chains, and the good-paying jobs that rightfully belonged on American soil. And in certain cases, they became a quiet but effective tool for peace — pressuring badly behaving nations and helping stop conflicts before they could spiral into something far worse.

The result was nothing short of electric. Nearly twenty trillion dollars in new economic energy surged through the nation: shuttered plants began the process of roaring back to life, communities long forgotten began to hum again, and American workers once more prepared to stand at the center of the world's greatest engine of prosperity.

Then came the spring of 2026. The Supreme Court, in a closely watched ruling, struck down the narrow emergency authorization Trump had used for some of those tariffs. For a moment, the critics celebrated, certain that the momentum had been broken. But they underestimated the quiet resolve of a determined cabinet.

Within days — almost as if they had prepared for this very moment — the team pivoted with precision, shifting to different, rock-solid legal frameworks that accomplished the exact same purpose. The factories kept coming home. The jobs kept returning. The Golden Age kept unfolding.

It was a powerful reminder that in America, when one door is closed by law, resourceful and freedom-loving leaders simply find another open window — just as the Founders themselves had done time and again when the path forward looked blocked. The flame of self-reliance burned even brighter, proving once more that the American spirit is bigger than any single ruling, and that the greatest comeback stories are written not by those who give up, but by those who simply find a better way.

ENERGY DOMINANCE DETERMINES THE FUTURE

That unyielding drive carried over to energy, where Trump pushed forward with nuclear and oil advancements, rolling out mini-reactors to feed the hungry data hubs driving the AI surge.

Elon Musk, with his eye on the stars, talked about tapping endless solar energy from space and beaming it down, a wild but brilliant way to satisfy tech's endless thirst without relying on unreliable outsiders. This push locked in real independence, cutting loose from shaky foreign sources that had always hung like a sword over our security. AI grew strong on domestic power, and bigger dangers—like being held hostage by supply cuts or price games—started to lose their grip as our own resources ramped up.

Sarah is from North Dakota's oil patches. She is an oil worker who suffered through years of scarce employment but finally saw a turnaround under new policies that opened up drilling. She'd come up in those endless fields, taking over the family trade from her dad, a tough soul whose quiet faith got him through freezing storms and lean times to provide for them all. But when restrictions tightened, rigs went silent, and Sarah's days turned hollow, piecing together whatever work she could find while her children asked why the good jobs had vanished.

It felt like the end of a way of life. Then the changes came—approvals for smarter oil pulls and nuclear setups, including those small reactors geared for tomorrow's needs. Sarah was hired for a new project, handling rigs that reached depths once off-limits. The work was demanding, with real hazards in the biting cold, but as the oil began to flow, she thought back to her father's evening blessings for abundance. Channeling Marcus Aurelius's insight, "The impediment to action advances action. What stands in the way becomes the way," she turned every obstacle into fuel for progress.

Word of her comeback spread through the camps, drawing more workers back, as the country's energy surged forward—a powerful reminder of how sacrifice and steadfast pursuit can keep the flame of self-sufficiency burning strong.

RISING STARS

J. D. VANCE

In the heart of Middletown, Ohio—a once-thriving steel town shadowed by the Rust Belt's decline—James David "J.D." Vance was born on August 2, 1984, into a world of grit and hardship that would forge his unyielding spirit. His early years were marked by turmoil: his parents divorced when he was young, his biological father Donald Bowman faded from the picture, and his mother struggled with addiction, cycling through unstable relationships that left young J.D. shuttling between homes. But it was his maternal grandparents, "Mamaw" and "Papaw"—fierce, faith-filled Appalachians from Kentucky's Breathitt County—who became his anchors, raising him with tough love, Bible stories, and lessons in resilience amid economic woes and family chaos. Vance later adopted their surname as a tribute, embodying the compassion he felt for the forgotten working-class folks like his own kin, whose dreams were crushed by job losses and cultural decay. After graduating from Middletown High School, he enlisted in the U.S. Marine Corps in 2003, serving as a combat correspondent during a 2005 deployment to Iraq, where he honed discipline and a sense of purpose that pulled him from the brink of despair.

The Corps, he often says, kept him honest and gave him lifelong bonds, a testament to his gratitude for institutions that lift people up. From there, Vance powered through Ohio State University, graduating summa cum laude in just two years, before earning his law degree at Yale in 2013, where he learned the ways of America's elite but never forgot his roots.

Venturing into Silicon Valley as a venture capitalist at firms like Mithril Capital under Peter Thiel, Vance built a successful career investing in innovation, but it was his 2016 memoir "Hillbilly Elegy"—a raw, heartfelt chronicle of his family's struggles with poverty, addiction, and the erosion of American values—that catapulted him to national fame, becoming a bestseller and Netflix film that resonated with millions facing similar trials. Drawn back to public service by a desire to advocate for the overlooked, he ran for U.S. Senate in Ohio in 2022, winning with Donald Trump's endorsement as a Tea Party-aligned voice against establishment excess, championing fiscal responsibility, strong borders, and a robust national defense that prioritizes American workers. As senator, Vance pushed "America First" policies, confronting threats from China and rogue regimes, authoring legislation to curb globalization's harms like cheap labor outsourcing, and earning conservative praise for his hawkish stance on trade and security while showing empathy for families battered by economic shifts.

In 2024, Trump selected him as vice presidential running mate, and their victory ushered in Vance's role as the first millennial VP in Trump's second term starting 2025, where he serves as a "Swiss army knife" enforcer of the MAGA agenda—securing cabinet confirmations, advancing religious freedom and pro-family policies, brokering Ukraine-Russia talks, imposing targeted tariffs for industrial revival, and clashing with globalists on migration and censorship to restore U.S. sovereignty and traditional values. Through successes like revitalizing American manufacturing and protecting life at all stages, Vance draws from his own journey of redemption, remaining a devoted husband to Usha and father to their three children, blending interfaith harmony with Christian upbringing in a life that champions human dignity for all.

MARCO RUBIO

In the sun-drenched streets of Miami, where the echoes of freedom seekers from distant shores mingled with the rhythms of everyday struggle, Marco Rubio entered the world on May 28, 1971, as the son of Cuban immigrants who had fled Fidel Castro's oppressive regime in search of the American Dream. His father, Mario, toiled as a bartender, while his mother, Oriales, worked as a maid and cashier, instilling in young Marco the values of hard work, faith, and resilience amid financial hardships that saw the family briefly relocate to Las Vegas before returning to Florida. Raised Catholic after a short time as a Mormon, Rubio found solace in family and football, earning a scholarship to Tarkio College in Missouri before transferring to the University of Florida and later graduating with a law degree from the University of Miami in 1996. His early life, marked by the compassion he showed for his parents' sacrifices—helping them navigate language barriers and economic woes—shaped a man who understood the human cost of tyranny and the promise of opportunity. Entering politics with a heartfelt drive to give back, Rubio started as an intern for Rep. Ileana Ros-Lehtinen, then became a city commissioner in West Miami in 1998, where he focused on community improvements like parks and infrastructure. By 2000, he won a seat in the Florida House of Representatives, rising swiftly to become the youngest Speaker from 2006 to 2008, championing conservative reforms in education, property taxes, and criminal justice that empowered families and reduced government overreach—successes that conservatives praised for revitalizing Florida's economy and embodying the spirit of limited government.

Even as he taught political science at Florida International University, sharing stories of leadership with students, Rubio's compassion shone through in his advocacy for the vulnerable, drawing from his own family's immigrant journey.

Catapulted to national prominence in 2010, Rubio won a U.S. Senate seat as a Tea Party favorite, defeating establishment figures like Charlie Crist in a race that highlighted his charisma and firm stance against big government, earning him acclaim from conservatives as a fresh voice for fiscal responsibility and strong national defense.

As senator, he navigated challenges like the 2013 immigration reform push, which drew some conservative criticism for being too lenient but reflected his humane approach to border security and family unity, rooted in his parents' story. His 2016 presidential run, though ending after a home-state loss, showcased his vision for a "new American century," inspiring many with speeches that blended optimism and realism. Reelected to the Senate in 2016 and 2022, Rubio became a leading hawk on foreign policy, authoring the "Rubio Doctrine" that echoed Truman's anti-communism by confronting threats from China, Russia, and rogue regimes while bolstering alliances—efforts that conservatives lauded for protecting American sovereignty. In Donald Trump's second term starting in 2025, Rubio ascended to Secretary of State, where he has confronted Chinese aggression through economic decoupling, human rights advocacy, and Indo-Pacific alliances, restoring U.S. primacy in a way that honors his refugee roots by countering tyranny. He has strengthened Latin American ties to combat socialism and migration, advanced energy independence to weaken adversaries, and expanded the Abraham Accords for Middle East peace. Juggling a dual role as acting National Security Advisor after Mike Waltz's ousting, Rubio has integrated diplomacy with security, overseeing successes like obliterating Iranian nuclear sites, brokering Ukraine-Russia talks, intervening in Venezuela for stability, and eliminating DEI mandates at State—moves that have put adversaries on notice while promoting traditional values and U.S. interests with a compassionate eye toward global human dignity. Through it all, Rubio remains a devoted husband to Jeanette and father of four, his life a testament to how one man's empathy for the oppressed can fuel a career of principled triumphs.

In the grand hall in Munich, Germany, on a crisp February afternoon in 2026, Secretary of State Marco Rubio stood before leaders from across the old continent and spoke like a friend who loves you enough to tell the truth. He reminded everyone that America and Europe are not just partners on a map—they are family. **"Our home may be in the Western Hemisphere,"** he said, **"but we will always be a child of Europe."** The roots of our country run deep into this soil: the Christian faith that built cathedrals and inspired great minds, the ideas of liberty and rule of law that crossed the ocean and helped found a new nation, the shared blood and sacrifices from battlefields old and new. These are the real foundations—not fleeting trends or feel-good slogans, but the sturdy things that have carried Western civilization through dark times before.

Rubio spoke plainly about how the West had drifted. After the Cold War victory, too many leaders chased a dream of a world without borders, where nations slowly fade, and guilt over the past becomes a chain. He called it a "dangerous delusion" that led to empty factories, porous borders, and a quiet erosion of the very culture that gave us Beethoven and Shakespeare, the universities, and the spirit of invention. Mass migration without control, he warned, isn't kindness—it threatens the cohesion of societies and the future we owe our children. True freedom, he said, includes the sovereign right of every nation to decide who comes in, to protect its heritage, and to stand proud of its history instead of apologizing for it. Decline isn't destiny; it's a choice—and America has no interest in politely managing the decline of the greatest civilization the world has ever known.

Yet Rubio's words carried real hope, not scolding. He called on all of us—Americans and Europeans alike—to shake off the shame, reclaim our shared inheritance, and build something new together: a confident, self-reliant West strong enough to meet the challenges of this century. Rebuild our industries. Secure our borders. Unleash ingenuity in space, medicine, and technology. Stand shoulder to shoulder again, not as weakened dependents, but as proud partners defending the way of life worth passing on. In this 250th year of American independence, his message felt like a clear bell ringing across the Atlantic: the best of our past is still alive, and the best of our future is still possible. With clear vision and steady courage like this, the flame of freedom doesn't flicker—it burns brighter than ever, lighting the path for generations to come.

ROBERT F. KENNEDY, JR.: A MODERN CRUSADER'S PATH

Robert F. Kennedy Jr., born in 1954 amid his father's rising star, carried forward a legacy of advocacy but carved his own rugged trail through personal storms and public battles. As a young man, following the tragic assassination of his father, he grappled with addiction, finding redemption in the law after graduating from Harvard and the University of Virginia, then honing his skills as a prosecutor in New York. Turning to environmental causes, he founded the Waterkeeper Alliance in the 1990s, fighting corporate polluters and winning landmark cases to clean rivers and protect communities from toxic harm.

His activism expanded to children's health, launching the Children's Health Defense in 2011 to challenge what he saw as dangers in vaccines and pharmaceuticals, drawing both praise for his tenacity and criticism for his skepticism, all while echoing his family's commitment to the vulnerable.

In a twist few saw coming, RFK Jr.'s independent presidential run in 2024 led to an unlikely partnership with Donald Trump, suspending his campaign to endorse the former president and joining forces in a shared vision to shake up Washington's status quo.

This alliance gave rise to the MAHA movement—Make America Healthy Again—aiming to address chronic diseases by rooting out corruption in food, drugs, and Big Pharma, promoting clean eating and transparency. As Health and Human Services Secretary in the Trump administration, RFK Jr. wasted no time making waves: directing Medicaid to monthly checks that crack down on illegal immigrants' enrollment to safeguard resources for citizens, urging the FDA to confront China's influx of toxic nicotine products harming kids, and influencing the American Heart Association to drop opposition to barring soda and candy from food stamps, steps toward curbing obesity and addiction.

These early strides, from fluoride removal pledges to reversing disease epidemics, offer a glimmer of renewal, proving one man's resolve can spark real change for everyday Americans' well-being.

SECTION THREE

FORWARD PATHS

To keep America standing tall, we must cling to the government system our founders crafted—a framework that keeps power in check and puts individual rights at its core—while locking down our borders to shield the culture and resources that make us who we are. We can't let outside forces or insiders muzzle the truth through censorship, because open speech is the lifeblood of our society. Above all, we stay vigilant every day, remembering that this watchfulness is what guards our liberties, letting the flame of freedom glow steadily for those who come after us, rooted in the faith that goodness and resolve will always see us through.

THE IMPACT OF POLITICAL PARTIES THROUGHOUT AMERICAN HISTORY

In the early days of the American republic, as the ink dried on the Constitution, political factions emerged like rival clans vying for the soul of a fledgling nation. The Federalists, led by Alexander Hamilton in the 1790s, championed a strong central government, robust financial systems, and ties to Britain, appealing to merchants and urban elites who saw stability in centralized power. Opposing them were the Democratic-Republicans, organized by Thomas Jefferson and James Madison around 1792, who advocated for states' rights, agrarian interests, and sympathy for revolutionary France, drawing support from farmers and those wary of aristocratic overreach. By the 1820s, the Federalists had faded, and the Democratic-Republicans had splintered, giving rise to Andrew Jackson's Democrats in 1828—populists who advocated expanded voting rights for white men, westward expansion, and limited federal interference. However, they infamously defended slavery in the South.

The Whigs arose in the 1830s as a counterweight to the Democrats, advocating infrastructure projects, protective tariffs, and moral reforms, attracting industrialists and anti-Jackson forces until their collapse in the 1850s over divisions over slavery. In 1854, Republicans emerged from anti-slavery fervor, advocating free labor, the Homestead Act, and abolition, with Abraham Lincoln as their standard-bearer.
These parties weren't static; over time, Democrats evolved into champions of the New Deal's social welfare in the 1930s under FDR, while Republicans shifted toward pro-business conservatism, especially after the 1960s Southern Strategy, which realigned Southern conservatives with the GOP as Democrats embraced civil rights.

Fast forward to recent decades, and the parties underwent seismic shifts that left many traditionalists adrift. Donald Trump's ascent in 2016 reframed the Republican Party around economic populism, prioritizing working-class blue-collar voters with promises of trade protectionism, immigration restrictions, and an "America First" agenda that emphasized nationalism over free-market orthodoxy.

This alienated some old-school Republicans—like the country-club fiscal conservatives or foreign-policy hawks such as Dick Cheney and Mitt Romney—who viewed Trump's style as a departure from Reagan-era internationalism and decorum, even as his policies echoed their own priorities on deregulation and tax cuts. Meanwhile, Democrats veered leftward, embracing progressive stances on social justice, climate action, and identity politics, influenced by movements like Black Lives Matter and figures like Bernie Sanders, which some longtime moderates felt radicalized the party beyond its mid-20th-century labor-union roots. Many older Democrats, accustomed to the centrist pragmatism of Bill Clinton, remained unaware or in denial of this evolution toward more ideological extremes, as evidenced by rising independent identification—hitting 45% in 2025—among those disillusioned with both sides. Politics spans a spectrum: far-right reactionaries seek to restore traditional hierarchies, often resisting social change; conservatives prioritize limited government, free markets, and cultural traditions; moderates occupy the middle ground, favoring compromise and incremental reforms; liberals advocate for equality, social programs, and civil liberties; while far-left radicals push for systemic overhauls like wealth redistribution or dismantling institutions. History shows a pendulum effect, where extremes provoke backlash—from the progressive reforms of the 1960s leading to Nixon's conservative "silent majority" in the 1970s, or Obama's hope-fueled liberalism swinging to Trump's populism in 2016. Under Biden, border encounters surpassed 10 million, with debates over policies allowing humanitarian parole and asylum claims contributing to perceptions of lax enforcement, fueling a rightward swing as voters reacted to what some saw as unchecked migration straining resources. This cycle endures, with overreaches on one side often pulling the nation back toward balance, reminding us that democracy thrives on tension but risks fracture when the swing grows too wild.

The lesson to be learned from all of this is that American politics mirrors our Constitution, correcting itself whenever the pendulum swings too far in either direction. This balance is most likely what our founders intended, but we must always rein in the radical changes that, in the name of progress, thwart the American dream and threaten liberty itself.

IMMIGRATION WISDOM

In the path forward, immigration done right can strengthen us, welcoming those who bring skills and a drive to contribute through a merit system that selects contributors ready to build alongside us.

It's about assimilation too, where newcomers embrace the shared values that tie us together—respect for law, hard work, and a shared love for this land—because without that unity, divisions grow and threaten what holds America together.

"America gave the world the notion of the melting pot - an alchemical cooking device wherein diverse ethnic and religious groups voluntarily mix together, producing a new, American identity. And while critics may argue that the melting pot is a national myth, it has tenaciously informed the America's collective imagination." – Ivan Krastev

Borders aren't just lines on a map; they protect the culture we've nurtured, ensuring change comes slowly and thoughtfully. The task of removing those who've entered illegally and are already here seems nearly impossible, with millions woven into communities. Still, it's vital nonetheless to tackle it with justice and firmness, or we risk losing the rule of law that keeps everything fair. Upholding the law ensures justice for all, treating everyone by the same rules, so no one jumps ahead while others wait their turn. Cartels running drugs and smuggling people enrich themselves by putting countless others in danger or causing death.

Think of April Aguirre's path, drawn from her own words in hearings where she stood up for what's right. As the daughter of Mexican immigrants who came the legal way, waiting years through paperwork and patience to build a life here, she grew into a fierce advocate for crime victims, driven by a deep sense of fairness shaped by her family's hard-earned journey. When she saw the borders thrown open, letting in waves of unchecked arrivals—including those with dark intentions—she couldn't stay silent. Testifying before leaders, she shared the horror of an 11-year-old migrant girl named Maria, raped and strangled by someone who'd slipped across unchecked, her body so battered that April had to find a dress to hide the bruises for the funeral. "As a daughter of immigrant parents," she said, her voice steady but heavy with disappointment, "I am ashamed of what has been done to our country by opening our borders to all, including criminals." What burned in her was the injustice to those like her family, who played by the rules only to see others cut the line, giving honest migrants a bad name and endangering everyone. Fueled by a faith in doing right by others—echoing the biblical call to love your neighbor while upholding truth—she pushed for vetted paths, not chaos, her courage a reminder that true patriotism means defending the system that made her family's dream possible, even when it means speaking hard truths in rooms full of power.

KNOWLEDGE INTEGRITY

To keep our nation strong at its heart, we root our ideas of right and wrong in faith—a quiet guide that looks beyond our own wants to lasting principles, giving us something solid to lean on when life gets confusing. Without that kind of base, it's hard to see what really steers someone's decisions through tough times, and we've seen how societies without it can slide into a mess, like in Russia after communism fell apart, where graft ran wild. Folks were left scrambling for any sense of purpose in the wreckage.

We have to fight back against twisted messages, especially in the unseen struggles today, where some teachers, caught up in outdated communist ideas, steer young people toward splits rather than togetherness, turning learning spaces into closed-off zones that shut down open thinking. Those places, and a lot of the daily news, were supposed to stand guard over our freedoms. Instead, they've been overtaken by a small group peddling lopsided views, just like in communist setups, where a few decide what gets said and heard, squeezing out honest discussion and risking the freedoms that let us voice our thoughts freely.

When these key parts fail us, it's up to each of us to pick up the slack and hold onto the truth ourselves, since so many primary news sources have turned into pipelines for biased stories that push specific agendas, breaking trust and driving wedges between people. We hold our ground by insisting on straight talk everywhere, encouraging learning that's free and fearless, and gathering around simple facts that pull us closer, sparking anew the common understanding that holds our community together with hope. There's a saying that goes like this: "Nobody wants to hear your opinion. They only want to hear their opinion coming out of your mouth." That may be true, but we need to constantly encourage open discourse with room for both sides of a problem, without shouting down opposing views.

"Freedom is the right to tell people what they do not want to hear."
– George Orwell

Let me share the story of James O'Keefe, a guy whose passion for getting to the bottom of things made him a tireless hunter in a world full of secrets. From early on, he had this inner fire for fairness that wouldn't let him stand by, so he started Project Veritas, going undercover to shine a light on what big organizations wanted hidden. In one intense operation, he caught a CNN producer on secret video confessing that their nonstop push on unbacked Russia claims was more about pumping up viewership than actual reporting. This bombshell laid bare how stations could bend stories to suit their angle, leaving everyday viewers confused and split apart. The backlash hit hard: legal fights, getting banned from online spots, even dangers to his well-being, but O'Keefe pressed on because he believed deeply that exposing falsehoods was his call to serve his homeland, much like Patrick Henry's bold words, "Give me liberty, or give me death!" drove him to put his own safety on the line for everyone's. His trust in a greater truth gave him the strength to endure, transforming his hardships into a signal for others, showing how one individual's brave push against deceit can wake up many more, keeping alive the fire of honesty that guards our collective pursuit of truth and brighter days.

ETERNAL VIGILANCE

To hold onto the vigilance that keeps our freedoms alive, we start by asking hard questions without fear, probing the decisions around us to uncover what's real and what's hidden, because silence lets shadows grow. We stand tall for the principles that built this land—truth, fairness, personal responsibility—living them out in daily choices that show others the way, even when the winds push back.

We draw lessons from the past, remembering how nations fell when they forgot their roots, as in the slow rot of ancient Rome, where unchecked spending and moral drift invited invaders to topple an empire once thought unbreakable.

We rein in government waste, trimming the fat from bloated budgets that siphon hard-earned money into endless programs, while sparking private ventures that let people chase their own paths to prosperity, fueling growth from the ground up.

We keep the flame burning by passing on the American Dream—not just better chances for our kids, but teaching them to guard our Constitution, embrace a strong work spirit, and build on a moral base tied to faith, so they see why freedoms matter; without that, young hearts swayed by ideas like communism, which crushed millions under despots who starved their own in Ukraine's Holodomor or slaughtered dissenters in Mao's Cultural Revolution, might never grasp the fight needed to defend what we have.

Trump revived the Monroe Doctrine's spirit, stepping in to shield our hemisphere from outsiders—like pushing back Russian, Chinese, and Iranian meddling in Venezuela or Chinese grips on Panama—ensuring no foreign powers or tyrants plant roots close to home that could choke our independence.

We root out the rot of misuse in places like foreign aid arms or hidden agency ops, where funds meant for good twist into tools for undermining, and push for cleanups like the new efficiency drives to scrub government clear. We call out the slanted stories from big news that run counter to our founders' vision, spreading untruths that ruin lives in the rush to sway minds, as one cleared official once asked in despair, "Where do I go to get my reputation back?" after falsehoods shredded his name.

"America is beyond power; it acts as in a dream, as a face of God. Wherever America is, there is freedom, and wherever America is not, madness rules with chains, darkness strangles millions. Beneath her patient bombers, paradise is possible." – John Updike

We turn away from kindness that harms ourselves, as Gad Saad warned against "suicidal empathy," knowing a handful of repeat wrongdoers spark most troubles, so we end no-bail releases that let them roam free, while welcoming varied views but standing firm against clashing realities that could tear us into war, because only watchful hearts preserve the peace.

We remember the term "useful idiots" used by communists to describe people whose empathy clouds their judgment and ends up making situations worse—much like how young people today, particularly young women, are lured toward communism by its false promises, treating the government as a parent that will cradle them and shoulder all responsibilities, a seductive but dangerous illusion that erodes self-reliance and freedom.

"It is difficult to free fools from the chains they revere." - Voltaire

MIND CONTROL

Back in the hard years under totalitarian regimes like the Soviet Union, the people in charge learned a simple but frightening trick. They flooded everyday life with so many conflicting stories, slogans, and rules that after a while, nobody could tell what was true anymore. Words stopped meaning what they always had. History got rewritten, basic facts about men and women got twisted, and anyone who spoke plainly risked losing their job, their friends, or worse. The goal wasn't just to control what people did — it was to confuse them so badly that they gave up even trying to know the truth. When that happens, the rulers win without needing chains or guns.

In the fifteen years leading up to America's 250th anniversary in 2026, many people watched something similar take root here at home. What started as "woke" ideas in colleges and big corporations quietly spread through schools, workplaces, and even government. Suddenly, boys were told they could become girls and girls could become boys, and everyone was expected to use new pronouns or risk being called hateful. Merit — the idea that the best person should get the job or the scholarship — was pushed aside in favor of diversity, equity, and inclusion quotas. Free speech on campus and social media often meant you could only say approved things. Old communist ideas about class struggle and tearing down Western traditions found new life not just in colleges but even in elementary school classrooms. To many everyday Americans, it felt like a slow, deliberate effort to blur reality itself and move the country toward a softer kind of total control.

Aleksandr Solzhenitsyn, the great Russian writer who survived the Soviet gulags and was exiled in 1974, saw this danger clearly. On the very day he was arrested, he released his short essay "Live Not by Lies." In it, he gave ordinary people the simplest way to push back: personal non-participation in lies. He wrote, "The simplest and most accessible key to our self-neglected liberation lies right here: personal non-participation in lies. Even if all is covered by lies, even if all is under their rule, let us resist in the smallest way: Let their rule hold not through me!"

Solzhenitsyn then laid out a practical list anyone could follow, even the most ordinary or timid person. From that day on, he would not write, sign, or speak a single line he knew was false. He would not repeat lies in conversation, teach them, or act them out. He would not vote for something he didn't truly believe in or attend a rally pushing ideas he rejected.

He would walk out of any meeting, movie, or class the moment propaganda started. He would not buy or read newspapers that hid the truth. It might cost comfort or a job at first, he admitted, but it was far easier than hunger strikes or setting yourself on fire — and it was the one road still open to honest people.

When enough individuals simply refuse to cooperate with falsehood in their daily lives, the whole system of lies begins to lose its power and eventually crumbles. That choice — quiet, personal, and brave — is still open to every American today.

And we watch forever against those bent on unraveling our way of life, like George Soros pouring fortunes into causes that critics say fray borders and values, or Klaus Schwab championing resets that smell of global chains over personal choice, or Bill Gates funding sweeps that some fear tilt toward control over health and lives, or Reid Hoffman bankrolling lawsuits against political opponents that critics argue weaponize the courts to silence dissent, or international money barons who pull strings on banks that then dictate to companies, forcing them into unfair hiring rules that divide rather than unite, all demanding our constant guard to keep liberty's fire from being snuffed. Even late-night television, once a bastion of balanced satire where comedians poked fun at politics from all sides, has devolved into one-sided propaganda pushing hard-left agendas, shaping masses toward singular thinking and killing true comedy in the process.

We must never forget that freedom is not a possession we can lock away and forget about. It is a living flame that needs constant tending. History shows us that the greatest threats to liberty often come not from marching armies, but from quiet, clever ways of reshaping how people think. In his important 2026 book "Manufacturing Delusion", Buck Sexton shines a clear light on the old Soviet techniques of mind control that once confused and divided entire populations. Those same patterns, he warns, are being used again today in subtler forms, and we would be wise to recognize them before they take deeper root.

Sexton reminds us of the famous experiments with Pavlov's dogs. When the animals were repeatedly pushed to the edge of drowning and then rescued, something profound changed inside them. Their personalities shifted. The once-loyal, predictable dogs became anxious, confused, and unpredictable. The Soviets studied this carefully. They learned that if you flood people with fear, contradiction, and relentless messaging, you can break down their ability to know what is true. Over time, many simply stop trying to figure it out and accept whatever the loudest voices tell them. That is not ancient history. We are watching similar tactics at work right now.

Today, our freedom of speech — the very right our Founders gave us to protect us from tyranny — is sometimes turned against us. Voices that should be debating ideas are instead drowned out by noise, slogans, and emotional triggers designed to confuse rather than clarify. Old words are given new meanings, basic truths about human nature are called hateful, and anyone who asks simple questions is often shouted down or canceled. The goal is not to win an argument. The goal is to make people so weary and uncertain that they stop trusting their own eyes and ears.

Yet here is the hopeful truth: Americans have always been harder to fool than tyrants expect. We still carry that stubborn streak of independence that says, "I will think for myself." The answer is not fear. The answer is vigilance with open eyes and steady hearts. We protect our freedoms best when we refuse to participate in the lies, when we keep asking honest questions, when we insist on truth even when it is uncomfortable, and when we teach our children that clarity and courage still matter more than comfort. The flame our ancestors carried across stormy seas is still ours to guard. As long as enough of us refuse to be swept along by manufactured confusion and chaos, that flame will not go out.

Let me bring this to life with the tale of Brandon Straka, a man whose awakening turned him into a voice for truth amid swirling storms of division. Once caught in the pull of mainstream narratives, he stepped away from a life in the arts to question what he saw around him, founding the WalkAway movement to share stories of folks breaking free from one-sided views that stifled real talk. In the heat of 2018, as crowds clashed and media spun tales that painted one side as villains, Brandon went public with videos urging people to think for themselves, facing down arrests, smears, and even time behind bars over January 6 charges that later crumbled. What drove him wasn't fame but a raw love for the country that had given him chances, blended with a faith that called him to stand for honesty no matter the cost. As he endured interrogations and isolation, he held onto Thomas Jefferson's words, "The price of freedom is eternal vigilance," knowing he had to act now or watch the nation he cherished slip away. His grit inspired thousands to speak up, turning personal trials into a rally for others, a living proof that one citizen's brave push can sustain the flame of resilient liberty, guiding us all toward a future where courage wins out.

AMERICA AT 250 – LOOKING FORWARD TO THE NEXT 250 YEARS

As we stand on the edge of America's 250th year, a brave new world unfolds with leaps in science, technology, and healing that promise to reshape how we live and dream. Think of Elon Musk, a man whose bold visions have already pushed boundaries—from Tesla's cars that drive themselves through busy streets, learning from every mile to make roads safer, to Optimus robots stepping into factories and homes, handling tasks with a precision that frees people for more meaningful work. SpaceX rockets light up the skies, with missions gearing up to return us to the Moon and set foot on Mars, carrying the spirit of exploration that once drew pioneers across oceans. In medicine, strides in longevity whisper of turning back time—researchers unlocking ways to clear out aging cells, perhaps adding healthy years through treatments like gene therapies, stem cell therapies, and compounds that mimic fasting's renewal.

Quantum computers race ahead, crunching problems in seconds that once took lifetimes, opening doors to cures, secure communications, and insights into the universe itself. Grok and other AI tools, built to seek truth without bias, could guide us honestly through this rush, while America's role—rooted in freedom's spark—positions us to lead, ensuring these wonders serve humanity's reach among the stars, not chains that bind.

"America is the spirit of human exploration distilled." – Elon Musk

Our hopes for the next 250 years rest on nurturing that dream where each generation lifts the next higher, but only if we instill in them the tools to protect it: knowledge of our founding laws, a drive to work with purpose, and a spiritual grounding that fosters compassion and strength. We envision a land where innovation thrives under liberty's watch, families pass on stories of sacrifice that fuel resolve, and the flame of opportunity burns bright for all who cherish it.

Teach your children values, patriotism, kindness, and service. Give them a work ethic, but mostly surround them with patience, love, routine, and the foundation of family.

Pledge allegiance to the flag. Stand proudly for the National Anthem. Take off your hat and hold your hand to your heart. Do it all in reverence to the countless patriots who came before you and sacrificed their lives, their livelihood, their fortunes, and their futures so we can all continue to breathe free.

Like the American eagle, we must remain eternally vigilant.

With strength renewed and lighting our path, we turn now to the close, carrying that eternal flame ahead to secure America's promise as the beacon for all humankind.

CONCLUSION
ETERNAL FLAME
AMERICA'S PROMISE TO HUMANITY

SAFEGUARDING AMERICA'S FREEDOM

America started small, with settlers who risked everything to build something better. They crossed dangerous oceans, survived brutal winters without enough food, and fought tyrants who executed people without justice. Many today don't learn these stories, but they're real—they show what it took to win our freedoms. Those ancestors gave their lives on battlefields like Lexington and Gettysburg so future generations could live without fear. Freedom is more than something handed to us; it's a responsibility we protect, rooted in life, liberty, and the pursuit of happiness. This is what we inherit, and we have to work to keep it, or it fades away.

CURRENT CONCERNS

As we mark America's 250th anniversary, we're facing serious challenges from both within and without that threaten our freedoms. China is pushing hard—stealing inventions from our creators, using its military to intimidate countries in the South China Sea, and setting economic traps to weaken our position globally. Russia is attacking democracies directly, rolling tanks into Ukraine to destroy lives and homes, interfering in our elections to create division, and breaking down alliances that once kept aggressors in check. In the Middle East, while we have many friends and allies who share our values of peace and cooperation, certain regimes and groups continue to fuel instability—backing terrorism, oppressing their people with brutal laws, and pursuing weapons that endanger the region and beyond. North Korea's leader tests missiles that threaten us, runs a regime where people starve in camps for the smallest complaint, and casts a nuclear threat over our coast. Much of Islam, like other faiths, promotes peace and moral living, but radical Islamic terrorism from groups like ISIS and Hamas represents a twisted ideology, much as misdirected Christians committed atrocities like murder, rape, and pillage during the Crusades in the name of God. These extremists attack innocent people in public places to impose Sharia's strict rule, where women have no rights, and others face death for disagreeing—actions that clash with the Judeo-Christian principles of freedom, justice, and human dignity that underpin our society and directly clash with our American way of life. Even European countries we consider "friendly" are leaning towards totalitarianism and censorship in a dramatic way. Inside our country, divisions come from ideas like cultural Marxism spreading through education and media, prioritizing group identities over what unites us and weakening family and faith that have always held us together. No one has a monopoly on truth, and acting superior because of your beliefs doesn't convince anyone—it just comes across as small-minded.

God gave us all free will, strong enough that we can even turn away from Him. Tyrants throughout history have tried to take that away from people, and we must always stand against it.

We must bring American values back into education to preserve our children's futures.

"America's future will be determined by the home and the school. The child becomes largely what he is taught; hence we must watch what we teach, and how we live." – Jane Addams

Take Jocelyn Nungaray, a 12-year-old from Houston whose life was cut short in a violent attack by two Venezuelan men who entered the country illegally and faced capital murder charges. Her mother, Alexis, turned her heartbreak into purpose, speaking to lawmakers about the need for secure borders and real justice. With a deep commitment to the country that should have kept her daughter safe, and faith that loss can lead to change, she reminded everyone of Reagan's words about how easily freedom can slip away. Stories like hers show that regular people, facing external powers or internal conflicts, can step up and protect what matters, even when it's hard.

PRESERVING OUR AMERICAN WAY

Keeping our way of life means putting family first, building it around faith and the chance to achieve dreams—taking care of aging parents at home where they belong, instead of leaving them isolated in facilities. We resist the deep state, those unelected bureaucrats who operate behind the scenes, using regulations to block elected leaders and limit our choices. Big Tech companies become problems when they censor opinions, manipulate what we find online, and monitor our lives, giving too much power to a handful of people over information. Illegal immigration without controls strains our systems, brings in crime, and dilutes the culture we share, so we need to apply laws fairly and with care. We're seeing some progress with efforts to cut government waste, but we need more: require every program to expire and get reviewed every five years to eliminate unnecessary spending; fully audit agencies to stop fraud, like the massive losses in aid programs; limit debt to current levels unless voters approve more; move to a flat tax without special breaks for insiders; and reduce regulations on small businesses to let ideas grow. Running up endless debt burdens our children and makes it tougher to handle dangers from abroad.

Rachel Morin was a mother of five in Maryland, out for a jog, when an illegal immigrant from El Salvador with a criminal record allegedly killed her. Her brother, Michael, channeled the family's grief into advocacy, addressing national audiences to call for responsible borders and systems that respect legal processes. Grounded in American principles, they argued that genuine kindness means enforcing rules to protect everyone. With faith guiding them and love for the nation that shaped their lives, they pushed for unity based on merit, facing criticism to defend the future. Efforts like theirs highlight how protecting family, faith, and smart finances keeps us strong, voice by voice.

"Freedom prospers when religion is vibrant and the rule of law under God is acknowledged." – Ronald Reagan

EPILOGUE
KEEPING THE FAITH

FLAMES OF FREEDOM

Soldiers at Valley Forge wrapped rags around their bleeding feet just to march on through the bitter cold. Marines at Iwo Jima raised that flag amid relentless gunfire, paying a heavy price with thousands of lives lost. These moments capture the raw sacrifices people made to stand against tyranny and protect what matters. Now, it's our generation facing new threats that aim to chip away at our strength, and we have to step up—through faith, determination, and real action—to ensure these freedoms hold strong for another 250 years. Those old rally cries still echo: "Remember the Alamo," where a small band held back a massive army; "Remember the Maine," blown apart in a mysterious explosion that ignited a war; "Remember Pearl Harbor," hit out of nowhere; and "Remember 9/11," when towers crumbled, and so many innocent lives were taken. They remind us of the costs paid and push us to stay vigilant.

Younger folks, especially Gen Z and millennials, are rediscovering something deeper amid all this. Many Christians are turning back to Jesus in casual meetups and gatherings, Jews are reconnecting with their traditions, and people from other faiths are embracing core ideas like kindness, generosity, and treating others as they'd want to be treated. It's like they're filling a void after too much isolation. The shocking assassination of Charlie Kirk in September 2025—a young man who blended deep faith with love for his country—really rattled everyone. It woke people up, leading to a quiet surge of spiritual interest on college campuses, where kids are exploring personal beliefs in ways that feel real and urgent.

Looking forward, America's innovative drive gives us a real edge against those who want to undermine us. It's about harnessing rapid tech advances and big, bold ideas to stay ahead. In a recent "Moonshots" podcast on X, Peter Diamandis and Elon Musk shared some game-changing thoughts that could reshape everything. Musk sees artificial general intelligence—AGI—hitting by 2029 or even earlier, more intelligent than any human brain, solving problems we can't yet imagine. But they pointed out that rivals like China are surging ahead in AI computing power and solar energy, building massive infrastructure while we lag—it's a wake-up call to ramp up and reclaim the lead. Then there's the job shake-up from AI and robots, which might displace work but could usher in an era of plenty, where machines handle the grind, and people focus on creativity, wiping out scarcity as we know it.

"In the twenty-first century, the robot will take the place which slave labor occupied in ancient civilization." – Nikola Tesla

Clean energy is another frontier: exponential leaps in solar panels and batteries could make power basically free, cutting off resource fights that fuel conflicts with our global competitors. On health, new longevity studies are pushing boundaries—using biotech like gene editing and AI to discover drugs that could let us live twice as long as we do now, giving future generations more time to build and innovate. Musk's work with xAI and Grok is all about creating honest AI that hunts for truth, fighting back against the lies and propaganda our adversaries spread to divide us. Space is key too: projects like Starship heading to Mars make humanity multi-planetary, a safeguard against any Earth-bound disasters from threats we face.

They talked about shifting to an abundance mindset—using these tech explosions to tackle huge problems and turning rivalries into opportunities rather than win-or-lose battles. AI alone could rescue America by multiplying our productivity tenfold, helping us innovate faster than competitors in defense, the economy, and healthcare. And it all starts with curiosity: Musk says his breakthroughs come from never-stopping questions, a habit we need to adopt as a nation to reinvent ourselves against those who hold us back.

We must tackle the absurd national debt and rein in government spending. This reminds me of Ronald Reagan's famous comment:

"You know, we could say they spend money like drunken sailors, but that would be unfair to drunken sailors—because the sailors are spending their own money."
- Ronald Reagan

My father had a saying: **"Everyone's a genius; only in different subjects."** Now imagine something that takes that idea further—an intelligence that's expert in every field at once, from science and medicine to philosophy and ethics, connecting it all instantly to fix humanity's toughest issues. It's like having a room full of the greatest minds on the planet, but they're all wrapped up in one.

That's what Artificial General Intelligence, or AGI, could be: a human-made system that doesn't just copy our brains but goes beyond them. It could analyze huge amounts of information in moments to find cures for long-standing diseases, literally reverse our aging process, or devise new, never-conceived energy strategies that prioritize national security and economic independence. But as thoughtful people point out, this kind of power has downsides: if we don't ensure it aligns with our core values, it might challenge our identity, making us wonder what it means to be human when machines outthink us. In the end, AGI could drive massive progress, boosting economies and advancing science for everyone's benefit, as long as we steer it carefully with a focus on what makes us human.

Going even further, the future past AGI might bring superintelligent machines that change everything we know, possibly triggering a rapid "intelligence explosion" that lets us explore space, settle other worlds, and eliminate resource shortages. Leaders and experts warn that we need to keep tight control to stop bad actors from misusing it, so it helps us instead of replacing us. We could build societies where smart AI rules prevent mass job losses from turning into bigger problems, while encouraging new ideas that value individual effort and strong communities. Still, the dangers are real: if things go off track, it could lead to serious threats that turn potential gains into disasters, especially if we put power ahead of people's well-being. At this turning point, we're on the edge of incredible possibilities—like ending aging, achieving real global peace, or achieving unlimited energy—but we'll only get there if we move forward thoughtfully, protecting our essence as humans amid these advances.

This is America's narrative—one of rising above, from shattering slavery's chains in bloody fights like Antietam to triumphing in world wars. We live it out like Jimmy Stewart in "Mr. Smith Goes to Washington," worn out but unyielding against corruption, or Lincoln at Gettysburg, honoring the dead to keep government by the people alive. Jefferson nailed it in the Declaration: life, liberty, and the pursuit of happiness are God-given rights no one can strip away. Picture the troops storming beaches, soaring into storms, holding the line when the odds were stacked against them—their faith and guts carried them through for our sake. We honor that by pushing ahead, bolstering our foundations against every challenge. With bravery, belief, and these groundbreaking innovations, the American dream doesn't just survive—it thrives for centuries, lighting the way for everyone. Godspeed as you work to safeguard these liberties well beyond my time. Keep the faith!

Picture this: you're walking through an old family home, one that's stood strong for generations, its walls etched with stories of triumphs and close calls. That's America, built by our Founders with lessons carved from the ruins of ancient empires like Athens, Sparta, Rome, Egypt, Persia, and Babylon. They saw how those mighty civilizations crumbled—not from outside invaders alone, but from inside rot: unchecked power, moral decay, rigid systems that couldn't bend, and leaders who forgot they served the people. So, our Founders crafted our Constitution with safeguards—checks and balances, equal laws for all, protections for faith and speech without letting any group dominate—to keep us from those same pitfalls. It was like installing fire alarms in every room, hoping we'd never need them but knowing human nature sometimes sparks trouble. For over 250 years, it's worked, a testament to their wisdom drawn from history's harsh teachers.

But lately, those alarms have started beeping. We're seeing echoes of ancient mistakes creeping in: government overreach bloating agencies like the IRS with unchecked power, much like Rome's emperors seizing estates; a loosening of moral foundations where families fracture, and values shift, reminiscent of Athens' chase for pleasure over honor; borders left porous, straining resources as in Egypt's neglected defenses. Think of recent scandals—waste in USAID or politicized justice—mirroring Persia's greedy satraps hoarding taxes.

Remember Ronald Reagan's warning, "**Freedom is never more than one generation away from extinction.**" It's not doom and gloom; it's a compassionate call to wake up, because ignoring these signs lets the rot spread, undermining the liberty our Founders fought to secure.

Yet, here's the hope that keeps the light burning: America has always been resilient, a nation of comebacks built on the sacrifices of millions—from Revolutionary soldiers freezing at Valley Forge to everyday heroes today upholding truth. We count our blessings in a land where faith guides without force, where hard work still opens doors, and where we can course-correct through our enduring Constitution. As we step into this new age of challenges, let's honor those who died for our freedoms by staying vigilant—voting wisely, holding leaders accountable, and nurturing the values that make us strong. Remember, as Abraham Lincoln said amid our darkest hour, "**We shall nobly save, or meanly lose, the last best hope of earth.**" The choice is ours; let's choose to keep the flame alive.

And so, my friends, as we stand on the threshold of America's two hundred and fiftieth birthday, let us remember the deepest truth that the Founders knew in their bones: this nation was not built on politics or power or even brilliant ideas alone. It was built on faith — faith in a Creator who endowed us with unalienable rights, faith in one another when the night seemed darkest, and faith that ordinary men and women could rise and do extraordinary things.

We will face storms. We always have. There will be voices that tell us the dream is over, that freedom is too costly, that we should simply kneel and accept whatever comes. But Viktor Frankl, who survived the worst hell humanity ever devised, left us these immortal words: **"When we are no longer able to change a situation, we are challenged to change ourselves."** That is the American spirit in its purest form. No matter what is taken from us, no one can take our ability to choose hope, to choose courage, to choose faith.

So keep the faith! Stand tall in the face of tyranny and repression, just as the men and women of 1776 did. Speak truth with kindness. Love your neighbor even when you disagree. Work hard, dream bigger, and never stop believing that the American Dream is not a relic of the past — it is a living flame that each generation is called to carry forward. The story is not ending. It is only beginning again. And with God's help and our own steady hands, the best chapters are still ahead.

...with liberty and justice for all.

REFERENCES

Historical Documents and Primary Sources

Abrams, T. (n.d.). Work sample: Narrative of the life of Frederick Douglass. EdSpace. https://edspace.american.edu/ta0420a/work-sample

Adams, J. (n.d.). *Founders Online: Correspondence and papers*. National Archives. https://founders.archives.gov

Baker Institute. (n.d.). *James A. Baker III: Biography*. James A. Baker III Institute for Public Policy. https://www.bakerinstitute.org/about/james-baker

Bible (King James Version). (n.d.). *Genesis, Micah, Psalms*.

BlackPast.org. (2025, March 23). Stephen Bishop (1821-1857). https://blackpast.org/african-american-history/stephen-bishop-1821-1857

Bly, A. T. (2022, August 16). Education in enslaved communities. Library of Congress Blogs. https://blogs.loc.gov/teachers/2022/08/education-in-enslaved-communities

Brucker, R. (n.d.). Origins of the Stephen Bishop story. Roger Brucker. https://rogerbrucker.com/origins-of-the-stephen-bishop-story

Connecticut Colonial Records. (n.d.). *Public acts and election sermons*.

Declaration of Independence. (1776). https://www.archives.gov/founding-docs/declaration

Epictetus. (135 AD/ n.d.). *Enchiridion* (translated editions).

Federalist Papers. (1787–1788). Hamilton, A., Madison, J., & Jay, J.

Gehrz, C. (2019, July 9). The self-education of Frederick Douglass. Patheos. https://www.patheos.com/blogs/anxiousbench/2019/07/frederick-douglass-self-education

Jacobs, H. A. (1861). Incidents in the life of a slave girl, written by herself. Project Gutenberg. https://www.gutenberg.org/ebooks/11030

Kissinger, H. A. (1994). *Diplomacy*. Simon & Schuster. (As referenced in National Review analyses: https://www.nationalreview.com/2014/09/henry-kissinger-realist-fernando-herrera/)

Library of Congress. (2013, November 19). 12 years a slave: Primary sources on the kidnapping of free African Americans. https://blogs.loc.gov/teachers/2013/11/12-years-a-slave-primary-sources-on-the-kidnapping-of-free-african-americans

Marcus Aurelius. (180 AD/ n.d.). *Meditations* (translated editions).

Massachusetts Historical Society. (n.d.). *Samuel Allyne Otis papers and letters*.

Monroy, D. (2020, June 17). How literacy became a powerful weapon in the fight to end slavery. History.com. https://www.history.com/articles/nat-turner-rebellion-literacy-slavery

National Archives. (n.d.). *George C. Marshall: Secretary of State*. National Archives and Records Administration. (As cited in Heritage Foundation reports on post-WWII diplomacy: https://www.heritage.org/defense/report/the-marshall-plan-lessons-today)

National Archives. (n.d.). *Twenty-Fifth Amendment*. https://www.archives.gov/federal-register/constitution/amendment-25.html

National Archives. (n.d.). *Twenty-Fourth Amendment*. https://www.archives.gov/federal-register/constitution/amendment-24.html

National Archives. (n.d.). *Twenty-Second Amendment*. https://www.archives.gov/federal-register/constitution/amendment-22.html

National Archives. (n.d.). *Twenty-Third Amendment*. https://www.archives.gov/federal-register/constitution/amendment-23.html

National Park Service. (2021, March 25). Stephen Bishop. https://www.nps.gov/people/stephen-bishop.htm

New York Colonial Manuscripts (Dutch). (n.d.). *Documents Relative to the Colonial History of the State of New York* (translations). Albany.

Overton, C. (n.d.). Stephen Bishop: The legendary Black explorer of Mammoth Cave. Correy Overton. https://www.correyoverton.com/historys-hidden-gem/stephen-bishop-respected-cave-guide

Pennsylvania Historical Society. (n.d.). *Accounts of gradual abolition*.

Reagan Library. (n.d.). *Secretaries of State: Thomas Jefferson*. Ronald Reagan Presidential Library & Museum. https://www.reaganlibrary.gov/research/secretaries-state/thomas-jefferson

Rubio, M. (2025). *Senate Confirmation Hearing Testimony*. U.S. Senate Committee on Foreign Relations. (As covered in The Federalist: https://thefederalist.com/2025/01/15/marco-rubio-confirmed-secretary-state-trump-administration)Schwab, K. (1971). *Moderne Unternehmensführung im Maschinenbau* [Modern enterprise management in mechanical engineering]. (As cited in Burkett, C. (2013). *Remaking the world: Progressivism and American foreign policy*. Heritage Foundation. https://www.heritage.org/political-process/report/remaking-the-world-progressivism-and-american-foreign-policy)

Thirteen.org. (n.d.). Slavery and the making of America: The slave experience: Education, arts, & culture. PBS. https://www.thirteen.org/wnet/slavery/experience/education/docs1.html

United Nations. (1945). *Charter of the United Nations*. United Nations. (As cited in Fagan, P. F. (2001). *How U.N. conventions on women's and children's rights undermine family, religion, and sovereignty*. The Heritage Foundation. https://www.heritage.org/civil-rights/report/how-un-conventions-womens-and-childrens-rights-underminefamily-religion-and)

United Nations. (1948). *Universal declaration of human rights*. United Nations. (As cited in Fagan, P. F. (2001). *How U.N. conventions on women's and children's rights undermine family, religion, and sovereignty*. The Heritage Foundation. https://www.heritage.org/civil-rights/report/how-un-conventions-womens-and-childrens-rights-underminefamily-religion-and)
University of North Carolina at Chapel Hill. (n.d.). Incidents in the life of a slave girl. Written by herself. Documenting the American South. https://docsouth.unc.edu/fpn/jacobs/menu.html
U.S. Constitution and Bill of Rights. (1787–1791). https://www.archives.gov/founding-docs
Virginia Convention Records. (n.d.). *Contemporary letters on Patrick Henry's speech*.
Wikipedia. (n.d.). Education during the slave period in the United States. https://en.wikipedia.org/wiki/Education_during_the_slave_period_in_the_United_States
William Bradford. (1650). *Of Plymouth Plantation* (original manuscript excerpts). Library of Congress archives.
World Economic Forum. (n.d.). *History: A short history*. World Economic Forum. (As cited in Fagan, P. F. (2001). *How U.N. conventions on women's and children's rights undermine family, religion, and sovereignty*. The Heritage Foundation. https://www.heritage.org/civil-rights/report/how-un-conventions-womens-and-childrens-rights-underminefamily-religion-and)

Books and Monographs

Alexander, K. L. (2018). Betsy Ross. In National Women's History Museum biographies. https://www.womenshistory.org/education-resources/biographies/betsy-ross
Allan, H. S. (1948). *John Hancock: Patriot in purple*. Macmillan.
Asinof, E. N. (1963). *Eight men out*. Holt, Rinehart and Winston.
Berger, R. (1977). *Government by judiciary*. Harvard University Press.
Biskind, P. (1998). *Easy riders, raging bulls*. Simon & Schuster.
Bork, R. (1990). *The tempting of America*. Free Press.
Breen, T. H. (2010). *American insurgents, American patriots: The revolution of the people*. Hill and Wang
Brown, R. D. (1970). *Revolutionary politics in Massachusetts: The Boston committee of correspondence and the towns, 1772–1774*. Harvard University Press.
Canby, W. J. (1870). The history of the flag of the United States. Paper presented to the Historical Society of Pennsylvania, Philadelphia, PA. (As cited in multiple secondary sources, including USHistory.org transcription: https://www.ushistory.org/betsy/more/canby.htm)
Courtois, S., et al. (1999). *The black book of communism*. Harvard University Press.
Cruz, T. (2020). *One vote away*. Regnery.
Cutter, W. (1847). *Life of Israel Putnam*. Phillips, Sampson & Co.
Earle, A. M. (1893/1973). *Customs and fashions in old New England*. David & Charles (reprint).
Earle, A. M. (1898). *Home life in colonial days*. Macmillan.
Fischer, D. H. (1989). *Albion's seed: Four British folkways in America*. Oxford University Press.
Fischer, D. H. (1994). *Paul Revere's ride*. Oxford University Press.
Fischer, D. H. (2004). *Washington's crossing*. Oxford University Press.
Foner, P. S. (Ed.). (1945). *The complete writings of Thomas Paine*. Citadel Press.
Frankl, V. E. (2006). Man's search for meaning (I. Lasch, Trans.). Beacon Press. (Original work published 1946)
Goodfriend, J. D. (n.d.). *The Dutch colonial legacy*. In *New York divided*. New York University Press.
Hayek, F. A. (1944). *The road to serfdom*. University of Chicago Press.
Holton, W. (2009). *Abigail Adams*. Free Press.
Isaacson, W. (2011). *Steve Jobs*. Simon & Schuster.
Kaye, H. J. (2005). *Thomas Paine and the promise of America*. Hill & Wang.
Lee, M. (2017). *Written out of history*. Sentinel.
Leepson, M. (2005). Flag: An American biography. Thomas Dunne Books/St. Martin's Press.
Lomask, M. (1982). *Aaron Burr: The conspiracy and years of exile*. Farrar, Straus and Giroux.
Lovejoy, D. S. (1985). *Religious enthusiasm in the new world: Heresy to revolution*. Harvard University Press.
Lumen Learning. (n.d.). Primary source reading: Twelve years a slave. US History I (AY Collection). https://courses.lumenlearning.com/suny-ushistory1ay/chapter/primary-source-reading-twelve-years-a-slave
Martin, J. K. (1997). *Benedict Arnold, revolutionary hero*. New York University Press.
McCullough, D. (2001). *John Adams*. Simon & Schuster.
Meade, R. D. (1957). *Patrick Henry: Patriot in the making*. Lippincott.
Miller, M. (2010). Betsy Ross and the making of America. Henry Holt and Company.
Nicoletti, C. N. (2017). *Secession on trial*. Cambridge University Press.
Northup, S. (1853). Twelve years a slave: Narrative of Solomon Northup, a citizen of New-York, kidnapped in Washington City in 1841, and rescued in 1853. Documenting the American South. https://docsouth.unc.edu/fpn/northup/northup.html
O'Connor, S. D. (2002). *Lazy B*. Random House.
Radosh, R., & Milton, J. (1997). *The Rosenberg file*. Yale University Press.
Reagan, R. (1990). *An American life*. Simon & Schuster.
Rink, O. A. (1986). *Holland on the Hudson: An economic and social history of Dutch Manhattan*. Cornell University Press.
Scalia, A. (1997). *A matter of interpretation*. Princeton University Press.

Schiff, S. (2022). *The revolutionary: Samuel Adams*. Little, Brown.
Schlafly, P. (1964). *A choice not an echo*. Pere Marquette Press.
Sexton, B. (2026). Manufacturing delusion: How the Left uses brainwashing, indoctrination, and propaganda against you. Sentinel.
Shone, T. (2004). *Blockbuster: How Hollywood learned to stop worrying and love the summer*. Free Press.
Shorto, R. (2004). *The island at the center of the world: The epic story of Dutch Manhattan and the forgotten colony that shaped America*. Doubleday.
Solzhenitsyn, A. (2006). Live not by lies. In E. E. Ericson, Jr., & D. J. Mahoney (Eds.)
Unger, H. G. (2000). *John Hancock: Merchant king and American patriot*. Wiley.
Unger, H. G. (2010). *Patrick Henry: Lion of liberty*. Da Capo Press.
U.S. History Online Textbook. (n.d.). Betsy Ross and the American flag: Historical analysis. https://www.ushistory.org/betsy/flagpcp.html
Victor Davis Hanson. (2021). *The dying citizen*. Basic Books.
Weinberger, C. W. (1990). *Fighting for peace: Seven critical years in the Pentagon*. Warner Books.
Wirt, W. (1817). *Sketches of the life and character of Patrick Henry*. James Webster.
Wright, L. B. (Ed.). (1947). *The history and present state of Virginia* (1705 ed.). University of North Carolina Press.

Journal Articles

Ahrens, L. (2024). Dealing with evil—A continuing series on nurturing our emotional, physical, spiritual, and mental health. *American Jails, 38*(2), 77–79.
Hidayatullah, M. (2014). The methods used in delivering speech conclusion in Nelson Mandela's speeches. https://core.ac.uk/download/489566434.pdf
Journals of the Continental Congress. (1777). Journals of the Continental Congress, 1774–1789 (Vol. 8, p. 464). United States Continental Congress. (Resolution of June 14, 1777: "Resolved, that the flag of the thirteen United States be thirteen stripes, alternate red and white; that the union be thirteen stars, white in a blue field, representing a new constellation.")
National Review. (2007, June 19). The day the music died. National Review. https://www.nationalreview.com/2007/06/day-music-died-interview
National Review. (2013, November 22). Our lives with Kennedy. National Review. https://www.nationalreview.com/2013/11/our-lives-kennedy-interview
National Review. (2017, April 28). Dan Rather – Fake news. National Review. https://www.nationalreview.com/2017/04/dan-rather-fake-news
O'Rourke, M. (2012). Lost to history. *Risk Management, 59*(8), 4.
Short, E. (2020). The non-feminist Abigail Adams. *Human Life Review, 46*(2), 45–56.
Wiggins, J. R. (1988). Lawyers and journalists. https://core.ac.uk/download/229706468.pdf

Reports and Policy Papers

American Battlefield Trust. (n.d.). *1780: Sentiments of an American woman*.
American Battlefield Trust. (n.d.). *The Pequot War*.
American Battlefield Trust. (n.d.). *Trail of tears*.
American Chemical Society. (n.d.). *Penicillin*. *Chemical & Engineering News*.
American Enterprise Institute. (2015). *James Baker's diplomatic triumphs*. American Enterprise Institute. https://www.aei.org/foreign-and-defense-policy/james-baker-diplomatic-achievements
American Revolution Institute. (n.d.). *Deborah Sampson at war*.
Buckley, W. F., Jr. (2005, January 3). Publisher's statement. National Review. https://www.nationalreview.com/2005/01/publishers-statement-william-f-buckley-jr-2
Burkett, C. (2013). *Remaking the world: Progressivism and American foreign policy*. The Heritage Foundation. https://www.heritage.org/political-process/report/remaking-the-world-progressivism-and-american-foreign-policy
Cato Institute. (2015–2024). Analyses on historical tyrannies and freedom's foundations [Policy papers].
Cato Institute. (2015–2024). Analyses on historical tyranny and individual resolve [Policy papers].
Cato Institute. (2015–2024). Analyses on tyranny's impact on faith [Policy papers].
Cato Institute. (2015–2025). Analyses on government overreach, welfare failures, and economic policies [Policy papers].
CIA. (1987). *Damage assessment* (declassified).
Commission for Review of FBI Security Programs. (2002). *Webster Commission report*.
Congressional Budget Office. (n.d.). Reports on capital gains rate cuts revenue.
Department of Defense. (n.d.). Historical reviews of Cold War espionage.
Department of Energy Inspector General. (n.d.). Report on Solyndra.
Department of Justice Office of the Inspector General. (2012). Report on Operation Fast and Furious.
Department of Justice. (n.d.). Records on Robert Hanssen case.
Dobski, B. (2020). *America, the republican nation: A response to critics of the nation-state*. The Heritage Foundation. https://www.heritage.org/civil-society/report/america-the-republican-nation-response-critics-the-nation-state
Fagan, P. F. (2001). *How U.N. conventions on women's and children's rights undermine family, religion, and sovereignty*. The Heritage Foundation. https://www.heritage.org/civil-rights/report/how-un-conventions-womens-and-childrens-rights-underminefamily-religion-and

FBI. (n.d.). Official case artifacts and summary (John Walker Jr.).
FBI. (n.d.). Official case files (Atom Spy Case, Julius and Ethel Rosenberg).
FBI. (n.d.). Official case files (Robert Hanssen).
FBI. (n.d.). Official case summary (Aldrich Ames).
FBI. (2024). Reports on Trump assassination attempts.
Federal Deposit Insurance Corporation. (n.d.). *FDIC History (1930–1939)*.
Federal Election Commission. (n.d.). Official results (1992, 2000, 2016, 2024 elections).
Federal Reserve History. (n.d.). *Banking panics of 1930-31*.
Federal Reserve History. (n.d.). *Stock market crash of 1929*.
Federal Reserve History. (n.d.). *The great inflation*.
Gilder Lehrman Institute of American History. (n.d.). *Remember the Maine, 1898*.
Government Accountability Project. (n.d.). Reports on whistleblower protections.
Greenway, R. (2024, November 8). A new strategic service for a new cold war. Heritage Foundation. https://www.heritage.org/sites/default/files/2024-11/IB5361.pdf
Greenway, R. (2024). A new strategic service for a new cold war. The Heritage Foundation. https://www.heritage.org/defense/report/new-strategic-service-new-cold-war
Harford County State's Attorney. (n.d.). *Maximum penalty imposed for brutal 2023 MA-PA trail murder*.
Health Canada. (2024). *Sixth annual report on medical assistance in dying*.
Heritage Foundation. (n.d.). *A conservative pathway for immigration reform*.
Heritage Foundation. (n.d.). *Biden's border crisis*.
Heritage Foundation. (n.d.). *Biden's pardon abuse*
Heritage Foundation. (n.d.). *Defeating ISIS under Trump*.
Heritage Foundation. (n.d.). *Election integrity scorecard*.
Heritage Foundation. (n.d.). *How Obamacare raised premiums*.
Heritage Foundation. (n.d.). *How the first 'Green New Deal' flopped*.
Heritage Foundation. (n.d.). *IRS abuses*.
Heritage Foundation. (n.d.). *January 6: The truth*.
Heritage Foundation. (n.d.). *Judicial activism in the lower courts*.
Heritage Foundation. (n.d.). *NAFTA's legacy*.
Heritage Foundation. (n.d.). *Obamacare has doubled the cost of individual health insurance*.
Heritage Foundation. (n.d.). *Reagan's Cold War strategy*.
Heritage Foundation. (n.d.). *Reagan's faith*.
Heritage Foundation. (n.d.). *Showstopper: Department of Justice report*.
Heritage Foundation. (n.d.). *The Biden administration's weaponization of government*.
Heritage Foundation. (n.d.). *The Biden Afghanistan debacle*.
Heritage Foundation. (n.d.). *The high cost of Biden's energy agenda*.
Heritage Foundation. (n.d.). *The Laffer curve: Past, present, and future*.
Heritage Foundation. (n.d.). *The most glaring flaws in Obama's Iran deal*.
Heritage Foundation. (n.d.). *The origins of COVID-19*.
Heritage Foundation. (n.d.). *The real Reagan economic record*.
Heritage Foundation. (n.d.). *The Trump economic miracle*.
Heritage Foundation. (n.d.). *The war on poverty after 50 years*.
Heritage Foundation. (n.d.). *Trump's foreign policy achievements*.
Heritage Foundation. (n.d.). *Understanding the hidden $1.1 trillion welfare system*.
Heritage Foundation. (n.d.). *Welfare reform report card*.
Heritage Foundation. (n.d.). *Why returning to the JCPOA is a dangerous mistake*.
Heritage Foundation. (n.d.). *Wisconsin welfare reform success story*.
Heritage Foundation. (n.d.). Reports on founding principles, Judeo-Christian values, and modern threats (various articles, 2020–2025).
Heritage Foundation. (n.d.). Reports on judicial activism.
Heritage Foundation. (n.d.). From constitutional interpretation to judicial activism: The transformation of judicial review in America. The Heritage Foundation. https://www.heritage.org/the-constitution/report/constitutional-interpretation-judicial-activism-the-transformation-judicial
Heritage Foundation. (n.d.). How the United States government lost its liberalism. The Heritage Foundation. https://www.heritage.org/political-process/commentary/how-the-united-states-government-lost-its-liberalism
eritage Foundation. (n.d.). The Constitution created the District of Columbia and only the Constitution can make it a state. The Heritage Foundation. https://www.heritage.org/the-constitution/report/the-constitution-created-the-district-columbia-and-only-the-constitution
Heritage Foundation. (n.d.). Thomas Jefferson: Champion of liberty. The Heritage Foundation. https://www.heritage.org/american-founders/leading-founders/thomas-jefferson-champion-liberty
Heritage Foundation. (n.d.). D.C. statehood: Not without a constitutional amendment. The Heritage Foundation. https://www.heritage.org/political-process/report/dc-statehood-not-without-constitutional-amendment

Heritage Foundation. (n.d.). DC statehood: Not without a constitutional amendment. The Heritage Foundation. http://static.heritage.org/1993/pdf/hl461.pdf
Heritage Foundation. (n.d.). America's broken foreign aid apparatus. The Heritage Foundation. https://www.heritage.org/global-politics/report/americas-broken-foreign-aid-apparatus
Heritage Foundation. (n.d.). Saving America by saving the family: A foundation for the next 250 years. The Heritage Foundation. https://www.heritage.org/marriage-and-family/report/saving-america-saving-the-family-foundation-the-next-250-years
Heritage Foundation. (n.d.). The Heritage guide to the Constitution, second edition: What has changed over the past decade, and what lies ahead? The Heritage Foundation. http://static.heritage.org/2015/pdf/HL1260.pdf
Heritage Foundation. (n.d.). The crisis of American national identity: Part of the Lehrman lectures on restoring America's national identity. The Heritage Foundation. https://www.heritage.org/political-process/report/the-crisis-american-national-identity-part-the-lehrman-lectures-restoring
Heritage Foundation. (n.d.). The Constitution of the United States. The Heritage Foundation. https://www.heritage.org/initiatives/rule-law/judicial/the-constitution
Heritage Foundation. (n.d.). Checks and balances: Safeguarding liberty. The Heritage Foundation. https://www.heritage.org/the-constitution/report/checks-and-balances-safeguarding-liberty
Heritage Foundation. (2005, September 16). The formation of the Constitution. The Heritage Foundation. https://www.heritage.org/initiatives/rule-law/judicial/constitution
Heritage Foundation. (2009, February 11). Lincoln's conservative vision. The Heritage Foundation. https://www.heritage.org/political-process/commentary/lincolns-conservative-vision
Heritage Foundation. (2012, May 1). Understanding the three branches of government. The Heritage Foundation. https://www.heritage.org/political-process/report/understanding-the-three-branches-government
Heritage Foundation. (2012, April 19). A federal republic: Lincoln's first inaugural and the nature of the Union. The Heritage Foundation. https://www.heritage.org/political-process/report/federal-republic-lincolns-first-inaugural-and-the-nature-the-union
Heritage Foundation. (2013, November 19). A government 'of the people' or 'over' the people? The Heritage Foundation. https://www.heritage.org/political-process/commentary/government-the-people-or-over-the-people
Heritage Foundation. (2014). *The war on poverty after 50 years*.
Heritage Foundation. (2014). Guide to the Constitution.
Heritage Foundation. (2015). *The most glaring flaws in Obama's Iran deal*.
Heritage Foundation. (2016). Intelligence and national defense. https://www.heritage.org/military-strength-topical-essays/2016-essays/intelligence-and-national-defense
Heritage Foundation. (2017). *Obamacare has doubled the cost of individual health insurance*.
Heritage Foundation. (2017). *How Obamacare raised premiums*.
Heritage Foundation. (2018, June 1). Judicial activism: Legislating from the bench. The Heritage Foundation. https://www.heritage.org/courts/commentary/judicial-activism-legislating-the-bench
Heritage Foundation. (2018, October 22). The origins of "hate speech". The Heritage Foundation. https://www.heritage.org/civil-society/commentary/the-origins-hate-speech
Heritage Foundation. (2018, December 7). An epic American life. The Heritage Foundation. https://www.heritage.org/conservatism/commentary/epic-american-life
Heritage Foundation. (2018). *Understanding the hidden $1.1 trillion welfare system*.
Heritage Foundation. (2018). *The role of secretaries of state in American history*. The Heritage Foundation. https://www.heritage.org/american-founders/report/secretaries-state-american-history
Heritage Foundation. (2019, January 14). Lawless federal judges are winning their war against the Trump administration. The Heritage Foundation. https://www.heritage.org/courts/commentary/lawless-federal-judges-are-winning-their-war-against-the-trump-administration
Heritage Foundation. (2019). What is national security? https://www.heritage.org/sites/default/files/2019-10/2015_IndexOfUSMilitaryStrength_What%20Is%20National%20Security.pdf
Heritage Foundation. (2021, September 8). Yes, we're safer from terrorism because of intelligence reforms after 9/11. However... https://www.heritage.org/terrorism/commentary/yes-were-safer-terrorism-because-intelligence-reforms-after-911-however
Heritage Foundation. (2022, July 5). The Durham investigation: A primer. https://www.heritage.org/crime-and-justice/report/the-durham-investigation-primer
Heritage Foundation. (2022, July 15). The Dobbs decision: Restoring constitutional balance. The Heritage Foundation. https://www.heritage.org/life/report/the-dobbs-decision-restoring-constitutional-balance
Heritage Foundation. (2023). *The 2020 riots: Causes and consequences*.
Heritage Foundation. (2023). *The origins of COVID-19*.
Heritage Foundation. (2024). *Biden's border crisis*.
Heritage Foundation. (2024, March 21). The House Tax Relief for American Families and Workers Act: A welfare catastrophe. The Heritage Foundation. https://www.heritage.org/welfare/report/the-house-tax-relief-american-families-and-workers-act-welfare-catastrophe
Heritage Foundation. (2024, January). The Tax Relief for American Families and Workers Act: Light on tax relief and heavy on welfare expansion. The Heritage Foundation. https://www.heritage.org/sites/default/files/2024-01/BG3811.pdf

Heritage Foundation. (n.d.). *DACA is unconstitutional, as Obama admitted*.
Heritage Foundation. (n.d.). *It's time to end DACA*.
Heritage Foundation. (n.d.). *Six issues the U.S. should not concede to Cuba*.
Heritage Foundation. (n.d.). *The Biden Afghanistan debacle*.
Heritage Foundation. (n.d.). Analyses on budget, foreign policy, judicial reviews, tech policy, terrorism.
Heritage Foundation. (n.d.). Reports on colonial repression and early settlements (2020–2024).
Heritage Foundation. (n.d.). Reports on merit-based immigration and assimilation.
Hoover Institution. (n.d.). Essays on divine providence in settlements (2020–2025).
Hoover Institution. (n.d.). Essays on faith in early American history (2020–2025).
Hoover Institution. (n.d.). Essays on moral governance and generational shifts (2020–2025 publications).
Hoover Institution. (n.d.). Studies on historical lessons, AI future, and foreign policy (essays, 2020–2025).
House Judiciary Committee. (n.d.). Reports (2023–2025).
House Judiciary Committee. (2024, July 9). New report: How Manhattan DA Alvin Bragg and Judge Merchan violated the constitutional and legal rights of President Donald J. Trump. House Judiciary Committee. https://judiciary.house.gov/media/press-releases/new-report-how-manhattan-da-alvin-bragg-and-judge-merchan-violated
House Select Committee on Benghazi. (2016). *Final report*.
House Select Subcommittee on Coronavirus Pandemic. (2023). *Report*.
House Ways and Means Committee. (n.d.). Timeline on IRS targeting.
Imperial War Museums. (n.d.). *Gas in the First World War*.
Imperial War Museums. (n.d.). *Shell shock*.
Iran JCPOA Criticisms (funding terrorism): Heritage Foundation "The Most Glaring Flaws in Obama's Iran Deal" (2015); "Why Returning to the JCPOA Is a Dangerous Mistake".
Joint Committee on Taxation. (n.d.). Reports on tax cuts.
Korean War Legacy Foundation. (n.d.). *The forgotten war*.
Landis Ban and Reforms: MLB official history; Heritage Foundation cultural impact analyses (aligned with conservative views on integrity).
Levy, J. (2022). *The pandemic was a grand rehearsal for the Great Reset*. American Thinker. https://www.americanthinker.com/articles/2022/09/the_pandemic_was_a_grand_rehearsal_for_the_great_reset.html
Levy, J. (2023). *The WEF and the great reset of capitalism*. American Thinker. https://www.americanthinker.com/articles/2023/01/the_wef_and_the_great_reset_of_capitalism.html
Library of Congress. (n.d.). *The Zimmermann telegram*.
Lyndon B. Johnson Presidential Library. (n.d.). *The Great Society*.
Manhattan Institute. (n.d.). Studies on 1996 PRWORA impacts.
Margaret Thatcher Quote ("run out of other people's money"): Recorded in 1976 interview; Oxford Reference; Goodreads verified quotations.
Mayo Clinic Proceedings. (n.d.). *Howard Walter Florey—Production of penicillin*.
Media Research Center. (2019–2025). Critiques on media bias [Studies].
Miller, T. (2010). *The United Nations and development: Grand aims, modest results* [Special report]. The Heritage Foundation. http://static.heritage.org/2010/pdf/sr0086.pdf
Mises Institute. (2000–2024). Articles on monarchical oppression and colonial escapes.
Mises Institute. (2000–2024). Articles on monarchical religious control.
Mises Institute. (2000–2024). Writings on repression under monarchies and escape to liberty [Articles].
Mises Institute. (2000–2025). Writings on banking history, Patriot Act abuses, and liberty [Articles].
Mueller, R. S. (2019). *The Mueller report*.
NASA. (n.d.). Official report on Challenger disaster.
NASA History. (n.d.). *Apollo program*.
National Archives. (n.d.). *Japanese relocation*.
National Archives. (n.d.). *The Zimmermann telegram*.
National Archives. (n.d.). *Twenty-seventh amendment*.
National Center for Education Statistics. (n.d.). *Long-term trends in reading and mathematics achievement*.
National Park Service. (n.d.). *Harry Truman's decision to use the atomic bomb*.
National Review. (2013, November 6). Cut spending by . . . cutting spending. National Review. https://www.nationalreview.com/2013/11/cut-spending-cutting-spending-michael-tanner
National Review. (2015, May). Listen up, listen up. National Review. https://www.nationalreview.com/wp-content/uploads/2015/05/20150601-2.pdf
National Review. (2015, October 15). Pope Francis and Latin American economics. https://www.nationalreview.com/2015/10/pope-francis-latin-american-economics-conrad-black
National Review. (2015, November 19). Sixtieth-anniversary issue. https://www.nationalreview.com/wp-content/uploads/2015/10/20151119-1.pdf
National Review. (2017, July 3). The genius of the Constitution's separation of powers. National Review. https://www.nationalreview.com/2017/07/constitution-separation-powers-genius-founders
National Review. (2020). *Henry Kissinger's enduring legacy*. National Review. https://www.nationalreview.com/2020/05/henry-kissinger-legacy-realism-american-power

National Review. (2020, August 13). When George Washington met Moses. National Review. https://www.nationalreview.com/2020/08/george-washington-champion-religious-freedom
National Security Archive. (n.d.). Documents on the Pollard case.
National WWI Museum. (n.d.). *American Expeditionary Forces*.
National WWII Museum. (n.d.). *Attack on Pearl Harbor*.
National WWII Museum. (n.d.). *D-Day and the Normandy Invasion*.
National WWII Museum. (n.d.). *Japanese atrocities in China*.
National WWII Museum. (n.d.). *Rosie the Riveter and women in the workforce*.
National WWII Museum. (n.d.). *USO and entertainment during WWII*.
Nations Report Card. (n.d.). *NAEP long-term trend assessment results*.
Nobel Prize Official Site. (n.d.). *The Nobel Prize in Physiology or Medicine 1945*.
Office of Special Counsel. (n.d.). Case summaries; annual reports to Congress.
Pew Research Center. (n.d.). *A look at U.S. bank failures throughout history*.
Phillips, J. (2021). *The World Economic Forum's 'Great Reset' is a blueprint for socialism*. The Daily Caller. https://dailycaller.com/2021/01/25/world-economic-forum-great-reset-socialism-klaus-schwab/
PragerU. (2019). *Lessons from great American leaders: Frederick Douglass and Helen Keller*. PragerU. https://www.prageru.com/video/american-heroes-overcoming-adversity
Reagan Presidential Library. (n.d.). Campaign materials for "Morning in America" ad.
Reagan Presidential Library. (n.d.). Nomination records for Sandra Day O'Connor.
Reagan Presidential Library. (n.d.). Speeches on democracy promotion.
Reagan Presidential Library. (n.d.). Statements on Poland martial law sanctions.
Reagan-Gorbachev. (n.d.). Summit transcripts.
Ronald Reagan Presidential Library. (n.d.). *Ronald Reagan's military service*.
Rosa Parks Museum / National Park Service. (n.d.). *Rosa Parks biography*.
Science History Institute. (n.d.). *Howard Walter Florey and Ernst Boris Chain*.
Senate Intelligence Committee. (n.d.). Reports on Russia collusion.
Senate Judiciary Committee. (n.d.). Hearings on Clarence Thomas confirmation.
Shurk, J. B. (2022). *The globalist 'Great Reset' is a war on sovereignty*. American Thinker. https://www.americanthinker.com/articles/2022/12/the_globalist_great_reset_is_a_war_on_sovereignty.html
Smithsonian Magazine. (n.d.). *The wartime organization that brought Hollywood stars*.
Smithsonian Magazine. (n.d.). *We used to recycle drugs from patients' urine*.
Society for American Baseball Research. (n.d.). Biographies on Joe Jackson.
State Department. (n.d.). Inspector General report on email (2016).
State Department. (n.d.). Records on Abraham Accords.
State Department. (n.d.). Records on Condoleezza Rice/Colin Powell roles.
Supreme Court. (n.d.). Opinions (e.g., Heller 2008, Lopez 1995).
Tax Foundation. (n.d.). Historical data on Reagan economic policies.
Tax Foundation. (n.d.). Historical rates on US top marginal tax rates.
Tax Foundation. (n.d.). Historical revenue effects.
Tax Foundation. (n.d.). Retrospective on 1981 ERTA.
The Federalist. (2026). *Marco Rubio's first year as Secretary of State*. The Federalist. https://thefederalist.com/2026/01/20/marco-rubio-secretary-state-review
Treasury Department. (n.d.). Collections data on capital gains rate cuts.
Treasury Department. (n.d.). Revenue collections on tax cuts.
Trump administration. (n.d.). Statements on Afghanistan withdrawal timeline.
Trump. (n.d.). Memoirs *The Art of the Deal*.
U.S. Army Center of Military History. (n.d.). *Korean War POWs*.
U.S. Department of Agriculture. (n.d.). SNAP FY2023 data.
U.S. Department of Defense. (n.d.). Reports on troop levels 2017–2021.
U.S. Department of Energy. (n.d.). *Our history*.
U.S. Department of Energy Office of Science. (n.d.). *History*.
U.S. Department of Health and Human Services. (n.d.). *Head Start impact study* (2010/2012).
U.S. Department of Justice. (n.d.). Office of the Inspector General report on Robert Hanssen case.
U.S. Department of Justice. (n.d.). Records on post-Civil War treason considerations for Jefferson Davis.
U.S. Department of Labor History. (n.d.). *Chapter 8: Carter Administration 1977-1981*.
U.S. Department of State Office of the Historian. (n.d.). *Milestones: The Spanish-American War*.
U.S. Department of State Office of the Historian. (n.d.). *Milestones: Yellow journalism*.
U.S. Department of State Office of the Historian. (n.d.). *Truman Doctrine*.
U.S. Department of Veterans Affairs. (n.d.). *America's wars*.
U.S. Holocaust Memorial Museum. (n.d.). *The Holocaust*.
U.S. Holocaust Memorial Museum. (n.d.). *The rise of the Nazi Party* and *Axis powers*.
U.S. House of Representatives. (n.d.). Impeachment articles (2019, 2021).
U.S. Naval History and Heritage Command. (n.d.). *Admiral George Dewey*.

U.S. Naval History and Heritage Command. (n.d.). *USS Maine (1895–1898)*.
U.S. Naval Institute. (1998). *A special report: What really sank the Maine?* *Naval History Magazine*.
U.S. Navy History. (n.d.). *Pearl Harbor attack*.
U.S. Office of Special Counsel. (n.d.). Case summaries.
U.S. Senate Historical Office. (n.d.). *Censure of Joseph McCarthy*.
U.S. Senate Historical Office. (n.d.). *Margaret Chase Smith*.
U.S. Senate Historical Office. (n.d.). *Sam Ervin biography*.
U.S. Senate Historical Office. (n.d.). *Senators witness the first battle of Bull Run*.
U.S. Senate Select Committee on Intelligence. (1994). Assessment on Aldrich Ames.
U.S. Senate. (n.d.). Letters on nonprofit funding scrutiny.
U.S. Senate. (n.d.). Records on Ted Cruz positions.
U.S. Senate. (n.d.). Speeches on Mike Lee positions.
U.S. Supreme Court. (n.d.). *Korematsu v. United States* (1944).
USO Official Website. (n.d.). *USO history*.
USO Official Website. (n.d.). *USO tours in Vietnam* and *Bob Hope legacy*.
United Service Organizations (USO) Official Website. (n.d.). *USO history*.
University of Washington. (n.d.). *Mapping American social movements project: Communist Party USA history and geography*.
Victor Davis Hanson quotes: From "The Dying Citizen" (2021) and related historical commentaries.
WallBuilders. (n.d.). *The founding fathers on Jesus, Christianity and the Bible*.
WallBuilders. (n.d.). *Founding fathers on prayer*.
WallBuilders. (n.d.). *Resources on faith of the founders*.
WallBuilders. (n.d.). *The pilgrims thanksgiving*.
Wikipedia. (n.d.). *Fireside chats*.
Wisconsin Welfare Reform Success (1990s Tommy Thompson, employment increases, child poverty drop): Heritage Foundation "Wisconsin Welfare Reform Success Story" (1990s-2000s reports); Manhattan Institute studies on 1996 PRWORA impacts; U.S. HHS data on caseload declines post-1996.
World Wide Web Invention: CERN history; Tim Berners-Lee W3C records.

News Articles and Opinions

American Battlefield Trust. (n.d.). *Spectators witness history at Manassas*.
American Thinker. (n.d.). Articles on Trump's tariff strategy and economic reset.
Breitbart. (n.d.). *A desperate plan that changed the course of the revolution* (on rally cries in American history).
Breitbart. (n.d.). *DOGE: Musk, Ramaswamy lead effort to slash government waste* (on Department of Government Efficiency).
Breitbart. (n.d.). *Elon Musk: Tesla full self-driving beta wide release coming this year* (on Tesla self-driving advances).
Breitbart. (n.d.). *FTC launches investigation into 'un-American' big tech censorship* (on Big Tech censorship).
Breitbart. (n.d.). *North Korea says latest missile tests involve hypersonic weapons system* (on North Korea's nuclear provocations).
Breitbart. (n.d.). *Project Veritas undercover investigation: CNN producer admits...* (on O'Keefe's exposé).
Breitbart. (n.d.). *Repeat offenders and no-bail policies fuel crime waves* (on repeat criminals and bail reforms).
Breitbart. (n.d.). *Trump accuser E. Jean Carroll backed by Democrat mega-donor* (on Reid Hoffman's funding of political lawsuits).
Breitbart. (n.d.). *#ExposeFacebook: Project Veritas reveals...* (on media bias exposés).
CBS News. (n.d.). *Transcript of Charlie Kirk murder suspect's closed hearing from October released* (recent).
CityNews Montreal. (n.d.). *Judge orders release of transcript of closed hearing for man accused of killing Charlie Kirk* (recent).
Educaloi. (2025). *Charlie Kirk's murder: Can you lose your job over comments posted on social media?*
Fox News. (n.d.). *Brandon Straka's WalkAway campaign: From arrest to advocacy* (on Straka's story and courageous stand).
Fox News. (n.d.). *Charlie Kirk's killing, Idaho murders plea and Karen Read verdict* (on Charlie Kirk's assassination).
Fox News. (n.d.). *Elon Musk unveils Tesla's Optimus robot prototype at AI Day* (on Optimus robots).
Fox News. (n.d.). *Gad Saad warns of 'suicidal empathy' in Western societies* (on suicidal empathy and crime policies).
Fox News. (n.d.). *James O'Keefe ousted from Project Veritas...* (on O'Keefe's challenges and courage).
Fox News. (n.d.). *Raymond Donovan, Reagan labor secretary acquitted in fraud case, dead at 90* (on the "Where do I go to get my reputation back" quote and media falsehoods).
Fox News. (n.d.). *Trump's DHS touts massive number of illegal immigrants deported, Dems lash out at ICE* (on illegal immigration strains and security risks).
Fox News. (n.d.). *xAI's Grok: Elon Musk's push for truthful AI* (on Grok and AI integrity).
Fox News. (n.d.). Opinion: *Here's how Trump can take on surging antisemitism in America* (on ISIS and Hamas ideological hatred).
Fox News. (n.d.). Opinion: *What it means to be an American this Fourth of July* (on American sacrifices from Valley Forge to Iwo Jima).

Fox News. (2005, February 15). Sources: FBI doing intel work overseas. https://www.foxnews.com/story/sources-fbi-doing-intel-work-overseas
Fox News. (2012, November 9). Lincoln -- our eternal president. Fox News. https://www.foxnews.com/opinion/lincoln-our-eternal-president
Fox News. (2015, December 21). Articles – December 21, 2015. Fox News. https://www.foxnews.com/html-sitemap/2015/december/21
Fox News. (2019, May 15). Dispute erupts over whether Brennan, Comey pushed Steele dossier, as DOJ probe into misconduct begins. https://www.foxnews.com/politics/dispute-erupts-over-whether-brennan-comey-pushed-steele-dossier-as-doj-probe-into-misconduct-begins
Fox News. (2020, September 17). How the Founders designed a balanced government: Lessons from 1787. Fox News. https://www.foxnews.com/politics/founders-constitution-balanced-government-1787
Fox News. (2023, May 18). Durham's damning report assails FBI leadership, media for enabling Hillary Clinton's alleged Russia hoax plan. https://www.heritage.org/crime-and-justice/commentary/durhams-damning-report-assails-fbi-leadership-media-enabling-hillary
Fox News. (2023, May 10). Activist judges and the threat to democracy: From Roe to nationwide stays. Fox News. https://www.foxnews.com/opinion/activist-judges-threat-democracy-roe-nationwide-stays
Fox News. (2024, November 23). Trump administration takes shape: President-elect completes top 15 Cabinet picks. Fox News. https://www.foxnews.com/politics/trump-admin-takes-shape-president-elect-completes-top-15-cabinet-picks
Fox News. (2024, December 20). Trump's controversial Cabinet picks: Fox Nation takes stock in new series. Fox News. https://www.foxnews.com/media/new-fox-nation-episodic-series-dives-deep-trumps-controversial-cabinet-picks
Fox News. (2025, July 8). FBI launches criminal investigations of John Brennan, James Comey: DOJ sources. https://www.foxnews.com/politics/john-brennan-james-comey-under-criminal-investigation-doj-sources
Fox News. (2025, November 7). Brennan, Strzok, Page subpoenaed as part of federal Russiagate probe: Sources. https://www.foxnews.com/politics/brennan-strzok-page-subpoenaed-part-federal-russiagate-probe-sources
Fox News. (2025, July 28). FBI's controversial Trump-Russia actions predicted with 'alarming specificity' by foreign actors: Sources. https://www.foxnews.com/politics/fbis-controversial-trump-russia-actions-predicted-alarming-specificity-foreign-actors-sources
Fox News. (2025, July 31). Soros' alleged ties to Russiagate exposed in declassified annex of Durham report. https://www.foxnews.com/politics/soros-alleged-ties-russiagate-exposed-declassified-annex-durham-report
Fox News. (2025, July 9). Trump says Brennan, Comey 'crooked as hell' amid FBI probe, may have to 'pay the price'. https://www.foxnews.com/politics/trump-says-brennan-comey-crooked-hell-amid-fbi-probe-may-have-to-pay-the-price
Fox News. (2025, July 10). Obama officials used dossier to probe, brief Trump despite knowing it was unverified 'internet rumor'. https://www.foxnews.com/politics/obama-officials-used-dossier-probe-brief-trump-despite-knowing-unverified-internet-rumor
Fox News. (2025, July 10). Obama officials admitted they had no 'empirical evidence' of Trump-Russia collusion: House Intel transcripts. https://www.foxnews.com/politics/obama-officials-admitted-had-no-empirical-evidence-trump-russia-collusion-house-intel-transcripts
Fox News. (2025, August 4). WILLIAM SHIPLEY: What the Durham Annex tells us about the Russiagate hoax. https://www.foxnews.com/opinion/william-shipley-what-durham-annex-tells-us-about-russiagate-hoax
Fox News. (2025, August 13). Clapper allegedly pushed to 'compromise' 'normal' steps to rush 2017 ICA, despite concerns from NSA director. https://www.foxnews.com/politics/clapper-pushed-compromise-normal-steps-rush-2017-ica-despite-concerns-from-nsa-director
Fox News. (2025, July 15). John Brennan emerged as prominent anti-Trump media figure long before latest DOJ probe into Russiagate origins. https://www.foxnews.com/media/john-brennan-emerged-prominent-anti-trump-media-figure-long-before-latest-doj-probe-russiagate-origins
Fox News. (2025, July 26). JONATHAN TURLEY: The key players in the Russia collusion hoax, and why they're sweating now. https://www.foxnews.com/opinion/jonathan-turley-key-players-russia-collusion-hoax-why-theyre-sweating-now
Fox News. (2025, July 30). Patel found thousands of sensitive Trump–Russia probe docs inside 'burn bags' in secret room at FBI. https://www.foxnews.com/politics/patel-found-thousands-sensitive-trump-russia-probe-docs-inside-burn-bags-secret-room-fbi
Fox News. (2025, January 19). Trump inauguration: Cheryl Hines embraces RFK Jr.'s MAHA mission. Fox News. https://www.foxnews.com/entertainment/trump-inauguration-cheryl-hines-embraces-rfk-jr-s-maha-mission
Fox News. (2025, March 13). Dr. Marty Makary advances out of key committee in bid for FDA confirmation. Fox News. https://www.foxnews.com/politics/trumps-fda-nominee-advances-full-senate-vote
Fox News. (2025, September 25). Michigan Democrat Rep. Stevens cites 'health care chaos' in impeachment move against RFK Jr. Fox News. https://noticias.foxnews.com/politics/michigan-democrat-rep-stevens-health-care-chaos-impeachment-move-rfk-jr
LiveNow from FOX. (n.d.). *Charlie Kirk murder: Judge rules redacted transcript, audio from closed hearing released* (recent).
NBC News. (n.d.). *Judge orders release of closed-door hearing transcript in case of man accused of killing Charlie Kirk* (recent).

National Postal Museum, Smithsonian Institution. (n.d.). The legend of Betsy Ross. In Long may it wave: The evolution of the American flag. https://postalmuseum.si.edu/exhibition/long-may-it-wave-the-evolution-of-the-american-flag/the-legend-of-betsy-ross
National Review. (n.d.). *America was always diverse* (mentions Salomon's role and sacrifices).
National Review. (n.d.). *Crispus Attucks and the American Revolution* (archived article on conservative historical views).
National Review. (n.d.). *Different realities: How polarized views threaten civil discourse* (on differing realities leading to unrest).
National Review. (n.d.). *Education is socialism's only antidote* (on indoctrination and youth).
National Review. (n.d.). *Forcing Ukraine's surrender to Russia won't bring lasting peace* (on Russia as adversary).
National Review. (n.d.). *Klaus Schwab and the great reset: A threat to freedom* (on Schwab's initiatives).
National Review. (n.d.). *Liberal indoctrination on campus isn't working* (on campus propaganda).
National Review. (n.d.). *Samuel Adams: He made a revolution*.
National Review. (n.d.). *The family is still America's most crucial institution* (on the family as America's core).
National Review. (n.d.). *The Monroe doctrine is back, and it's about time* (on Trump's revival of the Monroe Doctrine in Latin America).
National Review. (n.d.). *The promise of longevity science: Age reversal on the horizon* (on longevity and age reversal research).
National Review. (2019, January 14). Lawless federal judges are winning their war against the Trump administration. National Review. https://www.nationalreview.com/2019/01/lawless-federal-judges-are-winning-their-war-against-the-trump-administration/
National Review. (2020, September 18). Abraham Lincoln & American founding: Self-interest is not enough. National Review. https://www.nationalreview.com/2020/09/abraham-lincoln-american-founding-self-interest-not-enough
National Review. (2022, June 24). Dobbs overturns Roe: A victory against judicial activism. National Review. https://www.nationalreview.com/2022/06/dobbs-overturns-roe-a-victory-against-judicial-activism
National Review. (2023, April 5). Bragg's case against Trump hits a wall of skepticism—even from Trump's critics. National Review. https://www.nationalreview.com/2023/04/braggs-trump-indictment-folly/
PBS NewsHour. (n.d.). *Court releases closed hearing transcript for man accused of killing Charlie Kirk* (recent).
The Federalist. (n.d.). *Bill Gates's global agenda: Control through philanthropy* (on Gates's influence).
The Federalist. (n.d.). *Brandon Straka's fight against media narratives and January 6 persecution* (on Straka's experiences and faith-driven patriotism).
The Federalist. (n.d.). *Charlie Kirk's death is filling churches across the country* (on faith resurgence among Gen Z and millennials).
The Federalist. (n.d.). *It's important to be honest about what today's media actually are* (on media as propaganda).
The Federalist. (n.d.). *Saving America from the propaganda industrial complex* (on combating propaganda).
The Federalist. (n.d.). *SpaceX's Starship: The future of Mars colonization* (on SpaceX Moon and Mars missions).
The Federalist. (n.d.). *Trump admin stops Iran from sending terrorists more guns and oil* (on Iran's sponsorship of terrorism).
The Federalist. (n.d.). *Trump's Latin America policy is a return to the Monroe doctrine* (on influence against foreign powers in the hemisphere).
The Federalist. (n.d.). *Yes, I still want to live long and burden my children* (on caring for aging parents).
The Federalist. (n.d.). Articles on the importance of law in immigration policy.
Utah News Dispatch. (n.d.). *Questions about media access still open in early stage of Charlie Kirk murder case* (recent).
Victor Davis Hanson. (n.d.). *Facing facts about race* (on racial division).

License Link References

Public Domain Images- courtesy of PICRYL or Creative Commons. (n.d.). Attribution-ShareAlike 4.0 International (CC BY-SA 4.0) [License]. Retrieved from https://creativecommons.org/licenses/by/4.0/ or https://creativecommons.org/licenses/by/2.0/
Bucks County Choral Society. W.E.B. DuBois Quote, (n.d.). *African American spiritual 14*. https://www.buckschoral.org/african-american-spiritual-14

Other

2 Timothy 2:3 You therefore endure hardness, as a good soldier of Jesus Christ.

Roe v. Wade, 410 U.S. 113 (1973).

Dobbs v. Jackson Women's Health Organization, 597 U.S. 215 (2022).

Various Quotes throughout book: BrainyQuote. (n.d.). Retrieved from https://www.brainyquote.com

Diamandis, P. H. (Host). (2026, January 6). Elon Musk on AGI timeline, US vs China, job markets, clean energy & humanoid robots (No. 220) [Audio podcast episode]. In Moonshots with Peter Diamandis. https://podcasts.apple.com/us/podcast/elon-musk-on-agi-timeline-us-vs-china-job-markets-clean/id1648228034?i=1000743987690

Note: Josiah Quincy's story is based on factual elements from his life as a multi-generational colonist and patriot, humanized with historical context from the above sources; he was indeed a descendant of early settlers and involved in pre-Revolutionary activities.

The family anecdotes about my ancestors is personal and not drawn from published sources—it's shared as a firsthand illustration of the era's human toll. All other details are grounded in these historical records to ensure accuracy and compassion in telling the story.

The personal childhood memory of the base playground and father's service is a family anecdote not drawn from published sources. All other details are grounded in these verified historical records.

The personal family anecdote about my father as a Navy medic in the South Pacific is a cherished firsthand story and not drawn from published sources—all other details are grounded in these verified historical accounts to ensure accuracy and compassion in the telling.

The personal family story about my parents is a cherished memory and not drawn from published sources. All other details are grounded in these historical records.

These sources provide verified historical grounding for the compassionate, human-centered storytelling in the sub-section. The personal childhood memory of the assassination is a family anecdote not drawn from published materials.

Vietnam USO and Personal Anecdote: USO Archives: Hope tours, Raye, Wayne, etc. Personal family story not published.

DISCLAIMER

This book is a work of non-fiction based on the author's research, personal experiences, and interpretations of historical events, faith, and principles of freedom. While every effort has been made to ensure the accuracy of the information presented, history is complex and subject to varying interpretations. The author and publisher have thoroughly researched historical records, but acknowledge that omissions, errors, or differing viewpoints may exist due to the limitations of available sources or unintentional oversights. Readers are encouraged to conduct their own research and consult primary sources for verification.

Anecdotes and personal stories shared herein are drawn from the author's best recollection and knowledge and are intended to illustrate themes rather than serve as verbatim accounts. Conversations, timelines, and details may have been reconstructed or condensed for narrative purposes, but they reflect the author's sincere understanding of events.

Any references to individuals, whether historical or contemporary, are based on public records and the author's analysis. Any reflections or comments on specific individuals — including their character or actions — are gleaned solely from publicly available references, news reports, court records, and other documented sources. These comments represent the author's good-faith interpretations and opinions on matters of public interest and are not intended to harm, injure, or defame any person. Public figures are held to a different and higher legal standard under United States law. No statement in this book is made with actual malice, knowledge of falsity, or reckless disregard for the truth (see *New York Times Co. v. Sullivan*, 376 U.S. 254 (1964)). The author and everyone connected with the publication of this book expressly disclaim any and all libelous intent whatsoever.

No fictional characters or events are intended to resemble or depict any real persons, living or deceased, beyond those explicitly identified as such. If any resemblance occurs, it is purely coincidental.

The views, opinions, and discussions on faith, freedom, politics, and related topics expressed in this book are those of the author and do not constitute legal, financial, medical, religious, political, or professional advice. Readers should seek qualified professionals for guidance in these areas. The author and publisher disclaim any liability for actions taken or decisions made based on the content of this book, including but not limited to any loss, damage, or injury resulting therefrom.

This book is protected under copyright laws, and reproduction without permission is prohibited. The author and publisher make no warranties, express or implied, regarding the completeness, reliability, or availability of the information contained herein.

Published in the spirit of open dialogue and the pursuit of truth, this work aims to inspire reflection and discussion, not to incite division or harm.

ABOUT THE AUTHOR

Tad Sisler is an award-winning American Author, Composer and Producer of feature films and music. More than a thousand of his original works are available through *iTunes, Amazon* and virtually every other major marketplace. Through the years, **Tad** created and released independent feature films and documentaries, television shows, developed a music store and vast collection of music for film and television usages, in addition to published screenplays and books.

Tad is a voting member of *The Academy of Recording Arts & Sciences.* **Tad** invented a wireless karaoke all-in-one microphone that became a best-seller on *Amazon.* A child prodigy, Tad was playing advanced piano pieces at the age of 8, and rating superior in Classical piano competitions at 12. Tad won his first scholarship for singing at 12, attending the Idyllwild School of Music and the Arts, then affiliated with the University of Southern California.

President and Mrs. George H.W. Bush with Tad Sisler

FEATURE FILMS
Tad produced, edited, and released **"The Ghosts of Brewer Town"**, a mystery feature film, currently available on *YouTube.* **Jesse Davis – A Life in Song** is another of Tad's documentaries of a legendary jazz singer, also on *YouTube.*

DOCUMENTARIES
Tad launched the **Journey To An Extraordinary Life-Legends Among Us** documentary series, which chronicles the lives and careers of legendary artists, actors, sports figures and heroes of medicine, in a feature-film format.

BOOKS
Books, Audio Books and Podcasts released by **Tad** include **"Reflections in the Key of Life-The Steve Madaio Story"**, chronicling the life and times of America's most prolific trumpeter. This book garnered a **Readers' Favorite Book Award** for Tad.

President Gerald R. Ford and Tad Sisler

"Mafia Baby" is a shocking true story of a woman raped by a Mafioso, who then raised his child alone. Tad's autobiography, **"It's a Long Climb to The Middle"** *is* available currently on *Amazon* and *Barnes & Noble*. Screenplays in development by Tad Sisler include **"The Incredible Spark of Franklin Benjamin"**, and **"Please Don't Forget".** **Tad's** latest **Music Mastery** collection of books is designed to educate and inspire musicians to become masters. His **Health and Longevity Mastery** series of books is crafted to educate on longevity, age reversal, and general wellness. Tad's **Faith and Freedom Mastery Series** aims to educate and inspire readers to remember the basic tenets on which our society was built.

MUSIC
Tad's production music catalog tripled in size with the addition of thousands of excellent production music tracks, as well as hundreds of sound-alike tracks for the DJ/Karaoke industry, now distributed on **iTunes, Amazon Marketplace, CD Baby, Spotify, Rdio, Xbox Music** and dozens of other outlets Worldwide.

Tad produced and released a high-quality original jazz music project entitled "The Barcelona Sessions" to 1000 radio stations Worldwide, with never- before-heard original performances by Tad with Miles Davis' bassist Marshall Hawkins, Bill Evan's drummer Marty Morell, Frank Sinatra's saxophonist Pat Rizzo, Maynard Ferguson's guitarist Michael Higgins, and Andrae Crouch' flutist/saxophonist Glen Myerscough, produced by Tad Sisler in his recording studio.

Tad Sisler with Congressman/HUD Secretary Jack Kemp

Tad Sisler composed the full score to "**The Encore Of Tony Duran**", an indie feature film starring **Elliott Gould, William Katt, Nicki Ziering and Cody Kasch**, along with his co- composer Andrew Fraga, Jr. After having the distinction of being the first film to sell-out at the prestigious *Palm Springs International Film Festival*, the film won the **Jury Award** for **Best Feature Film** at the *Las Vegas Film Festival* and the *Santa Fe Film Festival*, as well as the **Indie Spirit Award** at the *Fort Lauderdale Film Festival* and the **Audience Favorite Award** at *Tallgrass Film Festival*, in conjunction with a **Lifetime Achievement Award** for **Elliott Gould.** The film is available on *Amazon Prime.*

Tad completed the music and audio editing for the TV Series "**American M.C.**". The first 7 episodes are complete and in the process of distribution through **iTunes**. Tad scored the Main Title theme to **American M.C.** as well as underscore and providing Music Supervision and source music.

Vice President Dan Quayle, Tad Sisler, and Pro Golfer Tom Weiskopf

PRODUCTION

Tad Sisler has been a valuable member of the team of specialists and project developers for **Yamaha Corporation of America**, delivering hundreds of intricate projects to exact **Yamaha** specifications over a 10-year period.

Tad received accolades in 2011 after being given the honor and challenge of doing the "official" remake of the iconic "**Andy Griffith Theme**" for the estate of the composer **Earle Hagen** as a perfect sound-alike, along with his composing associate Andrew Fraga, Jr. Following a stint composing for a series entitled **"Famous Families"** on **Foxstar** and working as assistant to composer Jeff Edwards on the television series "**Silk Stalkings**" and "**Renegade**" in the late 1990's, Tad Sisler and founded & developed a production music catalog, containing thousands of high-quality music tracks available for sync licenses in film, television and advertising in more than 150 genres.

Secretary of State, General Colin Powell with Tad Sisler

In addition to handling Music Supervision on "**The Encore Of Tony Duran**", and on **"American M.C."**, **"The Ghosts of Brewer Town"**, **"Tis' The Season"**, the **"Journey To an Extraordinary Life"** series, **Tad** placed his original music on **NBC, ABC/Disney, Warner Brothers Television**, **TNT**, US National Infomercial campaigns through **Guthy/Renker** and **Script To Screen**, as well as custom composing for the TV and Advertising industry.

The Most Reverend Archbishop Jose Gomez with Tad Sisler

Tad released contains hundreds of top-quality soundalike tracks produced by **Tad** and his associates, for DJ and Karaoke usages, currently on *ITunes, Amazon Marketplace, Spotify, Rdio, Xbox Music,* and many other outlets.

LIVE PRODUCTION

In the 1980's and 1990's, **Tad** and his team produced a series of live headliner events at multiple venues from the ground up, including sold-out performances by **Kenny Rogers, Earth, Wind & Fire, Los Lobos, Glen Campbell, The Righteous Brothers, Lou Rawls, Tito Puente,** the **Power Jam** featuring **Timmy T, Tara Kemp, Candyman, Soul To Soul** and more.

Tad Sisler with Arizona Senator Dennis Deconcini

HISTORY

As a very young man, Tad Sisler worked as a performer for **Frank Sinatra**, studied music in choreography under world-famous Broadway Dancer/Choreographer **Jacque D'Amboise**, received superior ratings in classical piano performance in tough **Joanna Hodges** international competitions, and received private acting lessons from **Richard Burton**, a friend of his family.

Tad attended the prestigious **Idyllwild School of Music and the Arts** on vocal music scholarships during the period when it was affiliated with the **University of Southern California**. In High School, Tad was one of 100 statewide vocalists elected to the prestigious **All-State Choir** in Missouri.

During his storied career, Tad has also had the honor of performing with and working among such greats as **Gladys Knight, Rita Coolidge, B.B. King, Marilyn McCoo, Johnny Mathis, Kenny Rogers, Tito Puente, Sonny and Mary Bono, Gene Barry, Terry Cole-Whittaker, Shecky Greene, Peter Marshall, Mary Hart, Blackwell, Herb Jeffries, Trini Lopez, Glen Campbell, Jennifer Hudson** and other legends.

Congressman Scott Peters and Tad Sisler

Tad Sisler's extensive experience, state of the art facility and history of delivering quality feature films and music on time and on budget, as well as the ability to draw from an extensive catalog of production music, allow his experienced team to offer complete services in custom film and television production as well as in music composition and production efficiently.

Tad is proud and humbled to be a voting member of the **Academy of Recording Arts & Sciences**, which allows him to have a voice to vote for great artists worthy of winning a **Grammy Award**. Many of Tad's works have been placed into Grammy consideration.

In 2023, Tad won a prestigious **Telly Award** for creative excellence in his *Journey to an Extraordinary Life* film series.

Legendary Broadcaster Larry King and Tad Sisler

Modern Renaissance Publishing is at the forefront of a new intellectual awakening, dedicated to fostering a renaissance of ideas that resonate in today's world. Our mission is to bring cutting-edge concepts and timeless wisdom to the public through a diverse array of publishing formats, including books, eBooks, and audiobooks.

We are proud to launch our **Music Mastery** series, offering comprehensive guides and insights for musicians of all levels. Our **Health and Longevity Mastery** series highlights the latest discoveries and insights into extending the human healthspan and lifespan. Our **Faith and Freedom Mastery Series** aims to educate and inspire readers to remember the basic tenets on which our society was built. In addition to our literary endeavors, we also publish original music, enriching the cultural landscape with creative expressions… whether you're seeking to expand your knowledge, enhance your skills, or simply be inspired.

Modern Renaissance Publishing provides the resources and content to empower your journey. Join us as we bridge the rich heritage of the past with the innovative spirit of the present to shape a brighter, more enlightened future.

©2026 by Tad Sisler
Publisher: MODERN RENAISSANCE PUBLISHING
IN USA +1 (818) 845-6700
modernrenaissancepublishing.com
Email: modernrenaissancepublishing@gmail.com
ISBN# 978-1-966258-36-0
All Rights Reserved

www.ingramcontent.com/pod-product-compliance
Lightning Source LLC
LaVergne TN
LVHW081314110826
845149LV00006B/1507

* 9 7 8 1 9 6 6 2 5 8 3 6 0 *